AF361342

THE *EN YAAQOV*

THE *EN YAAQOV*

Jacob ibn Ḥabib's Search for Faith in the Talmudic Corpus

MARJORIE LEHMAN

WAYNE STATE UNIVERSITY PRESS DETROIT

© 2012 by Wayne State University Press, Detroit, Michigan 48201. All rights reserved.
No part of this book may be reproduced without formal permission.
Manufactured in the United States of America.

16 15 14 13 12   5 4 3 2 1

Library of Congress Cataloging-in-Publication Data

Lehman, Marjorie Suzan.
The En Yaaqov : Jacob ibn Abib's search for faith in the talmudic corpus /
Marjorie Lehman.
p. cm.
Includes bibliographical references and index.
ISBN 978-0-8143-3480-5 (cloth : alk. paper)
1. Ein Ya'akov. 2. Aggada—History and criticism. 3. Ibn Habib, Jacob ben Solomon,
1445?–1515 or 16. I. Title.
BM516.E433L44 2011
296.1'276—dc22
2011016271

Typeset by Maya Rhodes
Composed in Adobe Garamond Pro and Serlio LH

CONTENTS

Acknowledgments

As I complete this book, the first in what I hope will be more books on the *En Yaaqov,* I long for details that will never be available to me. My relationship with Jacob ibn Ḥabib, the original compiler of the *En Yaaqov,* feels an intimate one. The powerful images of his life, its noble strivings, seemed to compress the centuries between us as I submerged myself within his medieval world and plowed through his introduction, commentary, and anthology of aggadot with great intensity. But a certain distance does and should remain. I will never know the details of ibn Ḥabib's daily life, what it felt like for him to be torn from his home in Spain, what he thought as he resettled in Lisbon and then, in Salonika, as a father and as a husband—what moments of humanity sustained him. As scholars, we are sensitive to the fact that we can draw out only so much about an individual from the texts that he or she leaves behind. But as people we are always searching for the human being who thinks and feels as we do. If I were to describe ibn Ḥabib based on what I have read, I would conclude that he was not a man who looked back on his past experiences, wishing to recount its travails. He was an optimist, a man who lived in the present and who thought only of how best to prepare his readers and his community for an uncertain future. To look backward on the traumas that being dislocated from his home surely conjured up for him would pull him into a shadowlike world that no longer existed for him. He could never return to Spain. But he could look forward into the future with a sense of hope.

My Jewish identity is informed by history. I cannot look forward in time unless I am looking back, and in this regard, I am different from Jacob ibn Ḥabib. For him, the details of his past experiences were not as significant as the mission of drawing new messages for his generation from the aggadot of the Talmud. But ibn Ḥabib reminded me that not everyone wants to record the traumas of their past. Some prefer to connect and reconnect to something that could survive, that did survive, unconnected to time and place—the aggadah, Talmud, faith.

Today there is little left of the Salonikan Jewish community that ibn Ḥabib worked to build in those early years of the sixteenth century. Few Greek Jews survived Hitler's Holocaust. But the Talmudic texts ibn Ḥabib studied and the work that he compiled in Salonika, the *En Yaaqov*, have outlived him. He understood that it was these familiar texts of the Talmudic corpus and the spiritual messages that could emerge from one's study of them that would have a better chance of survival than the physical place of Salonika, where he began life anew. In a similar act of bestowal, I leave this book as a legacy to my children, Jonah and Gabriel Klapholz. It is a testament to the values that I, along with my husband, Ari Klapholz, hold dear. While we want our children to look back on their rich Jewish history as they walk forward into the world, we also want them to understand that the ancient texts of the Talmud can, as they once did for ibn Ḥabib and his generation, continue to speak to them, inspire them, even lead them to faith.

Over the past several years I worked independently to write this book, but I gratefully acknowledge that it took a small village of people to complete it. A seminar on popular culture at Columbia University, given by Michael Stanislawski, sparked my interest in the *En Yaaqov*, and the support, encouragement, and scholarship of my mentor in the Religion Department at Columbia University, David Weiss Halivni, enabled me to make it the subject of my dissertation. Most fortunate to be trained as a Talmudist by Dr. Halivni, I committed myself wholly to this discipline, delaying considerably my return to the sixteenth century and the *En Yaaqov*. I am indebted to my colleague Burton Visotzky for insisting that seminars on the *En Yaaqov* be taught as part of our program in Talmud and Rabbinics at the Jewish Theological Seminary. And so it was that I began to teach what had always fascinated me. But it was the graduate and rabbinical school students in these seminars who convinced me that I had much to say about the *En Yaaqov*. Through them, I was able to hone my views and mold my thoughts. Each one of them inspired me with their contagious interest in the *En Yaaqov*. Without them I would never have completed this book. Thanks are therefore due to each and every one of them.

I began work on this book under the guidance of two supportive provosts at the Jewish Theological Seminary. Jack Wertheimer, recognizing the value of writing a book on the *En Yaaqov*, secured sabbatical time for me so that I could progress uninterrupted. Our more recent provost, Alan Cooper, continues to encourage my scholarly interests and guides me in his profound respect and understanding for the tension that my scholarship generates in the wake of my deep commitment to and love for teaching.

I am also exceedingly fortunate to be a member of one of the largest faculties of Jewish scholars in the country at the Jewish Theological Seminary in New York City. So many members of this faculty have been gracious with their time, ideas, and guidance. They have shared their observations with me during lectures on the *En Yaaqov* at JTS and at conferences; they have read numerous drafts and have given me invaluable advice on all the stages of writing and publication. I believe I have piqued their interest in this collection and have prompted them to think more about its contribution to the history of Jewish literature in their own research and classes. I am deeply appreciative of their generosity to me.

While it is very difficult to single out any one faculty member at JTS, I am particularly indebted to Judith Hauptman for her unwavering support. As a member of my dissertation committee, she consistently reminded me of the contribution that a book on the *En Yaaqov* could make to our field and encouraged me to commit myself to its completion. Burton Visotzky read every page of my manuscript, offering the most detailed comments. Without his keen eye and constant belief in me, I never would have finished this book. Richard Kalmin made me believe that with hard work and single-minded devotion I could produce a significant book on the *En Yaaqov.* In the moment when I was about to walk away from it all, he restored me to the right course. He advised and encouraged me throughout all my years at JTS, finding the time to read whatever I gave him. David Kraemer enthusiastically became my mentor, poring over my manuscript with utter care, offering me the advice of a scholar of Talmud anxious to see our field grow beyond the sixth century. He gave me the confidence to enter the medieval world as a woman trained as a Talmudist. Benjamin Gampel, who stands out in my mind as my first teacher of medieval Jewish history at the Brandeis High School, read my introduction and proposed goals with utter care, pointing me in the right direction and preventing me from veering off course. Joel Roth, as the chair of the Talmud department at JTS, spent the years of his chairmanship making sure that I had the space to think about and write about Jacob ibn Ḥabib. Carol Ingall took care of me, making sure that my emotional well-being remained intact, even when the completion of this work seemed almost unachievable. Edna Nahshon became another important colleague and friend, generously introducing me to Kathy Wildfong at Wayne State University Press, a caring reflection of her belief in the contributions of my work to our field. David Fishman graciously assisted me with reading material that was in Yiddish. There are few whose scholarship and generosity match that of Menahem Schmelzer. His continued interest in my research on the *En Yaaqov* inspired me to keep improving my work. I thank him for always being an invaluable resource. Finally, other colleagues at JTS have been enormous sources of inspiration. I thank Beth Berkowitz, Shira Epstein, Amy Kalmanofsky, Jeffrey Kress, and Jonathan Milgram. I look forward to an exciting future devoted to sharing ideas about our scholarship and our teaching. And thanks to Ute Steyer, a descendent of Jacob ibn Ḥabib, for assisting me with translating German.

I have also been fortunate to have received help and direction from numerous colleagues outside of JTS, including Daniel Abrams, Carole Balin, Elisheva Carlebach, Matthew Goldish, Tal Ilan, Elka Klein (*z"l*), Rebecca Kobrin, Sharon Koren, Leonard Levin, Jonathan Schorsh, and Nancy Sinkoff.

I am ever so indebted to Mindy Brown, Baynon McDowell, and Adam Parker, without whom I could not have put the finishing touches on this manuscript. Their care with regard to my work has been invaluable.

I would especially like to thank Joseph Hacker, whose work on the *En Yaaqov* and on sixteenth-century Ottoman Jewry has informed my research more than the work of any other scholar. My meeting with Professor Hacker during his sabbatical from Hebrew University, at the Center for Jewish Studies at the University of Pennsylvania, spurred me to depart from the conclusions drawn in my dissertation and to rethink my approach to the *En Yaaqov*. Because of him, my book became a better book.

The Lillian Goldman scholars' working group on the History of the Jewish Book, at the Center for Jewish History in New York City (2009–10), became, during the final year of writing this book, a productive forum for thinking about the *En Yaaqov* and its history following the death of Jacob ibn Ḥabib. Through this forum I met Yoram Bitton, the cataloguer of Hebrew manuscripts at Columbia University, who graciously pointed me to relevant manuscripts and rare books. Many thanks to Adam Shear, who invited me to participate in this workshop and convened useful and productive sessions, as well as to Judith Siegel, the senior educator at the center, for creating such a valuable forum.

I am indebted also to many individuals in the library at the Jewish Theological Seminary, all of whom I cannot name here. But I must extend special thanks to reference librarians Jeremy Meyerowitz and Ina Cohen, who were ready and available to answer my questions. Many thanks to Yevgeniya Dizenko, who prepared the scans of the pages of the editions of the *En Yaaqov* that have enhanced this book and its publication. I also would like to thank all the members of the Rare Book Room staff for their knowledge, unflinching care, and ready assistance, including Sarah Diamant, Jay Rovner, Jerry Schwarzbard, David Sclar, and David Wachtel. They provided me with important information, pulled books for me at a moment's notice, and graciously lengthened hours in the Rare Book Room when I most needed them to meet my deadlines. So much of what I know about rare books I learned from them. Thanks also to Sharon Mintz, curator of Jewish Art at the Library of the Jewish Theological Seminary, for her invaluable assistance.

Friends have stood by me throughout this project, believing at every turn that they would one day read a finished work, even before I believed it myself. Thanks to dear and devoted Wellesley friends Carole Balin, Beth Notar, Carrie Goodman Pianin, Kirsten Russell, and Rahmawati Sih. Thanks to Amy Kalmanofsky, Jane Kanarek, Abby Knopp and Freddy Slomovic, Rebecca Kobrin, Muriel and Alexander Seligson, and Nancy Sinkoff. You have seen me through this project with unconditional love and support. Thank you, thank you.

In the end, though, it comes down to the power of family. Mine has sustained and continues to sustain me at every turn. This book is as much theirs as mine. No one could be more fortunate to have such parents as Sheila and Wallace Lehman, who believe in being passionate about an idea, utterly value and share my commitment to the field of Jewish studies, and take enormous pride in my devotion to it. They raised me to love learning and to love the Talmud, all the while instilling in me a sense of responsibility to share what I have learned. I am exceedingly fortunate to have wonderfully supportive and caring in-laws, Leah and Henry Klapholz; understanding and highly devoted siblings, Nancy and Samuel Leibowitz, Daniel and Deborah Lehman, and Marc Klapholz; as well as lively and loving nieces and nephews, Alexander, Doria, Joshua, Aviva, Rachel (and yes, Fenway, too!), who have kept me laughing during those moments spent away from my work. It is because of my husband, Ari, and our children, Jonah and Gabriel, that my days are filled with the best that life has to offer. As I bring this book to its conclusion, I feel nothing but gratitude to and love for each and every one of them. It is to all of them that I dedicate this book.

INTRODUCTION

For Christians, Muslims, and Jews in the medieval world, religion and faith were wedded intimately. The nature of this relationship was defined and redefined by an array of thinkers, each searching for religious meaning. A combined sense of fidelity to the past and of sensitivity to the intellectual, social, and political contexts in which they found themselves resulted in the creation of different expressions of religious spirituality. One such gesture, quite unique for its time, is the *En Yaaqov,* the Talmud-based work of the late-medieval Spanish rabbi Jacob ibn Ḥabib (d. 1516). Approximately a decade after resettling in the Ottoman city of Salonika following the expulsion of the Jews from Spain in 1492, ibn Ḥabib devoted himself to removing the majority of the Talmud's legal portions from the Talmudic corpus. His intention was to produce a new "Talmud-like" collection containing only aggadic passages (that is, nonlegal material). The resultant text, the *En Yaaqov,* resembled the Talmud in the sense that ibn Ḥabib preserved the order of the aggadic material as it was within the Talmud's original chapters and tractates. His introduction and running commentary to the aggadic passages show that his devotion to the *En Yaaqov* project was rooted in his desire to portray the Talmud as more than Judaism's foundational legal tract. His goal was to characterize the Talmud as a theological document, its aggadah having the power to mold and sustain a believing Jewish community.

Ibn Ḥabib's dramatic editorial and creative efforts emerged in reaction to the traumatic events of Jewish expulsion and forced conversion as well as to the diminishing status of Talmudic aggadah, the Jewish preoccupation with the study of legal codes, the prominence of Maimonidean intellectualism and Kabbalistic esotericism. During the medieval period Jewish legists, philosophers, and mystics objected to what they viewed as an exclusive Talmudism or a "Talmudo-centric" spiritual orbit[1] and proposed alternative approaches to religious reflection that were not focused on the Talmud alone. Ibn Ḥabib produced the *En Yaaqov* in reaction to medieval thinkers who were challenging the Talmud's status as Judaism's sole normative text. In fact, the *En Yaaqov* emerged in part out of this longstanding debate over the Talmud's canonical status within the curriculum of Jewish learning. Its publication offered a unique alternative text through which to answer the questions that had been reverberating throughout the Jewish community for centuries: What is rabbinic Judaism, and what are the texts that define it?

To be sure, the Talmud's very nature—that is, its complicated dialectical style and its interweaving of legal and nonlegal material—came into conflict with a desire to foster a practice-based Judaism whereby Jews could readily gain access to a set of legal decisions. To observe the commandments properly, the Jewish community needed a more straightforward guide. As a result, the production of legal codes began. However, an increased focus on their study within the curriculum led to a decline in the study of the Talmud, reshaping the curriculum into one that did not necessarily require avid Talmud study and Judaism into a religion represented by another set of canonical texts,[2] such as *Hilkhot Harif,* the eleventh-century legal code of Isaac Alfasi (Rif); *Mishne Torah,* Maimonides' twelfth-century legal work; *Pisqe Harosh,* Asher ben Yeḥiel's late thirteenth/early fourteenth-century summary of earlier legal decisions; and *Tur,* Jacob ben Asher's fourteenth-century code.[3]

While Maimonides never doubted the Talmud's significance as a work of Jewish law, he did not envision the Talmud as the central text of Jewish theology. He argued that it was a spiritual error to view the Talmud as the only text worthy of study.[4] His remedy regarding the "limitations" of the Talmud involved far more than the production of a new legal code.[5] He also produced a system of thought rooted in Aristotelian philosophy, which he laid out in his philosophic treatise the *Guide for the Perplexed.* In the *Guide,* Maimonides charts the path toward an intellectual form of spiritual perfection. In such a system the external disciplines of physics and metaphysics became the preferred means for achieving an understanding of God, and Aristotelian philosophy, rather than Talmudic discourse, was considered the highest expression of the human spirit.[6] That Maimonides did not hide his preference for the study of philosophy over and above studying Talmud[7] would arouse anger and discomfort among many Jews, including ibn Ḥabib, for generations to come.

But the debate over the centrality of the Talmud was multipronged and came to include the Kabbalists as well. With the publication of the Zohar near the end of the thirteenth century, Kabbalists posed an array of positions regarding the Talmud that ranged from a desire to supplement Talmud study with Kabbalah to a need to supplant the Talmud altogether. Ecstatic Kabbalists interested in achieving *devequt,* or a state of unity with God, found that the intellectual demands of Talmud study impeded their desire for self-negation. They found it difficult to immerse themselves in God or to achieve a sense of divine communion with Him when they were preoccupied with the intricacies of complicated Talmudic legal arguments. Those who were more committed to a theurgic form of Kabbalah, one that held them responsible for securing the unity of the divine realm through the performance of commandments, objected to a type of exclusive Talmud study that ignored the esoteric meaning of halakhah (Jewish law). In their minds, Talmud study did not necessarily yield an understanding of the idea that fulfilling the commandments had cosmic significance.[8]

Ibn Ḥabib's interest in spiritual matters and specifically in faith did not lead him to philosophy or to Kabbalah. Instead, his spiritual concerns led him directly to the Talmud. The image of the Talmud as a work primarily of halakhah, not to mention the fact that many felt the need to explore philosophy and/or Kabbalah in order to engender a relationship with God, left ibn Ḥabib with the sense that something had gone awry in the development of the curriculum of Jewish study, especially with respect to theological matters. In his introduction to the *En Yaaqov,* ibn Ḥabib expresses his discomfort with the study of law codes in particular, which focus only on the legal aspects of the Talmud to the exclusion of its aggadic texts. In addition, his commentary explicitly lambastes those who are overly involved in the study of philosophy.[9] Furthermore, Kabbalistic esotericism did not inform his textual analyses. In ibn Ḥabib's mind, the loss of focus on aggadah generated by the study of codes, for example, and the dependency of Jewish thinkers on philosophy and Kabbalah, were every bit as much about the loss of the Talmud itself. For him, aggadah was an integral part of what made the Talmud the Talmud. For him, without a collection of aggadah to match Alfasi's code of Jewish law, the messages contained within the aggadot would be overlooked indefinitely.[10] Indeed, until ibn Ḥabib's *En Yaaqov,* no one had attempted to produce a Talmudic/aggadic equivalent to Alfasi's code with the goal of rebalancing Talmudic tradition. No one had directly challenged codificatory endeavors like Alfasi's from the perspective of its effect on aggadah in quite the same way as ibn Ḥabib.[11] It seems that for him the Talmud and Judaism had been sold short when its aggadic sections were ignored, and this called for a corrective.

Furthermore, Talmudic aggadah had also been a casualty of fifteenth-century Spanish Jewry's commitment to philosophy and to its connection to the Jews' anti-Christian polemic. In fifteenth-century Spain, the aggadot of the Talmud had served as philosophers' prooftexts to confirm the rational integrity of Judaism. Indeed, philosophers used aggadic material in an atomized and indiscriminate way when needed; they pulled aggadic passages out of their contexts in the Talmud for use in their philosophic treatises. Anyone who studied these philosophic collections approached such works for their philosophic ideas rather than for the purpose of studying aggadah itself. Indeed, for some members of the learned elite, aggadic material found in the Talmud proved to be no more than trivial, foolish, and irrational. Aggadah was the Talmud's "vulnerable spot." Moreover, converts to Christianity and Christians themselves had viewed aggadah as well-suited fodder for challenging the authority of the Talmud, rabbinic hegemony, and even the integrity of Judaism.[12] In the Talmud's defense, rabbis pushed the study of Talmudic aggadah to the periphery of the curriculum, claiming its value to be secondary to that of the Talmud's halakhic contents.[13]

The *En Yaaqov* was uniquely intended not only to reintroduce Talmudic aggadah into the world of Talmud study but also to establish the Talmud as a core text of Jewish culture through the medium of aggadah. From ibn Ḥabib's perspective, thinkers increasingly had looked outward and beyond the Talmud, to other disciplines, for guidance in their spiritual quests. To overcome the sense of dissatisfaction experienced by philosophers and mystics with regard to the centrality of Talmud study, ibn Ḥabib suggested that the Talmud was a theological document capable of responding to the spiritual needs of his community. Now they could look to the *En Yaaqov* and find spiritual insights, especially during difficult times. In its form as a version of the Talmud, the *En Yaaqov* became a meta-halakhic document with supra-literal references to non-halakhic ideas. In a world where Talmud study seemed to be under fire and its intrinsic worth challenged,[14] ibn Ḥabib planned to reorient the impressions of his community by offering them a version of the Talmud containing only its nonlegal content. In other words, by making them aware that the aggadot of the Talmud contained important theological messages that could be unveiled without relying on philosophy or Kabbalah or law exclusively, ibn Ḥabib proposed a cultural orbit that claimed the Talmud as its core text. To accomplish this, he used the aggadot of the Talmud to renegotiate the parameters of "what is" the Talmud, with the overarching goal of reshaping it. The Talmud would be more than simply a legal text. It would also become the site of rabbinic theology.

The En Yaaqov: *A Response to Crisis*

There is a strong relationship between the *En Yaaqov* and the world in which it was produced. This collection of Talmudic material, the first volume of which was printed in Salonika in 1516, came into being at the precise moment in history when the memories of the Spanish expulsion (1492) and the traumas of conversion were fresh in the minds of Iberian Jews. The inner religious thoughts of ibn Ḥabib developed amid the political events that formed the society around him.[15] While there is no predictable literary response to catastrophe and no assurance that new books or collections arise in response to historical trauma per se,[16] the *En Yaaqov* offers an opportunity to explore the link between historical catastrophe and literary creativity precisely because of when it was printed and who created it.

That said, in studying the *En Yaaqov,* one is hard pressed to find ibn Ḥabib reflecting on the expulsion from Spain or on his resettlement in the Ottoman empire in a direct way. Nowhere in his commentary, which flanks the pages of the *En Yaaqov,* or in his introduction to this work does he describe the specific events that brought him out of Christian Spain and to the shores of the Ottoman empire. In comparison to many of the spiritual leaders of ibn Ḥabib's day who interpreted the expulsion in religious terms, seeing it as a divine punishment and as God's abandonment of His people,[17] ibn Ḥabib offered no reasons for the events that had displaced the Iberian Jewish community. In addition, messianic consolation and a sense of yearning for spiritual redemption, which had also preoccupied many of ibn Ḥabib's contemporaries, do not surface in the *En Yaaqov.*[18] Any anguish felt by him somehow never provoked the type of question that another refugee of Spain, Solomon ibn Verga, stated quite explicitly in his work *Shevet Yehudah:* "Why [did] this enormous wrath [occur to us]?"[19]

Ibn Ḥabib also distinguished himself from such contemporaries as Isaac Abarbanel. Abarbanel saw the biblical curses invoked upon the Israelites for failing to observe God's commandments in Deut. 28:15 as midrashically connected to the punishment outlined in Lev. 26:17, "you shall perish among the nations." In his mind the afflictions and slaughters that occurred to the Jews in exile were God's punishment for transgression. In his torment, Abarbanel went so far as to equate the expulsion from Spain with the Jews' forced exile from Israel and into exile in Babylonia; Spain was his Jerusalem.[20]

This historical catastrophe also prompted Abarbanel to search for a providential reason for its occurrence. In his desire to explain why the Spanish expulsion was a culminating event that marked the emptying of Jews from all of Europe, he wrote that God had "roused the spirit of the kings of the lands of the West to expel all the Jews from their territory . . . in such a way that they emerged from all sides of the West and all of them passed toward the Land of Israel." The expulsion from Spain was just one final event that prepared the Jews for a national migration to Israel. To console the exiles, Abarbanel also asserted the "innate superiority of the Jewish people" and involved himself in calculating a date for the arrival of the messiah.[21]

Unlike Abarbanel, ibn Ḥabib made no attempt to explain away the travails that he had encountered or that his community had faced. Optimism pervades his commentary. Refusing to look backward by specifically naming and describing the traumas of his past, he searches for ways to strengthen the faith of his present community. Yet one cannot ignore that ibn Ḥabib's theological interest in reorienting the character of the Talmud plays out at the precise time when many were trying to make theological sense of their past experiences. The fact that ibn Ḥabib takes such a strong interest in faith and ties this interest to the texts of the Talmud in such an intimate way suggests that if he wasn't asking ibn Verga's question, he was writing for an audience who was, at the very least, troubled by the question. And while one cannot take for granted that any historical circumstance singlehandedly provokes the authorship of an entire document,[22] the degree to which ibn Ḥabib involved himself in the daily issues of rebuilding communal life in Salonika following the expulsion, as evidenced in his legal responsa, indicates that he was preoccupied with issues of deep concern to a postexpulsion community.[23] For example, such responsa indicate that ibn Ḥabib was concerned with, aware of, and devoted to the issues generated by the conversos. At a time when history had proven that the survival of Jewish identity did not necessarily depend on the performance of commandments but rather on the strength of one's faith, the *En Yaaqov* represented a fitting means for cultivating believing Jews.

The *En Yaaqov* offers its readers insight into the mind of one rabbi who was responding to and participating in the events that were occurring around him in a manner quite different from ibn Verga and Abarbanel.[24] Instead of understanding the banishment of Iberian Jewry as a mere historical circumstance that could be set aright through a correct behavioral system or viewing the expulsion as part of a wide-ranging, comprehensive religious process that ultimately could bring about messianic redemption, ibn Ḥabib's *En Yaaqov* conveyed something else. For ibn Ḥabib, the expulsion of the Jews from Spain was not an unprecedented event that had changed the course of Jewish history.[25] It was an event that had happened before and could occur again. In an effort to transmit a timeless message that paralleled the nature of the aggadot of the Talmud, ibn Ḥabib chose not to call attention to the events that had just befallen Iberian Jewry.

Ibn Ḥabib's ultimate goal was to use his aggadic commentary to instruct his constituency regarding how to believe in God. The work was preparatory, designed to cultivate a populace that would grow and sustain a strong and simple internal faith of the heart. Reverberating throughout his comments is a concern for strengthening their faith in the hope that no future tragedy or political calamity would undermine it. Indeed, the comments are devoted to describing how it is that God ultimately comes to protect His constituency.[26] His goal was to describe the nature of the relationship that one was to have with God. Toward this end, ibn Ḥabib promises to unearth "within the sections [of the Talmud that deal with] monetary laws . . . the principles of faith, [that are] like good jewels or hidden pearls stored away within a bundle of silver,"[27] thereby making the Talmud the core text in accomplishing his goals. The *En Yaaqov* represents ibn Ḥabib's desire to move on following catastrophe and to focus on cultivating a Jewish community that could withstand the trials that might test its faith in the future.

In conceptualizing a definition of faith rooted in the texts of the Talmud, ibn Ḥabib argued that faith was not dependent on any discipline external to the Talmud or, for that matter, on external reward. One was not to rely on philosophy or Kabbalah or the expectation of reward, including the coming of the messiah, in a faith-based commitment to God. The coming of the messiah would not radically alter the lives of the Jews, as God's power was not to be substantiated through any form of material gain.[28] It was religious fantasy to believe that good deeds resulted in material rewards as part of a perfect retributive system.[29] Instead ibn Ḥabib intended, through the aggadot of the Talmud, to develop self-sufficient believers with strong attachments to God who would not lose faith even if they did not receive the type of rewards they expected. If their identity as Jews was challenged due to forced conversions, or their communities were torn apart due to expulsion decrees and the like, their faith would define them as committed Jews and prepare them to rebuild their lives.[30] An internal faith of the heart, devoted in some measure to recapturing elements of biblical and rabbinic theology, as opposed to one rooted in the science of reason, had the ability to speak to a larger population, even unite Jews one to the other, in a way that an intellectualist approach to faith could not. In moments of hardship and communal disarray, when explanations seemed unachievable, ibn Ḥabib gravitated to a faith of feeling and to a God of the human conscience and heart.

A Response to Fifteenth-Century Jewish Thought

Intriguingly, ibn Ḥabib's interest in an emotional type of faith rather than in an intellectualist approach parallels developments in fifteenth-century thought.[31] Indeed, some of ibn Ḥabib's contemporaries had viewed philosophy as the discipline that weakened Jewish identity, because one needed to reach outside the library of Jewish texts to effectively engage in its study. Many blamed philosophy in order to explain away the painful reasons for both the surge of forced and voluntary conversions to Christianity by Jews and their resistance to returning to Judaism or escaping from Spain. They believed that philosophers and the study of philosophy had not succeeded in preparing their followers to withstand the ordeal of persecution and expulsion.[32] Although ibn Ḥabib never found fault with the study of philosophy in quite this way and even sanctioned its study for those who chose to rely on it,[33] his anti-intellectualist position on faith develops within a milieu where the power of philosophy had become worrisome for some. It had not generated the appropriate spiritual context within which a broad portion of Jews could develop a robust relationship with God.[34] Therefore, rather than thinking about what Jews had done to deserve their misfortune, ibn Ḥabib preferred to think about what would strengthen the Jewish community. His response was to use the medium of the aggadic commentary to communicate his vision of a faithful Jew who trusted God, who did not question God's punishments, who believed that God dispensed more goodness than one deserved, and who acknowledged that he could not understand all that God did in the world. God's goodness was to be taken on faith.[35] Ibn Ḥabib devoted himself to the creation of a timeless message that was to be rooted in a timeless document; it was a message that he hoped would serve Jews under any circumstance.

Despite ibn Ḥabib's weddedness to the Talmud and to revealing the messages of faith contained within its texts, he sidestepped the rabbis and rabbinic theology in a manner that was driven not only by the intellectual developments of his era but also by the events of his time. Biblical and Talmudic texts offered a vision of religious faith in terms of an unwavering loyalty and trust in God that was, for the most part, expressed through practice. However, while professing to uncover messages of faith found within the words of the Talmud's rabbis, ibn Ḥabib opted to embrace the agenda of Spanish Jewish philosophers of the fifteenth century who strove to develop a systematic rabbinic theology rooted in dogmatics. Unlike the rabbis of the Talmud, thinkers of this time were preoccupied with defining Judaism in accordance with a set of propositions or principles of faith. These thinkers reduced belief to a set of declarations in their understanding that it was sufficient for a person to hold such beliefs implicitly without expressing them necessarily through behavioral acts.[36] Maimonides' earlier set of thirteen principles were the point of departure, but fifteenth-century Jewish thinkers were far more engaged in the study of dogma, proposing their own sets of principles in an attempt to define Judaism, prove its rationality, and/or provide a rational refutation of Christian dogma. Various catechisms were proposed by a spectrum of fifteenth-century Jewish intellectuals, including Ḥasdai Crescas, Joseph Albo, Abraham Shalom, Isaac Arama, and Abraham Bibago,[37] all of whom ibn Ḥabib mentions in the *En Yaaqov*.

When ibn Ḥabib decided to integrate elements of this dialogue into his commentary and to shift his understanding of rabbinic theology in the direction of dogmatics, he embraced an approach to faith that was not rooted in external behavior, that is, in the performance of mitsvot alone. He also chose to reveal his interest in dogmatics within the context of a document that did not contain the Talmud's legal passages.[38] This is not to say that he was advocating for faith over practice, because surely one finds throughout his commentary mention of the importance of observance as a true reflection of one's faith.[39] However, for a man reared in the Iberian Peninsula, where conversion to Christianity was a significant factor and a constant threat, it is not surprising to find that he embraced an understanding of faith that was propositional. The idea that one could define one's Jewishness on the basis of a set of principles of faith made sense to those who, like ibn Ḥabib, had experienced a world where some Jews had not been able to practice Judaism openly.

Although scholars have disagreed on the impetus for the Jews' interest in dogmatics, one view connects persecution and forced conversion with a desire to define a minimum set of beliefs that define a Jew as a Jew.[40] Maimonides, in particular, authored his set of thirteen principles amid Almohad fanaticism, persecution, and forced conversions. The fact that the greatest activity in the study of dogmatics occurred during the fifteenth century in Spain, at a time of forced conversions and persecution, supports the notion that Jews became interested in authoring creeds in the wake of historical circumstances that threatened their identity as Jews. That ibn Ḥabib remains interested in dogma even after resettling in the Ottoman city of Salonika is, in part, a reflection of his concern that history could repeat itself and that Jews needed to have an understanding of what defined them as Jews.

Nonetheless, it is important to note that this theology or commitment to dogmatics was not presented in a systematic fashion. While many of ibn Ḥabib's predecessors and contemporaries had written dogmatic treatises containing rationalist proofs and reflections (both positive and negative) on Maimonidean philosophy and had communicated their positions in the form of well-ordered dogmatic treatises arranged in accordance with the dogmatic principles, ibn Ḥabib imposed no thematic or ideational structure onto the *En Yaaqov* based on his interest in dogma.[41] In fact, to locate ibn Ḥabib's references to the principles of faith, one needs to sift through his aggadic exegeses one by one. In the interest of claiming the Talmud as the most central text of Jewish authority and identity, ibn Ḥabib ensured that the order of the aggadot as they were found in the Talmudic corpus was primary. He began with the aggadic passages found in the Talmud and claimed that the "principles of faith" were to be found "within the words of our ancient rabbis."[42] In this regard, he proposed a dramatic change in the way dogma had been studied and discussed in the Jewish communities of Spain. He believed it was the aggadot of the Talmud that posed the questions and offered the answers regarding how one could embrace faith in the wake of life's challenges.[43] The texts of the Talmud were to direct theological thinking; for ibn Ḥabib, dogmatics would no longer be a subset of philosophy that stood outside the context of the aggadot of the Talmud.

Opportunity and the Ottoman Context

The historical trauma that brought ibn Ḥabib to the shores of the Ottoman empire also created an important moment of opportunity in the history of Jewish literature. It enabled the *En Yaaqov* to emerge and to achieve a high level of popularity. The Jews' forced expulsion from Christendom and their resettlement within the multiethnic and multireligious milieu of Ottoman society made the period of the early sixteenth century a ripe one for developing new modes of study and for proposing new ideas. Jews gained more freedom and protection under Islamic law than they had during the previous century in Christian Spain.[44] Freed of the Christian cultural context, where Talmudic aggadah had been used to discredit Judaism and the Talmud, a renewed interest in Talmudic aggadah and in aggadah more generally emerged. Ibn Ḥabib's *En Yaaqov* was part of a literary surge in the early sixteenth-century Ottoman empire that included the transition from manuscript to print of older collections of midrash aggadah and the appearance of commentaries written on aggadah as well as homiletical works that included aggadah within them. Jews also had access to libraries filled with Jewish books and manuscripts. As Hebrew print shops disseminated works that had never been obtainable in print before,[45] the production of collections like the *En Yaaqov* became possible, and these volumes were more available to a wider audience. In comparison to works that had remained in manuscript for years with very limited opportunities for dissemination, the *En Yaaqov*'s emergence in print gave a much larger readership access to Talmudic aggadah. Moreover, the development of an urban middle class eager to learn[46] greatly increased the demand for the *En Yaaqov*. People clamored for its contents and purchased quires of material even before its printer, Judah Gedaliah, produced a bound book.[47] In this cultural atmosphere, a work filled with Talmudic aggadah and a running commentary that showed little commitment to the rationalist program or to Kabbalah, or even to integrating aggadah with halakhic analysis, was able to emerge and to be embraced.

During the early sixteenth century in the Ottoman empire, the *En Yaaqov* was among the very few Jewish works to be printed as a book; certainly it was the first work of Talmudic aggadah published in the city of Salonika.[48] None of the new aggadic works authored at the same time as the *En Yaaqov* was printed during these early years of the printing press, and none became as well known.[49] Many of these new aggadic commentaries were lost or remained in manuscript.[50] And although there is no record of a reprinting of the *En Yaaqov* in Salonika until the end of the sixteenth century,[51] printed editions were published in Venice (1546, 1566) and in Cracow (1587) during the sixteenth century. These editions also reached Ottoman Jews.

The *En Yaaqov* is the product of the intersection of text, history, and culture. It offers a unique opportunity to explore the effects of the Spanish expulsion on Jewish theology and, more specifically, on the relationship between that theology and a curriculum of Jewish studies centered on the Talmud. Ibn Ḥabib produced the *En Yaaqov* in reaction to medieval thinkers who questioned the spiritual value of studying the Talmud alone and who had challenged its status as Judaism's sole normative text. He hoped that, through his collection of Talmudic aggadah and his anthology of running commentaries, he would contribute to the spiritualization of the Talmud and ensure that the study and the understanding of one's relationship with God was centered on the study of the texts of the Talmudic corpus.

The First Printed Edition of the En Yaaqov

To date, I have not been able to locate any full-length or even legible fragments of manuscripts of the *En Yaaqov*.[52] Because the printer, Judah Gedaliah, took an interest in ibn Ḥabib's project and began printing portions even before ibn Ḥabib completed his work, manuscripts were presumably lost or not preserved. I have, therefore, made reference throughout this book to the first printed edition, *En Yaaqov* (Salonika, 1516), volume 1, citing it as *EY* (Salonika, 1516), with the name of the tractate on which ibn Ḥabib comments, along with section and folio references, where applicable. Although this edition has been digitized and is now available on the website of the Jewish National University Library,[53] I have also cited parallel references to the texts of the *En Yaaqov* found in the Vilna edition of 1883 (repr. Jerusalem, 1961), prepared by the Press of the Brothers and the Widow Romm, in order to enable readers to locate these texts with greater ease. Although there are many editions of the *En Yaaqov* that differ considerably one from the other, the editors of the Romm edition of the *En Yaaqov* (1883) paid careful attention to producing a "best text" of the aggadot by comparing different versions of the *En Yaaqov,* and to compiling the most comprehensive anthology of commentaries and essays written on the aggadot of the Talmud. As a result, this edition was reprinted more often than any of the other editions of the *En Yaaqov*.[54] In the conclusion to this book, I discuss the differences between the Romm edition of the *En Yaaqov* and ibn Ḥabib's original work.

In compiling the *En Yaaqov,* ibn Ḥabib had at least one collection of Talmudic aggadah available to him, *Haggadot Hatalmud* (Constantinople, 1511).[55] Some scholars have suggested that it served as a base text for him in compiling the *En Yaaqov*. Indeed, the question of the relationship between *Haggadot Hatalmud* and the *En Yaaqov* has been explored by Shamma Friedman and Stephen Wald in the context of their larger research into finding textual evidence for the *Bavli* (Babylonian Talmud). In this regard, both *Haggadot Hatalmud* and the *En Yaaqov* provide evidence of versions of the *Bavli* that are no longer extant. Although Wald detects a great deal of dependence on the part of ibn Ḥabib on the texts of *Haggadot Hatalmud* in his study of the third chapter of *b. Pesaḥim,* Friedman cautions that each tractate needs to be compared on its own. One can make no presumptions, Friedman argues, that ibn Ḥabib relied on *Haggadot Hatalmud* consistently or exclusively throughout his work on the *En Yaaqov*.[56] In fact, a comparison between tractate *Berakhot* as found in the *En Yaaqov* (Salonika, 1516) and the same tractate in *Haggadot Hatalmud* indicates that ibn Ḥabib did not depend on *Haggadot Hatalmud* alone when he collected the material for tractate *Berakhot*. Not only does the *En Yaaqov* contain more aggadic material from the Talmud than *Haggadot Hatalmud*, it also contains different aggadic selections. Passages found in the *En Yaaqov* cannot be found in *Haggadot Hatalmud*. At the same time, there are aggadic passages found in *Haggadot Hatalmud* that are absent from the *En Yaaqov*. In addition, viewed from the perspective of lower criticism, the two versions of tractate *Berakhot* possess significant differences, suggesting a reliance on different manuscript traditions. In support of Wald's claims, however, it is possible that as ibn Ḥabib got older and weaker, he relied more heavily on *Haggadot Hatalmud* in order to expedite his work on the collection, specifically with respect to tractate *Pesaḥim*.[57] He seemed more ambitious at the beginning of the process, relying on more sources,[58] including the Oxford manuscript (Opp. Add. Fol. 23 [366]) and the Soncino printed edition of *b. Berakhot* (1483–84).[59] It is also clear that he relied on sources that are presently unknown.

Jacob ibn Ḥabib died before he could complete the *En Yaaqov*. Its first volume, which includes an anthology of the aggadot found in *Seder Zeraim* and *Seder Moed,* as well as a commentary and an introduction, is his own work.[60] He drew most of his aggadic material from the *Bavli* (Babylonian Talmud) and a far more limited amount of aggadot from the *Yerushalmi* (Jerusalem Talmud).[61] His anthology of commentaries, including primarily those of Rashi, Tosafot, and Rabbi Solomon ibn Adret (Rashba) on the aggadot of the Talmud, reflects his commitment to the development of a larger conversation regarding the aggadot, one that extends beyond that of his own views. His anthology of tractate *Berakhot* and his commentary on the aggadot found there convey a more serious and more directed commitment to his initial objectives than his work on the other tractates.[62] Indeed, ibn Ḥabib ponders his frustration that he cannot accomplish all that he set out to do in his introduction. As he brings his work on *Seder Zeraim* to a close, he laments his inability to write extensively on every aggadic passage. He expresses the travail of an author in recognizing that, for every printed interpretation, one thousand more exist. He also bemoans the page limits set by his printer, Judah Gedaliah. Ironically, his freedom to author lengthy comments was curtailed by the very invention that made his work possible. He feels compelled to speak out to his constituency and apologizes for the truncated presentation with respect to the tractates of *Seder Moed,* which differed so greatly from his work on *Seder Zeraim*. But mostly ibn Ḥabib feels the limits of time as he nears the end of his life. In response, he pleads both for monetary assistance from his constituency in order to continue the project and for a continuous commitment to the explication of aggadah from his colleagues.[63]

After ibn Ḥabib's death, his son, Levi ibn Ḥabib, completed the project. However, in Levi's introduction to the second volume of the *En Yaaqov* (Salonika, 1522–23), titled *Bet Yaaqov,* one finds the anguished words of a son unable, or maybe unwilling, to follow in the footsteps of his father. Indeed, the second volume fails to reflect Jacob ibn Ḥabib's theological vision. In addition, there are far fewer aggadic passages in volume 2, and Levi's commentary lacks the passion and the commitment to aggadah displayed in the lengthy excurses of his father. It is apparent that father and son had different agendas and different commitments to the study of aggadah.[64] The second volume represents a later contribution to the history of the *En Yaaqov* that bears no resemblance to the objectives of the first. Because the primary focus of this book is on the inception of the *En Yaaqov* and not its reception history, the chapters that follow focus on the contribution of Jacob ibn Ḥabib alone.

The Present Study

The En Yaaqov: *Jacob ibn Ḥabib's Search for Faith in the Talmudic Corpus* is devoted to exploring the first printed edition of the *En Yaaqov* and to Jacob ibn Ḥabib's initial contribution to the complex reception history of the collection following his death. To date, Joseph Hacker is the only scholar who has devoted serious attention to ibn Ḥabib and the *En Yaaqov,* in his article "*Rabbi yaaqov ibn ḥabib: Lidmutah shel hahanhagah hayehudit besaloniqi bereshit hameah ha-16.*"[65] This book broadens, deepens, and expands on Hacker's observations, shedding further light on the intricacies of ibn Ḥabib's strategy of spiritual and intellectual adaptation following the traumas of 1492.

This foray into the world of the *En Yaaqov* consists of five chapters. The first three chapters are devoted to a discussion of the factors that cultivated ibn Ḥabib's interpretive and anthological consciousness. Indeed, his editorial decisions and interpretive enterprise reflect an implicit agenda that represents a reaction to his own historical circumstances and to the intellectual trends circulating in Spain throughout the fifteenth century. These chapters construct the matrix that nurtured ibn Ḥabib's impulse to compile the *En Yaaqov.* Chapter 1 describes the factors that led ibn Ḥabib to author and produce the *En Yaaqov* as an adaptive strategy, in response to the political turmoil he encountered following the expulsion of 1492 and to the challenges of resettlement in the Ottoman arena where the Sephardim lacked authority. The chapter includes a discussion of ibn Ḥabib's confrontation with the conversos and the extent to which this experience molded his attitude toward aggadah, informed his theological views, and influenced his decision to produce a new version of the Talmud. Chapter 2 focuses on the intellectual framework within which ibn Ḥabib's attitude toward Talmudic aggadah developed and explains why few running commentaries explicating the aggadot of the Talmud existed prior to his early sixteenth-century commentary titled *Hakotev*. When ibn Ḥabib produced the *En Yaaqov* and authored a commentary to it, he nurtured a new area of interest among Iberian Jews of his era. This chapter examines why the early sixteenth century was particularly ripe for the reception of this type of work. Chapter 3 discusses ibn Ḥabib's editorial decisions in choosing to construct the *En Yaaqov* as a Talmud "lookalike." The chapter presents the creation of the *En Yaaqov* as a reaction to the way the Talmud was studied (and not studied) during the fifteenth century in Spain, and highlights ibn Ḥabib's commitment to reorienting the curriculum of Talmud study to include aggadic material.

These discussions lay the groundwork for chapter 4, which presents ibn Ḥabib's theological perspective through an analysis of key passages in his commentary to the *En Yaaqov*. The goal of chapter 4 is to examine how a single Spanish Jewish leader during the postexpulsion period integrated text and context to provide a resource that Jews could delve into for spiritual growth and continuity of faith. This chapter presents ibn Ḥabib's view of aggadah as a pedagogically self-conscious medium with a strong theological-pedagogical thrust.[66] Examples will show how ibn Ḥabib used the aggadot to construct the questions he believed to be on the minds of his constituency and to find the answers to those questions within these texts. The intention is to characterize the aggadic passages as ibn Ḥabib saw them—that is, as texts capable of guiding his constituency toward an enlightened conduct rooted in faith—and to portray him as a pedagogue interested in designing an approach to the Talmud that would speak to the Jews of his day.

Finally, chapter 5 will address the printing history of the collection, which was quite different from that of the Talmud. The goal of the chapter is to illuminate and evaluate the extent to which ibn Ḥabib succeeded in his plans for the *En Yaaqov* and to provide an image of what ultimately became of ibn Ḥabib's endeavor to produce a Talmud-based document of faith.

1

Fʀᴏᴍ Sᴘᴀɪɴ ᴛᴏ ᴛʜᴇ Oᴛᴛᴏᴍᴀɴ Eᴍᴘɪʀᴇ

The Life and Contexts of Jacob ibn Ḥabib

Rabbi Jacob ibn Ḥabib, the original creator of the *En Yaaqov,* authored this work in response to a particular Spanish intellectual orbit. But the development of his ideas about the nature and meaning of the aggadot of the Talmud was also an outgrowth of his encounter with the challenges that Iberian Jews faced during the fifteenth century. Like many in his generation, he confronted the rise of a class of conversos,[1] Inquisitorial strife, the tumultuous expulsion of the Jewish community at the hands of the Spanish monarchs in 1492, the Portuguese edict of forced conversion in 1497, the agonies of resettlement, and the internal social conflicts that defined Jewish communal life in the Ottoman empire. Through the *En Yaaqov,* ibn Ḥabib responded to this turbulent moment in Jewish history, offering his perspective on how the Jewish community should cope. Thus it is necessary at this juncture to explore the context that shaped ibn Ḥabib's life and that contributed to his decision to compile the *En Yaaqov.*

Ibn Ḥabib's life story spans four cities—Zamora, Salamanca, Lisbon, and Salonika—beginning with his birth in Zamora, a Spanish city in Castile, in the middle of the fifteenth century (between 1440 and 1450). He was a student of Rabbi Samuel Valensi, who had trained under the well-known rabbinic figure Rabbi Isaac Canpanton. Valensi had succeeded Canpanton as head of the Jewish academy in Zamora. After completing his studies ibn Ḥabib assumed a leadership role in the academy of Salamanca. The expulsion of Spain's Jews in 1492 resulted in his relocation to Lisbon and his confrontation with a decree of forced conversion instituted by the

17

Portuguese monarchy in 1497. By the year 1501, ibn Ḥabib had again relocated. Along with many other Iberian Jews, ibn Ḥabib resettled in the Ottoman city of Salonika.[2] In Salonika he resumed his role as a prominent rabbinic leader and began his work on the *En Yaaqov*. As noted earlier, he was unable to complete this work before his death in 1516; his son, Levi ibn Ḥabib, produced the second volume of the *En Yaaqov*, titled *Bet Yaaqov*, beginning with tractate *Yebamot* of *Seder Nashim*.

Life Alongside Conversos

In Castile, ibn Ḥabib had lived among such men as the Jewish-born Diego de Zamora. Diego had become a monk in the Order of San Jeronimo, and eight of his siblings followed the same course. Inquisition documents attest both to the fact that Diego was a devout Christian as well as to his commitment to performing certain mitsvot. When accused of observing Jewish practices, Diego was brought to trial in 1489 before Spain's Inquisitorial court. While Diego was never allowed to reassume his duties within the order, he was acquitted of the accusations against him. In the end, his good (Christian) name was restored among the men of the order, with whom he continued to identify.[3]

To examine ibn Ḥabib and Diego even in a most cursory way is to observe something common to Jewish communal life of the fifteenth century. Both committed Jew and convert lived side by side, each able to align himself with a competing religious institution, each in tension with the other. Without specific documentation it is difficult to determine what provoked these two men to follow the paths they did. Jacob ibn Ḥabib's family may have been more fortunate than that of Diego de Zamora, possibly escaping from the fanatical zeal of the anti-Semitic clerics who forcibly were converting Jews to Christianity. Yet the divergent stories of these two men may be due to the ability of one man and the refusal of another to withstand anti-Jewish decrees that affected the religious, political, and economic lives of Jews. Indeed, to be labeled a Christian offered converts many privileges denied to Jews, as it provided them with opportunities to enter occupations, acquire wealth, and reside in communities once forbidden to them. Conversion was an attractive option for some and not uncommon.[4] That Diego become a monk in the Order of San Jeronimo may, however, attest to his sincere desire to live as a Christian, in contrast to ibn Ḥabib, who chose to remain a Jew.

Converts like Diego, whether sincere or otherwise, posed great challenges to the rabbinic elite who led academies and headed communities in

Castile, among them ibn Ḥabib. On one level, the conversos never emerged as a monolithic group of crypto-Jews who led a secret Jewish existence nor as full-fledged Catholics. Indeed, the religious beliefs of the conversos varied greatly. There were many different privately held reasons for conversions to Christianity, and many types and degrees of forced situations that led Jews to live different religious lives.[5] As Richard Popkin has argued, there were conversos who upheld a partial Christian faith intermingled with Judaism. Theirs was a "Jewish Christianity" that involved the rejection of Christian dogma, like Trinitarianism, in favor of a type of Christianity that was more acceptable to Jews wishing to hold on to Judaism on some level. In addition, he notes that some converts chose not to embrace either religion and failed to fit comfortably anywhere.[6] In this regard, conversos blurred the lines of religious identity and ethnicity.[7] In a society where religion was used as a way to construct clear boundaries, the converso violated them by failing to be wholly Jew or Christian.[8]

On another level, it was the crypto-Jews who generated an additional set of complex religious and sociocultural challenges. Despite the fact that they identified as Jews, they exhibited no common ritual practice and adopted no unified curriculum of Jewish study. As a result, they engendered alternative Judaisms that were individualized and varied greatly from family to family.[9] The individual choices they made and the communal options they ignored, including the rejection of a life lived within the framework of neighboring Jewish communities, were reminders that there were other standards on which Jewish identity could be judged. Crypto-Jews suggested that one did not need to live amid the Jewish community, or to ally oneself with its leaders or its institutions, or even to take part in its intellectual culture, in order to consider oneself Jewish. Therefore, assessing one's observance of Judaism's precepts or one's commitment to the study of its sacred canon no longer proved to be a realistic or practical means of judging who was a committed Jew.[10]

In effect, the conversion of many thousands of Jews to Christianity destabilized the traditional categories of religious identity,[11] prompting the development of a "cultural gray area" that threw Jewish and Christian self-definition into question.[12] Conversions raised, for the first time, systemic doubt not only about who was a Christian and who was a Jew, but also about what defined Judaism.[13] For ibn Ḥabib, such uncertainties became most pronounced as he grappled with conversos wishing to return to the Jewish fold in the years following the expulsion.

Upon resettling in the Ottoman city of Salonika at the beginning of the sixteenth century, ibn Ḥabib confronted a variety of communal tensions intimately tied to the question of Jewish self-definition. Was the Jewish ancestry of a converso enough to identify him or her as a Jew? Were second- and third-generation conversos also Jews? Did a converso's commitment to Jewish praxis matter? Was faith a central component in making determinations as to whether a converso was a full-fledged Jew? The answers to these questions governed the ease with which conversos who wished to reidentify as Jews could do so. And yet no consensus emerged to quell the popular perceptions of conversion fostered not only by the native Romaniot Jewish community in the Ottoman empire but also by Iberian refugees.[14] (Romaniot Jews were members of the original Jewish community of the Ottoman empire, present from Byzantine times.) This situation worked against building and maintaining communal cohesion. It was difficult to break down the barriers that existed in the cities of the Ottoman empire between the Jewish community and the conversos.

Ibn Ḥabib took on this challenge and became deeply involved in the quagmire of problems posed by converts wishing to return to the Jewish fold. Many components of the discussions that arose in Salonika, interestingly, were not new. In fact earlier, well-entrenched legal positions informed ibn Ḥabib's own stance. Thus before one can discuss ibn Ḥabib's response to the conversos in the wake of the resettlement of Jews in the Ottoman empire and its impact on the *En Yaaqov*, it is important to address the legal decisions and religious perspectives that influenced him.

Confronting the Crisis of Religious Identity

During the fifteenth century in Spain, several prominent Spanish rabbis began to grapple openly with issues of Jewish identity in their legal writings, setting them out in responsa (legal responses to communal questions) and giving them visibility. They drew on earlier legal positions, as Jews had a history of confronting Jewish conversion to Christianity. The forced conversions during the eleventh century at the hands of the Crusaders prompted Rashi (d. 1040), the biblical and Talmudic exegete, to reinterpret an aggadic passage found in the Talmud (*b. San.* 44a) to make the argument that "a Jew is a Jew, even though he sinned." As Jacob Katz notes, it was Rashi who gave these words legal authority, valuing ancestry as the most powerful determinant of one's Jewishness.[15] During the twelfth century Maimonides, in response to the forced conversions of Jews by the Almohads, protectively warned against making accusations regarding a Jew's ancestry as a way of questioning it; ancestry was not to be used as a foil against itself in the religious polemics of the day. A convert remained a Jew if he had been forced to change his religion. For Maimonides, the crux of the issue was one of intent, borne out by individual decisionmaking.[16] By the fourteenth century, Rabbi Solomon ibn Adret (1235–1310) of Barcelona relied on Rashi's stance to argue that converts to Christianity who wished to return to Judaism did not need any type of reconversion ceremony such as, for example, immersion in the *mikve* (Jewish ritual bath). He maintained that "all Jewish families must be held as fit and emanating from the children of Israel."[17] Indeed, the legal responses of these rabbinic figures reflected the fact that for them one's Jewishness was an inherent characteristic that could not be rooted out by external means.[18]

Jews continued to be divided in their attitude toward conversion. Ibn Adret believed that one's election to Israel was indelible, arguing that a gentile son born to an apostate mother was a Jew, and yet maintained that the son was also loathsome.[19] In Adret's legal comments one senses his desire to uphold a belief in God's election of Israel. A sense of pragmatism runs through his legal declarations as he makes room to "allow" converts back into Judaism based on the notion of lineage. On the other hand, for ibn Adret the convert is still "other"; he is suspect. He is an individual whom the Jewish community cannot entirely embrace. It was this sense of "otherness" that continued to fuel tensions between Jews and conversos for generations, most especially as conversos from the Iberian Peninsula arrived in Salonika during the early sixteenth century.

Arguably, the Jews' interest in lineage became most pronounced following the 1391 massacres in Spain, which resulted in the conversions of many Jews. Lineage was the most significant way of emphasizing the continuing "Jewishness" of the converts at a time of great religious insecurity. One rabbi, Isaac ben Sheshet Perfet (1326–1408), who fled Valencia for North Africa after the massacres of 1391, insisted that all forced converts were to be considered Jews and to be forgiven. His successor, Simon ben Tsemaḥ Duran (1361–1444), a rabbi from Majorca who was trained in Spain and who fled after 1391, also argued that the conversos should not be judged negatively.[20] Such rulings were of crucial importance in grappling with communal questions related to marriage, divorce, inheritance, and ritual. In this regard, as David Nirenberg indicates, there were "two emerging genealogical emphases amongst the Sephardic rabbinate [during the fifteenth century], the one stressing the purity of certain lineages, the other insisting on the genealogical integrity and continued Jewishness of the converts and their descendents."[21] Interestingly, according to Nirenberg, it was this commitment to lineage that provoked new forms of historical consciousness and historical writing even prior to the expulsion from Spain. It also set the stage for first-generation Sephardic exiles like Solomon ibn Verga (mid-fifteenth century–early sixteenth century) and Abraham Zacuto (1452–1515) to produce historiographic works that were fitting examples of this literary trend. These were works that valued lineage as a way to narrate the history of the Jewish people.[22]

However, during the fifteenth century there was also another noticeable shift in the rhetoric surrounding the discussion of Jewish identity. The issue of Jewish lineage became integrated with questions about a convert's religious volition. Lineage was measurable and traceable; it even enabled Jews to embrace an authoritative belief in their origins and to be convinced of a stable transmission of their traditions.[23] But what about their faith? Was one's Jewish status related to one's choice regarding what he wished to believe about God and Torah? Concerns about Jewish identity and status provided the impetus to think about whether faith could be used as an adequate gauge to determine Jewish self-definition. Spain's rabbinic authorities wrestled with this question in their legal discussions as they contended with their discomfort over the converso issue,[24] opening the way for ibn Ḥabib to think about Jewish identity both from the perspective of lineage and from the perspective of one's inner religious convictions.

Several late fifteenth-century Spanish rabbinic authorities, including Abraham Saba, Isaac Caro, Joel ibn Shu'eib, Joseph Jabetz, and Isaac Abarbanel, authored responsa on the issue of the Jewish status of the conversos. Their rhetoric was both harsh and sympathetic as they tried to balance their suspicions with a sense of hope and pragmatism. Some argued that the conversos were sinners. They believed that in abandoning their Jewish faith the conversos had committed a "wicked" act.[25] In fact, as Joseph Hacker contends, the rise of the Inquisition prompted rabbinic leaders, such as Joel ibn Shu'eib and Isaac Arama (1420–1494), to argue that Israel had failed to live up to the ideal: that is, they had refused to view martyrdom as more preferable to succumbing to the accusations posed by their inquisitors. Was it truly better to have resisted one's enemies than to have surrendered their identities to the whims of Spanish religious zealousness?[26] For Arama and ibn Shu'eib, the idea that one's lineage remained intact or even that one possessed a degree of internal faith in his heart did not counter the fact that one had sinned by converting and refusing to martyr oneself.[27]

On the other hand, Spanish rabbis of the fifteenth century also understood that they could not pretend to know or to understand the motivations of each and every converso. Who had converted wholeheartedly? Did Jews convert in the wake of mob violence? Were they officially baptized?[28] When did they "cross the line" from Jew to Christian, if at all?

Answers to these types of questions led rabbis to distinguish between the external acts performed by the conversos and their chosen internal convictions, especially regarding those who were forced to convert. In spite of his negative views, Isaac Arama advocated that "the essence of the perfection of a man and [the essence of] his [religious] zeal is his faith." While conversos practiced idol worship in public, he believed they worshiped the God of Israel in their hearts.[29] Arama envisioned an unbreakable link between sincere faith and Jewish identity.[30] Driven by the desire to define that which unified all Jews and to construct a form of Judaism with which many could identify in spite of their converso status, rabbis discussed Judaism in terms of its essence. Abarbanel, for example, argued that faith was inseparable from the essence of Judaism; it could never be stripped away in the face of persecution. Although those who broke from the daily performance of commandments were sinners, they were still Jews, according to Abarbanel. As long as the act of conversion did not root out their inner faith and they preserved this faith clandestinely, they were Jews worthy of messianic redemption.[31] Ibn Verga reflected similarly when he wrote in *Shevet Yehudah:* "And what will it profit our lord and king to pour holy water on the Jews, calling them by our names 'Pedro' and 'Pablo' while they keep their faith like Akiba or Tarfon? . . . Know, Sire, that Judaism is one of those incurable diseases." In this world, Iberian Jewish thinkers argued that one's Judaism could not be rooted out by the holy waters of baptism as long as one's faith was steadfast.[32]

The goal in taking this view, on the part of rabbis like Abarbanel, was to create a more transcendent or immutable identity that would be "relevant across a range of diverse situations." Therefore it was necessary to make efforts to evaluate which of Judaism's values were the most enduring.[33] Rabbinic authorities thus found a way for Jews who had converted to continue to be considered Jews, thereby changing the scope of Jewish identity to include something less measurable than lineage or even praxis. At the same time, they envisioned a type of Judaism that was more "concise" in nature ("*yehadut shel tamtsit*"),[34] one that was able to defy or to rise above the times in which Jews of the fifteenth century found themselves.

It was this way of thinking that led Abraham Saba, a contemporary of ibn Ḥabib from Zamora, to conceptualize the *Shema,* a daily prayer through which Jews declared their faith in God each day, as one composed for the situation in which the conversos found themselves. While Saba never ignored the indelibility of God's election of the Jewish people, elevating circumcision as the one commandment that could protect a Jew's soul in the afterlife,[35] it was the *Shema,* in his opinion, and its statement of faith, that enabled Jews during times of persecution to pronounce silently the essence of their ancestral faith. The recitation of this prayer offered conversos the assurance that they could perform at least one commandment secretly that would not expose them as professing Jews. In addition, in the event they forgot or could not read the Torah, the *Shema* encapsulated the Torah itself. Through a quiet, daily, repetitive utterance of the prayer, they could invoke their belief in the entire Torah and in God.[36] This meant that for Saba the mere declaration of one's faith in God through prayer, rather than by the performance of external deeds (mitsvot), became a mechanism by which one of the two religions, Christianity or Judaism, claimed the will of its worshipers. Indeed, Saba's argument reflected his hope that the conversos would return to Judaism.[37]

Evidence of the struggle over the religious identity of the conversos pervaded many genres of literature, including legal literature (responsa literature), biblical exegeses,[38] and even philosophical treatises, throughout the fifteenth century. For example, the Jewish philosopher Ḥasdai Crescas, following the massacres of 1391, transformed the earlier legal ruling that converts are Jews despite the fact that they have sinned into a philosophical-theological category. For Crescas, one's inner desire to perform a commandment became an exercise in free will. In other words, if one's free will coincided with his desire to carry out commandments, he was rewarded, even if he did not actually perform them. In Crescas's mind conversion was predetermined by divine causation; it was part of God's plan. There was nothing the Jews could do to prevent it, and thus they should strive inwardly to believe in God and plead for divine mercy.[39]

Moreover, Crescas's work *Or Adonai* (3:2) appeared to offer guidance to the converso on how to remain Jewish in essence. One was to pray in church while keeping God in mind. Torah learning was valued less; one's devotion and faith in God mattered far more. Crescas believed that God's providence was in evidence in the way He took care even of those who sinned. He also offered words of encouragement to convince individuals that they had the ability to turn transgression into merit. Crescas viewed "rebelliousness" and subsequent repentance as a force that could prompt one to cling to God with greater strength. In this way he hoped to embolden his readers to always remain faithful Jews at heart.[40]

Whether through lineage or through arguments about the importance of one's inner faith, rabbinic leaders of the fifteenth century wrestled to define the boundaries that differentiated Jew from non-Jew and in the process nourished a conversation about Jewish self-definition. But the problematic status of the conversos did not disappear, even as Jews left Spain and resettled elsewhere. Each Jewish community following the expulsion continued to confront the issue of the conversos in some form. Their concerns evolved and took on new characteristics as Jews traveled from land to land, just as Jacob ibn Ḥabib had moved from Spain to Portugal and then to the Ottoman empire in search of a safe haven.

The Expulsion from Spain, Migration to Portugal, and Forced Conversion

The decree of expulsion issued by the Iberian monarchs King Ferdinand and Queen Isabella in 1492 marked the end of Spanish Jewry in Spain. Ibn Ḥabib chose to migrate to Portugal, as the signs of a rich Jewish communal life were in evidence there.[41] Its myriad synagogues and Jewish academies, not to mention its Hebrew printing presses, set the stage for continuity rather than disruption in the Jews' attempts to begin life anew. Cultural similarities—as Portugal was also a part of the Iberian Peninsula—eased the transition. Furthermore, in Portugal, unlike Spain, there appeared to be no forced conversions or uprisings against the Jews.[42]

In the end, however, ibn Ḥabib miscalculated in choosing Portugal as his country of refuge.[43] By 1497 he had to confront forced conversions at the hands of the Portuguese. After the death of King John II of Portugal in 1495, Ferdinand and Isabella had renewed their efforts to unite the entire peninsula. The Spanish monarchs made the marriage of their daughter to King John II's successor, Manuel I, conditional on the expulsion of the Jews; they would have to leave Portugal by October 1497.[44] However, once the decree was established, the king made every attempt to mold its outcome to suit the needs of his kingdom, which was on the brink of becoming an important European power. Manuel I was aware that if the Jews were expelled, his kingdom would lose an "active and enterprising minority" possessing both significant knowledge and wealth. His act would, therefore, threaten Portugal's continued growth.[45]

History did not repeat itself: The Spanish decree of expulsion of 1492 had provided Jews with the option to leave Spain or to stay, albeit with consequences. They could remain in Spain only as Christians. In the case of Portugal's Jews, there was little choice.[46] To protect his interests, in 1497 King Manuel I decided to forcibly baptize the entire Jewish community rather than to expel them, making it difficult, if not impossible, for Jews to leave.[47] It would appear, therefore, that ibn Ḥabib and his family were forced to confront the baptismal font with no choices and no means of escape.

There are no documents attesting precisely to what occurred to ibn Ḥabib in Lisbon in 1497, as even the descriptions of forced baptisms recorded by the Jewish and Portuguese chroniclers do not provide adequate or comprehensive accounts of the process. Maria José Pimenta Ferro Tavares attributes this lack of clarity to the "shock and chaos of the events [that] wiped out the specific memories of time and place."[48] In addition, there was great confusion over what was initially a decree of expulsion, which King Manuel ultimately retracted in 1497. Ports of embarkation had been set up to carry Jews to other places. However, when the Jews arrived to board these ships, they were instead forcibly baptized[49] as part of King Manuel's campaign to maintain his Jewish constituency in the form of a new Christian population.

Yet there is evidence that a number of Jews managed to escape.[50] Indeed, Abraham Saba narrates such an escape in his commentary on the Book of Ruth, *Eshkol Hakofer:*

> In short, they stripped me, and took away my sons and daughters, and all that I had remained there and I was left with nothing. And I and the (Ms. Parma: forty) others were imprisoned and chained (Ms. Parma: so that we would convert), and after six months (Ms. Parma: when the king realized that he did not succeed), the king ordered to give us one broken ship to take us to Arzila (near Tangiers), and I remained here, in El Kasar El Kebir, and this holy community clothed my nakedness and supplied me with all my needs . . . and I was here for a long time while sick with a heavy head and eyes, for I remembered my sons and books that I left behind, especially, those books that I composed [and lost].[51]

Whether ibn Ḥabib resisted the Portuguese authorities and was imprisoned like Saba is shrouded in mystery, and scholars continue to speculate about the events that led to his release from Portugal. The scholar Isaiah Tishby cites a fragmentary piece of genizah disclosing a group of eight individuals in Portugal who refused to convert; they were imprisoned, eventually released, and, finally, sent to North Africa. Tishby concludes that ibn Ḥabib was one of them.[52] Tishby cites as further evidence ibn Ḥabib's introduction to the *En Yaaqov,* where he states that he could not prepare his work until he arrived in Salonika because he did not have the appropriate Talmudic books available to him. For Tishby, ibn Ḥabib could not have been referring to Lisbon in his introduction because tractates of the Talmud were obtainable there. He concludes, therefore, that ibn Ḥabib must have been describing his experience in North Africa, in a place where there was a dearth of manuscripts and printed tractates of the Talmud.[53]

A legal source authored by ibn Ḥabib, which refers to "a few days when the [Jews] could attempt bravely to leave the turmoil,"[54] supports the idea that he had a small window of opportunity to escape from Lisbon in 1497. But the fact that there is no document that explicitly outlines the details of ibn Ḥabib's flight or offers details regarding the course of his travels between 1497 and 1500 means that Tishby's argument remains conjecture.[55] Certainly, ibn Ḥabib was embroiled in the traumas that defined the period and was caught in the throes of Manuel's decree, but the details remain unclear.

Some information is available regarding ibn Ḥabib's son, Levi ibn Ḥabib, who was forcibly baptized in 1497, although the details of that conversion also remain unclear. Scholars have argued that Levi ibn Ḥabib was abducted by the Portuguese authorities as part of a decree imposed on children under the age of fourteen, whom they forcibly converted and placed into Christian homes.[56] This would account for the fact that Levi ibn Ḥabib and his father may have become separated and therefore suffered different fates, even arriving in Salonika at different times.[57] However, it is more likely that by 1497 Levi ibn Ḥabib was an adult and was converted when separated from his father in the wake of the confusion that accompanied Manuel's decree.[58] The evidence that Levi ibn Ḥabib began to teach in Salonika immediately on his arrival there in 1498, and that he lived in Salonika for several years prior to the resettlement of his father in 1501, supports the notion that he was forcibly baptized as an adult.[59] It is hard to imagine that he escaped as a child with enough knowledge to begin teaching in Salonika as soon as he arrived, as the responsum quoted below attests. The depth of the tragedy that had occurred to Levi ibn Ḥabib, like that of the Jews who were forced to convert under similar circumstances, remained with him for decades. Despite the forced nature of his conversion, he reflects on it with a sense of unending regret and guilt in this responsum, which he authored forty years after his arrival in Salonika, while serving as a rabbi in Jerusalem:

> Not for my sake am I, God forbid [writing this], but for the sake of all the forced converts who have found themselves in the same unfortunate situation, who placed themselves in great dangers and escaped [Portugal] and did not see any goodness until they returned to Judaism. And many of them died [and

inherited] life in the World to Come. And even if others chose to change my name, I did not change it. And, anyone who examines [my] heart and searches my conscience will know that I always feared God. And, if I did not merit [by dying in order to] sanctify God's name[60] [know that] my heart will grieve inside me in the face of His anger. . . . And inasmuch as He [God] succeeded in saving me from destruction and brought me to this praiseworthy city [Salonika] in the selfsame year [of my conversion] in order [that I could] teach the law every day until this day, that there are [now] more than forty years, so I have merited in returning to Judaism.[61]

This responsum indicates the extent to which forced converts like Levi ibn Ḥabib, who returned to Judaism, struggled personally. They felt pangs of guilt for resisting martyrdom. Prominent rabbinic figures like Jacob Berav (1474–1546) also posed additional challenges. Berav's support for the reestablishment of the ancient Sanhedrin (Jewish court) would have granted the Jewish community the power to sentence individuals, including converts, to punishment in order to clear them of sin.[62] Did Levi ibn Ḥabib deserve to be punished? As a prominent rabbinic figure who had become an accepted member of the Jewish community, why could he not find solace? What were the effects of his experience with conversion on Jacob ibn Ḥabib, his father?

One should not readily dismiss the effects of conversion on a father who was unable to protect his son from the tragic realities of a monarchical decree.[63] Although Jacob ibn Ḥabib may not have converted, he could understand the pain it caused those who underwent conversions and later attempted to return to Judaism. It was this concern that had a pronounced impact on his legal decisions regarding conversion. The section that follows analyzes the manner in which ibn Ḥabib dealt with conversos on his arrival in the Ottoman city of Salonika.

Grappling with Conversos in Salonika: The Legal Sources

In the early sixteenth-century Ottoman empire, the debate surrounding the status of the conversos continued despite the fact that the players had shifted. Admittedly, there were no forced conversions or monarchical decrees targeting the Jews in the Ottoman cities of Constantinople (Istanbul) and Salonika during ibn Ḥabib's day which could parallel what had occurred to them in Spain and then in Portugal. Jews were welcome to return to their ancestral roots. And yet there were instances where conversos returned to Spain and Portugal,[64] as well as cases of Jews who converted to Islam. In one instance of note, Elijah Mizraḥi, the *marbits torah* (rabbinic leader) of the Romaniot Jewish community in Constantinople, and ibn Ḥabib's opponent in matters of conversion, was personally affected by the conversion of his own son to Islam.

Mizraḥi's son, Gershon, was rumored to have converted voluntarily during the course of an illness. Within a responsum where Mizraḥi discredits the rabbinic leaders of Candia (Crete) for slandering one of their rabbis, Joseph Algazi, he defends his son, arguing that Gershon had no intention of converting.[65] In Mizraḥi's mind, Gershon had been maligned and rejected by a community that believed him to be a sincere convert to Islam. He pleads desperately for understanding in the wake of circumstances that were beyond his son's control. In Mizraḥi's portrayal, Gershon left his family in Tokat and paid large sums of money to bribe the local authorities so that he could flee to a place where he could return to Judaism willingly. Mizraḥi also claims that Muslim functionaries and subjects from Amasya, Tokat, Ankara, and Bursa struggled fiercely to ensure that Gershon remained a Muslim.[66] However, these facts did not prevent his son's community from lambasting him. So incensed was Mizraḥi by the way his son was treated that he spoke out against his community through the language of *b. B. Metsia* 58b: "All who descend into Gehinnom [subsequently re-ascend] except three who descend but do not re-ascend, [including] . . . [he who] publicly shames his neighbor." And, furthermore, "He who publicly shames his neighbor is tantamount to he who sheds blood."[67] While the details of the events surrounding Gershon's connection to Islam will never be known, it is clear from the strength of Mizraḥi's language that he found the reaction (or potential reaction) of the Jewish community to his son just as disconcerting as the conversion itself.[68]

Mizraḥi's response illustrates how matters related to conversion weighed heavily on the rabbis of the early sixteenth-century Ottoman empire. Mizraḥi testifies to the fact that while the Ottomans did not issue decrees that led to the forced conversion of the entire Jewish community to Islam, the threat of conversion during this period extended well beyond the Iberian exiles and their attachments (whether sincere or in name only) to Catholicism. The potential for Jews to convert remained a possibility even in the Ottoman empire. Gershon's conversion, in particular, underscores the power of the *qadis* (local governors) and even the local Muslim population to place pressure on the administrative and legal functionaries in various cities regarding conversions to Islam.[69] Furthermore, as long as religion was wedded to ethnicity, which was true during this period, and certain religions made allowances that others did not (whether economic or social), conversion remained a possibility.[70] Even the freedoms afforded Jews in the Ottoman empire did not override the desire for opportunities that being Muslim could offer.[71]

Ibn Ḥabib's transition to the Ottoman world was marked by concerns about the conversos that were similar to those that had surfaced during the fifteenth century in Spain. He encountered the distrust of those who wondered why Jews had not fled Portugal in greater numbers, or why conversos who chose to remain in Spain in 1492 did not find their way to the Ottoman cities sooner. The question why more Jews had not chosen to martyr themselves loomed once again. There was also a feeling of discomfort, certainly expressed by Elijah Mizrahi, over Jews being drawn to Islam.

The conversos themselves also wrestled. For some, like Levi ibn Ḥabib, as noted in the responsum quoted earlier, the power of self-reproach weighed heavily. Could they ever repent for their past transgressions even if Christianity had been forced on them? Some ex-conversos who had lived as Christians for longer periods of time than Levi ibn Ḥabib also had difficulty readjusting to Judaism. The realities of adult circumcision, their unfamiliarity with the synagogue service, their inability to read Hebrew, and the extent to which Jewish texts (Bible and Talmud) began to govern their lives was frustrating. This led to varying degrees of resistance to Judaism on the part of the ex-conversos, including attacks on rabbinic culture.[72] Some ex-conversos converted back to Christianity and some to Islam. Some returned to Spain and Portugal.[73]

Questions of Jewish status were also vital as, for example, in cases where converso wives left their husbands and attempted to remarry Jews on their arrival in the cities of the Ottoman empire. Could a once-converso wife, even if she returned to Judaism, marry a Jew? Could the Jewish community comfortably welcome and absorb these ex-converso wives? Indeed, ibn Ḥabib's writings present a rabbinic figure who was concerned about the legal and psychological challenges posed by the conversos. In reaction ibn Ḥabib authored *haskamot* (legal ordinances that reflected the consensus of various members of the Jewish community) in the hope of countering the challenges that conversion posed. In addition, his aggadic commentary reflected an underlying concern for reintegrating conversos into the Jewish community.

Ibn Ḥabib was faced with a staunch anti-converso current that was upheld even by refugees of the Spanish expulsion. From as far away as North Africa, Spanish Jews like Jacob Berav claimed that a Jew who had converted was "worse than a full-fledged Christian." This led Berav to argue that synagogue donations should not be accepted from converts. But the strength of his position against the conversos is reflected more strongly in Berav's demand for the reinstitution of the ancient rabbinic punishment of lashes to punish and assuage the guilt of conversos who desired to return to Judaism.[74] Moreover, the Spanish rabbi Judah Benveniste argued that leniencies toward the conversos on the part of rabbis with the power to invoke legal decisions would preclude "a share in the God of Israel."[75]

In the Ottoman empire the Romaniot *marbits torah*, Elijah Mizraḥi, fueled the debate. Romaniot Jews laid claim to authority in matters of Jewish law over and above the newly arrived Spanish and Portuguese exiles by virtue of their ancient roots in Constantinople and its environs. For Mizraḥi in particular, evaluating whether a Jew was a full-fledged convert was important for maintaining Romaniot hegemony throughout the region.

On one level, ibn Ḥabib shared Mizraḥi's views. A *haskamah* signed by ibn Ḥabib and several other rabbis who were part of a central governing body in Salonika at the beginning of the sixteenth century[76] supported Mizraḥi's position invalidating all marriages that took place during the years of religious persecution.[77] Women would thereby not be compelled to acquire divorce contracts (*gittin*), normally required for purposes of remarriage, from their converso husbands who remained abroad as new Christians in the lands of the Iberian Peninsula.[78] Women who would have needed to perform either Levirate marriage, which required that widowed women marry their brothers-in-law, or *ḥalitsah*, which freed women from this requirement, were also exempt from Levirate marriage and *ḥalitsah* if the original marriage had taken place in Spain or Portugal in front of witnesses who were conversos. Each woman was allowed the freedom to remarry.

There should be little doubt that leniency was granted to women who were connected to converso husbands or brothers-in-law living in Spain or Portugal. It spared them the dangers involved in trying to locate their husbands abroad and released them from acquiring documents necessary for obtaining divorces. In this way, the *haskamah* gave them tremendous latitude with respect to remarriage. The legal ruling allowed women who had converted to Christianity and who wished to return to Judaism to assimilate into the Jewish community more readily. Becoming the wives of Jews enabled their seamless readmission into the Jewish community. The *haskamah* also reduced the risk that they would distance themselves from Judaism on the grounds that the Jewish community had created impenetrable legal boundaries.

The *haskamah* signed by ibn Ḥabib was constructed on the premise that all marriages performed between conversos after 1492 in Spain and after 1497 in Portugal were performed in front of invalid witnesses who were also converts. Therefore, they were null and void. As a person's halakhic observance was a primary requirement for serving as a valid witness, no converso could legitimize any marital union. Ironically, the very same ruling that released female conversas from their marriages abroad so that they could remarry cast aspersions on male conversos by disqualifying them on the basis of their external behavior.[79] But this dissonance attests to the level of pragmatism that drove ibn Ḥabib's decisions. Reentry into the Jewish community via remarriage was paramount for conversas.

But the essence of ibn Ḥabib's attitude toward the conversos comes to the fore more clearly in the second *haskamah* he authored several years later. Directly challenging the Romaniot leader Mizraḥi, this *haskamah* issued a legal stringency requiring that all widowed women who were married in the Ottoman empire in the presence of valid witnesses perform Levirate marriage or *halitsah,* even if their brothers-in-law were in Spain or Portugal and living as non-Jews.[80] In other words, if a woman's husband died in Salonika before she was able to have children with him, and her marriage to him had been performed in front of valid witnesses, she was legally required to marry her husband's brother (levir), or closest male relative, to ensure that his family line continued (Deut. 25:5–6). A childless widow in Salonika was not free from the commandment of Levirate marriage—that is, marriage to her Iberian or Portuguese brother-in-law—until he performed the ceremony that released her, *halitsah.* This gave every childless, widowed Jewish woman who had relatives living as conversos abroad the responsibility of tracking them down before she could think about remarriage to another man. The difficulties in accomplishing this task were considerable. If the childless widow could locate her brother-in-law, she would need to bring him to Salonika, for example, where a Jewish court existed, so that either a legal Jewish marriage could be performed or, as was more likely the case, *halitsah* could be legally executed to allow her to enter into another marriage union. This was an unlikely scenario. Conversos could not readily leave Spain and Portugal, nor did many wish to do so. In addition, the lines of communication were not always open between Jews in the Ottoman empire and conversos in the Iberian Peninsula, who had to conceal all attachments to their Jewish past. In other words, ibn Ḥabib's ruling that a widow had to perform either Levirate marriage or *halitsah,* even when her levir was a convert, severely curtailed her ability to remarry following the death of her husband.

On the surface, this ruling seems to undermine the leniencies proposed by ibn Ḥabib in the earlier *haskamah,* in that remarriage became more difficult, if not impossible, for Jews who had entered into legal Jewish marriages in the Ottoman empire with familial connections to conversos living abroad. But when ibn Ḥabib chose to take a stance regarding Levirate marriage, he entered into a longstanding debate that had prevailed among earlier rabbis, specifically, the geonim. He opposed the ruling set forth by Yehudai Gaon and upheld by Elijah Mizraḥi[81] that labeled the convert a full-fledged Muslim or Christian who deserved to be cut off from the Jewish community. Regarding the issue of the childless widow whose marriage had been performed in front of valid witnesses and whose levir was a convert, Rabbi Yehudai ruled that Levirate marriage and *ḥalitsah* should not be performed. Under such circumstances the childless widow was free to remarry whomever she desired as a result of a ruling that also promised to diminish the number of *agunot* (women who were bound to marriages they could not dissolve and who therefore could not remarry).[82]

On the surface Yehudai and, later, Mizraḥi fostered a more lenient position regarding the childless widow than ibn Ḥabib by allowing widows the freedom to remarry without performing Levirate marriage. This was in spite of Mizraḥi's consistently stringent attitude in regular cases of Levirate marriage, where over and over again he defended the rights of deceased husbands and their brothers against the rights of widows.[83] However, the underlying motivations for Yehudai's position, as elaborated upon by Mizraḥi, represented a negative attitude toward anyone who converted to Christianity or Islam. Mizraḥi's position reflected a desire to admonish the levir for having chosen to convert, castigating him not only for rejecting Judaism but also for having subsequently severed the familial relationship between brothers necessary for the proper performance of Levirate marriage, as noted in Deut. 25:5–6. According to Mizraḥi, when one brother converted, he broke all familial bonds. He was no longer a Jew.

Mizraḥi's negative opinion was rooted in his discomfort over converts who violated the Sabbath in public or who had engaged in "idolatrous worship."[84] They violated the framework of Jewish practice that pervaded and defined Judaism at that time. It was troublesome to think that people were making their own decisions regarding which commandments to observe and which to reject. This threatened not only Mizraḥi's authority but also the definition of Judaism he espoused. Mizraḥi writes: "If it happens in my lifetime that people rely on their own opinion to justify the desecration of the Sabbath . . . what will happen after my death? . . . People who have never seen the light of Torah issue faulty instructions contrary to religion on their own authority."[85]

Mizraḥi's attitude toward the conversos was connected to his discomfort with the idea that Jews could make choices without any superimposed rabbinic authority. The presence of conversos who wished to return to Judaism endangered the development and preservation of a cohesive, even monolithic type of Judaism, where people not only observed the same mitsvot but also performed them in the same way. The conversos, in particular, had no common religious identity and few of the characteristics that generally define social groups.[86] They characterized themselves in a myriad of ways that ranged from those who wished to remain Catholic to those who desired a full return to Judaism. Indeed, Mizraḥi's comment conveys that he felt his authority being threatened by those who were selective in what they observed, not to mention by rabbis like ibn Ḥabib, who arrived in the Ottoman empire from the Iberian Peninsula possessing different attitudes regarding the status of conversos. In studying the conversos, one might even begin to hear the early strains of criticisms regarding modern-day Jews and the way they have asserted their own autonomy and challenged rabbinic authority. Indeed, Yirmiyahu Yovel has argued that these converts "pre-illustrate[d] or anticipate[d] main features and claims of Western modernization."[87]

Yet Mizraḥi did encourage conversos to return to Judaism with the promise of the reward of the World to Come and the understanding that their repentance would earn them greater honor than that received by a righteous person.[88] Mizraḥi argued that "idolators" who had repented could reintegrate into the Jewish community, even be appointed as cantors and discharge worshipers of their obligations in prayer.[89] His attitude, however, cannot be seen outside of his view that conversos were converts who had sinned completely. Indeed, in his mind these converts could not move seamlessly back into the Jewish fold without repenting before God in a manner that characterized their past lives as fully transgressive. That Mizraḥi refused to see his own son as a person who had chosen to convert voluntarily may have been due to his negative views on the subject of conversion and his more limited exposure to it, as compared to ibn Ḥabib's firsthand knowledge.

Influenced by his own experience with the conversos, ibn Ḥabib thought differently. While he viewed conversion as strong enough to disqualify someone as a valid witness, it was not, in his mind, powerful enough to sever one's relationship to Judaism or, more specifically, the relationship between two brothers who were born Jews. This explains ibn Ḥabib's decision to sign two *haskamot* that, on the surface, appear to be contradictory in their effect on women desirous of remarriage. However, when viewed from the perspective of a rabbi who wished to view the conversos as full-fledged Jews, the two *haskamot* convey a coherent perspective. Conversos who serve as witnesses invalidate marriages because they are disqualified by Jewish law even though they are full-fledged Jews. Therefore, women who enter into these legally invalid marriages can, upon their return to Judaism, marry freely and are not required to perform Levirate marriage. However, if a Jewish marriage is performed in front of valid witnesses in the Ottoman empire, the husband and wife of such a union are required to perform all the legal requirements incumbent upon them, including Levirate marriage, should the marriage dissolve for any reason. It did not matter that the levir might be living as a convert abroad because, in ibn Ḥabib's mind, his conversion was not powerful enough to sever the tie between him and his brother. Internally, he was still a Jew.

For Mizraḥi, conversion to Christianity or even Islam was exclusionary and deemed the convert as "other." For ibn Ḥabib, conversions were to be categorized as forced, insincere acts, done in name only. These acts did not reflect what was truly in the hearts of those who converted, as he writes:

> And surely it has been fifteen years . . . since the days of religious persecution and forced apostasy, when many of our brethren were brought [to experience] by necessity the violation of [their] bod[ies] and their fortune[s] in order to present themselves as true converts who had publicly denied the existence of God and the Torah of Moses . . .
>
> And also many of the unlearned who until this day have [remained] intermingled [with others] in the land of their enemies, who knows what is in their hearts? And it is necessary to place them on the scale of merit as forced converts through and through [who did not voluntarily choose to convert]. And tomorrow they [will] come to us [in order to live lives as openly professing Jews] and now we insult them by judging them as full-fledged converts [capable of allowing their sisters-in-law to remarry without performing levirate marriage or *ḥalitsah*]? Please, may God save us from such a thought.[90]

Ibn Ḥabib's ability to overlook the legal transgressions of the conversos emerged from his commitment to integrating the concept of lineage with an understanding that Jewishness exists in one's heart. The performance of external deeds did not necessarily prove one's Jewishness. Surely this view paralleled the position of many of his Spanish predecessors and contemporaries. The idea was to create an unbreakable link between converts and Jews. Therefore in his legal writings he invoked the centuries' old dictum that even though the conversos had sinned, they were still to be considered Jews.[91] In his refusal to doubt their Jewishness, he also held that the conversos "and their children and their grandchildren, [were] by law for all time, Jews."[92] At the same time, he placed converts on a "scale of merit," believing that in their hearts they had always identified as Jews. And once lineage was intertwined with a belief that one could identify inwardly as a Jew without performing mitsvot, ibn Ḥabib undermined the sense that conversos who wished to return to Judaism were somehow "other." He did not view identity in binary terms; instead he embraced a position that broadened and deepened Jewish self-definition in the direction of greater inclusivity.

While for Mizraḥi conversos who wished to return to Judaism needed to repent for their sins, ibn Ḥabib made no such demands. In fact, by taking a more stringent position on the issue of Levirate marriage, ibn Ḥabib was also able to uphold a longstanding legal view shared by Sherira Gaon and other Spanish Jewish authorities, including Rashi, Moses Maimonides (1135–1204), Moses Naḥmanides (1194–1270), and Solomon ibn Adret,[93] in the name of what mattered to him: integrating conversos back into the Jewish community.[94] The psychological benefits of such a perspective could be felt by conversos who, like Levi ibn Ḥabib, were ashamed of their past deeds. They could look back and remind as well as comfort themselves that internally they had always identified as Jews.

More significant, however, was ibn Ḥabib's plea in the preceding passage not to judge the conversos too harshly. With full knowledge that group cohesion required each of its members to accept the other, ibn Ḥabib warned against harboring negative sentiments against the conversos. Armed with the ultimate objective of integrating returning conversos into the Jewish fold, ibn Ḥabib exposed the largest threat to the construction of a cohesive group: the failure to judge the members of one's community properly.[95] If the conversos were dismissed as willing apostates in all legal matters, they became further stigmatized, and the chances of their acceptance within the Jewish community remained remote.

But ibn Ḥabib's legal rulings could only go so far in overcoming the stigmas already in place regarding the conversos. He needed to do much more to create a cohesive new community in Salonika that not only would welcome the conversos but would also adapt to the multiethnic Jewish community that Iberian Jews encountered there.[96] Ibn Ḥabib was also well aware that there were no assurances. The political situation could change; Jews could once again face the threat of forced conversions and expulsion. He thus turned to work on the *En Yaaqov*. There, in his commentary, one observes a man who wished to speak to a broad Jewish community and to help them compassionately to strengthen their faith. The *En Yaaqov* cast legal analysis aside in favor of an examination of Judaism's nonlegal classical texts in an attempt to respond to many of the issues the conversos brought into focus: communal dissension, stigmatization, Jewish self-definition, and the value of faith. In this regard, the *En Yaaqov* became a prime example of religious adaptation following the expulsion from Spain. It represents one strategy employed by a rabbinic leader engaged in rebuilding life in a new locale.[97]

The Impact of the Conversos: Evidence from the En Yaaqov

Ibn Ḥabib's involvement in matters pertaining to the conversos—whether as a witness to forced conversions, as the head of an academy in Salamanca living alongside conversos, as a Jew in Portugal exposed to a decree requiring that all Jews convert, as a rabbi grappling with the halakhic issues that arose as a result of the presence of conversos in Salonika and abroad, as the father of a son who had converted, or as a welcoming and supportive force to those desirous of returning to Judaism—had a significant impact on his analyses of Talmudic aggadah in the *En Yaaqov*. His interest in the inner religious lives of Jews and the contours of faith emerged at the precise moment when reintegrating conversos into the Jewish community was most acute. He penned his commentary in Salonika at the beginning of the sixteenth century, hoping to encourage Jews to harbor strong inner and outer religious convictions. In many of his comments, one observes the wide experiential lens of a rabbi who had little interest in calling attention to his time and place, but who was centrally informed by the events that occurred there.

Ibn Ḥabib makes no explicit mention of the conversos in his introduction to the *En Yaaqov* or in his commentary to the aggadot of the Talmud. Instead, ibn Ḥabib's messages bear the timeless quality so evident in many of the documents produced in his day. Not surprisingly, he uses the destruction of the Temple as a paradigm for tragedy and as a basis for discussing religious and spiritual renewal, instead of disclosing the time-dependent historical and current details that characterized his historical moment.[98] His exegeses offer comfort to those who sinned in the face of extenuating circumstances without ever mentioning the conversos explicitly. Ibn Ḥabib exonerates biblical figures from sin and operates to instill inner faith in the hearts and souls of his constituency without fully revealing a connection to his life experience. But the link is undeniable by virtue of the ideas he continuously raises in his commentary. His concern for the inner conviction of Jews and their faith emerges against the historical backdrop of religious conversion. This experience was one factor that triggered his interest not only in faith but also in the relationship between inner belief and Jewish identity. Although chapter 4 reflects more fully on ibn Ḥabib's commitment to cultivating faithful Jews, the discussion below offers an example of ibn Ḥabib's compassion for those not able to observe mitsvot due to circumstances beyond their control.

An aggadic passage (*b. Ber.* 7a) portrays Moses questioning God as to why unfortunate circumstances occur to righteous people. In response ibn Ḥabib, not unlike his predecessors Isaac Caro and Isaac Abarbanel,[99] labors to prove that one cannot possibly know the innermost thoughts of the people with whom one comes in contact. Recalling the experience of the converso, albeit implicitly, ibn Ḥabib makes the argument that a person can pretend to be on the outside what he is not on the inside.[100] Therefore one should refrain from trying to understand God's system of reward and punishment based on external deeds. By citing in his commentary a midrash found in *Shemot Rabbah* regarding Moses's discovery of three treasures, ibn Ḥabib elaborates on his position.[101]

When Moses asks in *Shemot Rabbah,* "To whom does this first treasure belong?" God answers, "To those who fulfill my commandments." And when Moses points to the second treasure and asks, "To whom does this treasure belong?" God answers, "To the orphans." Finally, Moses points to a third treasure and asks one more time, "To whom does this great treasure belong?" God replies, "This is the treasure that I have set aside for those who have no credit in order to dispense reward to those who may not necessarily have earned it." Ibn Ḥabib made the following remarks with regard to this midrash:

> [And this text from *Shemot Rabbah*] alludes to [the case of] the man who desires in his soul to better his understanding and his deeds. [But] this man doesn't have the preparation [so as to] fulfill his desire due to the many external obstacles which confront him and prevent him from acting as he wishes. And because of this he does not have the means [by which] he can become [a] gracious servant. But God knows [the] thoughts [that people

possess], [and He] prepares a large treasure for the man [who is in this situation]. And from this [treasure] he gives [this man] a free reward and [God] does so with righteousness, justice, graciousness, and mercifulness.[102]

This source makes no explicit linguistic reference to the converso (*meshumad, anus*) or to the lands of persecution (*artsot hashemad*), and the larger comment is not limited to the issues raised by conversos. However, the implicit reference here to those who experience "external obstacles" that impede study and observance conjures up the image of the converso. Although such a person cannot be considered a "gracious servant" of God, according to ibn Ḥabib, he can be the recipient of God's graciousness; he can receive a grand reward, greater than if he had "raised orphans" or "performed mitsvot," as *Shemot Rabbah* intimates. Despite ibn Ḥabib's decision to leave the category of "external obstacles" undefined, the comment conjures an image of the situation of Jews who were forced to convert. These were Jews who were unable to lead observant Jewish lives due to obstacles that were beyond their control. Indeed, the source corroborates ibn Ḥabib's view, as communicated in his legal writings, that one's thoughts or inner disposition can inform—even define—one's identity. He wrote this comment believing that no enemy of Judaism could forcibly convert a Jew who did not want to be converted. While monarchs and clerics had the power to convert Jews in name only, they had no control over the conversos' inner religious lives. For this reason, if a converso did not embrace Christianity internally, there was no divine punishment.[103] Rather, there might even be great reward. The source implies that the average person, in ibn Ḥabib's opinion, did not have the ability to predict who would be rewarded and who would be punished based on observable behaviors. So much depended on what was internal and visible to God alone.

In establishing that one's commitment to God and Jewish tradition is based on one's inner volition, ibn Ḥabib warns against misjudging oneself and one's fellow Jews. When external behaviors are dismissed as a workable gauge for membership within the community, a place is carved out for those who are different. According to ibn Ḥabib, the prophet Isaiah's remark, "Who is among you that fears the Lord, that obeys the voice of his servant, that walks in darkness and has no light?" (Is. 50:10), refers to those who fear God despite the fact that the "spirit of the times [stands] in opposition to [them]." In ibn Ḥabib's opinion, while God-fearing individuals stand in darkness and have no light, they also continue to trust in the name of God, who has the power to bring "darkness" to an end.[104] This belief in God earns them the right to be considered sincere Jews despite external transgressions like conversion.

Ibn Ḥabib also turns to the figure of King David who, in an aggadic passage found on *b. Ber.* 4a, refers to himself as "devout" in spite of his own moral infractions. Certainly David's relationship with Batsheva, resulting in his decision to murder her husband, Uriah, calls the personal integrity of this Israelite king into question. What of such hubris? What of the fact that, in the aggadic passage in *b. Ber.* 4a, a quote from Ps. 86:1–2 presents David begging for God's protection as if he deserves it? In response to this aggadic pericope, ibn Ḥabib emerges not only as a commentator bent on searching for a way to excuse David's sordid behavior (as was typical of rabbinic commentators desirous of whitewashing biblical figures)[105] but also as a rabbi committed to describing the inner workings of the relationship between God and human beings. Ibn Ḥabib moves the figure of David beyond the character description constructed in the *Bavli* (Babylonian Talmud), where the king proves his righteousness through a set of external acts, including giving up sleep to thank God in prayer, advising women regarding issues of marital status, and consulting his teacher and advisor, Mefiboshet, about the propriety of his judgments. David is reconstructed by ibn Ḥabib as a perfect man of internal faith who acted against his true "instinct" when confronting Batsheva and Uriah. God knows the "secrets of [a man's] conscience and has the ability to pardon a person for his sins if and only if he has the proper disposition as David did." Ibn Ḥabib writes:

And when [a person] concedes [his sinful behavior] and abandons [it], he says before Him [God], may He be blessed, "surely you know that I am perfect in this thing, may it be your will to pardon [this] sudden transgression." And this was the intention of David in [putting forth] the [following] request, ["Protect my soul because I am devout" (Ps. 86:2)] because since [God], may He be blessed, knows that [David] was devout in an all-encompassing [way] toward Him,[106] it was fitting to pardon him from the sin of Batsheva and Uriah. [This is] because his [true] instinct was violated in order to do this [act].[107] And similarly, [David prayed to God for vindication because God had not punished him for any of his actions saying], "Probe me, O Lord and test me" (Ps. 26:2).[108] [But, God did not test David because He knew that his] "inside was like his outside."[109] [And David continued,] "my eyes are on your steadfast love" (Ps. 27:3), that is, it was inscribed in [David's] heart that there is no assistance except from the God who does mercy for thousands, may He be blessed. And second, [that David] was perfect in his ideas about faith[110] and expressed [this] point when he said [the following]: "I always walk in your true [path]" (Ps. 26:3). These are the thoughts that are hidden in [David's] heart and that are known before Him [God].[111]

In ibn Ḥabib's mind David is a blameless man of faith who acted against his true "instinct"; he is a man who keeps his true thoughts hidden in his heart. Most significant, however, is ibn Ḥabib's desire to highlight the relationship between God and human beings by stressing that only God knows a person's "true" inclinations and thoughts. David was a devoted servant of God in spite of his sins against Batsheva and Uriah, according to ibn Ḥabib. His actions did not reflect his natural instinct for piety and faithfulness. They were exceptional, extenuating, fleeting, and therefore also forgivable. In fact, it was David's positive instincts, hidden thoughts, and God's knowledge of the "secrets of his conscience" that prompted God's pardon. This left David in the right position to label himself a pious and devoted servant of God, as noted in the aggadic passage. In fact, by invoking the same phrase used by Rabban Gamaliel in an aggadah found in *b. Ber.* 28a to describe those upright students who deserved admission to the academy, ibn Ḥabib transforms David into a man who, like these impeccable students, can be described as having an "inside" that is exactly equivalent to his "outside." His contradictions are therefore resolved. Ibn Ḥabib grasps this Talmudic image to emphasize that David's internal qualities can be seen by God, who alone knows the true intentions of His servants. And so, David is forgiven.

The ideological latitude offered here by ibn Ḥabib is remarkable. The internal, emotional, and spiritual aspects of one's relationship with God are able to override outright external transgression, even murder. Certainly the dangers of such an ideology are self-evident. Ibn Ḥabib's concern for such hazards surfaces in his final interpretive stance as he begins to grapple with the portion of the aggadic passage that presents David in doubt over whether he will be counted among the righteous in the future. By relying on Rashi's midrashic reinterpretation of Ps. 27:13, ibn Ḥabib's David, while confident about his present spiritual devotion, also emerges as fearful that he will once again sin in the future. With a tinge of unease, ibn Ḥabib indicates that the pardoning of one's past transgressions can promote assumptions about the vindication of one's future actions as well. For this reason, ibn Ḥabib warns, one cannot look into the future with self-assurance about the way God will view one's actions based on the past. The figure of David, as ibn Ḥabib sees him, speaks only to those transgressions that had already occurred. Even David could not be assured that God would pardon him again in the future.

No doubt the message conveyed here through King David has a timeless tone; ibn Ḥabib did not compose his commentary for only a narrow audience of returning conversos. However, the tenor of the text and the description of David offered by ibn Ḥabib reflect the same attitude that underlies his legal responsa regarding the significance of one's internal character in making evaluations about Jewish status. God judges human beings on the basis of their thoughts, temperaments, instincts, and attitudes toward God rather than on their external actions. This was an idea that developed among medieval thinkers who were searching for the means to vindicate conversos and to make sense of the phenomenon of conversion in all its facets. Ibn Ḥabib's interaction with the conversos and the problems they evoked played a role in ibn Ḥabib's desire to define what constituted upright character in his portrayals of rabbinic figures and in his analyses of aggadic texts. He was struggling to locate the core ingredients of one's relationship with God. Ibn Ḥabib used the aggadot of the Talmud to propose a template for spiritual and religious "perfection,"[112] valuing internal intention. Furthermore, whether the conversos who returned to Judaism harbored self-inflicted feelings of guilt or experienced the chidings of a community unable to accept their pasts, ibn Ḥabib's image of David could speak to them and inform them that, in one's relationship with God, one's hidden thoughts, conscience, and true loyalties were apparent to Him. If one's instincts were sincere, repentance was possible, and one's transgressions were forgivable. Fellow Jews had no right to offer judgments.

Building a New Jewish Community in Salonika

Dealing with the conversos was surely not the only challenge ibn Ḥabib faced in the aftermath of the expulsion from Spain. A more complete picture of him and his motivations for compiling the *En Yaaqov* emerges from his attempt to grapple with the resettlement of Iberian Jewry and the restructuring of Jewish communal life in the Ottoman city of Salonika.

The converso poet, historian, and exegete Samuel Usque, who left Spain in 1492 and who described the experience as "my hell on earth," pointed to Salonika as the "true mother-city in Judaism." He also wrote that when the Jews of Europe who had been persecuted and banished came to find refuge in Salonika, the city "received them with love and affection, as if she were

Jerusalem, that old and pious mother of ours." The Jews of Spain came to feel "at home in exile" once again as they established synagogues named after the places they had abandoned and preserved their names, clothing styles, and food customs. They were linked to their heritage and sought to preserve vivid reminders that Sephardic Jewish culture had outlived its time on Spanish soil. In fact, the strength of Iberian Jewish identity could be found as late as the nineteenth century. Spanish visitors of this era reported their discovery of a "miniature [Jewish] Iberia alive and flourishing."[113]

However, the process of transforming the city of Salonika into a replacement home for Sephardic Jews did not happen immediately and certainly did not occur in full measure during ibn Ḥabib's lifetime. The potential for Sephardic hegemony was threatened from the outset by the established community of Romaniot Jews who, since Byzantine times, had been present in the Ottoman empire (in spite of the fact that the majority of Romaniot Jews were not in Salonika in ibn Habib's day).[114] Jews in Salonika from France, Germany, and Italy had also fled persecution and expulsion decrees.[115] The history of Salonika includes the efforts of many Jewries to implant their communal identities, often at odds with one another.

Traditionally, Jews conformed to the rites and customs of their new home (*minhage hamaqom*) and relinquished their past customs to those of their new community. However, in the Ottoman empire Sephardic Jews embarked on a campaign to spread Sephardic Jewish culture even as they encountered other Jews who wished to preserve their own traditions, including prayer rites, kashrut laws, and marriage customs. Sephardic Jews also had to contend with a strong Romaniot Jewish community that wished to maintain their own hold on the Jewish community at large.[116] So distinct were the Romaniot Jews that even the Ottoman authorities perceived of the Jewish community as composed of two main groups, the Romaniots (*surgun*) and the Jews who came from Catholic Europe (*kendi gelen*).[117]

The tension that existed and that was fueled by Sephardic Jews who wished to assert their authority over and above any other European group can be surmised from an eyewitness report of an argument that took place at a communal fish stall in the early "moments" of daily life in the sixteenth century. Jews had gathered around the stall to debate whether the fish being sold had scales or not. If it had scales, it was a kosher fish. Apparently the scales were not readily seen by the naked eye. "The newcomers from Spain" accused the others of lax observance after hearing their legal opinion rendered. To avert a physical brawl, several Jews took the fish to be inspected further.[118] This form of socioreligious mayhem, which brought even fish sellers into the center of Jewish communal debate, represents the lack of cohesion in Salonika at the beginning of the sixteenth century. Such debates over everything from fish scales, the lungs of kosher animals, prayer rites, and gifts sent by a groom to his bride prior to their betrothal were indications of a wider struggle over communal jurisdiction and the character of communal life. What drove the tension is a form of cultural arrogance not only on the part of Romaniot Jews, Ashkenazic Jews, and Italian Jews, but also on the part of Iberian Jews who hoped, more than their contemporaries, to transform the Ottoman empire into a land that was "uniquely theirs."[119] This position resounds in the words the Sephardic rabbi Moses Aroquis of Salonika wrote to the community of Edirne in 1509:

> It is well known that Sephardic Jews and their sages in this kingdom, together with the other congregations who join them, comprise the majority here, may the Lord be praised. The land was given uniquely to them, and they are its majesty, its radiance and splendor, a light unto the land and unto all who dwell in it. Surely, they [the Sephardim] were not brought here in order to depart! For all these places are ours too, and it would be worthy of all the minority peoples who first resided in the kingdom [Romaniots] to follow their example and do as they do in all that pertains to the Torah and its customs.[120]

And while Sephardic custom was not universally accepted by 1509, as it took many more years before Sephardic hegemony was in evidence throughout the region,[121] this type of egotism spurred ibn Ḥabib to confront issues of identity from another vantage point. Ibn Ḥabib's concerns had revolved around the conversos' reintegration into the Jewish community at large as well as with what identified them as Jews, rather than with what distinguished them as Sephardim. Rebuilding a Jewish communal existence that was Iberian in character provoked a different type of struggle. The core of the matter for ibn Ḥabib centered on the question of whether intracommunal accord, that is, fostering respect for the Romaniot Jews and adopting their customs, should take precedence over the legacy of Sephardic Jewry. To what extent should he work to preserve the heritage that his Iberian Christian neighbors had worked strongly to eradicate? Maybe it was better to adopt Romaniot ways in order to build a larger cohesive community.

To some extent the tensions over how to assert Sephardic hegemony were reduced by the fact that Jews were able to organize themselves into autonomous communities according to their country or area of origin.[122] The composition of each community, or *qahal,* depended exclusively on geographic location, as Jews redrew the map of Europe in the city of Salonika. The Jews of Spain divided themselves into self-sufficient communities: the Gerush Sefarad community, the Castilian community, the Aragonese community, the Catalan community, and the Majorcan community. The Portuguese arrivals established three different communities. Among the Italian Jews there were as many as six communities. The principle that "*kol qahal veqahal keir bifne atsmo*" (each community is a city unto itself) meant that each community conducted its own legal, social, and cultural affairs; supported its own poor; appointed its own rabbinic leader (*marbits torah*); had its own synagogue and yeshivot (academies); and even spoke its own language.[123] Each *qahal* (community) guarded its autonomy. Supported by the Ottomans who sanctioned the existence of this organizational structure, this communal diversity enabled those who had left their mother countries to continue to live together with those who shared similar historical memories, languages, and customs.[124]

However, the system was also quite unstable. There were inner rifts that prompted members to leave one *qahal* to join another.[125] *Marbitse torah* were free to issue ordinances and excommunications that promoted reshuffling. This was a power that they abused at times. Individual rabbis were also forced to rule on matters that often affected members of other communities, creating tensions in matters of family law (marriage and divorce), inheritance, and business (probate and commercial law).[126] In fact, marriages took place between Jews of different nationalities, complicating matters still further.[127] In addition, rabbis did not necessarily serve the communities that matched their own nationalities.[128] Jacob ibn Ḥabib became the *marbits torah* of the Calabrian Jewish community, despite the fact that its members were Sicilian Jews who had been expelled in 1493.[129] Whether he was drawn to this congregation because there were Sephardim who had joined this community in Calabria following their own expulsion from Spain in 1492 is not clear. What is clear is that Jacob ibn Ḥabib was not the leader of a community of Castilian Jews, as one might have expected given this communal framework. It was not until the Calabrian rabbi David ben Judah Messer Leon arrived in Salonika in 1505 that ibn Ḥabib became the leader of the Gerush Sefarad community (made up of Spanish exiles); he held this position until his death in 1516.

Indeed, an attempt was made as early as the first decade of the sixteenth century to temper the existing factionalism through the institution of a central board of rabbis or *qehillah*. This "umbrella group" authored a number of *haskamot,* such as those regarding Levirate marriage and divorce discussed earlier, and handled dietary issues as well as taxation challenges.[130] When this organization was first established, many of the rabbis appointed to oversee its operations were of Sephardic origin. They included Meir Arama, Joseph Fasi, and Jacob ibn Ḥabib.[131] However, it was not until the middle of the sixteenth century, under the direction of rabbis like Joseph ibn Lev and Samuel de Medina, that the *qehillah* assumed sufficient power over the individual congregations in dealing with supercommunal issues, including taxation, communal education,[132] marriage, and kashrut.[133] It was at this point that de Medina could finally claim that the "communities of Calabria, Provence, Sicilia, and Apulia [had] adopted the ways of Spain" and that only the German Ashkenazic Jews remained steadfast in their own customs.[134] De Medina could comfortably speak out in favor of his own Sephardic heritage, claiming that its customs were "the foundation of the kingdom of Turkey."[135] By the 1570s, the process of Sephardization had come full circle, with Sephardic traditions eclipsing the others in its midst.[136]

Still it is important to note that, during the first two decades of the sixteenth century, when ibn Ḥabib assumed a leadership role, the impact of Sephardic custom on the community was more tenuous. Many disputes between the various communities in the early sixteenth century were subject to a degree of cross-fertilization, whereby Sephardim adopted the customs of the Romaniot Jews as well as of the Ashkenazim and vice versa.[137] In fact, ibn Ḥabib's legal rulings in the area of kashrut and marriage law offer insight into a Sephardic rabbi who was caught between the desire to implant his own Sephardic customs in contradistinction to Romaniot ways while preventing the establishment of a fragmented community comprised of people observing different customs.[138]

When ibn Ḥabib argued for the implementation of Sephardic custom, he recognized that dietary issues were likely to promote polarization in the Salonikan Jewish community. For example, it had been the custom of Romaniot, Italian, and Hungarian communities to refuse to allow those who ritually slaughtered animals to practice *nefiḥah,* a procedure whereby air was blown into an animal's lung to check for blemishes. As soon as a blemish was detected, the animal was disqualified and deemed unkosher. In contrast, Sephardim allowed *nefiḥah:* they permitted the slaughterer to check to see whether the blemishes that were visible to the eye were indeed complete perforations or surface abrasions by blowing into the animal's lungs. If the slaughterer found only surface abrasions, the animals were deemed valid for sale to kosher patrons. Ibn Ḥabib was aware that if he decided to support a lenient ruling, in keeping with Sephardic kashrut custom, he would drive a wedge between Jews who accepted *nefiḥah* and those who did not.

He would contribute to a situation in which Sephardim and their non-Sephardic neighbors could not eat together. Business challenges would also arise whereby some butchers would have more meat available to them than others. Despite ibn Ḥabib's desire to support Sephardic custom, he relied on another Sephardic principle demanding that one follow the stringencies of one's new locale. He argued that his community should therefore not render an animal kosher on the basis of *nefiḥah* and required the adoption of the Romaniot custom.[139]

Ibn Ḥabib also embraced the Romaniot stringency that denied slaughterers the ability to deem an animal kosher in instances where its lungs were stuck to its ribs or chest walls. Carrying out *nefiḥah* to determine whether there were any abrasions required the removal of the lung altogether in a process that risked further injury. Romaniot authorities preferred to render the animal invalid rather than attempting to remove its lungs. According to Joseph Caro's discussion of this issue in his collection of responsa titled *Avqat Rokhel,* ibn Ḥabib uttered no objection to the custom he had encountered in Salonika, although by Caro's day there were communities practicing the more lenient Sephardic custom that allowed *nefiḥah*.[140]

In the case of *sivlonot,* gifts that were sent by a bridegroom to his intended bride, ibn Ḥabib tried a different legal strategy in his efforts to respect Romaniot custom without abandoning Sephardic custom entirely.[141] During this period Jewish marriages took place in three stages. First, there was an engagement where the parties agreed to the marriage and its financial terms. This was followed by *qiddushin,* which bound bride and groom to each other with an item that had some monetary value, such as a ring. The couple was able to live together after *nissuin,* the final stage in the marriage process, was performed, which involved a ceremony under a marriage canopy. The Romaniot custom was for the groom to send *sivlonot* to his bride at the time of *qiddushin* or after it. Women who received these gifts were considered legally married; they needed divorce contracts to end their relationships with grooms. Iberian Jews, however, sent *sivlonot* before *qiddushin;* thus when brides received these gifts, they did not become legally bound to the grooms who sent them. No divorce contract was needed to end the couple's engagement.[142] Difficulties ensued when grooms from one community became engaged to brides from another community. Such cases prompted concerns as to whether divorce contracts needed to be issued in the event that the final stage of marriage (*nissuin*) had not yet taken place.[143]

Caught in the conflict between preserving Sephardic custom and promoting some degree of communal cohesion, ibn Ḥabib deferred to the Romaniot Jews and adopted a more stringent position, at least for those

Sephardic Jews living outside Salonika who became engaged to Romaniot Jews. Within his own city of Salonika, however, ibn Ḥabib argued persuasively for preserving the original Sephardic custom. Despite Talmudic cases that advised newcomers to adopt the customs of their new locale, ibn Ḥabib suggested that Salonika was different from other Ottoman cities. In contrast to Constantinople, he argued, Salonika was a city without well-defined Romaniot traditions. The fact that it was populated by Iberian exiles and not Romaniot Jews during ibn Ḥabib's day allowed him to argue that the local custom (the *minhag hamaqom*) was, in fact, Sephardic custom. Additionally, *sivlonot* was a monetary matter. Newcomers to a given locale were allowed to follow their own customs if the issue was entirely monetary and not a religious prohibition.[144] These were the arguments that ibn Ḥabib made in his 1509 responsum regarding the issue of whether a groom who had sent *sivlonot* to his bride needed to write a divorce contract for her following their broken engagement.[145] His tone is one of a man nostalgically recalling his past and desperately trying to find a way to hold on to it. The legal issue of *sivlonot* forced ibn Ḥabib to confront the potential for great cultural loss. The adoption of new customs endangered the very survival of Sephardic Jewish culture. And yet ibn Ḥabib's responsum also reflects his anxiety over a decision that challenged the Romaniot rabbinic leader Elijah Mizraḥi, and that threatened the establishment of communal cohesion in a place that had offered Iberian Jews a new home.[146] Was it not incumbent upon them to adopt Romaniot custom fully? Ibn Ḥabib's grief resounds in the final words of his responsum. With a feeling of resignation, he writes, "This is the speech of a man who recognizes his humility because he is a stranger in the land, a guest who has turned aside to tarry for a night. I am the worm [*tolaat*]."[147]

Such feelings of inferiority surface again in ibn Ḥabib's commentary on the following aggadic text from *y. Sheqalim* where, as Joseph Hacker notes, ibn Ḥabib shows an unusual sense of admiration for the Romaniot Jews: "Rav Abba bar Munah said to Rabbi Zera: If our earlier scholars were like angels, we are the sons of men; and if [earlier scholars] were like the sons of men, then we are like donkeys. And we are not like the donkey of Rabbi Pinḥas ben Yair."[148]

In his response in the *En Yaaqov,* ibn Ḥabib refers to the Romaniot rabbis as the latest generation of ancient rabbis who thought of themselves as equals to the donkey of Rabbi Pinḥas. If this was the case, ibn Ḥabib asks, "then what of us? What is it that we know in comparison to them? Of the two types of citizens living in this kingdom, surely I [ibn Ḥabib] raise my head to them, but nevertheless my heart bleeds."[149]

Battling against the loss of Sephardic distinctiveness and identity in the face of his respect for the Romaniot community, ibn Ḥabib made difficult legal choices. His responsum on *sivlonot* reveals these signs of struggle. Not surprisingly, his strong interest in aggadah—and his decision to view the Talmud as more than the basis from which to develop Jewish law—intensified within this milieu. He understood the potential for the customs surrounding the implementation of halakhah to divide Jews. The less particularistic messages of the aggadot were appealing. The aggadot defied geographical boundaries and ethnic differences, offering up ideas of interest to a broad audience. Indeed, one of ibn Ḥabib's goals in his own commentary was to find what united one Jew with another, and not to focus on what divided them. For ibn Ḥabib, anthologizing the aggadot and writing a commentary were the literary means for exposing core Jewish values that could potentially bind all Jews within a complicated communal structure in which Jews from many different places lived side by side. Rarely in the *En Yaaqov* did he make reference to his own particular historical experience or to his ethnic identity as a Sephardic Jew. In fact, a sense of optimism and hope surfaces in ibn Ḥabib's introduction to the *En Yaaqov,* where he cites the example of Rabban Gamaliel (*m. Abot* 1:18) to express his ultimate desire that everyone "exercise truth in the name of peace."[150] Through Rabban Gamaliel, ibn Ḥabib recalls a time following the destruction of the Temple when troubles intensified and people were not as upright as they had once been. This prompted Rabban Gamaliel to insist on three "pillars" (*amudim*) that would construct a strong society—justice, truth, and peace. Ibn Ḥabib uses Rabban Gamaliel symbolically to express his hope that communal accord will one day deem courts of law unnecessary. He employs this tannaitic figure to convey his lofty wish for a cohesive and peaceful Jewish society. Given this view, ibn Ḥabib's reverence for the Romaniot Jewish community is not surprising. Factionalism concerned him greatly and strained his commitment to protect Sephardic identity.

Joseph Hacker, in his use of the *En Yaaqov* to construct a biographical portrait of ibn Ḥabib, correctly attests to ibn Ḥabib's quest to appeal to a broad audience. He argues that such a concern prompted ibn Ḥabib to challenge Maimonidean philosophy in the hope of widening his audience of readers.[151] However, one must also consider the societal and religious challenges of daily life that ibn Ḥabib was able to confront with his *En Yaaqov.* More than communicating messages about faith in a nonphilosophical manner (which will be discussed in greater detail in chapter 4), he located through the aggadot of the Talmud a common spiritual center capable of speaking to all Jews, regardless of geographical origin.

Ibn Ḥabib spent the final years of his life in the city of Salonika, where he completed the first volume of the *En Yaaqov*. He authored numerous responsa and wrote a commentary to the *Tur*. There is also evidence in responsa literature that he wrote a legal compendium on kashrut law.[152] Unfortunately, no manuscript or printed compilations of his responsa exist. His halakhic commentary to the *Tur* can be found only in illegible manuscript form, and knowledge of his compendium on kashrut law comes from passing references in responsa, written after his death, by Joseph Caro and Joseph ibn Lev.[153] Some of ibn Ḥabib's responsa have been preserved in the collections of others, including those of Elijah Mizraḥi, with whom he debated, and Samuel de Medina, who lived in the generation following ibn Ḥabib (and who eventually succeeded him as the *marbits torah* of the Gerush Sepharad community), as well as in Joseph Caro's *Bet Yosef*. In many responsa, including one written by Moshe Feinstein as late as 1977 on the issue of fish scales, ibn Ḥabib is cited as a central rabbinic authority for matters that run the spectrum from dietary concerns to issues of marriage and divorce, the conversos, prayer leadership, Torah reading, the building of synagogues, and tenant law.[154] He was referred to in various sources by the rabbis of his era as a "great [man] of his generation," as a "paragon of the generation," and as a "gaon."[155] But, despite ibn Ḥabib's status as a significant rabbinic figure in Salonika in the first two decades of the sixteenth century, not to mention his stance as a rabbinic authority in Castile prior to his arrival in Salonika, printers took a greater interest in his work on Talmudic aggadah than in his halakhic contributions. Later rabbis were more apt to cite his legal conclusions than to insist on the value of printing his material in one authoritative collection. Perhaps ibn Ḥabib's willingness to abdicate Sephardic custom and to consider ways of adopting the customs that were more indigenous to Ottoman Jewry made him less attractive in later years, when Sephardic hegemony became more pervasive.

The *En Yaaqov* project grew out of this milieu. It was the product of a man embroiled in the challenges Sephardic Jews faced in the years preceding their expulsion from Spain and during its aftermath. It offered his strategy of religious adaptation. And yet the forces that influenced ibn Ḥabib to compile the *En Yaaqov* extend beyond this historical and social context. The fifteenth-century Spanish intellectual orbit also played a large role in molding this project. The next two chapters analyze how prior attitudes toward aggadah, the development of legal codes, and the Jews' interest in philosophy and Kabbalah also contributed to ibn Ḥabib's decision to compile the *En Yaaqov*.

2

THE *EN YAAQOV*

A Response to the Problems and Challenges of Aggadah

The *En Yaaqov* entered the Jewish world during the early decades of Spanish Jewish resettlement in the Ottoman empire. As an early sixteenth-century anthology of the Talmud's nonlegal (aggadic) passages, it was a unique document in that it also contained the first anthology of aggadic commentaries. In the postexpulsion era, the collection emerged to fill a recognizable gap in the history of Spanish Jewish literature. With few exceptions, Spain's Jews had not been preoccupied with compiling collections of Talmudic aggadah, nor did they write running commentaries on the aggadot of the Talmud.[1] Despite the intensive and well-developed scholarly output of legal anthologies of the Talmud (codes) and Talmud commentaries from the eleventh to fifteenth centuries, there was little progress made in the area of Talmud commentaries on the genre of aggadah until the beginning of the sixteenth century in the Ottoman empire. After the expulsion there was a noticeable shift as Jews became more interested in compiling collections containing Talmudic aggadah and in writing commentaries on these sources.[2] Ibn Ḥabib's collection, however, was the most prominent and popular among them, as one of the very few collections of Talmudic aggadah not only to emerge as a printed book in the early sixteenth century but also to be reprinted numerous times in the centuries that followed.

To make sense of this literary shift it is necessary to explore the status of Talmudic aggadah prior to the emergence of the *En Yaaqov*. It is important to understand the formation of an intellectual culture that, for the most part, approached Talmudic aggadah in a manner quite different from that

51

of ibn Ḥabib. Indeed, such an overview will expose the intrinsic challenges that, prior to the sixteenth century, prevented this portion of Talmudic literature from assuming the prominent, central role that ibn Ḥabib envisioned for it. The goal of this chapter is to target the problems that the Talmud's genre of aggadah raised for centuries of Jews.

Terminological Clarification: Aggadah versus Midrash Aggadah

Before a more nuanced history of aggadah can be explored, it is important to point out that ibn Ḥabib was firmly committed to the explication of Talmudic aggadah, that is, to the aggadot of the *Bavli* (Babylonian Talmud) and *Yerushalmi* (Jerusalem Talmud) alone.[3] The *En Yaaqov* is not a work of midrash aggadah, arranged with the distinct purpose of explicating biblical verses. It is a work of aggadah organized to focus attention on the Talmud's nonlegal material. From as early as the rabbinic period, midrash aggadah and aggadah developed side by side. Midrash aggadah emerged as an exegetical discourse focused mainly on explicating the texts of the Bible in the form of either running commentaries[4] or homilies that followed the weekly Torah lection.[5] Aggadah, on the other hand, was a more loosely defined genre of text that encompassed any type of material that was neither legal nor exegetical. Rabbinic maxims, discussions about ethical concerns, fanciful stories containing hyperbolic descriptions, and narratives about rabbinic figures characterized aggadah.[6] One finds this type of material interspersed throughout the *Bavli* and *Yerushalmi* within the halakhic discussions. Although it was not uncommon to find selections of midrash aggadah alongside aggadic passages in the *Bavli* and *Yerushalmi,* these midrashim were intermittently dispersed, without a coherent organizational pattern. At the same time, midrashic compilations contained aggadic material. Midrashic exegetes used these aggadot to support their midrashic analyses. They integrated parables, ethical statements, analogies, and narratives in their larger midrashic pericopes. Indeed, it was this amalgamation of aggadah and midrash aggadah throughout the rabbinic corpora that often blurred the distinction between the two genres.

However, there is also much evidence to support the idea that, for many of the early rabbis (tannaim and amoraim of the first through fifth centuries), aggadah was a genre distinct from that of midrash aggadah. When rabbinic sources of that era describe the curriculum, midrash and aggadah are listed as separate disciplines alongside scripture, halakhah, Mishnah, and Talmud.[7] They are distinct components governed by different interpretive strategies and techniques that had to be mastered in their own right.[8]

These differences resulted in the compilation of separate collections of midrash aggadah and of aggadah.[9]

The fact that scholars throughout the generations have used the terms *midrash aggadah* and *aggadah* interchangeably should not undermine the distinction noted here. Scholars such as ibn Ḥabib erected categories even when they were not entirely perfect.[10] They made sincere attempts to make sense of what they included and excluded. Creating categories helped them to define their objectives and to distinguish their works from others. Ibn Ḥabib embraced the category of aggadah, drawing aggadic material from the Talmud alone.[11] He viewed the Talmud as a work of aggadah, that is, one that encapsulated a large variety of types of aggadot and one that was distinct from the midrashic collections he had encountered. Despite the fact that he found sections of midrash in the Talmud, he did not allow the verses around which these midrashim were constructed or the fact that they were strewn throughout the Talmudic corpora to dictate how he organized his collection. Ibn Ḥabib also never drew material from any of the classical collections of midrash aggadah,[12] even though he had access to them in Salonika.[13] The Talmud and the order in which it presented the aggadic material governed ibn Ḥabib's organizational approach to the *En Yaaqov*. This editorial decision reflects his desire to fill a void with respect to collections of Talmudic aggadah in the wake of the availability of a pronounced number of medieval collections of midrash aggadah.[14]

As it happened many of these medieval midrashic collections were anthologies. Editors over time gathered ancient midrashic materials, as in the case of *Yalqut Shim'oni,* or compiled midrashic collections that contained several compositions like *Midrash Rabbah,* or rewrote ancient sources; indeed, these compilers produced new compilations of older material.[15] This large-scale tendency toward anthologization had been common throughout the medieval period[16] and led some scholars to associate the emergence of the *En Yaaqov* with this midrashic anthological literary phenomenon.[17] However, it is important to recognize that these midrashic anthologies exemplified an urge to reestablish a connection between rabbinic tradition and scripture, while the *En Yaaqov* displayed no overall commitment to this agenda. Midrashic anthologization had emerged because the connection between rabbinic texts and scripture had begun to weaken during the medieval period. This was due, in part, to the fact that medieval Bible commentators did not necessarily rely on the prior ancient midrashic exegeses in their analyses. Anthologizers feared that these early classical interpretations, as well as the interpretive strategies used to produce them, would be lost, so they endeavored to preserve them.[18]

But ibn Ḥabib was not interested in contributing to the preservation of the relationship between midrash and biblical exegesis. He viewed himself as a Talmudic exegete committed to the hermeneutical explication of aggadah found in the *Bavli* and *Yerushalmi* Talmudim. For this reason the Talmud, and the order in which he found the aggadot contained within it, guided his anthological endeavor. Midrash, centered as it was on biblical texts, never captured his anthological interests.

Ibn Ḥabib's lack of interest in midrash emerges in a more pronounced way in his commentary where he uses the interpretive terms *remez, nigle,* and *nistar* with far greater frequency than the term *derash.* This suggests a desire to shift the meaning and authority of aggadah away from a direct tie to scripture. The word *remez* connotes that the *peshat,* or literal sense of the text, alludes to a hidden idea that is masked by the *peshat.* Unlike the term *derash,* which signifies that the starting point of an interpretation is the biblical verse, ibn Ḥabib used the term *remez* to unravel a nonbiblical source. He also used the terms *nigle* (exoteric meaning) and *nistar* (esoteric meaning) to explain away the exoteric or surface meaning of a particular aggadic text in the name of unveiling a deeper, hidden (*nistar*) meaning. While the terms *remez, nigle,* and *nistar* were commonly used by philosophers and Kabbalists, ibn Ḥabib, for the most part, did not use them to signify philosophical or Kabbalistic ideas. Rather, he employed *remez* and *nistar* to signify an interpretation that did not emerge straightforwardly from the literal sense of the words on which he was commenting, in the name of drawing out from the aggadot messages of spiritual guidance.

To be sure, ibn Ḥabib's decision to use the terms *remez, nigle,* and *nistar* rather than *derash* calls attention to his desire to distinguish himself as an exegete of Talmudic aggadah and not as a scholar interested in the midrashic exegesis of biblical passages. And yet, despite his focused goals, ibn Ḥabib exhibits terminological slippage on occasion in his commentary, using the term *derash* from time to time. The clearest example of this terminological conflation surfaces in ibn Ḥabib's introduction, where he describes nonlegal passages found in the Talmud as *derashot* and also as *aggadot,* without distinguishing one form from the other. At one point in his introduction, ibn Ḥabib refers to his project as one devoted to distancing his constituency from the desire to view *derashot* as somehow of minimal importance, with an unclear purpose. In another instance he mentions his intention to offer interpretive remarks on all of the "*aggadot* [of the Talmud] upon which Rabbi Solomon ibn Adret commented" in his thirteenth-century running commentary on Talmudic aggadah.[19] Also in his introduction, ibn Ḥabib compares his own work to those of his predecessors, claiming that there "is nothing new" in his work on aggadah. He lauds those who lived before his time and who devoted their energies to compiling books of material found in the midrashic collections available to them, stating his intention to follow in their footsteps.[20]

On the surface, the terminological slippage is bothersome, given ibn Ḥabib's commitment to a new project that bore no relationship to the discipline of midrash aggadah. However, this lack of consistency is also revealing when considered within the larger context in which ibn Ḥabib made his comments. Fully aware that he was charting new ground, ibn Ḥabib strove to situate himself within a well-established intellectual sphere of individuals who had engaged in the preservation and creation of midrashic works for centuries. Ibn Ḥabib wished for credibility.[21] As Jacob Elbaum argues, anthologists wanted to see their works as part of the continuum that began with the classical midrashim of *Bereshit Rabbah* and *Vayiqra Rabbah*. To consider their compositions and compilations as distinctly non-midrashic works ran the risk that these new collections would be characterized as somehow belated or even second-tier to those that preceded them.[22]

Furthermore, the term *midrash* was a "consciously rehabilitated" one, used in an entirely different manner during the Middle Ages from the way it was applied during the period of the classical midrashim. Many involved in the process of anthologizing rabbinic material, like ibn Ḥabib, failed to use more specific or descriptive terminology to distinguish their collections from those of others.[23] Collections fell under the rubric of "midrash," such as *Midrash Aseret Hadibberot,* even though they did not necessarily fit comfortably into this category. Although *Midrash Aseret Hadibberot* was organized around the Ten Commandments, it was primarily a collection of aggadic stories drawn from the Talmud and non-Jewish folktales that were rewritten for a Jewish audience.[24] Anthologizers used the term *midrash* somewhat freely and quite loosely referred to their interpretations as *derashot* for the purpose of granting their works a degree of authority, despite the fact that *midrash* did not necessarily characterize the way an anthologizer used his materials or approached his sources.[25]

For this reason, ibn Ḥabib did not intend for his reference to the *En Yaaqov* as a work composed of *derashot* to be taken literally. Rather, he uses terms such as *midrash, derashot,* and *derash* more loosely, with the purpose of establishing his work as part of a recognizable tradition, which was marked by anthologies of midrashic exegeses. While trying to forge new ground with respect to the production of an anthology of Talmudic aggadah and its associative commentaries, he was also trying to garner support for the study of the Talmud as a document of aggadah within a context that held midrash aggadah in high regard.

The Rabbinic Period: The Problems Begin

From as early as the tannaitic period (approximately 30 BCE–220 CE), the genres of halakhah and aggadah were wedded to each other and continued to be so throughout the rabbinic period. This is especially pronounced in the Talmudim where one finds aggadic material regularly interspersed with halakhic passages. The tannaitic collection, *Sifre*, argues quite eloquently that the words of both halakhah and aggadah have been uttered by God, saying, " 'Man does not live on bread alone' (Deut. 8:3), referring to midrash; 'but by everything that issues from the mouth of God' (Deut. 8:3), referring to halakhot and aggadot."[26]

And yet the amoraim (approximately 220–500 CE) viewed the genres of halakhah and aggadah as distinct forms of rabbinic pedagogy. For example, in the following aggadic source, two amoraim vie for the primacy of one genre over the other, using different genres in order to teach:

> Rabbi Abbahu and Rabbi Ḥiyya bar Abba once came to a place. Rabbi Abbahu expounded narrative material [aggadah] and Rabbi Ḥiyya expounded legal material. All of the people abandoned [the discourse of Rabbi Ḥiyya bar Abba] and went to the [discourse of] Rabbi Abbahu. [Rabbi Ḥiyya bar Abba] was disheartened. Rabbi Abbahu said to him: "I will tell you a parable. . . . [This matter] is [analogous] to [the case of] two people. One sells precious stones, while the other sells small wares [such as pins and needles]. To whom do more [buyers] go? Isn't it to the one who sells small wares?"[27] (*b. Sot.* 40a)

According to this story, the people prefer aggadah. Rabbi Ḥiyya bar Abba is disappointed. He does not understand why people would gravitate toward aggadah at the expense of halakhic discourse. To comfort him, Rabbi Abbahu defends their choice. He explains through the parable that the populace will always approach the merchant selling goods they need and can afford. The merchant selling precious stones has little to offer them; they have no immediate use for such items, nor can they afford to buy them. In other words, the richness or complexity of halakhic discourse was beyond what the people desired; it was beyond their cognitive reach. Because they had difficulty comprehending it, they opted for the more palatable, simple, and readily understandable messages of aggadah.

This source from *b. Sotah* reflects that halakhah and aggadah were not perceived as complementary genres but rather as independent mediums.[28] Each medium spoke to and even attracted different segments of the Jewish community—one intellectual and the other common. And yet sources in the Talmudim convey that aggadah was attractive even to the rabbinic elite. Some rabbis emerged in Talmudic literature as masters of aggadah, including Rabbi Samuel bar Naḥman.[29] There were also academies, like that of Rav Pappa and Rav Huna, devoted to the investigation of aggadic sources. No doubt this is why Rav Kahana was advised to go to the academy of Rav Pappa and Rav Huna when he answered a question unsatisfactorily about the connotation of the word "Sinai" in its reference to the mountain where Moses received the Torah. It was understood that Rav Pappa and Rav Huna would be more able to answer the question because of their knowledge of aggadah.[30] Interestingly, Rabbi Joshua ben Levi assured those who gave charity that their sons would be wealthy, wise, and versed in aggadah rather than in halakhah.[31] In *b. Ḥag.* 14a, the masters of the Talmud are compared to those who offer bread to their students, whereas the masters of aggadah draw their students' hearts "as one draws water." The significance of bread notwithstanding, aggadah is necessary to delight the heart (*b. Ḥag.* 14a). In addition, the Talmud refers to the existence of a *Sefer Deaggadeta* (Book of Aggadah), suggesting that members of the rabbinic elite were producing collections of aggadah for the purpose of spreading the messages contained within the aggadot to the people.[32]

The tension between the value of halakhah in contrast to that of aggadah plays out still further in the figure of Rabbi Joshua ben Levi. He surfaces in the *Bavli* (*b. B. Qam.* 55a) as a master of aggadah, whereas in the *Yerushalmi* he lodges a severe attack on those who write, preach, or listen to aggadic discourse (*y. Shabb.* 16:1, 15c).[33] Several other sources express similar negative sentiments toward aggadah. For example, in *b. Ḥag.* 14a, Rabbi Eleazar ben Azariah accuses Rabbi Akiva of offering an erroneous aggadic interpretation; he advises Rabbi Akiva to desist from such teachings and to continue, instead, to focus on legal matters. In *y. Shabb.* 1:4, 3d, Rabbi Ba bar Aḥa, in the name of Rebi, claims that one should not teach aggadah at all. In *y. Peah* 2:4, 17a, there is a warning against deriving binding legal conclusions from aggadic material. Additionally, when Rabbi Jeremiah asks Rabbi Zera to teach him, Rabbi Zera responds that he does not feel well enough to teach halakhah. Therefore, Rabbi Jeremiah asks him to teach something aggadic because it is simpler.[34] Moreover, in an amoraic discussion about whether one needs to say a blessing before studying Mishnah or Talmud, the question of whether the study of aggadah needs any benediction at all is simply not addressed. This silence connotes that in some rabbinic sources, aggadah was valued less than halakhah.[35]

And so the problem of evaluating the authority of aggadah began. Should one believe in the divine status of both halakhah and aggadah? In other words, had both mediums "issue[d] from the mouth of God," as noted in *Sifre Devarim*? Or was aggadah somehow less significant, less complex, less instrumental in usefulness, and even less sacred than halakhah?[36] Furthermore, if aggadah was a distinct type of rabbinic literature, was there a particular hermeneutical approach that was to be employed in interpreting it?[37] Generations of Jews in the years following the Talmudic period continued to ask these questions. Legal codifiers, philosophers, and Kabbalists, not to mention Karaites as well as converts and non-Jews, constructed a large arena where they wrestled with the nature and authority of aggadah. It was this ongoing struggle that led Isadore Twersky to point to aggadah as one of the topics capable of constructing a "phenomenology of medieval Jewish intellectualism."[38] In this regard, the history of aggadah highlights the main intellectual currents of the medieval period, as the forthcoming discussion underscores. It also sets the stage for ibn Ḥabib's response, in the form of a compilation of Talmudic aggadah in the early sixteenth century.

In the Aftermath of the Talmud

The geonim (the rabbinic scholars recognized as the highest authority from the end of the sixth century to the eleventh century) were major contributors to the view that aggadah and halakhah were separate disciplines governed by different rules of interpretation. Beginning with Yehudai Gaon (eighth century), who compiled the first code, *Halakhot Pesuqot,* the geonim recorded timely halakhic decisions in individual collections.[39] Yehudai, among others, believed that a more concise record of legal parameters would make halakhah more accessible than it was in the Talmudic corpus. But the commitment to this task on the part of the rabbis of the geonic period had a penetrating effect on the status of Talmudic aggadah. In their codes they left out many of the Talmud's aggadic digressions, homilies, and stories, presenting instead collections of legal decisions that the Talmudim (*Bavli* and *Yerushalmi*) had never clearly cited.[40] To legitimize this decision, the geonim warned against relying on aggadot with respect to halakhic issues. In fact, Saadya Gaon (889–942) developed the following guiding rule for making legal decisions: "*En somekhin al divre aggadah*" (one cannot rely on aggadah). A half-century later, Sherira Gaon (968–98) referred to aggadot as mere guesses, from which one could not derive any rules.[41] Hai Gaon (998–1038), the son of Sherira Gaon, in his comments on *b. Ḥag.* 14a, went so far as to say: "Know that aggadic sayings are not like received tradition; they are simply what an individual expresses (*doresh*) regarding what occurs to him personally—[such as] 'it is like,' 'it is possible,' 'one may say.' [Aggadot] are not decisive statement[s] and that is why we do not rely on their [authority]. These . . . views are neither a received tradition nor a halakhic ruling, they are no more than perhapses."[42]

Such statements over time formalized the status of aggadah as second to that of halakhah and diminished the authority of aggadic passages. But the effect on aggadah was most pronounced in instances where the study of legal codes took precedence over the study of the Talmud itself. The adoption of this type of curriculum, whereby students learned from documents which, for the most part, excluded aggadic passages, undermined the value of aggadah.[43]

The effects were far-reaching. Even four centuries later ibn Ḥabib found himself arguing for the significance of Talmudic aggadah. In his introduction to the *En Yaaqov,* ibn Ḥabib complains about the way code literature diminished the degree to which Jews could easily familiarize themselves with the aggadot of the Talmud. The emphasis on codes suppressed Talmudic aggadah's emergence as a serious discipline of study.[44] Discussing the impetus for the *En Yaaqov* in his introduction, ibn Ḥabib writes:

> The student that I have referred to above saw [what occurred during the] many years that have passed since the day when this great compilation that was mentioned above [the Code, *Hilkhot Harif*][45] was compiled by the great and extraordinary sage [Rabbi Isaac Alfasi] of blessed memory—[that] what came forth from and spread throughout some of the populace was an ignorance in the absence of the acquisition [of knowledge from the aggadot of the Talmud]. [This is] because the part [of the books of the Talmud] that remained [and were excluded from Alfasi's code, that is, the aggadic portions] were in the eyes [of the populace] as small [incompletely formed clusters of] grapes [*olelot*] that remained on the vine at harvest time [for the poor because they] were not [part of] an eatable [fully formed] cluster.[46] [The material that] remained was only seen as peripheral[47] stories and aggadot. . . . And now they will see that I am the student whose soul yearns with a hunger that is sweet to the soul and chooses

the good thing and commands himself to write [another collection] on the special book [the Talmud containing] all of the pericopes that lend themselves to being interpreted and that are written in the six orders that comprise the Mishnah, most of which Alfasi did not include in his great collection. . . .

My eyes and my heart [were focused on] these pericopes all of my days in order to arrive at and pay attention to the intentions of the learned rabbis in their faithful interpretations. This was my second reason for calling this book *En Yaaqov.*[48] It discloses the legacy of my heart although I am the worm, Jacob.[49]

The metaphorical reference *olelot,* which ibn Ḥabib uses to describe Alfasi's treatment of the aggadot, equates this body of material with the undeveloped clusters of grapes and therefore with the refuse of a harvest to which only the poor were entitled. It points to ibn Ḥabib's sense of the negative consequences of codification. He yearns to salvage the clusters or aggadot. In this regard, ibn Ḥabib sets himself up as the person who will grapple with all the material Alfasi left out.[50] His intention is to "open the eyes of the blind and to encourage all students who are upright in their hearts to understand the words of the sages [of the Talmud with respect to] their [use of] metaphor[s], flowery language, and riddles."[51] Ibn Ḥabib envisions that he will produce a work of aggadah that will complement Alfasi's code and that will "right the wrongs" of Alfasi's editorial decisions. In so doing he will reclaim aggadah as a valuable and holy medium equal to that of halakhah.

This goal, however, did not emerge without a good deal of thought regarding how his collection would be received. After all, ibn Ḥabib not only left out all the halakhic material contained in the Talmud, but also created another derivative text of the Talmudic corpus that contained little of the material which the legal codifiers had anthologized. For the most part, ibn Ḥabib stood on shaky ground, with few precedents to legitimize his efforts. The closest earlier model was *Haggadot Hatalmud,* a far more modest compilation of Talmudic aggadah published in Constantinople five years before ibn Ḥabib's collection.[52] In fact, ibn Ḥabib specifically mentions in his introduction to the *En Yaaqov* his desire to fend off "devious talk from those who want[ed] to open [their mouths]" against him.[53] He feared they would criticize him, imagining they would say, "What is this endeavor that you have undertaken in that you thought to compile a book, [that is], also a large composition of statements that are [already] laid out before us like a set table? Surely they [the legal codifiers Alfasi and Rosh] have [already] written [collections] using the books of the Talmud that are in our hands?"[54]

In defense, ibn Ḥabib conveys that what he is offering is a corrective. His collection will parallel the legal codes but not replace them, so that he can bring to light what the codes had pushed aside.

Additional Challenges to Aggadah

There were other attacks against the credibility of aggadah throughout the medieval period, both from within and outside the Jewish community. The Karaites, for example, latched onto the medium of aggadah as a means for undermining the authority of rabbinic Judaism. The absurdity of the contents of many of the aggadic sources as well as their use in connection with matters of halakhic significance enabled the Karaites to attack rabbinic hegemony and the Talmud where they were particularly vulnerable.[55] In their eyes aggadic sources that described God in anthropomorphic terms, with passages that narrated fanciful stories about demons and ways to ward off their evil effects, and that included references to rabbis who heard divine voices, were not credible.[56] After all, did Elijah the prophet really appear before Rabbi Yose at the entrance to a ruin (*b. Ber.* 3a)? Did God really "coo like a dove" to express His anguish over the destruction of the Temple (*b. Ber.* 3a)? Were there heavenly watches each night where God roared like a lion to signify each of them (*b. Ber.* 3a)? Did the sound of donkeys braying and dogs howling communicate something about the transition from one heavenly watch to another (*b. Ber.* 3a)?

Muslims, and eventually Christians, also relied on aggadic sources, especially those drawn from the Talmud, to discredit Judaism. Even Jews who converted to Christianity, in their desire to undercut Judaism, used aggadic sources to assail the Talmud. For example, the Spanish convert Peter Alfonsi (b. 1062) devoted the first chapter of his polemical work against Judaism to a critique of aggadah.[57] Aggadic references to God's corporeality were the fuel for his attack:

> Do you see, therefore Moses [my adversary], how far all this type of thing is from true theology? For if it is indeed true that God weeps for you, roars like a lion, beats the sky with His feet, sighs in the manner of doves, moves His head and cries, "woe to me" out of excessive grief; that He furthermore strikes His feet in His grief, claps His hands and every day prays that He may pity you—what then stands in the way of your being set free from captivity [other than God Himself]? To believe [all] this about [what] God [does and thinks] is blasphemy.[58]

Once Alfonsi could deem the words of aggadah as "nothing other than the words of jesters in schools for children," he was able to extrapolate from this diminished image of aggadah to judge halakhah. How could anyone, Alfonsi claimed, trust the laws of a group of men who had authored such foolish ideas and then canonized those concepts alongside their halakhic excurses on the pages of the Talmud?[59] In this regard, aggadah became the fodder for an even larger attack lodged by non-Jews and converts against Judaism. But Alfonsi was not the last to contribute to the assailment. For centuries the attacks lodged against Judaism by way of aggadah placed Jewish intellectuals on the defensive and weakened the value of aggadah.

One of the most prominent attacks on aggadah occurred in July 1263 in the royal palace of Barcelona. A disputation took place between the Dominican friar Pablo Christiani, himself a convert to Christianity, and the Geronese rabbi Moses Naḥmanides. During the course of the disputation, Naḥmanides was prompted to defend an aggadic passage claiming that the messiah had been born on the day when the Temple was destroyed. Naḥmanides stated:

> Know that we have three categories of books. The first is the Bible, and all of us believe in it fully. The second is called the Talmud, and it is a commentary to the commandments of the Torah. . . . We further have a third book, which is called Midrash, that is to say sermons. [This is] akin to the bishop standing and giving a sermon and one of the auditors finding it favorable and writing it down. This book—he who believes in it, well and good; but he who does not believe in it does no harm. . . . We further call this book Aggadah, that is to say, stories, meaning that they are only things that people tell one another.[60]

Whether Naḥmanides' claims reflected his desperate attempt to defend Judaism or his sincere views on the subject of aggadah is less important here than the role aggadah played in the friar's attempts to discredit Judaism.[61] To counter the Christian usurpation of rabbinic material used to undermine Judaism, Naḥmanides reinforced the secondary, even tertiary, nature of aggadah as compared to the Bible and the halakhic portions of the Talmud.[62] In this regard, Naḥmanides pushed aggadah aside publicly in the eyes of the Christians and Jews who witnessed the disputation unfold.[63] In addition, Naḥmanides' response, focused as it was on diminishing the sacredness of aggadic material, signified that for many Jews there was no choice but to discredit aggadah if they were to survive direct attacks on their very identity as Jews.

The Effects of Philosophy on the Status of Aggadah

Although the image of Talmudic aggadah suffered from the perspective of those interested in legal codification, and it was often discredited in an attempt to defend Judaism, geonim and later medieval Jews embraced and defended aggadah in conjunction with their interest in the study of Greek philosophy. Hai Gaon, for example, granted Talmudic aggadah greater authority than aggadot found in other collections. He also created a framework for interpreting these aggadot by embracing the rabbinic notion that the Torah "spoke in the language of men" (*b. Ber.* 31b). In his mind, nonsensical expressions of God laughing, speaking, weeping, or sighing were "analogies and comparisons with things known to us by the senses."[64] God did not actually laugh, speak, weep, or sigh. The aggadot merely "spoke" in a language that the average person could comprehend.

Sherira Gaon and Saadya Gaon expanded on this approach to aggadah and argued that many aggadot could be rationally confirmed using the tools of philosophical evaluation.[65] Saadya's philosophy, in particular, depended on finding the rational core of the difficult aggadic references. To accomplish this he viewed aggadot as metaphors representing some level of knowledge that was acceptable to the rational mind, each text conveying something beyond its literal meaning. For example, visions of an anthropomorphic God became "purely psychic phenomena" that had occurred in the mind of the beholder and had no objective reality perceivable by anyone else.[66]

Arguably, the geonim were responsible for reducing the value of aggadah, in contrast to halakhah, but they were not responsible altogether for diminishing its study. Their interest in and familiarity with Greek philosophy, which emerged from their close contact with their Islamic neighbors, fueled their desire to prove the rationality of questionable aggadot. In fact, this objective played a central role in Saadya Gaon's overall mission. He was committed to transforming those whose beliefs were based on religious authority alone into individuals who held beliefs that could be confirmed through arguments of reason.[67]

For the geonim, the conviction that meaning lay beneath the surface of sacred texts—that is, that one word or idea could stand for something else—enabled them to explain away problematic texts without rejecting them outright. In later years, Maimonides drew on their ideas, fostering the belief that the literal sense of aggadah was merely an allusion to a deeper meaning that conformed to the dictates of reason.[68] Maimonides argued that an aggadic passage could convey an explicit meaning that was markedly different from its implicit or esoteric meaning. This was due to the nature of language. According to Maimonides, language was limited in its ability to describe the intangible—that is, temperaments, feelings, and essences. Thus it was in the nature of language to conceal inner meanings and to convey messages more figuratively.[69] Maimonides applied his understanding of language to his study of aggadic passages and granted them the status of "poetical conceits." In other words, the ideas expressed in the aggadot were communicated in much the same way as poets conveyed their ideas through poetry, that is, metaphorically. Illustrating this point, Maimonides describes an aggadic passage found in *b. Ketub.* 15a: "Would that I knew whether, in the opinion of these ignoramuses, this *tanna* believed this to be the interpretation of the text, that such was the purpose of this commandment. . . . I do not think that anyone of sound intellect will be of this opinion. But this is a most witty poetical conceit by means of which he instills a noble moral quality . . . and he props it up through a reference to a [biblical] text, as is done in poetical compositions."[70]

According to Maimonides it was only by means of one's rational faculty that the literal formulation of the aggadot, which on the surface appeared illogical, could be transcended and the inner truth obtained. If an individual were to encounter aggadic references that contradicted reason, he was to ascribe them to his own deficiencies.[71] In this regard, Maimonides limited his audience and turned the study of aggadah into a "negatively loaded" intellectual exercise for most. Only the scholarly elite had the ability to understand these hidden meanings that would, in turn, lead them closer to attaining an intellectual perception and understanding of God.[72] The literal sense of the aggadot was merely a protective coating that shielded hidden philosophical truths from the masses.[73] In fact, so committed was Maimonides to explicating aggadic literature that he set out initially to write a commentary to the aggadot of the Talmud.[74] He abandoned the idea out of fear that the messages would be misunderstood by the populace.[75]

Clearly, by Maimonides' time the very character of aggadah had undergone a change in the years since Rabbi Abbahu described its popular appeal in *b. Sot.* 40a. Philosophers from Saadya to Maimonides drove a permanent wedge not only between the genres of halakhah and aggadah but also between the elite and the masses. Their interest in philosophy turned aggadah into a medium that served the larger goals of their discipline and the needs of the intellectual elite they strove to influence. It was not a means employed merely to charm the masses.[76]

The Jews' absorption of philosophy from their non-Jewish neighbors beginning in the geonic period effectively transformed the study of aggadah into a subset of philosophy. Aggadah became the source material used by the geonim and later by medieval scholars to prove that Judaism conformed to the tenets of reason; it was the rabbinic medium around which philosophic controversies were played out most effectively.[77] Philosophers studied aggadah through the lens of the subject matter that was on their philosophic agendas, whether they were unique to Jews (for example, the special character of the prophecy of Moses, the future arrival of a Davidic messiah, the afterlife, and revelation) or more common to Jews, Christians, and Muslims alike (for example, the existence of God, divine attributes, the creation of the world, the human soul, and the nature of the composition of the universe).[78]

The Jews' interest in philosophy had a significant impact on their production of running commentaries on the aggadot of the Talmud and on their failure to study aggadah as a subject in its own right. Jewish philosophers were not necessarily looking to explain away the types of difficulties found within the texts of the Talmud, which might appeal to an aggadic exegete. Philosophers were less interested in grappling with superfluous words, repetitions, and contradictions within the Talmudic texts themselves in order to clarify the difficulties found within an aggadic text.[79] Maimonides, in particular, recognized that not all aggadot were philosophically informed. In those instances, it was better not to formulate a perfect equation between aggadah and philosophy.[80] Resisting the running commentary preserved a comfortable distance between aggadah and philosophy that allowed philosophers more freedom to pick and choose those aggadot that informed their philosophical positions. It also allowed them to begin with a set of philosophic questions that did not necessarily emerge naturally from the classical Jewish sources. Even the answers to their questions were not necessarily rooted in the texts of biblical and rabbinic literature. Jewish philosophy evolved into an intellectual discipline devoted to systematic reflections about Judaism, using philosophical categories to answer philosophical questions and not to explicate the ambiguities and contradictions found within aggadic texts. For example, queries about the existence of God and the nature of His oneness fueled their treatises. Was it possible for God's existence to be proven? Was His existence identical with His essence? Were anthropomorphic references to God to be taken literally? Was free will compatible with divine foreknowledge? Could the nature of eternity and of God's providence be defined?[81]

Jewish philosophers also studied Greek philosophical works and engaged in an intellectual struggle to determine their own relationship to these sources. For example, was Aristotle's doctrine of the ethical mean outlined in his *Nicomachean Ethics* compatible with halakhah? Did a life lived in accordance with halakhah comply with Aristotelian ethics?[82] Once Jewish philosophers determined that the conclusions the Greek philosophers drew were correct, it was necessary to demonstrate that Judaism did not contradict those conclusions. If they discovered that Judaism did, in fact, overturn these sources, then it was their responsibility to expose these errors in their writings. They harbored heartfelt concerns that, if Judaism was not compatible with philosophy, the discovery could undermine the faith of the philosophic-minded.[83] It could also challenge the viability of Judaism in the eyes of the non-Jewish elite, with whom they believed themselves to be in direct conversation. Although Jewish philosophers never ignored aggadah and used Talmudic sources to strengthen their claims in many instances, the aggadot of the Talmud did not serve as the starting point for their philosophical analyses.

As philosophy was the medium through which Jews conversed with the surrounding cultures, there was always the risk that placing the Talmud, and therefore Talmudic aggadah, front and center would weaken this link. In keeping with the primary objective of philosophy, which was to "articulate the desired relationship between the Jewish religious tradition (believed to be grounded in historical divine revelation) and the secular, universal truth-claims of philosophy (grounded in the natural rational capacity of humans),"[84] many philosophers distanced themselves from the genre of the running commentary on Talmudic aggadah. The fanciful and illogical aggadic passages found in the Talmud called attention to the Talmud's weaknesses. It was better to begin with a philosophic point or question and to interweave aggadot as needed, using philosophic interpretive methods that dismissed literal readings of aggadot in favor of nonliteral ones. No doubt philosophers preferred to overlook the Talmud's warnings against philosophical speculation. They pushed aside the blatant admonition found in tractate *Ḥagigah* that "whoever speculates about four matters [concerning God], it would have been better had he not come into the world [and they are]: what is above, what is below, what is before and what is after."[85] To be sure, the genre of the running commentary thwarted philosophers in their desire to create a bridge between divine revelation and the truth-claims of philosophy. Philosophers were looking for a way to bolster Judaism in the eyes of the philosophically minded Jew *and* non-Jew alike. The authors of many philosophical works justified their contributions by noting how important their works were for the sake of the dignity of the Jewish people. They wished to combat the notion that Jewish culture was inferior to that of their Christian neighbors. For this reason, their philosophical reflections needed to be presented in a way that would gain them credibility in the eyes of the Christian learned elite. Their objective was to articulate Judaism in a manner that was intelligible within their own philosophic circles as well as to the surrounding society.[86] Therefore Talmudic aggadah remained no more than the "handmaiden" of philosophy, a subordinate medium, most especially within the Hispano-Jewish/Christian orbit into which ibn Ḥabib was born.

Many philosophers had followed in the footsteps of Maimonides; they had looked beyond the external sense of the aggadot that appeared to contradict their sense of the truth and read aggadic material nonliterally or allegorically for the sake of revealing a philosophical idea.[87] But challenges arose. What were the credible boundaries of such an approach? At what point did the philosopher sacrifice the aggadic texts out of existence as well as the basic ideas of Talmudic tradition that were communicated in those texts? How did nonliteral philosophic interpretive strategies affect understandings regarding whether the messiah would come, or whether Jewish souls would be resurrected, as conveyed in the aggadic sources of the Talmud? To what extent did philosophy work to undermine the integrity of the Talmudic corpus? Further, would philosophical reflections extend to promote nonliteral readings of halakhic passages? After all, if Maimonides could argue in his "Letter on Astrology" that the aggadic views of the sages could be rejected,[88] might one say the same about the Talmud's halakhic points?

And so, for centuries, the power of Maimonidean philosophy fueled a great degree of controversy that included a debate about the nature of aggadah.[89] Maimonides' powerful influence placed those who preferred more literal readings of aggadah on the defensive.[90] It was not enough merely to embrace an aggadic passage as literally formulated and to comment on it. One needed to defend this position in light of the philosophic stance. Staunch critique emerged within Spain and in the communities of Provence, Northern France, and Germany.[91] For example, at the end of the twelfth century, the prominent Spanish rabbi Meir Halevi Abulafia (1164–1244) accused Maimonides of heresy in an epistle he wrote to the Jews of Provence. This was part of an attempt to organize a countermovement against Maimonidean philosophy.[92] Abulafia blamed Maimonides for promoting an excessively rationalistic eschatology.[93] He was instead committed to the plain sense of the Talmudic text, especially with regard to aggadot written about the World to Come and the afterlife. Exceptions, he argued, were to be made only when a literal interpretation endangered a fundamental theological principle, such as God's incorporeality, perfection, omniscience, or omnipotence.[94]

Years later, a rare Spanish Talmudic commentary on aggadah was penned by a rabbi embroiled in the Maimonidean controversy.[95] The prominent Talmudist Solomon ibn Adret (1235–1310) authored not only a running commentary on the halakhic portions of the Talmud but also a separate, albeit less comprehensive, commentary on the Talmud's aggadic passages in which he opposed philosophic inquiry.[96]

Ibn Adret's involvement in the controversy over Maimonidean philosophy emerged most prominently in the ban he issued in 1305, prohibiting its study.[97] In a letter to the Spanish communities of France and Germany, he made his position quite clear.[98] No one was allowed to study philosophy until they reached the age of twenty-five and could "appreciate fully the delicacies of the Law." Ibn Adret was fearful that philosophy would overpower halakhah. He viewed those who studied the Bible through the lens of philosophy as having reduced it to "useless allegories." He argued that they "perverted all of the commandments in order to make the yoke of their burden lighter." He also lambasted young boys who began to study natural science and who thereby upheld Aristotle as the "Chief Cause." Thus he found it necessary to strengthen the "fence" around the Torah and to "make a strong hedge around the vineyard of the Lord of Hosts."[99]

Not surprisingly, ibn Adret turned to the aggadot of the Talmud, as they stood at the core of the controversy that ensued over the role of philosophy. Placing the aggadot of the Talmud front and center by using the genre of the commentary to "go on the offensive" was not only ibn Adret's way of building "a strong hedge around the vineyard" of God's words but also a way of speaking the "same language" as his Provencal contemporaries who had embraced Maimonidean philosophy. Indeed, the impetus for his authorship of this commentary on the aggadot of the Talmud was rooted in the conversation about philosophy that was taking place across geographic lines.

Ibn Adret wrote his commentary within the context of the close cultural relationship between his own city of Barcelona (in the Spanish province of Catalonia) and Provence.[100] By the time he began to write his commentary, the thirteenth-century Provencal rabbi Isaac ben Yedayah had already dedicated his scholarly energies toward the explication of material drawn exclusively from the Talmud for the purpose of spreading philosophy. Ben Yedayah diverged from Maimonides' literary scheme of the philosophical treatise with the main goal of propagating philosophic themes among those unwilling or unable to immerse themselves in the *Guide for the Perplexed.* As Marc Saperstein points out, ben Yedayah was a rabbi committed to legitimizing the study of philosophy within popular Jewish circles.[101] The Provencal rabbi Yedayah Hapenini Bedersi wrote a rationalist commentary that included comments on *Midrash Rabbah, Tanḥuma,* and *Pirqe Derabbi Eliezer,* in what Isadore Twersky refers to as a "comprehensive compendium" of aggadah.[102] The emergence of these works was part of an awakening of interest in aggadic sources during the thirteenth century, primarily in southern France. Some scholars interested in philosophy wrote treatises that were devoted to exploring the topic of aggadic exegesis. And while many of these works were not running commentaries on the Talmud similar in form to ben Yedayah's, they point to the existence of a school of philosophy that was specifically oriented toward aggadic exegesis.[103]

In contrast, ibn Adret used the medium of the aggadic commentary to combat philosophy and his Provencal colleagues. He spoke out through the same medium in an attempt to reverse the trajectory in evidence in Provence. In his opinion Talmud study was primary, as opposed to the opinions of his Provencal contemporaries who believed that the commentary was a useful means for spreading philosophic ideas.[104]

Moreover, in Spain at this time, the aggadic commentary did not become a primary means for disseminating philosophy.[105] There was no school of philosophy in Spain devoted to the exegesis of Talmudic aggadah or aggadah more generally. As a result, the philosophical study of aggadah was fragmentary.[106] The commitment to philosophy there seems to have produced a firmer set of barriers in Spain than in Provence with respect to the study of Talmudic aggadah. Possibly the availability in Provence of translations into Hebrew of Spanish philosophical works, grammatical-lexicographical treatises, and translations of the works of Aristotle and Averroës enabled philosophy to spread beyond the confines of the intellectual aristocracy.[107] For Spanish Jews philosophy may have been a discipline of the upper class.[108] This may account for the fact that philosophy was more at odds with the genre of the running commentary on Talmudic aggadah in Spain than in Provence, where such commentaries surfaced more comfortably.[109]

And yet given ibn Adret's involvement in the ban against the study of Maimonidean philosophy, his commentary is replete with philosophic terms and references indicating that he was quite comfortable with philosophic sources and principles.[110] While ibn Adret argued that he was committed to revealing the plain sense of the aggadot, his commentary indicates that he was not always an aggadic literalist.[111] Drawing to some degree from Maimonides, he viewed the *peshat*, or literal meaning, as a mere symbol of a deeper meaning; it was the *nigle* (exoteric presentation) that protected what was *nistar* (hidden). In ibn Adret's opinion, the rabbis spoke in the language of the parable, and it was the responsibility of those who studied their words to decipher their meanings.[112] For this reason one finds ibn Adret upholding the corporeal descriptions of the World to Come, as put forth in the Talmud, which portrayed an actual feast (*b. B. Batra* 74b–75a). Yet one also quickly discovers that ibn Adret did not entirely ignore the philosophically oriented view of this aggadic text, arguing that the food and drink consumed by the righteous at this feast strengthened the intellectual power of the soul.[113] While ibn Adret interpreted many aggadot according to their plain sense, others he interpreted allegorically.

That said, ibn Adret's philosophic interests were not strong enough to undermine the tenor of his commentary, which reflected his fear of the spread of philosophy. He believed that the traditions displayed in the texts of Talmudic aggadah could not be overturned by philosophic inquiry. He maintained that the aggadot of the Talmud were more valuable in their literal form than any interpretation that could be uncovered by philosophic means. Arguably, ibn Adret did not accept philosophy on axiological grounds, that is, on the basis of an acknowledgment of the superior worth of philosophy. Rather, he embraced philosophy from a phenomenological perspective, that is, by using familiar philosophic terms and concepts selectively to explicate aggadah. In other words, ibn Adret struggled to strike a balance among traditional Talmudic exegesis, philosophy, and even, at times, Kabbalah.[114] He worked with difficulty to define the boundary which, if crossed, would undermine Talmudic aggadah and even halakhah. Surely the difficulty he had in locating that boundary—living as he was within a sphere where philosophy played a major role in the intellectual current of his day—resulted in his straddling two approaches. Two centuries later, ibn Ḥabib would be more successful in distancing his aggadic interpretations from philosophy, but not without anthologizing the commentary of ibn Adret and characterizing his own work on aggadah as an effort to build on it.

Ibn Adret never completed his commentary, and it never generated a stream of followers. For two centuries his students and other scholars failed to take an active interest in producing running commentaries and super-commentaries (commentaries that comment on earlier commentaries) on Talmudic aggadah. Interestingly though, ibn Adret's brief foray into the study of Talmudic aggadah in Spain emerged because of his concern about the spread of philosophy. It seemed that those who were more philosophic-minded wrote philosophic treatises and those who were less so, such as ibn Adret, were more interested in Talmudic aggadah, though philosophic thought was part of their intellectual life. Philosophy managed to push the running exegesis of Talmudic aggadah to the margins of medieval Spanish Jewish intellectual culture; it was what prevented the interpretation of Talmudic aggadah from developing into an active discipline in its own right.

In fact, at the beginning of the sixteenth century, ibn Ḥabib's contemporary Isaac Abarbanel lauded ibn Adret for being the first systematic interpreter of the aggadot of the Talmud. He described ibn Adret as the one who successfully filled in the "necessary" gaps resulting from scholars' neglect of aggadah. In his mind, ibn Adret had "completed the work of God."[115] Abarbanel argued that ibn Adret had combated the approach of the philosophers of his generation who had used the aggadot as mere "pegs" for their interpretations. This had led them to ignore the actual content and intention of the aggadot they relied on. Abarbanel was also bothered by the fact that Talmudic commentators paid no attention to aggadah and instead focused their attentions on explicating the legal material of the Talmud to clarify prohibitory and acceptable behaviors.[116] Abarbanel looked back to ibn Adret as the model of an individual who had taken both Talmudic halakhah and aggadah seriously. Ibn Adret had authored a comprehensive Talmudic commentary that focused primarily on the halakhic contents of the Talmud as well as a separate aggadic commentary on the aggadic material.[117]

However, the dearth of interest in the authoring of running commentaries on Talmudic aggadah would change in the sixteenth century when the Talmudic commentary emerged as a significant literary genre due, in large measure, to the contributions of Jacob ibn Ḥabib. At a time when Abarbanel was bemoaning the lack of available commentaries on Talmudic aggadah, ibn Ḥabib began to compile the *En Yaaqov* in Salonika. In addition to writing his own running commentary, where he quoted and discussed aggadic passages, ibn Ḥabib collected the commentaries of his predecessors in what became the first anthology of aggadic commentary on the Talmud to exist in the medieval world.[118] Taking an ideological stance, his commentary reflects a desire to distance aggadah from philosophy. In fact, in his anthology of commentaries he chose to include only those passages from ben Yedayah's work that were not philosophical,[119] and he drew heavily from ibn Adret's commentary as well.[120] Furthermore, ibn Ḥabib's anthology of aggadic passages and his commentary did not focus solely on the problematic aggadot that fueled philosophic reconstructions or even on the issues that were at the center of philosophic and antiphilosophic debates. Ibn Ḥabib was far more concerned with his desire to produce a work containing Talmudic aggadah and a running commentary governed solely by the aggadot that he encountered. Therefore, while discussion of issues such as anthropomorphism, God's unity, the World to Come, the messiah, and faith surfaces in his commentary, ibn Ḥabib also wrote and commented on the issues of prayer, exile, the Land of Israel, and Torah study, which were not necessarily the foci of the philosophical disputes of his day.

Kabbalah and Talmudic Aggadah

When ibn Ḥabib began to prepare his anthology, he had at his disposal running commentaries on Talmudic aggadah that had been written by Kabbalists interested in disseminating their ideas through the words of the Talmud, such as the thirteenth-century Spanish aggadic collections of Azriel of Gerona and Todros ben Joseph Halevi Abulafia. However, ibn Ḥabib chose not to include passages from Kabbalistic commentaries either alongside or within his own commentary, despite the fact that there were more running commentaries on the aggadot of the Talmud available to him that were written by Kabbalists than by Talmudists and philosophers. Instead, ibn Ḥabib made infrequent references in his aggadic commentary to Kabbalistic works as well as to the ideas contained therein.[121] These sporadic references suggest that ibn Ḥabib was opposed to the way Kabbalists approached aggadah. Indeed the primary role of their aggadic commentaries was to sanction an esoteric program rather than to explicate aggadah for the sake of aggadah.[122] In their eyes, aggadah was not a medium in its own right, analyzed for the sake of bringing the messages of the aggadot to the fore; rather, they were committed to revealing the mystical potential of the aggadic material.[123] Aggadah granted Kabbalists the ability to disseminate an "utterly non-existent tradition as the most important truth of Judaism."[124] The aggadot linked Kabbalah to Judaism's classical texts because it had no antecedents in the known Jewish tradition.[125] In this regard, aggadah was a powerful resource. Ibn Ḥabib, however, differed in his objectives and envisioned a different role for aggadah. He did not want to cultivate Kabbalah or even develop a circle of philosophers who studied aggadah for that matter. He did not want aggadic interpretation to be dependent on one of these external disciplines; he believed in the self-contained status of the Talmud and in the ability of the aggadot to represent his understanding of the theology of the rabbis, as will be discussed in chapter 4. All of this can be interpreted to mean that ibn Ḥabib was not deeply influenced by the theurgic writings of the thirteenth-century Castilian and Catalonian mystics, which culminated in the production of the *Zohar* (1280–86), nor by the theosophic Kabbalistic literature that emerged in the aftermath of its compilation. The notion that God emanated ten aspects or *sefirot* from His infinite self and that, by understanding these *sefirot,* the mystic could learn to influence God and the world was not on ibn Ḥabib's theological or spiritual agenda.

Ibn Ḥabib readily admits to his inability to understand Kabbalistic ideas in his commentary to *b. Shabb.* 10a. There he quotes a passage from Joseph Gikatilla's Kabbalistic work, *Sefer Shaare Orah,* where Gikatilla integrates the idea of uniting the *sefirot* with an aggadic passage about God's gift of the Sabbath to the Jewish people (*b. Shabb.* 10b). This comment provoked the following response from ibn Ḥabib: "Here I have written what I did not understand in order to set a table before the one who will understand, [that is], if we can find someone in our generation [who can understand Kabbalistic ideas of this nature]."[126]

Although ibn Ḥabib rarely quotes directly from Kabbalistic works, he defends his decision to quote from *Sefer Shaare Orah* by revealing his hope of providing Kabbalistic insight to the person who might be interested and able to understand it. And yet ibn Ḥabib immediately qualifies his editorial decision by noting that a person knowledgeable in Kabbalah would be difficult to find. He then moves on to express his preference for the literal rendition of the aggadic passage as he sees it, and not the mystical.

More telling of ibn Ḥabib's desire to minimize the influence of Kabbalah in the *En Yaaqov* was his decision to refrain from writing his own interpretive comment on the classic aggadic text of Jewish esoterica found in *b. Ḥag.* 14b about "four [rabbinic sages who] entered paradise."[127] Instead he quotes two interpretations of this passage: one comment (or entry) from the *Arukh Hashalem* (a late eleventh- and early twelfth-century dictionary of Talmudic terms written by Nathan ben Yeḥiel of Rome)[128] and another passage from an unnamed work by a Catalonian rabbi who had quoted from a *teshuvah* of Hai Gaon, presumably to discredit Kabbalah.[129] As a Talmudic text that surely lends itself to Kabbalistic explorations, *b. Ḥag.* 14b has remained a *crux interpretum* in the study of early Jewish mysticism. Ibn Ḥabib's citations on the spiritual adventure into paradise taken by ben Azzai, ben Zoma, Elisha ben Abuya, and Rabbi Akiva thus reveal much about his relationship to Kabbalah.

In the text written by Nathan ben Yeḥiel which ibn Ḥabib quotes from, the ascent of these four rabbis into paradise is described as an inner vision and not as a detachment of the soul from the corporeal body necessary for penetrating the supernal worlds. In other words, in Nathan ben Yeḥiel's opinion, relying on Hai Gaon, the experience of these four rabbis was not an ecstatic or otherworldly event. Instead of a physical ascent, theirs was a psychological one.[130] Hai Gaon was clear to point out that Rabbi Akiva did not "ascend on high" but rather envisioned God "in the inner chambers of the heart." Moreover, Hai Gaon believed that God revealed Himself to the prophets through the "understanding of the heart" (*ovanta delibba*), and that such men did no more than contemplate the divine throne.[131] It was *as if* they had entered God's inner precincts, traveling from one *hekhal* to another, but indeed they had not actually done so. Certain righteous individuals, according to Hai Gaon, were able to experience God in some otherworldly/mystical manner. However, he warns that if a person were to become overly dedicated to achieving this type of mystical experience, or were to became devoted to the study of the mystical works *Hekhalot Rabbati* and *Hekhalot Zutrati,* such a commitment would envelop him and draw him away from his commitment to the study of Mishnah and Talmud, from his observance of the commandments, and from an honest and straightforward relationship with God.[132]

As a rabbi engaged in the process of compiling the *En Yaaqov* at the beginning of the sixteenth century, when Kabbalah was already a well-developed system of thought, ibn Ḥabib pointedly chose to ignore the Kabbalistic commentaries written on the passages from *Ḥagigah* and to rely instead on Hai Gaon's approach. Reflective as it is of Hai Gaon's adherence to rationalist thinking rather than to mysticism, the decision to cite him situates ibn Ḥabib outside the circles of Kabbalistic study and the interests of Kabbalists in aggadic exegesis.

Ibn Ḥabib's Intellectual Milieu: Fifteenth-Century Iberian Culture and Its Effect on Aggadah

The final stage of medieval Hispano-Jewish philosophy and, along with it, the development of ibn Ḥabib's interest in aggadah, was cultivated in the wake of a political, economic, and religious crisis that had begun decades before him. Mounting pressures experienced by Jews throughout the fourteenth century came to a disastrous head in 1391 with the eruption of riots driven by the populace, which turned into massacres of Jewish communities throughout Castile and Aragon. Many Jews were forcibly baptized, and many communities were attacked and plundered.[133] With little time to rebuild and to reestablish themselves, Spanish Jews were confronted with the charismatic anti-Jewish preacher, Vincent Ferrer, who incited both forced and voluntary conversions of Jews to Christianity. The failed disputation at Tortosa (1413–14) also overwhelmed the royal court's attempts to quell the violence that continued. Christianity triumphed while Judaism appeared to hobble behind in a desperate and helpless state that provoked shifts in the intellectual milieu of the time.[134]

To be sure, these events prompted Jewish intellectuals to consider their fate. Were they being punished for their religious transgressions? The self-examination that began in the Hispano-Jewish orbit targeted philosophy—specifically Maimonidean philosophy—for its engagement with the "foreign wisdoms" (*ḥokhmot ḥitsoniyot*) of Aristotle and Averroës. The accusations heaped on Maimonidean philosophy for being the catalyst of the moral and spiritual transgressions of Spanish Jewry emerged from both those with limited exposure to philosophy and those steeped in its traditions and ideas. The strongest attack came from the prominent halakhist and rabbi of Saragossa, Ḥasdai Crescas. The loss of his only son in the riots heightened his desire to move Jewish thought in a new direction, away from Maimonidean intellectualism and Aristotelian philosophy, and toward a theology that revolved around faith.[135]

Crescas devoted his treatise *Or Adonai* to overturning the Maimonidean notion that true knowledge (in other words, the universal truths of faith) could be obtained by means of philosophic speculation. He intended to achieve this goal by transforming the rationalist assimilation of knowledge and faith, which had been the cornerstone of Maimonides' philosophic system, in the hope of divorcing religion from philosophy. Whereas for Maimonides and the Jewish Aristotelians both the cognition of universal truths and the perfection of the human intellect were intimately connected with personal immortality, Crescas purposefully severed this relationship in the hope of creating a system that could be embraced by the learned elite and the populace as well. In so doing, he claimed that the ultimate end of life—that is, the union of the incorporeal, eternal soul joined with God in the afterlife—depended not on metaphysics but on the human love of God. This love was to be found in the freedom that all men had to observe God's commandments, which were given as a reflection of God's infinite will and love of His people. In contrast to the Maimonidean system, where praxis was viewed as inferior to speculation, Crescas insisted that the performance of God's commandments could assure one of personal immortality.[136]

In effect, Crescas reinvigorated the Maimonidean controversy. The strength of his arguments prompted his contemporaries to take sides in the debate. And there was a great deal at stake. To follow in the footsteps of Crescas meant that one needed to take seriously his refutation of the twenty-five propositions in Aristotelian physics which were outlined at the beginning of the second book of the *Guide for the Perplexed*. It also meant that the very image of Maimonides, a man "who epitomized the very cultural identity and leadership claims of the Jewish elite in Iberia," was to be overturned.[137] It was not easy to sever such a relationship. Just as in an earlier period ibn Adret had refused to relinquish his commitments to the philosophic tradition in its entirety, the same was true for rationalists of the fifteenth century, such as Crescas's students Joseph Albo, Zeraḥya Halevi, and Profiat Duran, as well as later rabbis including Abraham Shalom, Shem Tov ben Joseph, and Isaac Abarbanel. Although Crescas's insights left a permanent mark on the intellectual culture of the day, his influence never quite trumped the impact of Maimonidean philosophy.[138]

In fact, it was this very attachment to the rationalist tradition that thwarted, once again, the ability of aggadah to emerge as a serious discipline during the fifteenth century. Even Crescas's desire to move away from the Maimonidean philosophic tradition did not prevent him from arguing his position using the approach of a philosopher or the genre of the philosophic treatise. Such was the embeddedness of philosophical ways of thinking and conversing. The first book of his four-volume work, *Or Adonai,* deals with the *shorashim* (roots) of the religious beliefs of God's existence, unity, and incorporeality, and is divided into three sections, or *kelalim*. In the first section Crescas summarizes the stances of Aristotle and Maimonides. In the second section he critiques their positions. In the third section Crescas offers his own opinion. The second book focuses on the *pinot,* or cornerstones, of the Torah and is divided into six sections that deal with six beliefs. The third book presents Crescas's understanding of the "true" beliefs taught by the Torah. The final book presents thirteen questions that Crescas feels the Torah and/or tradition had never answered effectively.[139]

Crescas sought to reconstruct an outlook based on a prephilosophical religious experience of revelation rooted in the Bible and renewed through rabbinic texts. But he did so through the form of the philosophical treatise.[140] *Or Adonai* was all about Crescas's theological understandings as told by a man reared in the rationalist tradition of Spanish culture, and not about a desire to illuminate the nature, character, role, or meaning of Talmudic aggadah, unless it informed his larger goals. The disastrous political situation surrounding the riots of 1391 and the need on the part of the Jewish community to understand their plight influenced Crescas, but they did not provoke a desire to return to the Talmudic sayings of the rabbinic sages for inspiration in the form of a running commentary, as the expulsion and its aftermath would one day do for ibn Ḥabib.

Sermonizers, Dogmatists, and the Study of Aggadah

Sermons, which served as bridges between the elite culture and the general society, offer a glimpse into the hearts and minds of preachers of a particular era as they integrated their own ideas with the needs, expectations, and abilities of their constituencies.[141] No doubt preaching was also a genre that was well suited for aggadic explication given the lively, imaginative, moralistic, and value-laden character of aggadah. Although it is not possible to know conclusively to what extent preachers relied on aggadah, as many sermons remained oral, written records show that the philosophical sermon flourished[142] within popular circles. During the fifteenth century, sermonizers used philosophical modes of argumentation from their pulpits. They even made reference to Greek and Arabic philosophers about as often as they quoted from the Talmud and midrash. In a letter, Ḥayyim ibn Musa (1380–1460) writes of a "new type of preacher [who] rise[s] to the lecturn to preach . . . and most of their sermons consist of syllogistic arguments and quotations from the philosophers." According to ibn Musa the philosophers whom these preachers mentioned included Aristotle, Alexander, Themistius, Plato, Averroës, and Ptolemy. The Talmudic rabbis Abbaye and Rava were "concealed in their mouths."[143] This suggests that, by the fifteenth century, philosophy had emerged as an integral part of the more popular sector of the Spanish Jewish cultural milieu, possibly playing a larger role in the genre of the sermon than in the explication of Talmudic aggadah.[144]

Indeed, sermons attest to a desire to disseminate philosophical ideas to a broader audience.[145] Philosophically oriented sermons dealt with themes that were on the agenda of the intellectual elite, who hoped to stimulate a wider audience through them. While some of the sermons were more technical in their content and purpose—for example, resolving contradictions in the Aristotelian position on the essences of species, or showing concern for the inappropriate use of syllogistic arguments (sermon on *Vaethanan*, Deut. 3:23–7:11), or arguing for the superiority of intellectual pleasure over sensual pleasure (sermon on *Behuqotai*, Lev. 26:3–27:34)[146]—others concentrated on the discussion of important biblical themes, such as the binding of Isaac, and were apt to quote directly from Maimonides' *Guide for the Perplexed*. In one sermon on the binding of Isaac, it is clear that there was nothing controversial about quoting from Maimonides. The preacher had perceived in the *Guide* (3:24) a useful solution to a theological problem concerning whether or not God's knowledge was complete or incomplete. He felt the solution offered by Maimonides was worthy of sharing with all those who would hear his sermon.[147] The questions on the rationalist agenda of the learned elite were what fueled the sermonic exegeses of lectionary passages. In sermons such as these, the quotations from rabbinic literature functioned as mere "helpmates" brought in to aid in the process of grappling with issues not necessarily generated or resolved by the biblical and rabbinic texts quoted.

These observations prompt several questions: Why did aggadah take a backseat to philosophy in Spain? In the wake of the tumultuous events of the fourteenth century, which continued into the fifteenth century, and the wave of both forced and voluntary conversions to Christianity, why was there not a more intensive desire to embrace Talmudic aggadah? Why did even the few who authored commentaries on aggadot of the Talmud abandon this goal for the sake of their commitments to philosophy? For example, Abraham Shalom, the author of *Neve Shalom,* was among the few who chose to discuss his philosophic ideas in the form of homilies based on aggadot drawn from tractate *Berakhot.*[148] But even his plan to compose a commentary on all the aggadot of the Talmud that were deemed frivolous by philosophers was abandoned when he realized that tractate *Berakhot* provided sufficient source material for expressing his philosophic ideas.[149] In addition, why were the ideas of Aristotle, Averroës, and Maimonides more attractive than those of Rabbi Abbahu and Rabbi Joshua ben Levi at this time?

The continuous appeal of philosophy rather than of aggadah following the crisis of 1391 is due in no small measure to the sociocultural context of the Jews in fifteenth-century Christian Spain. During this time a startling change occurred in the intellectual culture due to the complicated political realities generated by a Christian monarchy as well as by a clerical class that threatened the viability of Jewish communal life and the veracity of the Jewish religion. The abrupt turn in the nature of fifteenth-century intellectualism speaks to the theological needs of a community living within a society where the Christian elite continued to determine the ground rules and to establish the framework for theological debate.[150] In this context the gravitational pull was toward the discipline of dogmatics. Dogmatics, more than aggadah, halakhah, Kabbalah, or straightforward philosophy, paralleled Christian interests and created a "playing field" on which Jews could hope for some chance of respectability. It was dogmatics—and the Jews' preoccupation with clarifying the definition of faith in the name of rooting Judaism in a set of dogmatic principles[151]—that enabled Jews to defend their refusal to adopt Christianity. It allowed them to develop a theology rooted in creed formulation, which paralleled Christian forms of self-definition. Indeed, the very essence of Christianity was defined by the adoption of a set of dogmas enforced by way of papal decree (i.e., Athanasian and Nicene decrees).

The Jews' interest in dogmatics was also prompted by the increasing number of Jews who were either forcibly converted to Christianity or who went to the baptismal font willingly. They harbored hopes that creed formulations would prevent Jews from converting to Christianity by protecting Judaism from Christian attacks on its theological underpinnings. In fact, many Jewish scholars who took an interest in dogmatics also authored polemical, anti-Christian tracts and recorded contentious exchanges with Christians.[152] In addition, crypto-Jews needed a way to identify with Judaism in the absence of the performance of mitsvot, and the Jewish community, in turn, needed a way to look on them as Jews.[153] To establish a minimalist version of Judaism, whereby a set of beliefs was identified, enabled crypto-Jews to think of themselves as Jews on accepting those beliefs, and allowed their Jewish neighbors to consider them as Jews as well.[154]

Furthermore, the confrontation with Christianity at this fragile moment in Jewish history also provoked a renewed interest in exploring the relationship between reason and faith. Dogmatics became the means by which Sephardic Jews worked through the conflict between philosophic knowledge and religious belief. The goal was to locate theology in the science of divine revelation by proposing a set of "principles" (*iqqarim*)—also called "foundations" or "roots" or "cornerstones" or "pillars," depending on the thinker[155]—thereby collapsing philosophy and theology to create a more organic synthesis. This led dogmatists to explore Maimonides' list of thirteen principles. Indeed, dogmatics became a way of employing or critiquing Maimonidean philosophy in the name of establishing a Jewish theology that reoriented philosophy to the needs of the day. Practically every Sephardic scholar trained in the rationalist tradition was preoccupied with the discipline of dogmatics during this period.[156]

All this limited the study of Talmudic aggadah in Spain during the century into which ibn Ḥabib was born. The explication of aggadah was less effective for building faith in the face of hostile Christian threats to the very definition of Judaism. It was preferable to develop a competing Jewish theology. Menachem Kellner argues that formal disputations and persuasive sermonizing on the part of Christian clerics prompted an increased need for Jews to respond to theological questions. This, Keller notes, trumped the learned Spanish rabbinic elite's preoccupation with halakhic issues[157] and certainly maneuvered the community's focus away from an aspect of their religion which caused unease and made them vulnerable—Talmudic aggadah.[158] Just as in the days of Naḥmanides, aggadah continued to be a source of embarrassment for the Jews within the Christian Spanish context. However, during this last chapter of Jewish history on Christian Spanish soil, the stakes were even higher. The great threat of both forced and voluntary conversions intensified the Jewish community's need for self-definition. The overarching framework of dogmatics and its relationship to philosophy spoke to this need more directly than aggadic literature. Dogmatists had little interest in framing their conversations around the aggadot of the Talmud, except to integrate them in an atomistic way where necessary. In this regard, Talmudic aggadah never emerged as a separate discipline of study in its own right.

When ibn Ḥabib considered Talmudic aggadah, he envisioned it as a source for rabbinic theology at a time when the Jews were in great need of spiritual reinvigoration. Following the expulsion from Spain, many were questioning their faith. However, it was the Jews' forced expulsion from Christendom and their resettlement within the multiethnic and multireligious milieu of Ottoman society that offered ibn Ḥabib the perfect opportunity to suggest that the Jewish community develop new modes of study that would be able to vigorously mold and strengthen faith. Jews were offered more freedom and protection by Islamic law than during the entire previous century in Christian Spain.[159] It is therefore not all that surprising that, outside of this Christian cultural context, where Talmudic aggadah had been used to discredit Judaism as well as the Talmud, and where the disciplines of philosophy, in particular, pushed Talmudic aggadah to the fringes of Spanish intellectual culture, a renewed interest in Talmudic aggadah could emerge. In fact, ibn Ḥabib's *En Yaaqov* marks the beginning of a new cultural trend in the Ottoman empire: a renewed, enhanced commitment to rabbinic aggadah.

The Ottoman Context

In the early sixteenth-century Ottoman empire, collections of midrash aggadah and of aggadah surfaced in printed form as both scholars and the literate public made demands on early Jewish print shops to produce already extant as well as new collections of aggadic material.[160] It was an important juncture in the history of Jewish literature, as the first printed editions of major midrashic works of aggadah, *Midrash Rabbah* (Constantinople, 1511), *Tanḥuma* (Constantinople, 1522), and *Yalqut Shim'oni* (Salonika, 1527), rolled off the presses. The following collections of aggadah were also printed: *Haggadot Hatalmud* (Constantinople, 1511), *Menorat Hamaor* (Constantinople, 1514), *Kad Haqemaḥ* (Constantinople, 1515), *En Yaaqov* (Salonika,

1516), and *Bet Yaaqov* (Salonika 1522).[161] The advent of the printing press in the Ottoman empire contributed to making aggadah highly visible in a way that it had not been historically.[162] Talmudic aggadah, in particular, became an area of great interest. As a result, Jews began to piece together collections of Talmudic aggadah and to take a greater interest in writing commentaries on the aggadot of the Talmud. For example, in ibn Ḥabib's search for tractates of the *Yerushalmi* when preparing the *En Yaaqov,* he mentioned the existence of another collection of aggadot drawn from the Talmud that was available to him and that contained aggadic texts from the *Yerushalmi.*[163] In his introduction he referred to *Haggadot Hatalmud,* a collection of Talmudic aggadah, also pointing to the availability of another printed collection of aggadah. At this time, even philosophers began to prefer integrating their philosophic ideas into rabbinic exegeses and produced fewer philosophic treatises than they had once produced in Spain.[164]

However, ibn Ḥabib intended for the *En Yaaqov* to overshadow any earlier efforts.[165] In keeping with his promise to expand on the efforts of his predecessor, the compiler of *Haggadot Hatalmud,*[166] he included more aggadic material drawn from the *Bavli* and *Yerushalmi* Talmudim, more commentaries, more indexes, and a lengthier introduction explaining his vision for the collection. In this regard, ibn Ḥabib's collection was the most successful exemplar of this flowering of interest in Talmudic aggadah. It was also the collection that was reprinted continuously in the centuries that followed ibn Ḥabib's death, and many scholars wrote new commentaries that were later added to its pages, as will be discussed in chapter 5.

Ibn Ḥabib was among those who initiated the momentum that surged throughout Ottoman Jewish culture regarding the relationship between the sacred texts of the Talmud and its commentary as Spain's Jews began to establish themselves there.[167] When ibn Ḥabib placed the aggadic texts of the Talmud front and center and aligned them with his own commentary, he made a statement, by virtue of that focus and adjacency, about the need for the explication of the aggadic texts of the Talmud. This image of embracing the aggadah within a document that resembled the Talmud stood in marked contrast to his fifteenth-century predecessors, who had used aggadic texts on an "as needed" basis merely to embellish their opinions or theses in treatises that bore no resemblance to the Talmudic corpus.

Within an environment where a greater interest was taken in Talmudic aggadah, ibn Ḥabib could reinvision dogmatics through the lens of the aggadot. He was able to argue that the principles of faith could be found within the aggadot of the Talmud.[168] He dismissed the need to prove the verities of a particular principle of faith, which had been central to the discipline of dogmatics for a century, or even to organize his collection thematically around the principles themselves. Instead he constructed lengthy exegeses on aggadic passages whereby, in the course of explicating the aggadic material, he revealed various principles of faith. His goal was to explain how one was to uphold such principles; he wished to dispel that which challenged one's belief in them. For example, he answered questions including: How was one to believe in a system of exact retribution when bad things happened to good people and even good people were forced into situations where they had sinned?[169] How could one believe in a messiah that had failed to come[170] or pray to a God who had not provided one with reward?[171] One did not need to rely on philosophy or Kabbalah to locate the core messages of the Talmud. Ibn Ḥabib wanted Talmudic aggadah, which had once been used by philosophers and Kabbalists in an atomistic way, to emerge as the voice of the Talmud itself. Said another way, the Talmud's theological messages were contained within the Talmud and needed only the efforts of a devoted exegete of aggadah to bring them to the surface. Ibn Ḥabib's *En Yaaqov* was, in many respects, a reenvisioning of dogmatics using aggadah as the starting point for the sake of a people in need of its personal theological messages.

The great success of ibn Ḥabib's efforts is reflected in the fact that the *En Yaaqov* became the most prevalent work of Talmudic aggadah in the years following its first printing. It charted a new path in the history of the study of aggadah in its response to the intrinsic challenges that this material brought to the fore. The prior lack of interest in the study of Talmudic aggadah—due to the attitudes toward aggadah held by legal codifiers, Talmudic commentators, and philosophers and Kabbalists—motivated ibn Ḥabib to advocate for a new intellectual trajectory for Jews.[172] Ibn Ḥabib's objective was to transform Talmudic aggadah into its own discipline of study independent of midrashic exegesis, philosophy, and Kabbalah.[173] He intended for the study of aggadah to emerge as a serious discipline tantamount to the study of the Talmud and equal in importance to the study of halakhah.[174] Ibn Ḥabib viewed aggadah, like halakhah, as a medium that had practical applications. In his mind, it was a body of sources that addressed issues facing Jews who were questioning how to believe in God. Thus, in creating the *En Yaaqov,* ibn Ḥabib committed himself to transforming the image of aggadah from a secondary, supportive, and at times problematic medium into a theological body of Talmudic material significant in its ability to inform one's relationship to halakhah.

3

Rethinking the Image of the Talmud

Judaism's textual practices are ontologically and historically at the heart of Jewish identity. Jacob ibn Ḥabib, who thought about this "textual fabric"[1] in terms of the Jews' development of an ongoing interpretive relationship with the Talmud, employed a textual strategy that reshaped the image of the Talmud. He made a conscious effort to design his collection of aggadah, the *En Yaaqov,* so that it would resemble the Talmudic corpora, the *Bavli* and the *Yerushalmi.* As every anthological act is ideologically charged, it is necessary to consider what ibn Ḥabib's chosen editorial form and his decisions regarding the organization of the material at hand mean.[2] More than what ibn Ḥabib said in his own commentary on the aggadic material, it is important to think about what he "did" when he undertook the project of compiling the *En Yaaqov.*[3] The process of anthologizing material, even when the act seems merely archival, as in the case of the *En Yaaqov,* is a powerful instrument of communication. The Jewish anthology as a form and a genre is every bit a reflection of the Jewish imagination. It is one way of making a statement about the meaning and shape of Jewishness.[4] Ibn Ḥabib's anthology of Talmudic aggadah was born out of ibn Ḥabib's desire to reshape Jewish identity through the lens of the Talmud.

Ibn Ḥabib's efforts represent a personal critique of the intellectual culture that was nurtured during the fifteenth century in Spain and then reconstituted in the Ottoman empire following the expulsion. Such a critique was leveled against many aspects of late-medieval Spanish Jewish culture with respect to its relationship to the Talmud, including the pronounced interest taken in the study of legal code literature in the Jewish academies that pushed Talmudic aggadah to the periphery; the widespread attention given to establishing a set of Jewish dogma or Jewish self-definition that took place outside the context of formal Talmud study; the emergence of a philosophical curriculum that was not centered around the Talmud; and the proliferation of the Talmud methodology of Isaac Canpanton, which was not easily applicable to the study of Talmudic aggadah. At its core, ibn Ḥabib's critique emerged from an understanding of Judaism as fundamentally Talmud-centered and from the idea that the Talmud is a self-contained work.[5] Discomforted by the characterization of the Talmud as a "book of law" rather than as a "book of faith" and by the fact that other disciplines outside of the Talmud, such as philosophy and Kabbalah, had become significant sources of Jewish spirituality, ibn Ḥabib strove to renegotiate the boundaries of what counted as formal Talmud study. In so doing, he entered into a longstanding debate over the degree to which the curriculum of Jewish study should be Talmud-focused and argued against its openness to other disciplines. This chapter is devoted to the significance of the relationship of the *En Yaaqov* to the Talmud and the nature of its critique.

A Talmud Lookalike

The collection that bears the closest resemblance to the *En Yaaqov* is *Haggadot Hatalmud,* a compilation of Talmudic aggadah published in Constantinople in 1511. In his introduction to the *En Yaaqov,* ibn Ḥabib bemoans the appearance of this earlier collection just as he begins his own work on the *En Yaaqov.* Yet despite the fact that many were willing to pay high prices to obtain *Haggadot Hatalmud,* ibn Ḥabib points to the need for a far more extensive, better collection. *Haggadot Hatalmud* had not achieved the goals for aggadah that ibn Ḥabib desired; thus he set out to distinguish his collection from this earlier effort. By attaching the aggadot to several running commentaries, including his own, he fulfilled the promise of the aggadot in the name of producing a more comprehensive collection of Talmudic aggadah than *Haggadot Hatalmud.* Although this earlier work contained a pithy, Rashi-like commentary, its brevity and the fact that its Talmudic text and commentary were difficult to distinguish from each other (both appeared in the same Rashi script) made it no model for ibn Ḥabib. In his mind aggadic commentary was to serve a far larger goal than that of mere clarification; it was to convey a theological agenda. Central to his vision was a desire to redefine the nature of the Talmud by using his commentary to offer spiritual messages that claimed the Talmud as a document of faith.[6]

In this regard, ibn Ḥabib stood in marked contrast to the author/editor of *Haggadot Hatalmud,* who was no more than a compiler of Talmudic sources and who did no more than elucidate aggadic passages for his readers.[7]

The first printed edition of the *En Yaaqov* (Salonika, 1516) is similar in appearance to early printed editions of the Talmud, in which the texts of the Talmud were set in block letters and placed alongside Rashi's commentary, which was printed in Rashi script.[8] Each page of the *En Yaaqov* includes not only large portions of commentary written in Rashi script but also texts of the aggadot printed in block letters (see appendix, figure 1). Like the compiler of *Haggadot Hatalmud,* ibn Ḥabib dismantled the Talmud's larger ideational units, or *sugyot,* and removed the legal material. In so doing, he preserved the order of the original aggadic pericopes as they appeared in the Talmud and situated these passages in the *En Yaaqov* within their tractates and chapters of origin. At the top of many of its pages are headings noting the Talmudic tractate and chapter from which ibn Ḥabib drew the aggadic material. At a glance, the collection looks like a version of the Talmud.

Ibn Ḥabib had several sources available to him, in addition to *Haggadot Hatalmud,* when he began to think about the organizational structure of the *En Yaaqov.* He showed little interest in relying on the existing midrashic collections' editorial arrangements or content. He not only rejected the idea of ordering the aggadot of the *En Yaaqov* in accordance with a set of biblical verses, but also decided that the Talmud would serve as his only base text.

Oddly, ibn Ḥabib also chose to reject the editorial precedents set by his Spanish Jewish predecessors, the authors of *Kad Haqemah*[9] and *Menorat Hamaor,*[10] who had produced Spanish anthologies of Talmudic aggadah during the medieval period.[11] The compilers of these works had drawn aggadic material from many rabbinic sources, including the Talmud, had constructed larger pericopes, and also had arranged the material according to theme.[12] These useful editorial tactics made aggadic literature found in many collections more accessible.

The author of *Kad Haqemah,* Baḥya ben Asher, had been concerned about promoting a broader-based interest in the study of aggadah which, he believed, would be accomplished by means of the sermon. By gathering together aggadot from various rabbinic texts, including the Talmud, and by organizing this material according to themes rather than biblical verses, Baḥya hoped to offer preachers easier access to aggadah. This he did by alphabetizing sixty topics beginning with the topic heading *"emunah"* (faith), which was followed by sections on *"ahava"* (love), *"orḥim"* (guests), and *"avel"* (mourning).[13] Despite the ease with which one could thus gain access to rabbinic aggadah, the collection did not promote greater interest in producing documents with a similar agenda. In fact, more than a century passed before another collection containing selections of aggadah drawn from rabbinic literature appeared in Spain, Israel ibn al-Nakawa's fourteenth-century work, *Menorat Hamaor.*

Yet ibn al-Nakawa's editorial embellishments—a rare attempt to synthesize aggadah with halakhah, using aggadah as its premise—did not entice ibn Ḥabib either.[14] Although ibn al-Nakawa's primary goal was to make the aggadic portions of the Talmud as well as passages from *Midrash Rabbah* and other more obscure collections of midrash[15] more accessible to those who studied halakhah,[16] he aimed to synthesize these aggadot with a set of authoritative rules regarding certain commandments. For example, when he dealt with the issue of prayer, ibn al-Nakawa drew not only from Jacob ben Asher's legal work, *Tur (Orah Ḥayyim)*, but also from various aggadot and midrashim that focused on the spiritual value of prayer.[17] It was important to ibn al-Nakawa to dispel notions that aggadah was somehow less important because it had no practical consequences for "real" life.[18]

But the impetus for the creation of *Menorat Hamaor,* ibn al-Nakawa wrote, came from his concern for the decline in learning among the populace and the Jews' growing indifference to laborious study. He also notes that there was desire for a comprehensive work of aggadah that would encourage its study.[19] And yet one still wonders why he embarked on this project with great trepidation, claiming himself unworthy of the role of gathering together scattered passages from different places.[20] While the admission is to some degree formulaic, as many authors were quite modest about their contributions, it is also plausible that he was proposing something new to an audience that was presumably less committed to the study of aggadah than to its more sacred counterpart, halakhah.

Even the second edition of *Menorat Hamaor,* which was produced by Isaac Aboab during the fifteenth century, did not draw the attention of ibn Ḥabib. Although Aboab relinquished ibn al-Nakawa's commitment to halakhah in favor of a collection committed to aggadah alone, ibn Ḥabib was apparently not swayed by what could have seemed an impressive shift. Aboab chose to adopt ibn al-Nakawa's overall thematic structure and even his title without sacrificing his independence as a compiler. He organized his collection according to seven themes that corresponded to the seven branches of the candelabrum: guarding against jealousy and lust; avoiding sins related to speech; performing mitsvot related to family (i.e., honoring one's parents, raising children, holiday observance, charity); studying Torah; practicing repentance; loving one's neighbor; and acting with humility.

The candelabrum was to be a reminder of the light that aggadah brought into the world of those who studied it.[21]

One would not be off the mark to recognize in Baḥya's *Kad Haqemaḥ,* and in ibn al-Nakawa's and Aboab's editions of *Menorat Hamaor,* attempts to create a context for the study of aggadah and to bring aggadah into the center of Jewish learning. That being said, none of these attempts was connected to a desire to situate the study of aggadah within the context of Talmud study. These compilers drew aggadah from an array of rabbinic sources. Ibn Ḥabib's ideological commitment to the centrality of the Talmudic corpus drove him to reject these templates, as he notes in his introduction to the *En Yaaqov.* As a result, his editorial strategy regarding the anthology of aggadic passages involved the exclusion of source material from any document other than the Talmud. He was willing to sacrifice thematic coherence despite the degree to which it severely curtailed one's access to the Talmud's aggadic passages. It mattered little to ibn Ḥabib that, without the legal core of the Talmud, one aggadic pericope did not necessarily build on the themes of its neighboring aggadic text. He did not even add words of his own to the aggadic texts in a manner that would link one passage to another and smooth the transition. There also is neither rhyme nor reason for the chosen aggadic texts. Ibn Ḥabib anthologized those aggadot about which he had something to comment. In this way, the aggadot from the Talmud he anthologized were no more than a large hodgepodge of nonlegal texts of different genres gathered together in the name of something more significant: the centrality of the Talmud and the significance of its aggadic passages.

Ibn Ḥabib fully understood the disadvantages of his editorial decisions, and he introduced strategies to overcome the deficiencies he had generated. For example, unlike the editor of *Haggadot Hatalmud,* he divided the aggadic material into numbered sections. He paid close attention to the seams that divided one conceptual piece of Talmudic aggadah from another and created smaller, organic units of aggadic material, each with its own number.[22] These new ideational pieces were then connected to a portion of commentary that lay beside or underneath them. Thus ibn Ḥabib's new version of the Talmud emerged—a Talmud with a fresh sense of what constituted the Talmudic *sugya* (an ideational unit of Talmudic material).

Ibn Ḥabib, in casting aside the idea of creating a "user-friendly" work of aggadah arranged according to theme, also relied on the power of indexes to lead his readers to the aggadot found therein. The two indexes ibn Ḥabib created also compensated for any limitations resulting from his editorial decisions by providing a thematic map to guide readers to the aggadot that were strewn throughout the Talmudic *sugyot* with no ideational organization. One index was conceptual: ibn Ḥabib designed it to divide the aggadic material into twelve ideational units, which he outlined in his introduction. He refers to each of the twelve concepts or themes as pillars to convey that these are the foundational concepts on which Judaism stands.[23] The themes included in this conceptual list signify the array of topics ibn Ḥabib found to be most useful to his readers within the aggadic contents of the Talmud: Torah study, worship, charitable deeds, the behavior of judges, truth, the maintenance of peaceful relations (on both an intercommunal and an intracommunal level), repentance, life in the Garden of Eden or Gehinnom in the afterlife, God's evaluation of the souls of man, the throne of God (the nature of God), the Temple, and the messiah (including the resurrection of the dead and the World to Come). This is not to say that every aggadic passage included in the *En Yaaqov* fit these twelve parameters, as the passages of Talmudic aggadah that ibn Ḥabib included exhibit a far greater diversity of themes than such an index reflects. The index, however, was merely an editorial strategy to make some of the contents of the *En Yaaqov* more readily accessible to those less familiar with the contents of the Talmud. Ibn Ḥabib arranged his second index according to the weekly Torah portions read in synagogues, paralleling, to some degree, the index found at the beginning of *Haggadot Hatalmud*.[24] Although ibn Ḥabib specifically states in his introduction that the *En Yaaqov* was to have a greater use than simply to guide preachers in their preparation of sermons for the Sabbath and holidays or for family life-cycle events, in devising this type of an index he was able to ensure that such a use would not be overlooked.[25]

The advent of the printing press made indexes both necessary and possible.[26] Printed books made large amounts of material more available to readers than ever before. Printers had to invent ways of making the material in books both usable and appealing to many types of audiences simultaneously. Every book had to be marketable. For ibn Ḥabib, however, who was working directly with his printer,[27] the indexes were about far more than catering to a large audience and to the economics involved in selling books. Ibn Ḥabib's indexes enabled him to maintain a commitment to the order of the aggadot as found in the Talmud, knowing his readers, from the preacher to the average synagogue-goer, would be able to find relevant material. This printing decision provided him the latitude to anthologize large portions of aggadic material simply because it was nonlegal or to include some passages that might be classified as legal—all in the name of exposing particular messages. He was not bound by the set of themes he posed in his index. He could create a template for a type of learning that was about the study of aggadah for the sake of study, and he could produce a book that made demands on its reader to begin at the beginning of the tractate and study until one reached its end—that is, to study the *En Yaaqov* as if one were studying the Talmud itself. The readers who encountered an aggadic passage followed by another aggadic passage would then conceptualize the Talmud in a new way. They would receive and incorporate deep within themselves an image of the Talmud as something other than a legal work.

The Talmudic Page

At the time the Salonikan printer Judah Gedaliah undertook the publication of the *En Yaaqov* in 1516, there was no standard, complete version of the *Bavli* or the *Yerushalmi* available to the Jewish world. The Italian printer Daniel Bomberg had not yet published what would become the first full, printed version of the Babylonian Talmud containing all its tractates. Bomberg's printed Talmud, published in 1520–23, was as much an attempt to standardize the Talmudic page as it was an economic move to publish a collection that would surely sell. But when ibn Ḥabib began his work on the *En Yaaqov,* the structure of the Talmudic page was still in flux. Some early manuscripts and early printed editions contained only the texts of the Talmud,[28] and some, such as those tractates printed in Spain, included Rashi's commentary; others had both Rashi and Tosafot, such as the Soncino edition of tractate *Berakhot,* printed in Italy in 1483–84.[29] Ibn Ḥabib, working together with the printer, made the editorial decision to include the comments of Rashi and Tosafot that corresponded to the passages of Talmudic aggadah which he had anthologized. Comments made by Rashi and Tosafot were quoted above ibn Ḥabib's commentary, *Hakotev.*[30] The significance of this editorial decision cannot be overlooked or underemphasized. The fact that ibn Ḥabib included Rashi and Tosafot means that he was using the *En Yaaqov* to take a stand not only on what constituted the Talmudic page but also on how the *En Yaaqov* would be characterized.

Indeed, Rashi's Talmud commentary had never been formally associated with the study of aggadah. Aggadah had never been the focus of Rashi's Talmudic interpretive agenda, in the sense that he took no interest in the interreligious polemical topics raised by the aggadot of the Talmud which engaged the geonim and his rabbinic contemporaries in their defense against Karaitic, Muslim, or Christian attacks.[31] Rashi never concerned himself with explaining away the Talmud's anthropomorphic references to God or even with the task of defending what appeared to be illogical aggadic references. He did not use the aggadot for homiletical purposes or to reveal theological messages. Instead he took the aggadot of the Talmud at face value. Although he rarely skipped over an aggadic pericope in its entirety without making at least one comment, his approach was entirely explanatory. He grappled with difficult words or phrases by adding short glosses for the purposes of clarification, but he rarely engaged in deep analyses of the aggadic passages found in the Talmud.[32]

Given ibn Ḥabib's stated intention to uncover the deep messages hidden within the Talmud's aggadot, his decision to include Rashi's comments may seem somewhat curious. After all, ibn Ḥabib did not share Rashi's *ad locum* explanatory approach to the study of aggadah. In ibn Ḥabib's eyes there was far more to say about the aggadot than Rashi illuminated, especially with respect to matters of faith. However, ibn Ḥabib's decision to include direct citations from Rashi's commentary prior to offering his own analyses,[33] as well as his utilization of Rashi's comments in his own commentary, *Hakotev,* indicate that he viewed Rashi's commentary as a serious interpretive effort with respect to aggadah as well as a significant part of the tradition of Talmud study.[34] In fact, in some instances ibn Ḥabib went so far as to construct his understanding of an aggadic text based on a comment Rashi had made. In the case of *b. Ber.* 6b, ibn Ḥabib built his entire analysis of an aggadic passage concerning whether the world was created for the sake of one person on Rashi's understanding of the word *litsevvat.* He saw this word as a verb form related to the medieval French noun *solaz,* which means "community."[35] Ibn Ḥabib began his interpretation of the aggadic passage by clearly stating that "from the brief language of Rashi, I learned what the three tannaim [in this passage] were arguing about."

Ibn Ḥabib's decision to anthologize Rashi's comments on the aggadot he chose to include in the *En Yaaqov* cannot be taken lightly. By ibn Ḥabib's day Rashi had become the Talmudic commentator *par excellence.* In fact, during the fifteenth century in Spain and Portugal, this observation led many in his scholarly circle to refer to Rashi as the *"parshandata,"* or the primary "exegete of the law." Within this context, Moses ibn Danon, who died in Portugal in 1493, advised exegetes who came after Rashi to "cast all of the commentaries of France on the refuse heap, save [those written by] *parshandata* [who he claims is Rashi]." While some have argued that Rashi may have earned this cognomen for his biblical commentaries alone, his commentary on the Talmud was also a contributing factor. Rashi's commentary had accompanied many of the printed editions of the Talmud by the time ibn Ḥabib began to piece together the *En Yaaqov* and had functioned as the main running commentary on the Talmud as well.[36]

By including an oft-studied commentator who had become intimately wedded to the study of the Talmud, ibn Ḥabib made a significant political decision as the editor and author of the *En Yaaqov*. By including Rashi he connected the *En Yaaqov* to the sphere of Talmud study. This decision also generated a closer relationship between the *En Yaaqov* and the Talmudic corpus than it had with any other extant collection of aggadah. Ibn Ḥabib's inclusion of Rashi signified his desire to create a readership that would engage in the study of Talmudic aggadah with the same degree of seriousness and attention to detail as they devoted to Talmudic/halakhic study. Ibn Ḥabib hoped his constituency of readers would, like those of Rashi, be committed to the study of the legal as well as nonlegal portions of the Talmud. To include Rashi was a curricular decision; it was a statement that the study of Rashi's commentary was an important step in the process of understanding the messages of the aggadot.[37]

Ibn Ḥabib also sifted through Tosafot and included those comments that were relevant to the aggadot he anthologized. Adherents of the Tosafistic school were even less devoted to the explication of Talmudic aggadah than Rashi. Within their academies they focused far more on scrutinizing the legal texts of the Talmud to locate a preferred interpretation and an acceptable halakhic outcome. Their methodology was rooted in a desire to see the whole of rabbinic-halakhic literature as a uniform corpus, each part agreeing with all the other parts such that no contradictions among its concepts, principles, arguments, and conclusions existed.[38] Tosafistic comments on the non-halakhic portions of the Talmud were minimal, and the instances where the methodology of the Tosafists extended to an in-depth look at the role of aggadah in the *sugyot* of the Talmud were rare. In addition, the facts that Tosafot had not played a central role in the Castilian Jewish academies during the fifteenth century, and that ibn Ḥabib's exposure to Tosafot occurred within the Ottoman context following the expulsion,[39] made ibn Ḥabib's editorial choice to include them even more surprising.[40] Why bother to include Tosafot at all? Did ibn Ḥabib believe that Tosafot were indispensable to the proper explication of the aggadot of the Talmud as well as to the analysis of the Talmud overall?

Part of the answer may lie in the fact that, at the precise time ibn Ḥabib was making decisions about which commentaries to anthologize in his *En Yaaqov*, others were thinking along the same lines as he was regarding the Talmud. Jews who had resettled in Salonika from various geographical locales valued different Talmud commentators. This is evident in the remarks of David Messer Leon, an Italian rabbi who settled in Salonika at the beginning of the sixteenth century.[41] He wrote in his book, *Kevod Ḥakhamim*, about how his approach compared to that of the Sephardic Jews he encountered:

> I entered within the boundaries of the Sephardic scholars, to debate the novellae of Naḥmanides, although it is not our custom in the German and Italian *yeshivot,* for all of our debates are on [the words of] Tosafot. . . . And as their debates are on [Naḥmanides'] novellae, so we do so on Tosafot. And just as they are not occupied with Tosafot, so we are not occupied with their novellae. But, even so, I concern myself very much with the novellae of Naḥmanides, whether on Torah or Talmud, because it is very sharp.[42]

Ibn Ḥabib, like David Messer Leon, exemplifies the cross-fertilization of intellectual traditions occurring in Salonika. His exposure to Tosafot in Salonika and his decision to include them in the pages of the *En Yaaqov* indicate that he was convinced of their value. The *En Yaaqov* offered the first printed presentation of Talmudic texts containing Tosafot to appear in Salonika.[43] Printed editions of several individual tractates of the Talmud did not roll off the presses in Salonika until after the first volume of the *En Yaaqov* was printed, and they did not contain Tosafot.[44] That said, ibn Ḥabib was able to locate in Salonika manuscripts and/or printed editions of various tractates of the Talmud that contained Tosafot or manuscripts of Tosafot alone that had been unavailable to him in Spain and Portugal. Commenting about the wealth of material accessible to him in Salonika, ibn Ḥabib writes in his introduction to the *En Yaaqov:*

> I found this multitude of books when I arrived at the home of the honorable scholar, Don Judah, the son of the pious and exalted prince, Don Abraham Ben Banvenest of blessed memory. . . . He supported writers and expert scribes who had skillfully copied all the books of the Mishnah and the Talmud many times. . . . His house is a gathering place for scholars and their students, to read, to study, to peruse them. He always spends a considerable amount of money on writing them, correcting them and proofreading them. Both of them generously lend me any book I need.[45]

From these manuscripts and printed books, ibn Ḥabib began to prepare the *En Yaaqov.* Generations of printers thereafter adopted the template of the Talmud that also contained Tosafot on its printed pages. Naḥmanides' commentary remained separate.

This is not to say that ibn Ḥabib overlooked Naḥmanides in favor of Tosafot.[46] He drew passages from Naḥmanides' novellae as well, although to a much lesser degree than he drew from Tosafot. But his editorial choice to include Tosafot, which was a less familiar tradition to him, and one that was born in the academies of Provencal Jews, was a clear indication of his desire to see Tosafot become more central.[47] The act of including Tosafot in the *En Yaaqov* constitutes a statement by ibn Ḥabib that his work was about more than explicating aggadah. It was also about participating in a conversation regarding what defined Talmud study more generally. To include Tosafot, despite their limited allegiance to aggadah, conveys that ibn Ḥabib approached the aggadic texts of the Talmud as purely "of the Talmud" and not as distinct aggadic texts in their own right.

Ibn Ḥabib's editorial decisions to include both Rashi and Tosafot were not, however, new in the history of Jewish literature. In the wake of the burning of the Talmud in France in 1240, copyists produced editions of Isaac Alfasi's code, *Hilkhot Harif,* which contained Rashi and abbreviated Tosafot in the margins in order to make the code more "Talmud-like."[48] While ibn Ḥabib may not have known of this collection, its emergence proves that, for medieval Jews, the inclusion of Rashi and Tosafot enabled collections to mimic the Talmud and even gain a level of credibility attributed only to the Talmud. The same was true for ibn Ḥabib. The organizational format of the Talmud, along with the inclusion of Rashi and Tosafot, gave aggadah a sense of integrity in an intellectual context where it had been sorely lacking. It served as a reminder that this material was *also* Talmudic and therefore should be studied with a similar type of devotion to its contents.

But the very fact that the *En Yaaqov* bears such a resemblance to the Talmud also suggests that ibn Ḥabib was reacting to the status of the Talmud in the intellectual culture in which he was reared. The boldness that characterized his decision to remove the Talmud's halakhic portions suggests that he wanted to broaden the perception of the purpose of the Talmud. Early sixteenth-century life in Salonika was not marked by Talmud burnings or by the confiscation of Jewish books. Therefore the emergence of the *En Yaaqov* does not constitute a substitute for a Talmud that was temporarily unavailable. Rather, it represents ibn Ḥabib's critique of the way the Talmud was studied, and not studied, by Jews who were interested in an array of disciplines, including practical halakhah, Talmudic casuistry, dogmatics, and philosophy. Although ibn Ḥabib did not intend for the *En*

Yaaqov to replace the Talmud, there is no doubt that he felt his community needed another Talmud-like work that would not only complement the legal codes but also prompt them to view the Talmud as a jumping-off point for theological discussion. The remainder of this chapter will focus on the way ibn Ḥabib produced the *En Yaaqov* to critique the intellectual culture into which he was born.

A Response to Alfasi

As noted in chapter 2, ibn Ḥabib followed in the footsteps of Isaac Alfasi, who had disrupted the *sugyot* of the Talmud and created, in essence, another version of it, titled *Hilkhot Harif*.[49] Pushing aggadah aside and focusing on the halakhah, Alfasi maintained the order of the legal passages as he found them in the Talmud and situated the halakhic material in their tractates and chapters of origin. In so doing, Alfasi proposed a type of Talmudic pedagogy focused on legal matters of a practical nature[50] rather than on illuminating the complicated Talmudic dialectic that had characterized the Talmudic corpus.

Alfasi's work met with great success in the academies of Spain, in particular. Whether this triumph was the result of a desire to unearth the Talmud's legal "bottom line," or because the study of codes left more time for pursuing the disciplines of philosophy and Kabbalah, or even because the Talmud was at many points under the threat of burning or confiscation, is hard to say. There is no clear evidence describing the curricula of these academies or an understanding of what factors motivated curricular decisions. Thus the extent to which rabbinic scholars focused on the study of Alfasi's code to the exclusion of the Talmud itself is not entirely known.

That said, from as early as the time of Abraham ibn Daud (1110–80), the author of *Sefer Haqabbalah,* and continuing until the early modern period, rabbinic scholars referred to Alfasi's *Hilkhot Harif* as a *talmud qatan,* a "little Talmud."[51] The title suggests that medieval thinkers considered his work as a version of the Talmud that could be studied on its own, without reference to the Talmud itself. Indeed, in the late eleventh and early twelfth centuries, the Spanish legal codifier Judah ben Barzillai al-Bargeloni argued that Alfasi's code was exactly like the Talmud. The fourteenth-century codifier Menaḥem ibn Zeraḥ, in the introduction to his work *Tsedah Laderekh,* noted that Alfasi's code was studied exclusively in Spain.[52] As late as the sixteenth century, Alfasi continued to have a strong influence in the codificatory arena. Maimonides states in the *Mishne Torah* that he relied extensively on Alfasi, and Joseph Caro considered him as one of three "pillars" on which his decisions in the *Shulḥan Arukh* were based.[53]

The image that ibn Ḥabib paints of Jewish learning in Castile in his introduction to the *En Yaaqov* is of a curriculum centered on the study of code literature, specifically *Hilkhot Harif,* remarking that it was to the detriment not only of Talmud study but of aggadah as well. Ibn Ḥabib describes the populace as at risk for never gaining exposure to the underlying messages contained within the Talmud's aggadic passages, because they were exposed to rabbinic leaders who studied codes and ignored aggadah. Even ibn Ḥabib's description of the earlier academies of the Talmudic rabbis Rabbi Ami and Rabbi Asi revealed his belief that they were studying halakhah to the exclusion of Bible and aggadah.[54] To overcome the casualty of this pedagogical choice, ibn Ḥabib devoted himself to producing a corrective work that would make Talmud study also about the study of aggadah. Pointing as a model to the work of Asher ben Yeḥiel (Rosh), who had arranged his fourteenth-century code, *Pisqe Harosh,* in Toledo in accordance with the tractates of the Talmud, and not to Rosh's son, Jacob ben Asher, who had opted for an entirely different organizational structure in his Toledan halakhic code, the *Arbaah Turim,* ibn Ḥabib communicated his intention to produce a Talmudic analog to halakhic codes that followed the structure of the Talmud.[55]

However, despite ibn Ḥabib's redactional decision to maintain the organizational structure of the Talmud, as Alfasi had done—that is, the names of its tractates and the order in which the material appeared—the *En Yaaqov* is not the exact inverse of Alfasi's code with the focus now on aggadah. Despite ibn Ḥabib's claims in his introduction to the contrary, he does not follow Alfasi's template exactly. Alfasi was more radical than ibn Ḥabib in the way that he interwove his own interpretations into the very fabric of the texts he quoted from the Talmud in order to communicate his position on the legal issue at hand. He seemed to make every attempt to preserve the language and structure of the Talmud, but nonetheless he edited and modified the texts he encountered. Within the texts of the Talmud that he quoted, Alfasi included his own analyses of the Talmudic discussions in relationship to those of his predecessors, as well as other relevant rabbinic texts, rather than relegating such analyses to a commentary, as ibn Ḥabib did years later. Alfasi aimed to resolve arguments left open in the Talmudim and often noted that his legal conclusions were correct beyond any doubt.[56] Although Alfasi did not state outright that he intended for his work to replace the Talmud, it would seem likely that, in rewriting the texts of the Talmud, along with reducing the impression that the aggadot were significant, he left little need for someone to study the Talmud alongside his own work. He hoped that his halakhic work would be seen as an end in and of itself, containing final legal conclusions.

In contrast, ibn Ḥabib did not insert his own words between the texts of the Talmudic aggadot, usurping no literary license from Alfasi in this regard. On the other hand, his decision to preserve the integrity of the Talmud's aggadic texts and distinguish them from his own interpretive remarks and anthology of commentaries suggests an editorial design more strictly parallel to the Talmud than Alfasi's code. Positioning ibn Ḥabib's commentary in a space beside the texts of the Talmud rather than within them was a pedagogical strategy to communicate that he had not said the last word, that the Talmud retained its sacredness, and that his was a human interpretation. Unlike Alfasi, ibn Ḥabib admits to his own fallibility and communicates his frustration that he can neither complete the *En Yaaqov* project nor capture in his collection all he believes there is to be said about the aggadot of the Talmud (both the *Bavli* and the *Yerushalmi*).[57] His decision to surround his anthology of the aggadic texts of the Talmud with not one but several commentaries—including those of Rashi and Tosafot; the late thirteenth-/early fourteenth-century commentary on the aggadot of the Talmud by Solomon ben Abraham ibn Adret (Rashba); a more limited number of comments drawn from the commentary on aggadah written by the thirteenth-century Provencal rabbi Isaac ben Yedayah[58]; and a small amount of material from the Talmud commentaries of Naḥmanides, Yom Tov ibn Ishibili (Ritva), and Rabbenu Nissim (Ran)—indicates that the *En Yaaqov* was as much an anthology of Talmud commentaries as it was an anthology of the aggadot themselves. That the commentaries were geographically heterogeneous, emerging from Provence, Catalonia, and Castile, indicates that ibn Ḥabib did not want to limit his messages to the Hispano-Jewish orbit alone. His aim was not to preserve or generate intellectual boundaries rooted in ethnic differences, especially at a time when the makeup of the Ottoman Jewish community was so diverse. He did not want to impose a sense of orthodoxy that would have entailed the presentation of one view to the exclusion of others. In this regard, the *En Yaaqov* was not about communicating a "bottom-line" interpretation, as was the case for Alfasi, but rather about the need for a continuous debate about the meaning of the aggadot of the Talmud.

One cannot ignore the fact that, because of the combined efforts of ibn Ḥabib and his printer, Judah Gedaliah, the *En Yaaqov* was the most extensive anthology of commentaries wedded to the texts of the Talmud that had ever been printed. In addition, no printed collection of Talmudic texts contained a contemporary commentary situated alongside the venerable commentaries of Rashi and Tosafot, as if to suggest that it was equally significant. Ibn Ḥabib's conscious fragmentation of both Talmud text and commentary and his inclusion of his own running commentary on the aggadot were bold editorial moves by a man who was imagining the potentiality of the Talmud. As an anthologizer he acted on the desire to gather the "dispersed sparks" of aggadic literary creativity to claim them as representative of the Talmudic imagination.[59] Reacting against the curricular success of Alfasi, ibn Ḥabib claimed the aggadot as canonical, sacred texts that had been overlooked. In his mind, the Talmud was far more than a work of halakhah.

The Talmud and the Challenges of Dogmatics and Philosophy

Ibn Ḥabib's editorial decision to create a collection of aggadah modeled after the Talmud, despite the availability of other thematic, midrashic, and sermonic collections of aggadah, was not only a reaction to the codificatory endeavors of scholars who had distanced the study of Talmud from its connection to aggadic discourse. It was as well the case that Jews of the medieval period participated in an array of scholarly pursuits, including ones that did not necessarily revolve around the study of Talmud. As Isadore Twersky argued, "The spiritual-intellectual chronicle . . . [was] so very rich in protagonists who push[ed] back the frontiers of study by *adding* subjects to Talmud," including philosophy and Kabbalah.[60] In his view not all Jews were "Talmud-centric"; the Talmud was not the only sustaining force of religious spirituality.[61]

Ibn Ḥabib's intention was to claim the Talmud as a central force in the cultivation of Jews' spirituality through its aggadic pericopes. Matters of faith, which had been on the agenda of the Spanish intellectual community throughout the fifteenth century in the form of dogmatics, would now lie at the core of the aggadic passages and therefore at the heart of the Talmud itself.[62] Many dogmatists had focused their attentions on the notion that Judaism, like Christianity, was creed-based. For this reason they were preoccupied with laying out the principles of Jewish faith, and their wish was to systemize Jewish belief. Using their own language of "pillars" (*amudim*), "foundations" (*yesodot*), "principles" (*iqqarim*), "cornerstones" (*pinot*), and "roots" (*shorashim*) of faith,[63] they attempted to define the minimal number of beliefs one needed to affirm in order to be considered a Jew.[64] In this regard, each dogmatist attempted to produce "their" definitions of Judaism.

However, these dogmatists also posed a particular challenge for ibn Ḥabib. With rare exceptions, they were not focused on the exegesis of the Talmud or on linking their study of Jewish dogma to the discipline of Talmud study. In fact, the seminal scholars of the fifteenth century who were interested in Jewish dogma and to whom ibn Ḥabib refers throughout his commentary—Ḥasdai Crescas, Joseph Albo, Joseph Jabetz, Abraham Bibago, and Isaac Abarbanel—did not write any commentaries on the Talmud, whether related to the issue of dogma or otherwise. Instead, they wrote treatises organized to reflect their interest in Jewish dogma, underscoring the fact that dogmatics was a subset of philosophy and not of Talmud. This meant that some of the most prominent Spanish scholars of the fifteenth century were thinking about Jewish self-definition and the character of one's belief in God *outside* the context of formal Talmud study.

To be sure, ibn Ḥabib's decision to integrate conversations about faith into the framework of the Talmud through his commentary on its aggadic passages was cultivated within a milieu where non-Talmudic disciplines received serious attention. For centuries many had embraced Maimonides' understanding that one attained human perfection through a curriculum that required the study of logic, mathematical sciences, and divine science.[65] Talmud study, while never ignored, was not considered sufficient in and of itself to unravel the mysteries of the Torah. His view was that the Talmud provided only "slight indications and pointers." Maimonides argued that there were no more than "a few grains belonging to the core which were overlaid with many layers of rind." Unfortunately, people were so occupied with these layers of rind that they missed what lay beneath them.[66] Maimonides pointed out that it was philosophy that directed the reader to a text's hidden meaning. Even fifteenth-century dogmatists such as Crescas, Albo, Arama, and Bibago, who captured ibn Ḥabib's interests and resisted, in varying degrees, Maimonidean intellectualism, did not commit themselves to producing works that focused on the interpretation of the Talmud as a form of Jewish spirituality. Crescas's stated plan to create a great Talmudic work, for example, was never realized in the wake of his more pressing devotion to developing a religio-philosophic magnum opus on Jewish faith, *Or Adonai,* and a critique of Christianity titled *Refutation of the Principal Dogmas of the Christian Religion.*[67]

For Joseph Albo, the author of the treatise on dogma *Sefer Haiqqarim,* it was essential to produce a work on faith to defend Judaism against its Christian opponents and to portray Judaism as more credible than Christianity.[68] Prompted by the yearlong disputation during 1413–14 with the Jewish apostate Joshua Lorki, Albo dedicated himself to outlining the fundamental principles of Jewish faith. This disputation had taken place before Pope Benedict XIII in Tortosa. The bull that ended the conference, titled *Et si doctoris gentium,* attacked the Talmud and other books believed by the Christians to discredit Christianity, prompting Albo's response.[69]

The bull resulted in the confiscation of copies of the Talmud throughout Aragon.[70] This act suggested that the papal authorities connected the strength and viability of Judaism with the Talmud. In fact, the decree diminished the role of Talmud study for a period of time. However, as Albo and other dogmatists attested, treatises that connected Jewish self-definition with a set of dogmas rather than with the statements of the Talmud alone communicated that the Talmud was not the sole curricular, cohesive focus of the Jewish community. Jewish faith was contingent on the internal disposition of the believer to embrace a set of principles that defined divine religion, and that was laid out in *Sefer Haiqqarim.* Such principles, as Albo claimed, were the fundamental principles on which Mosaic law was based.[71] While Albo was intimately familiar with the Talmudic corpus, studied it vigorously when able, and integrated rabbinic references into his *Sefer Haiqqarim,* he did not conduct serious discussions about the intricacies of faith in his treatise using Talmudic texts as his original focal point.

In later years, ibn Ḥabib's contemporary, the Castilian-born rabbi Isaac Arama (b. 1420), despite his excellent Talmudic training, turned to the medium of preaching rather than to authoring Talmud commentaries. On failing to raise sufficient funds to establish an academy in Aragon, Arama adopted the genre of the sermon to spread his teachings. His awareness that Jews were compelled to attend church services and to hear the sermons of preachers interested in converting them to Christianity also fueled his desire to embrace the synagogue as a significant pedagogical framework over and above the academy.[72] Although he eventually became head of a yeshiva in Calatayud, where he became known as a famed preacher as well as a rabbi who garnered many disciples, his primary contribution was the integration of his theological/philosophical ideas into the homiletic framework that he designed in *Aqedat Yitsḥaq.*[73] In this collection of sermons, his familiarity with philosophy is evident. He freely integrated biblical and rabbinic sources with material from Maimonides,[74] Ḥasdai Crescas,[75] Gersonides, and Joseph Albo,[76] not to mention Averroës and Aristotle. In fact, he made extensive use of Aristotle's *Nicomachean Ethics.*[77] Arama relied on the genre of the sermon to spread many of the basic elements of philosophical thought to the general public rather than focusing on disseminating rabbinic sources alone. His commentaries to the books of Esther, Song of Songs, Ruth, Lamentations, Ecclesiastes, and Proverbs[78] are also evidence that he was devoted to explicating the texts that were central to the life of the synagogue rather than to writing extensive interpretive remarks on the texts of the Talmud. In *Aqedat Yitsḥaq,* in a sermon devoted to the principles of faith, Arama presented these principles within the context of his interpretation of Lev. 23, where the festivals are discussed. In his mind, these festivals of biblical origin hinted at the basic beliefs of the Jewish faith.[79] In this way, Arama joined many of his contemporaries in discussing Jewish self-definition outside the context of Talmudic texts.

When ibn Ḥabib devoted himself to compiling the *En Yaaqov,* with its word-for-word citations from the Talmud, he offered a critique of his predecessors, who had failed to express their views through running commentaries on the Talmud. Ibn Ḥabib wished to show that the principles of faith were, in fact, rooted in the Talmud. Conversations about man's relationship to God were to take place within the context of Talmud study, bringing the two more intimately together.

At the same time, ibn Ḥabib's commitment to the production of a Talmudic collection of aggadah was a response to the longstanding tensions imposed on Talmud study by philosophers. Ibn Ḥabib had been exposed to assaults on a Talmud-centric curriculum and even after the expulsion remained concerned about the attraction of philosophy, which had pervaded Spanish Jewish culture throughout the fifteenth century. Those of Spain's philosophers who had rejected Talmud study outright in favor of a more conscientious commitment to the study of philosophic texts by a range of thinkers, including Aristotle, Porphyry, Boethius, and Galen, posed a threat to the centrality of Talmud study. They believed that Jews reared on the Talmud alone developed a false sense of devotion and a mistaken impression that they were "true Jews." They accused those who focused their studies on the Talmud of isolating themselves from the respected subjects that defined the rationalist agenda and functioned as a common intellectual discourse with their Christian neighbors. In the minds of such philosophers, the sense of sacral importance granted to the Talmud promoted the exclusion of subjects that formed the core of the philosophic program, including logic, physics, and metaphysics. Reflecting on this phenomenon in his introduction to a translation of the Neoplatonist Boethius's *Consolations of Philosophy (De Consolatione)*, Azariah ben Joseph ibn Abba Mari of Catalonia wrote in 1432: "I know that the common mass of foolish rabbis will find me guilty and will mock me because of this translation, but if these ignorant individuals, who pretend to be true Jews and who pretend to be devout with their absurd devotions, would read Maimonides, who translated many books by non-Jewish scholars, especially Galen, they would think otherwise."[80]

The fifteenth-century Spanish philosopher Abraham Bibago also expressed his dissatisfaction with Talmud scholars who ignored philosophy. He blamed them for reading Talmudic texts in accordance with their literal sense. Such a method, he argued, blinded them from considering more philosophically oriented interpretations and led them to ridicule Maimonides and his disciples.[81] For Bibago, these Talmudists claimed themselves to be pious before the masses despite their failure to examine the Talmud's inner meaning. He claimed that those who studied Talmud in this way labeled philosophers as heretics and unbelievers, when it was they who were sinners.[82]

But the extent of the Jews' interest in philosophy during the fifteenth century is best reflected in the remarks of ibn Ḥabib's contemporary Isaac Arama, himself a committed philosopher, regarding the academies in Spain.[83] He wrote that "the majority of students are like seedlings raised on [a] foreign language. . . . Today [this foreign language of philosophy] is the essence of [the curriculum] of our academies and regarding Torah and Talmud it negates learning." He complained bitterly that many Jews during his day were teaching "alien disciplines antagonistic to our Torah in their own language."[84] In Arama's mind it appears that some philosophers had gone too far and posed philosophic theories that were dangerous precisely because they were built on rejecting the texts of the Talmudic corpus.[85] He writes:

> If you approach one of them [who study philosophy] who had barely even heard of Porphyry's *Eisagoge* and inquire of him, "What is it that you are studying, the Bible, or the Mishnah, or the Talmud?" he would answer, "I concern myself with none of these things, but with wisdom alone." And all of this breeds vulgarity and pride. . . . For the men advocating this wisdom have stepped forward and prepared seductive words for thoughtless students and brainless children saying to them, "Why do you study the laws of ritual slaughtering with Abbaye and Rava; come with us and learn the marvelous wisdom of Aristotle and his disciples and commentators!" Blast the souls of these braggarts who say that in the [Talmudic] tractate *Neziqin* our blessed rabbis were dealing with secular and transitory matters.[86]

Surely, Arama desired boundaries. He was concerned about the fact that philosophy had the power to diminish the ontological status of the Talmud as well as the framework of observance that it symbolized.[87] But like many of his Spanish contemporaries, he was also drawn to it. At what point was one sacrificed for the other? In what way could one be integrated with the other? What role was philosophy to play in the curriculum of Jewish studies so as not to undermine the Talmud?

For Bibago the answer did not lie in the complete rejection of the texts of the Talmud. He had no intention of pushing the Talmud aside completely. On the contrary, Bibago proposed an approach to the study of the Talmud that exposed the deeper, rather than literal, meanings of the texts he encountered. The words of the Talmud were hints of some underlying meaning that exposed matters dealing with faith, and it was these matters that became central to his fifteenth-century treatise on faith titled *Derekh Emunah*.

But ibn Ḥabib saw Bibago in a different light in the *En Yaaqov*. In ibn Ḥabib's mind, Bibago became a thinker who intentionally contradicted the true sense of aggadah and did not believe in the validity of his own philosophic statements but made them rather to appeal to his constituency. His philosophic knowledge and desire to offer up philosophic interpretations were built, according to ibn Ḥabib, on the demands of a constituency that preferred philosophy to Talmud study. He used philosophy only to respond to a group of people whom he understood were more interested in and accustomed to "hearing rhetorical interpretations [about aggadic passages], even though [such interpretations] did not accord with the truth [of these original passages]." As ibn Ḥabib viewed Bibago, he was contradicting the true sense of aggadah and preferred a constituency that would devote themselves to the study of Mishnah and Talmud; it was through their study of Mishnah and Talmud that they would develop a way to withstand philosophic analyses.[88]

Although ibn Ḥabib was motivated to embrace Bibago because of their shared interest in matters of faith, his impressions of him were incorrect.[89] They were skewed by his fear that philosophy was powerful enough to sway rabbinic elites away from literal understandings of Talmudic aggadah in favor of more appealing philosophic renderings.[90] In an expression of wishful thinking, he attempted to convey through his sense of Bibago that the Talmud was primary. He wanted to portray the community as having dictated the nature of the curriculum to Bibago rather than the other way around.

It would seem that ibn Ḥabib wanted to push his readership in another direction, if only their knowledge of the Talmud and its more literal and nonphilosophic interpretations became strong enough to distance them from the need for philosophic explications.[91] Toward this end, the *En Yaaqov* would be the version of the Talmud that led them directly to the aggadic texts. It could spearhead conversations that were about the study of the Talmud and not informed, necessarily, by the discipline of philosophy in the adjacency of ibn Ḥabib's commentary to the aggadot. If discussions of Jewish theology had once been wedded to the larger discipline of philosophy, the *En Yaaqov* was an attempt to claim the Talmud as the focal point of such theological discussions.

Kabbalah

From another vantage point was the matter of Kabbalah, which presented its own challenges to the study of Talmud.[92] Kabbalists had criticized the exclusive study of Talmud. Although they did not deny that the Talmud played a vital role in Jewish life, Kabbalists argued that its study needed to be supplemented and sustained by Kabbalah.[93] Paralleling the position of philosophers, Kabbalists posed a similar view: instead of philosophy, Kabbalah was the discipline that provided access to the inner meaning of the Talmud.[94] They considered the Talmud an external manifestation of God's will. It was not the core medium capable of affecting a true communion with God.[95] The Kabbalist Shem Tov ibn Shem Tov, in the decades before ibn Ḥabib rose to the position of scholarly leadership in Salamanca, argued that the Talmud did not enable him to uncover an understanding of matters of faith.[96] Such concerns ultimately led him away from Talmudic study and toward Kabbalah. It was Kabbalah that would eventually guide him on his spiritual quest.

In the years following the expulsion, the Spanish-born Meir ibn Gabbai (b. 1480) argued that Talmud study prevented one from amassing theological insight and knowledge. He spoke out vehemently against the exclusive study of Talmud, claiming that the person who dealt with "the garment and the body of Torah" alone denied the essence of the Torah and should not have been created.[97] As Moshe Idel points out, for those Kabbalists of the ecstatic school who believed that the ultimate spiritual goal was to achieve *devequt,* a state of unity with God, the intellectualism of Talmud study thwarted their desire for self-negation. The theurgic trend among Kabbalists whereby its adherents were devoted to securing the unity of the divine realm, the *sefirot,* required the performance of God's commandments. Kabbalists of this school criticized Talmudists for not valuing the esoteric meaning of halakhah and for failing to recognize its cosmic significance.[98] They made forceful assertions that Talmudists were incapable of achieving perfection without the meta-halakhic approach provided by Kabbalistic doctrine.

Additional Challenges

Attacks on the Talmud continued to surface with respect to aggadah during the fifteenth century. The questionable nature of the truth of aggadic sources generated further critiques of the Talmud that resembled assessments of previous centuries. Moses Arragel, a figure more contemporaneous to ibn Ḥabib, translated the Bible into Spanish in the fifteenth century and in his commentary referred to Talmudic aggadah as *fablillas,* that is, "little fables or gossip." Arragel claimed that he ignored Talmudic exegesis simply because he could not "swallow" many of the Talmudic pericopes or their explanations.[99] He cast Talmud study aside entirely in an attempt to challenge its centrality.[100]

Objections to Talmud study also came from those more interested in biblical exegesis. Even as early as the beginning of the fifteenth century in Spain, opposition to Talmud study was raised by Profiat Duran, who favored the study of the Bible. Not unlike philosophers and Kabbalists, he pushed for a reformation in the educational curriculum, as he notes in his treatise *Maase Efod.* There, he censured Talmudists not only because, as he notes, they refused to study Bible but also because Talmud scholarship made them haughty. Talmudists, according to Duran, believed that Talmud study earned them the right to expect that "all should stand up before them." The presumed prominence of Talmudic scholars within the communities of Spain angered scholars like Duran who searched for a form of cultural transformation that placed the Bible on the highest educational rung.[101] For Duran it was the Bible that served as the instrument for understanding the divine and for achieving eternal felicity; it was the divine source of power and knowledge.[102] Duran's overarching objective was to integrate all religious and nonreligious study into one spiritual and intellectual curriculum, so that everyone would be occupied with the study of the Torah.[103]

In later years, scholars such as Isaac Arama, Isaac Abarbanel, and Abraham Saba authored Bible commentaries rather than Talmud commentaries. Neither Arama, Abarbanel, nor Saba wrote Talmudic novellae or running commentaries on Talmudic material.[104] Instead, they examined their ideas in light of biblical texts and integrated material drawn from the Talmud into their exegeses as they needed them to defend their points.

Ibn Ḥabib took a stance on the primacy of the Talmud as compared to the disciplines of biblical exegesis, philosophy, and Kabbalah. As Moshe Halbertal points out, the Talmud was not an exclusive item in the curriculum; it was not considered a self-contained text[105] that conveyed the sum total of what Judaism was. Ibn Ḥabib thrust himself right into the center of the debate over what constituted the curriculum of Jewish studies. In his desire to distance the Talmud from philosophy and Kabbalah, while at the same time claiming it as a book of faith through its aggadic passages, ibn Ḥabib argued for its self-contained status. He thus critiqued the status of the Talmud by attempting to retrieve it as Judaism's most central text.

Integrating Talmud and Philosophy: The Contribution of Isaac Canpanton

Scholars have also argued that Talmud study, despite these competing intellectual forces, thrived throughout Castile in the years prior to ibn Ḥabib's birth in Zamora and during the years leading up to the expulsion in 1492.[106] When John II of Castile (1406–54) and Alfonso V of Aragon (1416–58) rose to power, they overturned many of the anti-Jewish edicts that had been in place since 1391 and allowed Jews to begin to rebuild their communities. Jews seized this opportunity to restore their communal life to its pre-1391 stature. For example, Abraham Benveniste, the chief rabbi of Castile and the agent of John II, gathered a group of representatives from Valladolid in 1432 to issue a set of enforceable decrees that would rebuild the infrastructure of the Jewish community. The Castilian chief rabbi placed the status of Torah study highest on his agenda and set up an intricate tax system that was devoted to raising money for Torah learning. He further decreed that localities with fifteen families hire a teacher for their children. In any place where twenty or more families lived, they were to establish a place of worship and penalize those who did not attend morning and evening services. In areas where there were forty or more families, he required that they maintain a permanent scholar capable of imparting knowledge in the areas of Talmud, halakhah, and aggadah. Such scholars were expected to establish permanent academies where "they could teach all who wished to learn halakhah from them."[107]

One of the most prominent rabbinic leaders of this period was Isaac Canpanton (1360–1463), who set up an academy in Zamora.[108] Elijah Capsali describes Canpanton in his sixteenth-century overview of the history of the rabbinic elite, *Seder Eliyahu Zuta*, as the rabbi who "restored Spanish Jewry to its former glory and who raised many disciples." Abraham Zacuto adds in his own history of the rabbis, *Yuḥasin Hashalem*, that Canpanton was the "gaon of Castile." He further accentuates Canpanton's greatness by noting that "whoever saw [Canpanton's] face it was as if he had received the face of the *shekhinah*."[109] As head of the Jewish academy in Zamora, where ibn Ḥabib would ultimately become a student, Canpanton was responsible for producing some of the century's greatest rabbis, including Isaac Aboab II (head of the Jewish academy in Guadalajara), Isaac de Leon (head of the Jewish academy in Toledo), Abraham Saba, and Jacob ibn Ḥabib's teacher, Samuel Valensi (head of the Jewish academy in Zamora), each of whom adopted different foci of study.[110] Whereas Aboab produced Talmudic novellae on various tractates, wrote responsa, and penned a commentary on the *Arbaah Turim*,[111] de Leon became a Kabbalist.[112]

That Canpanton produced only one (known) work, *Darkhe Hatalmud*,[113] in his long lifetime, does not fit with the descriptions of his scholarly prominence that are found in the documents written by Spanish scholars. Oddly, Canpanton does little more than outline his Talmudic methodology. He does not expound on Talmudic texts in an extensive way. References to Talmudic passages in *Darkhe Hatalmud* flesh out his Talmudic approach, but are no more than references. They do not serve as jumping-off points for elaborate exegeses.[114] No commentaries, responsa, or code literature written by him exist. This lack of material reflects the larger reality that there simply are far more surviving texts written by Spanish Jews of the fourteenth century than of the fifteenth century in the areas of legal responsa literature, codes, and Talmudic commentaries. But this is surprising for such a prominent rabbinic figure.[115] Scholars, including Abraham Gross, who also noted this lack of fifteenth-century material, attribute Canpanton's success to his ability to cultivate many Talmudic scholars as he worked to restore Spanish Jewry to its former stature, rather than to the diminished prominence of Talmud scholarship in fifteenth-century Spain. In fact, Gross warns against judging "a personality or a period in the history of the Oral Law . . . by the quantity of his, or its, written legacy."[116] Evidence that Canpanton is frequently referred to in documents from this period as a central personality, and that his pedagogical approach continued to be used even after the expulsion from Spain, in Jewish academies inhabited by Spanish scholars in North Africa, Palestine, and the Ottoman empire, certainly supports Gross's claims.[117]

A closer look at the Talmud methodology that Canpanton proposed indicates that this rabbinic leader wanted more than to reestablish Talmud study as the communities of Castile began the process of rebuilding during the fifteenth century. He was also responding to a diminished interest in the study of Talmud, most especially among those engaged in the study of philosophy. For this reason, Canpanton designed an approach to the study of the Talmud that would appeal to the Iberian Jewish intelligentsia. He crafted a method of Talmud learning that conformed with the language and techniques of the highly regarded scholastic philosophic discourse in order to cultivate a renewed interest in Talmud study among those familiar with scholasticism. By showing that Talmudic logic was comparable to Aristotelian logic (or Aristotelian linguistic doctrine) in particular, Canpanton hoped to enhance the credibility and appeal of Talmud study in the eyes of those steeped in the philosophic curriculum but distanced from the study of Talmud.[118] In this regard, Canpanton offered one attempt to resolve the tension between traditional Talmud study and philosophy.[119] He created an environment that drew from the world of philosophy without setting it up as an independent discipline. He welcomed the study of philosophy; he believed that logic, in particular, because of its natural system of rules, must have informed the sages of the Talmud.[120] Since logic "determines the patterns and laws in human thinking and indicates the errors and proofs inherent in man's intelligence," Canpanton believed it was to be relied on to uncover the truth about the Torah.[121] The goal was to understand Torah with scientific precision.[122]

In employing Canpanton's method—that is, his *shitat iyyun*—a student viewed each *sugya* as a self-contained unit. His objective was to establish the rules that governed the formation of a *sugya* before attempting to understand all of its conclusions. In addition, Canpanton's method directed the student to pay close attention to the language of each text. No sentence, expression, or word in the language of the Bible, Mishnah, Talmud, or their commentaries was to be overlooked. Every word was purposeful. Each lacuna of language meant something. Operating with the belief that all possible alternatives needed expression in any Talmudic discussion, Canpanton encouraged his students to go so far as to consider why the Mishnah, for example, discussed four cases, while the Talmud ignored one of them. Possible interpretations not addressed by biblical commentators needed to be explained away and understood as erroneous, and the reasons for the inclusion of others required further interpretation. Finally, Canpanton required the implementation of logical analysis or the *ḥaluqah,* as he referred to it. To refrain from such a method deemed one an "ignoramus."[123] According to Daniel Boyarin, "The last generation of Spanish [Talmud scholars] and their students in the Spanish diaspora were saturated in the world of the study of philosophy and its operative tool, logic." The use of logic was their primary criterion for examining the Talmudic dialectic of the rabbis, even to the point of overturning approaches more typical of thirteenth- and fourteenth-century Talmud scholarship.[124]

Indeed, Canpanton made a strong ideological statement about the character of the Talmudic corpus and about the way it was to be studied. His insistence on a type of logical analysis built on scholastic philosophic discourse not only opened up Talmud study to external disciplines but also claimed the Talmudic sages as its profound adherents. That said, one cannot ignore the cultural critique that Canpanton promoted in his decision to affirm a type of Talmud methodology rooted in the non-Talmudic discipline of Aristotelian logic. He promoted a bridge that attracted many adherents within the walls of Castilian academies. He linked the meta-Talmudic discipline of philosophy, which had so profoundly engaged the Jews of his generation, with the Talmud. The attractiveness of Canpanton's method to so many conveys a sense of readiness on the part of Spain's Jews for something new and integrative with respect to the study of the Talmud.

The fact that Canpanton's method of *iyyun,* or casuistry, eventually spread throughout the Spanish academies and continued to influence Talmudic study in the aftermath of the expulsion was due to several factors. Scholars of the period embraced Canpanton's approach because he sanctioned philosophy, and especially logic, as essential modes of study in the achievement of Talmudic elucidation. In *Darkhe Hatalmud,* Canpanton claimed that all should own books dealing with philosophical matters in addition to Talmudic books. He who failed to do so was, in Canpanton's opinion, a person "who [did] not have the wisdom of God."[125] Canpanton continued to appeal to those who went so far as to argue that Torah would be forgotten by the Jews in all the kingdom of Spain if philosophy was not used as an interpretive companion tool to other forms of Talmudic exegesis.[126]

More conservative observers (of a later period) also embraced Canpanton. Elijah Capsali, for example, viewed Canpanton as a scholar who had produced a "godly medicine" to control "the plague of philosophy."[127] In describing the history of the period in Spain after 1391, Capsali rationalized that Canpanton had, in effect, constructed a "fence around the Torah." Instead of studying philosophy and Talmud independently, Capsali noted, Canpanton had successfully promoted the idea of integrating one with the other. As an acceptable consequence, Talmud study would hardly exclude the study of philosophy, but would control its impact.[128]

At the same time, Canpanton was also able to provide his students with the means for defending themselves against Christian scholastics who were apt to discredit the Talmud for its falsities. Once subjected to the rigor of scholasticism, Jews could guard themselves more effectively against challenges from the outside. The use of rules of logic in interpreting Talmud generated a sense of polemical superiority in fifteenth-century Jewish scholarship over and above Christian scholasticism. Judaism's sacred canon conformed to the rules of logic. It exhibited the distinguishing mark of scholasticism in its adoption of a dialectical method of inquiry that involved a three-step process. In the *sugyot* of the Talmud, one could find a question posed (*quaestio*), and an argument made for and against answers proposed by earlier authorities (*disputatio pro et contra*), followed by a logical conclusion (*sententia*). If the avowed purpose of scholasticism was a rational attempt to penetrate revealed data by using a logical apparatus,[129] it was well suited for the study of Talmud. Christian scriptures, on the other hand, could not live up to the same level of scrutiny.[130]

Finally, Canpanton's popularity also stemmed from his ability to assimilate the traditional Spanish focus in Talmudic study onto practical halakhah with his analytical approach. In other words, he blended the objective of reaching halakhic conclusions with some of the aspects of the analytical style of Talmud study that had flourished in Spain since the days of Asher ben Yeḥiel—a style aimed at resolving contradictions between texts, proposing questions and answering them, and noting superfluous language.[131]

Canpanton was not without his opponents. This opposition led some of Canpanton's contemporaries to view the academies that legitimized his approach as failures from a "religious-educational" perspective.[132] Even from as early as the fourteenth century, there were scholars who derided prior attempts to develop casuistic approaches to Talmud study. In their minds, it was useless for the pursuit of the Talmud's primary objective, that is, as an "interpretation of the precepts and legal rulings and prescriptions." Students of the academy were not to bother with novellae and Tosafot, "for they all waste man's time with vanities."[133] Ibn Ḥabib's contemporary, Joseph Jabetz, in particular, criticized Talmudists who "set their hearts on sophistries (casuistry) to show their argumentative strength, [so] that they could purify a reptile." Jabetz, who also spoke out strongly against the study of philosophy, not surprisingly noted that it was wrong to engage in the type of study that would draw one's focus away from practical legal matters. Despite the fact that Canpanton valued practical halakhah, his opponents focused their critiques of him on the rootedness of his methodology in a "foreign" discipline.[134]

Ibn Ḥabib's Relationship to Canpanton

Ibn Ḥabib was not opposed to the type of Talmud study that Canpanton proposed. As a student reared in Canpanton's academy and trained by Canpanton's student Samuel Valensi, ibn Ḥabib was skilled in his methodology. In fact, ibn Ḥabib's son, Levi ibn Ḥabib, lauded his father as someone whose knowledge of Talmud was empowered by his use of "*pilpul,*" or casuistry.[135] When Rabbi Joseph Garson eulogized ibn Ḥabib, it is not surprising that he praised him for his casuistry:

> The Torah that he [Jacob ibn Ḥabib] taught . . . was true [Torah] without any mistake. Whether [we speak of] his breadth [of Talmud knowledge][136] . . . or [of] the casuistry that he employed, [it] was not like the casuistry of others who relied on their own insights [rather than on a thorough knowledge of the texts of the Talmud] and erred. Rather his [method of study] befit [the texts that he examined] and [was] true. . . . And I would like to compare [his Talmudic] breadth to bread because it was large in quantity like bread and his casuistry to wine because it was refined [like wine]. . . . [So pure was his casuistry] that it was like good wine. [It was created] during the six days of Creation, and [it was of the type that produces the kind of pure knowledge that one finds as a] most lofty achievement [of life] in the world to come.[137]

Garson's eulogy conveys that ibn Ḥabib exhibited a refined type of casuistry, deserving of recognition and emulation.

Although ibn Ḥabib never mentioned Canpanton by name in his commentary on the aggadot, he makes reference to his method of using Aristotelian logic when he sanctions the use of *ḥokhmat hahigayon* (logic) outright. An aggadic passage where Rabbi Eliezer, on his death bed, gave the vague advice to his students, "Prevent your children from *higayon*" (*b. Ber.* 28b), became an opportunity for ibn Ḥabib to make allowances for and even encourage the study of philosophy more generally. By distinguishing between *ḥokhmat hahigayon,* which ibn Ḥabib claims is an intelligent means for explicating the texts that define Torah learning, and *higayon,* which ibn Ḥabib defines as the type of learning typical of children who "repeat [what they have studied] many times [over] without knowledge or intellection regarding the verse that was read to them," he narrows the definition of the term *higayon* used in the passage.[138] Ibn Ḥabib writes:

> And it is not suitable that one should think that the meaning of [prevent your children from] *higayon* [as noted on *b. Ber.* 28b] refers to *ḥokhmat hahigayon* [that is, logic] because surely it

> [*ḥokhmat hahigayon*] is enlightening wisdom [used] even [for the
> purposes of explicating] Talmud Torah. And if [the passage in
> *Berakhot* actually] stated, "Prevent your children from studying
> Greek philosophy," it would be correct [to think], in accordance
> with what [the rabbis] said, that [the passage in *Berakhot* means]
> cursed be the one who teaches his son Greek philosophy.[139] But
> because [the passage in *Berakhot*] did not mention [the word]
> *ḥokhmah,* but rather said, "Prevent your children from study-
> ing *higayon,*" this instructs that the correct [interpretation] is as
> Rashi [has suggested,[140] that one merely needs to prevent one's
> children from rote learning].[141]

A careful rereading of a passage in *b. Berakhot* with an educational warning
about *higayon* was an opportunity for ibn Ḥabib to cast the method of using
logic to study Talmudic texts in a positive light; the discipline of logic was
for him an "enlightened" form of wisdom useful in the sacred task of Torah
study. At the same time, ibn Ḥabib also encouraged the study of Greek
philosophy, *ḥokhmah hayevanit,* just as Canpanton had done years earlier.

However, within ibn Ḥabib's commentary one also finds a blatant critique of philosophical study[142] that reflects his desire to control the extent to
which Jews relied on it in their study of the Talmud. In fact, his commentary reads as if it were a critique of such an approach, as he time and time
again purposefully resists philosophy. Ibn Ḥabib's allowance for the use of
logic or Aristotelian philosophy in his comment on *b. Ber.* 28b should be
seen in this light. Although ibn Ḥabib never embraced Canpanton's methodology in his commentary on the aggadot of the Talmud, he seems here
to open the door to those who wish to apply it because it was an approach
rooted in the texts of the Talmud. In this way, he broadened his audience of
readers of Talmudic aggadah, but not without harboring some concern.

The reasons for ibn Ḥabib's discomfort emerge in his reflections on a
Talmudic passage found in *b. Avodah Zarah* 16b–17a. Ibn Ḥabib incorporates a reference to Rabbi Eliezer ben Hyrcanus[143]—who was accused in
this source of heresy (*minnut*)—in a comment that serves as an interpretive
remark in the *En Yaaqov* on *b. Ber.* 8a. Focusing on the somewhat comical
portion of the aggadic passage from *Berakhot* attributed to Mar Zutra, ibn
Ḥabib makes a more serious point about his fears regarding philosophy. On
b. Ber. 8a one is advised to pray to find something in a moment of need.
Mar Zutra adds that one should pray "'at the time of finding' (Ps. 32:6)]
that is, [when he finds] an outhouse [to relieve himself]." For ibn Ḥabib
the outhouse functions as a warning not merely to keep away from impuri-

ties found within it but to maintain a distance from anything that might lead one to heresy. Ibn Ḥabib defines heresy as "false ideas gleaned from the words of the philosophers"[144] and discusses the rabbinic narrative about Rabbi Eliezer ben Hyrcanus found in tractate *Avodah Zarah* to elaborate on this statement.

In *b. Avodah Zarah* 16b–17a, the Talmud narrates the details of Rabbi Eliezer ben Hyrcanus's seizure by the Roman authorities in response to some undefined form of heresy. Although the source is not entirely clear, Eliezer was presumably suspected by the Roman authorities (during the early second century CE) of an attachment to Christianity.[145] Upon Eliezer's fortunate release, he began to explore his past actions in an attempt to figure out why he, of all people, had been accused and taken. After some thought, Rabbi Eliezer attributed his misfortune to the circumstances surrounding an encounter with Yaaqov of Kefar Sekhanya, who is known from the version of the Talmudic text of *Avodah Zarah* found in the *En Yaaqov* as "a disciple of Jesus the Christian."[146] Yaaqov, who represents a Jewish Christian in this story, had engaged Rabbi Eliezer in a conversation regarding how to spend the earnings of a harlot, which she most likely donated to him. The question Yaaqov posed was whether funds such as these, which were earned in an inappropriate way, could be used to construct an outhouse for the high priest. When Rabbi Eliezer offered no legal solution, Yaaqov revealed advice he had gleaned from "Jesus the Christian." He responded that because the funds had come from a "place of filth," that is, from a harlot, they could also be used in the construction of a "place of filth," that is, for an outhouse. While the conversation between the two men did not seem to touch on topics that could be defined as heretical, such as Christian beliefs, Rabbi Eliezer attributes his arrest by the Roman authorities to the fact that he was pleased with Yaaqov's response. Eliezer not only accepted the legal recommendation from this Jewish Christian man but also failed to keep his distance from things associated with "forbidden women," such as harlots, despite the prohibition communicated in Prov. 5:3–8 against such actions. Through these transgressions Rabbi Eliezer came to understand his seizure as a punishment for the dialogue he had with Yaaqov.

Ibn Ḥabib refers to the story about Rabbi Eliezer to warn against listening to the words of philosophers. Ibn Ḥabib cautions that even the most benign conversation with the wrong person can yield unwelcome results. To be sure, the exchange between Rabbi Eliezer and Yaaqov was not about idolatrous practices, conversion, or even heretical ideas. It was an attempt to resolve a legal detail regarding the use of funds to prepare an outhouse for the high priest. Moreover, the issue revolved around the most menial and most impure architectural structure associated with the Temple, the priest's outhouse. And yet Eliezer wound up being accused of Christian heresy. This source conveys what ibn Ḥabib feared most: the dangers of fostering conversations with nonrabbinic teachers (symbolized by Yaaqov of Kefar Sekhanya) regarding internal Jewish concerns (symbolized by the outhouse for the high priest). Ibn Ḥabib was worried about students who did not spend all their time in the Jewish academy and who might, as a result, be lured from it by the questions posed and the answers offered by those who inhabited intellectual circles outside the academy walls.[147]

In fact, Garson's eulogy of ibn Ḥabib, noted earlier, supports this conclusion. He indicates that there was great interest among Castilian Jews to engage in the study of philosophy. In fact, Garson laments that students were willing to pay someone to teach them secular sciences instead of using those monies to pursue Torah learning. A strong interest in studying philosophy and its cognate disciplines, such as physics and metaphysics, outside the academy was common both before and after the Spanish expulsion.[148] Garson states that ibn Ḥabib was known to have raised money from members of his community to ensure that his students could study Torah at no cost to them. The funds paid for their food and housing, allowing them to devote themselves entirely to their studies within the academy.[149] Unfortunately, students preferred to pay teachers to instruct them in philosophy. This suggests that there were competing circles of study that challenged the centrality of the Jewish academy and, by extension, the prevalence of the study of the Talmud as well.

Garson's eulogy further underscores the fact that ibn Ḥabib wanted to erect boundaries between Torah learning and the study of philosophy. Like his contemporary Isaac Arama, ibn Ḥabib was concerned about the point at which philosophy undermined Talmud study and its messages. To what extent was a nonlegal discipline such as philosophy, which was nurtured outside the framework of the Talmud, allowable and even useful in unpacking the Talmud's ideas? To what extent was one to expand upon and apply Canpanton's synthesis to the study of aggadah?

Garson clearly describes ibn Ḥabib as the rabbi for whom only the study of the Torah "satiated the soul," and "not the external/foreign wisdoms [of Aristotle and Averroës]."[150] In ibn Ḥabib's opinion, the philosophy of Aristotle and Averroës did not fully inform Torah learning. For this reason ibn Ḥabib never became a serious student of philosophy even though the opportunity was available to him. He boldly admits that he never studied philosophy ("*lo lamadti ḥokhmah*").[151] In contrast to many of the Jewish philosophers whom he quotes in the *En Yaaqov*,[152] ibn Ḥabib never drew philosophic material from works outside the library of Jewish philosophic works. In an environment where Jews were actively engaged in the study of philosophy on many levels, it is clear that ibn Ḥabib made a conscious decision to resist it.

Despite the fact that ibn Ḥabib never fully objected to Canpanton's method, his interest in Talmudic aggadah and in the compilation of the *En Yaaqov* appears to be a critique of the synthesis that Canpanton proposed. The goal of Canpanton's method, whereby the language of the Talmud was evaluated using a consistent set of logical principles, did not guide ibn Ḥabib in his desire to unearth the Talmud's theological agenda.[153] It is also possible that Canpanton's method and its rootedness in Aristotelian logic made aggadah only more vulnerable in ibn Ḥabib's eyes. The illogical contents of so many of the aggadic narratives may have threatened the viability of aggadah more than it bolstered its relevance. In fact, Haim Bentov has suggested that Canpanton's methodology drove a wedge between the more intellectually minded in the academy who studied halakhah and those less so, relegating weaker students to the study of aggadah alone. In other words, students who could not employ Canpanton's method studied aggadah.[154] Whether Bentov is correct in this observation about the curricular decisions made in the academies of Castile is less significant than the fact that, in assessing Canpanton's method, he recognized its possible limitations in its application to the study of aggadah. It is therefore arguable that aggadah was pushed to the periphery of the curriculum of the academy not only by the study of code literature but also by Canpanton's Talmud methodology.[155]

One cannot ignore that the *En Yaaqov* was the work of a man with direct ties to Canpanton's students, including Samuel Valensi, who were well versed in Canpanton's method of casuistry. It is interesting, and not all that surprising, that ibn Ḥabib was drawn specifically to the aggadot of the Talmud in an environment where Talmud study was being reevaluated by scholars who were exposed to Canpanton's method. By producing a Talmud-like collection of aggadah, ibn Ḥabib appeared to be promoting the integration of aggadah into the curriculum of the academy in a more serious way. The organizational structure of the collection communicates a desire to entice students to study aggadah as if they were studying the Talmud. His anthology of Talmudic commentaries, which included Rashi and Tosafot, was an editorial strategy that would only enhance this goal. Through the *En Yaaqov*, one did not need to leave the academy or move outside the framework of the Talmud to find religious sustenance in the aggadot.

This is not to say that ibn Ḥabib was disinterested in the populace outside the academy walls. He anticipated at the outset that the messages of the aggadot would appeal to rabbis and preachers, who would then disseminate its messages to the community at large. In this way, ibn Ḥabib hoped to appeal not only to an intellectual elite but also to a popular audience.[156] In addition, a collection filled with Talmudic aggadah alone might also attract a nonscholarly but literate audience to study the Talmud more readily.

Indeed, ibn Ḥabib has been characterized by Joseph Hacker as "a representative of a halakhically inclined Jewish community" trying to revive a classical rabbinic tradition for a broad audience by discrediting philosophy. Such a perspective emerges quite correctly from the fact that ibn Ḥabib turned to the Talmud and drew material from it.[157] But ibn Ḥabib was trying to accomplish far more. In a time following the expulsion, when the nature of the Talmudic page was still in flux and the needs of the people were not necessarily met by the study of halakhah alone, the *En Yaaqov* filled a gap. Following a period of innovation in Talmudic study as put forth by Canpanton, it proposed another curricular approach to Talmud study, which included a serious commitment to the explication of aggadah, and therefore marked a new stage in the history of the study of the Talmud that was gaining momentum in the Ottoman empire, as noted in the previous chapter. By continuously viewing questions of faith through the lens of the aggadot of the Talmud, ibn Ḥabib not only committed himself to making the Talmud read like a document of faith but also constructed a new arena within which Jews both inside the academy and outside of it could discuss theology. He embraced aggadic material that might have been discredited for its irrational character and, through his commentary, drew from it the most essential points about faith without extensive philosophic prooftexts, strategies, and methods of presentation. He brought some of the core ideas of the dogmatists to the texts of the Talmud in a way that redirected conversations about belief away from their place in the philosophic treatise. Ibn Ḥabib replaced the sustained, rational discourse on God and his relationship to man that had taken place outside the context of Talmudic exegesis and made it so that the aggadic texts spoke directly about theological issues. The core points of the conversations that had once occurred outside the Talmudic corpus in the dogmatic treatises of Crescas's *Or Adonai,* Albo's *Sefer Haiqqarim,* and Bibago's *Derekh Emunah* were now found within the context of formal Talmud study. Indeed, the *En Yaaqov* emerged as a critique of a Talmudic culture that had long seen aggadah as secondary, and of a philosophic arena that was rooted to a far greater extent in the disciplines of physics, metaphysics, and logic than it was in the Talmud. Speaking about a later generation of postexpulsion Jews, Elisheva Carlebach cautions that when one studies rabbinic figures one needs to recognize that "subtle tensions [can] reside in the souls of the greatest men" which prompt them to rethink rabbinic Judaism.[158] What remains in the next chapter is to look at ibn Ḥabib's analyses of the aggadot and to explore how he grappled with matters of faith in his commentary through the texts of the Talmud in his effort to rethink this definition.

4

FROM TALMUDIC TEXT TO THEOLOGY
The Search for God, the Search for Home

In describing the survival of Judaism through the ages, George Steiner wrote, "The text is home; each commentary a return [to it]."[1] Steiner's words illustrate ibn Ḥabib's encounter with Talmudic aggadah. His journey "home" to the texts of the Talmud was motivated by a host of historical and intellectual biographical factors. As a witness to the end of Spanish Jewry on Iberian soil after decades of religious, political, social, and economic turmoil, and as a result of his experience living within an intellectual culture that did not always hold the Talmudic canon as its central text, ibn Ḥabib returned to the only home he knew. In his desire to contribute to Jewish continuity and to reshape Jewish identity after the expulsion from Spain, ibn Ḥabib adopted a textual strategy that allowed him to focus on classic categories of rabbinic theology, including messianism and the World to Come, exile and the Land of Israel, theodicy, the effectiveness of prayer, and the nature of God. In so doing, he produced a practical religious message for his troubled generation and created a new path of study. As ibn Ḥabib pointed out in his introduction to the *En Yaaqov,* he intended to unearth the messages of faith rooted in the texts of the Talmud.

Using the Talmudic commentary as his medium, ibn Ḥabib responded to the pressing theological questions of his day without aligning himself with any one preexisting system of thought. Quoting freely from thirteenth- and fifteenth-century philosophic, halakhic, and Kabbalistic thinkers, he responded to the same aggadic texts and questions that had provoked controversy among them. Where was the God who had affirmed His loyalty

117

to Israel?[2] If not in Salamanca or Lisbon, where would the Jewish community find God? On what basis would they form a relationship with Him? In a struggle to create a Jewish self in the absence of a safe physical home, ibn Ḥabib embraced the dialectic between core text and interpretation.[3] To ibn Ḥabib, identity was rooted in this indigenous dialogue far more than in the disciplines of philosophy or Kabbalah. As John Hirsh argued in his book on medieval spirituality, "The religious person never reaches forward so confidently as when he or she reaches back."[4] By returning to the ancient aggadic texts of the Talmud, ibn Ḥabib espoused a unique theological viewpoint intended to spiritualize existential circumstance and to supersede the intellectual approaches used by his predecessors to understand God and their relationship to Him. To read ibn Ḥabib's commentary is to discover a rabbi who, through the texts of the Talmud, was intent on shaping self-reliant, believing Jews out of the self-doubting and religiously insecure refugees who found themselves in the Ottoman empire.

For this reason, ibn Ḥabib molded references to daily prayers found in the texts of the Talmud, such as the recitation of Psalm 145 (*Ashre* [*b. Ber.* 4b]), into sources of consolation. The mere absence of one Hebrew letter (*nun*) in the psalm's alphabetic acrostic, as noted in the aggadic passage, became an opportunity for ibn Ḥabib to remind his readership that the psalmist did not want to call attention to the concept of defeat (*nefilah*). Rather, the psalmist intended for worshipers to understand that there would be a time when the people of Israel would rise up again. Stressing that the prior verse (Ps. 145:13) began with the Hebrew word *malkhut* (kingship), ibn Ḥabib noted that those who uttered the *Ashre* prayer were to recognize the eternal kingship of God. They were to know that "many days after the death of [King] David, Judah and Israel were exiled from their land." But they were not to make the "mistake and think that during this time of defeat there would be a lapse [of any kind] in the dominion of God"; as ibn Ḥabib writes, "God save us from thinking this way." Rather, they were to understand that God "supports all who stumble" (Ps. 145:14). In these words, one can hear ibn Ḥabib's desire to find comfort and to offer his community a sense of hope that God had not abandoned them during their years as Spanish exiles living in the Ottoman empire.[5]

Ibn Ḥabib's commentary regarding the *Ashre* prayer does not make mention of Spain or the expulsion. Indeed, ibn Ḥabib never explicitly states in his introduction or in his commentary that the *En Yaaqov* was a response to his generation's historical experience.[6] But his near-exclusive attention to theology belies his objective. He focused on faith at the precise moment when his fellow Jews were either questioning their own faith or had turned away from it entirely. Toward this end, he distanced himself from the Maimonidean goal of arriving at an intellectual perception of God through the acquisition of knowledge in the name of locating a more personal and achievable relationship with God; one could strengthen a conscious relationship to God by having faith in one's heart. He pushed aside mystical theology and its promise of unification with the Godhead for a more pragmatic and spiritual message. Moshe Idel is correct when he cautions against the notion that historical events automatically condition spiritual development. As he put it, the connection between outer events and the inner history of ideas is at best a nebulous one.[7] However, to ignore the historical context out of which the *En Yaaqov* emerged, knowing full well that its author survived the Iberian disaster of the late fifteenth century, is to miss an opportunity to explore not only how literature in general can function as a response to catastrophe but also how ancient texts in particular can be used to speak, to comfort, to persuade, to transmit, and even to reshape Jewish culture at specific times.

The study of ibn Ḥabib's commentary on the aggadot in the *En Yaaqov* provides the opportunity to explore those generative variables that can be associated with the emergence of profound works like the *En Yaaqov*. It offers an occasion to see how a commentator uses his work as a medium for change. By studying ibn Ḥabib's interpretive remarks in a thematic fashion—the pattern of a single rabbi's reliance on rabbinic images, categories, and ideas—one can observe his response to his era. Each thematic section shows how ibn Ḥabib used the aggadic texts of the Talmud to bring theological issues to the fore with which Jews had been struggling from as early as the inception of the Talmud, if not earlier, and which generated a crisis of belief during his time. Ibn Ḥabib's lack of explicit mention of the expulsion was not a reflection of his desire to ignore history. Rather, his concentration on theology while repressing historical circumstances mirrors the Talmud's own approach to context and situational background. The Talmud is not explicit about its historical milieu. Like the sages of the Talmud, ibn Ḥabib freed himself from time in the interest of showing that the Talmud and its insights were timeless, capable of speaking to generations of Jews.[8] In seizing hold of the texts of the Talmud, ibn Ḥabib sought a synthesis between Talmudic study and theology, that is, between sacred text and faith.

Ibn Ḥabib's "journey home" was far from simple. He did not return to the texts of the Talmud as an exegete with the agenda of merely turning his readers' attention to the aggadic texts of the Talmud, or resolving the texts' difficulties, or enlivening his community following the traumas of the expulsion. He also used the aggadic texts to address and respond to a medieval intellectual world where reason and faith were continuously in dialectic tension with each other. In his commentary he championed the side of "faith" in this debate, albeit without developing a systematic assault on any one thinker. It was his commitment to the medium of the Talmudic commentary that precluded an organized and systematic critique. Ibn Ḥabib's commentary grew out of his desire to distance religious spirituality and faith from philosophy. In so doing, he sought to displace Maimonides' religious ideal of attaining intellectual perfection with a religious objective which, he believed, was more true to the rabbinic texts he encountered.[9] According to ibn Ḥabib, cultivating pure faith that would result in the performance of mitsvot was a higher religious objective than Maimonides' philosophic ideal. Judaism was not a way of thinking; it was a way of "being" and, ultimately, of "doing."[10]

In rejecting the Maimonidean intellectualist view of a God who emerged out of philosophical argumentation and a set of proofs,[11] ibn Ḥabib advocated for an emotional commitment to faith that was not contingent on philosophic study and, for that matter, one that was open to a broader sector of the population. He resisted a God, as envisioned by philosophers, who had no personal connection to human beings. In other words, he distanced himself from the philosophic view of a God who extended no special providence to them and did no more than exist for those who could contemplate Him in a timeless state of pure intellectualism. It followed from the Maimonidean philosophic approach, for example, that prophets prophesied because they had the ability to attain intellectual perfection, as a consequence of their highly developed moral and intellectual capacity. The notion of life after death became a consequence of philosophical or intellectual excellence limited to an elitist few.[12] In contrast, ibn Ḥabib's interest in cultivating an emotional relationship with God was based on love rather than intellect. True faith hinged on a commitment of the heart rather than of the mind. Faith was to be "ingrained in one's heart," and individuals were "to direct their hearts toward heaven."[13] Anyone who possessed this faith could achieve life in the World to Come.[14] Dubious philosophic proofs that could be questioned and overturned[15] were simply not as powerful as a faith built on an utter trust and complete sense of confidence in God.[16]

The theological starting point for ibn Ḥabib was the development of a fear of God or a love of God. Although he used the concepts "fear" and "love" interchangeably in his description of the type of relationship with God he ultimately desired for his readers, both emotive concepts presupposed the existence of a nonrational faith. Ibn Ḥabib believed that an individual could fear God only through the development of a pure faith that was not contingent on or tied to the pursuit of philosophic knowledge.[17] When ibn Ḥabib used words like "thought" (*maḥshavah*), "understanding" (*deah*), or "wisdom" (*sekhel; ḥokhmah*), and stated that one should have God in his thoughts, he never meant in the philosophical sense.[18] Certainly, ibn Ḥabib believed in study, and he understood that the mind was central to that endeavor. However, ibn Ḥabib's path toward spiritual perfection was not a scholarly path with intellectual perfection as the final objective.[19] In this regard ibn Ḥabib's interpretive remarks are polemical in nature, as he draws from the intellectual culture that he inherited, redefining its language for the purpose of rethinking its religious goals.

The recognition that a philosophical and cerebral approach in the fifteenth century had coopted much of the religious dialogue and debate, and did not serve all Jews in terms of their spiritual issues, fueled ibn Ḥabib's desire to disconnect religious spirituality and faith from philosophy and intellectualism. Indeed, Maimonides' successors had, over time, prepared the ground for ibn Ḥabib in that he was not alone in his opposition. Like the work of the fifteenth-century Jewish dogmatist Ḥasdai Crescas, Maimonidean philosophy had disappointed ibn Ḥabib because it was rooted in the "foreign wisdoms" (*ḥokhmot ḥitsoniyyot*); it had not adequately strengthened Jewish faith.[20] For ibn Ḥabib, the tragic events he had witnessed made it abundantly clear that abstract principles did not govern, control, or secure human destiny.[21] Indeed, one rationalist proof could easily undermine another rationalist proof, threatening to destroy one's relationship with God more than it would enhance it.[22] The external discipline of science was being falsely used to understand God. Immortality was wrongly linked to the perfection of the human intellect, which could be achieved only through rationalist means. This was where Jewish philosophy had gone awry, according to ibn Ḥabib. This was what had undermined a secure and felicitous relationship with God. Human reason could not yield certainty.[23] To create a solid relationship with God, one was to turn inward; faith was to be an emotional disposition expressed in the observance of commandments.[24] The union of God and man was to be predicated on the fear or love of God. Therefore, to reject rationalism was to move toward molding a group of believing Jews who might accept life, and its joys and sorrows, on faith.

One might think that, for all of ibn Ḥabib's attention to spirituality, he would have gravitated toward Kabbalah, as did others who opposed philosophy, but he did not. He rarely quoted from Kabbalistic texts in his commentary. Instead, ibn Ḥabib was more attracted to the discipline of dogmatics. The riots of 1391 initiated a period of theological confusion and spiritual crisis among Jews and came to define their experience in fifteenth-century Spain. Aggressive missionary activity by the Church led to proselytizing fervor, anti-Jewish preaching, anti-Jewish legislation, and the rise of a social class of Jews who had been converted to Christianity, either by force or by their own choice. These individuals posed a host of legal, economic, and religious challenges to Jews in need of redefining their faith and status in society. Many fifteenth-century thinkers responded by taking a position on Jewish dogma, in an attempt to offer Judaism what they believed it lacked—a clear theological position on what Jews should believe—and ibn Ḥabib shared their objectives.

Despite his interest and shared concerns, ibn Ḥabib did not become a full-fledged dogmatist like Crescas, Albo, Bibago, or Abarbanel. His references to their works throughout his commentary are haphazard, and he never aligned himself firmly and comfortably with a single dogmatic thinker. Moreover, there is no coherent presentation of Jewish dogma at all in ibn Ḥabib's commentary, despite his explicit declaration in the introduction to the *En Yaaqov* that he would unearth the principles of faith buried within the Talmud's aggadic texts. For this reason, one finds references to various principles of faith interwoven into ibn Ḥabib's aggadic exegeses: that God exists,[25] that God is One,[26] that God created the world *ex nihilo*,[27] that God has no intervening helpers,[28] that the Torah is from heaven,[29] that God punishes transgressors and rewards the righteous,[30] that the messiah will come,[31] that one will be resurrected,[32] and that God performs miracles.[33] Ibn Ḥabib also includes blanket statements about his commitment to uncovering the principles of faith (*shorashe emunah*) and requests that his readers commit themselves to doing the same.[34] In fact, when ibn Ḥabib advised his readers to study the principles of faith, he warned against an approach like that of Joseph Albo who, he claimed, went too far in his investigation. The detailed investigative method embraced by Albo, in which general principles (*iqqarim,* or dogmas) had derivative principles (*shorashim,* or roots) and special principles (*anafim,* or branches), was not ideal in ibn Ḥabib's mind. It was better, ibn Ḥabib advised, to approach the study of the principles of faith as Maimonides did in his commentary on the Mishnah (*Pereq Ḥeleq*). Maimonides' list of thirteen principles, along with their definitions, was a more fitting template.[35]

One might theorize that ibn Ḥabib resisted systemization as a polemical act. He was, first and foremost, a Talmudic exegete; Crescas, to take a contrasting example, was a philosopher who launched a systematic critique on Maimonides without betraying his rationalist impulse. Like others before him, Crescas embraced the style of the philosophical treatise as his mode of communication. In contrast, ibn Ḥabib could not conceive of theology outside of the Talmud. To him, Jewish theology was rabbinic theology; they were one and the same. For this reason, the only "system" that ibn Ḥabib embraced was that of the Talmud. It, and only it, governed the order and content of his interpretations.

At the same time, the climate among Jewish intellectuals at the beginning of the sixteenth century in the Ottoman empire facilitated ibn Ḥabib's endeavors, as the preferred manner of expression was changing rapidly from the philosophical treatise to the commentary on seminal biblical and rabbinic texts. Philosophers, in particular, began to choose the genres of scriptural exegesis and the composition of homilies, interweaving philosophy with rabbinic aggadah and even Kabbalah.[36] Many commentaries now reflected the ideas of fifteenth-century dogmatic thinkers who cultivated their philosophic interests while, at the same time, emphasizing both the centrality of faith and the limitations of philosophy. Indeed, the content found in many of these commentaries did not constitute a radical departure from preexpulsion intellectual trends.[37] The shift was rather one of genre, from the treatise to the running commentary, where the use of biblical or rabbinic texts as starting points premised revealed texts over and above the external discipline of philosophy.[38] Ibn Ḥabib promoted this interpretive course, albeit in a manner that pushed philosophy aside, with greater force than many of his fifteenth-century predecessors and certainly with more force than many of his sixteenth-century contemporaries, who continued to revere Maimonides and value the *Guide for the Perplexed*.[39] In fact, in the Spanish academies of the Ottoman empire such as that of Joseph Taitazak, a contemporary of ibn Ḥabib in Salonika, students studied both halakhah and secular sciences.[40]

It would seem that the choice of the genre of the commentary was also a way for Jews to address their theological concerns during the years immediately following the expulsion. As doubts and anxieties grew over the relationship between God and human beings, it made sense that Jews chose a more "particularist tenor" of self-expression that drew them to and absorbed them in their ancient sacred texts. In essence, it was their years of suffering that drew them back to their biblical and rabbinic "home," which offered them comfort.[41]

Within this culture, ibn Ḥabib took a stand on how individuals were to exert themselves intellectually.[42] His antirationalist approach and comforting religious message emerged as Ottoman Jews were popularizing philosophy, halakhah, and aggadah for the masses. Beginning in the early sixteenth century, Jews began to reach out to the nonscholar to provide greater access to subjects that had long been closed off to them. For example, ibn Ḥabib witnessed the production of philosophic summaries[43] as well as the work of Talmudic aggadah, *Haggadot Hatalmud*. The anthologizers of these collections had the literate populace in mind when they composed them.

This interest in appealing to literate nonscholars, many of them Iberian Jews who had resettled in Salonika following the expulsions from Spain and Portugal, may have dissuaded ibn Habib from attempting a proof of God's existence, as Crescas had done, or from generating a carefully constructed and systematic analysis of Jewish dogma, as Albo had done. Instead ibn Habib devoted interpretive space to the challenges that various dogmatic beliefs proposed, hoping to appeal to a wider audience. Thus he cautioned his readers against calculating the coming of the messiah; comforted them regarding their presence in exile rather than in the Land of Israel; instructed them on what would occur when the messiah arrived; promised them that they would receive the reward of the World to Come (*olam haba*) if they fulfilled mitsvot; explained the concept of reward and punishment and the role of prayer in this world; and guided them in thinking about God. More important, he conveyed that developing true faith was intimately connected to the search for personal meaning.[44]

For ibn Habib, faith could be developed through an exegetical process. A skilled Talmudic commentator could guide individuals toward faith through the aggadic texts. Ibn Habib believed that the texts of the Talmud could unleash a theological transformation in much the same way that compilers of code literature sought to instruct individuals regarding their religious behaviors. Like the codifier Isaac Alfasi, ibn Habib believed that the aggadot "spoke to" his readers, giving them practical spiritual guidance. In his opinion, each aggadic passage revealed a personal spiritual message.

Moreover, ibn Habib taught that an ordinary life of faith was never to be an interior life cut off from social context. Faithful Jews lived within the Jewish community, and thus strengthening human connections was essential to ibn Habib. Spirituality emerged from the formation of a bridge between their personal relationship with God and their relationships with others.

The thematic discussion that follows, taken as a whole, represents ibn Habib's "journey homeward," as he unearthed what he believed to be the rabbis' theological message. Admittedly, such a thematic approach introduces an artificial sense of organization into what is a dissociative theological text. Within the Talmud-like canon he produced, ibn Habib wrote a running commentary that meandered from point to point without a coherent development of ideas. In fact, it is quite difficult for a reader to discern how one comment follows from another. But viewed together, his interpretive remarks reveal a rabbi embracing a pragmatic spiritual message for his generation. The following thematic presentation is a construct to illuminate ibn Ḥabib's theological perspective in a more readable fashion than his commentary appears to convey on the surface.

What Is Wisdom? Setting the Stage

In writing his commentary, ibn Ḥabib worked particularly to integrate rabbinic ideas with medieval philosophic concepts in order to distance the study of Talmudic aggadah from philosophy and to lay out an alternative, pragmatic, religious vision. Ibn Ḥabib reshaped terms such as intellect (*sekhel*), wisdom (*ḥokhmah*), knowledge (*deah*), and analytical study (*iyyun*) in a way that reflected his desire to dismiss rationalism as central to theological development. In this regard, ibn Ḥabib's terminology is the perfect starting point for unraveling his view of rabbinic theology and the overall goals he envisioned for his readers.

When ibn Ḥabib confronted the words of Rabbi Eleazar, who claimed that anyone who prayed Psalm 145 (*Ashre*) three times a day was assured of life in the World to Come (*b. Ber.* 4b), he labeled this worshiper a "person of intellect" (*ish hamaskil*), distinguishing him from the "common person" (*ish hahamoni*).[45] At first glance, ibn Ḥabib seemed to convey through his word choice that a preferred relationship with God was defined by intellection and that intellect divided the elite from the masses.[46] In actuality, ibn Ḥabib turned the notion of "intellect" on its head. Oddly, the "person of intellect," according to ibn Ḥabib, was not someone who had achieved intellectual perfection through the study of philosophy in the Maimonidean sense or who had gained Toraitic knowledge through the study of Talmud and halakhah. He was someone who "feared God with all of his heart." When God did not answer the person of intellect's requests, such a man would be silent. In other words, he would withhold his investigative complaints, saying "in his heart" that all that God did was for the best. This was because, as ibn Ḥabib argued, this worshiper filled his "thoughts" with an image of God's magnitude, just as the psalmist had described in Psalm 145 (*Ashre*).[47] Indeed, without ignoring the fact that the root of the word *maskil* is *sekhel*,[48] ibn Ḥabib noted that what was ingrained in the "intellect" of the person of intellect was nothing more than the indisputable belief that God was master of all.[49]

In contrast, the faith of the "common person," which was less desirable according to ibn Ḥabib, was based on whether God satisfied his desires. The common person took his own needs into consideration when forming a relationship with God in a manner that was just as problematic to ibn Ḥabib as the person who formed such a relationship based on intellection. Each could be easily undermined. The common person might not receive his requests; the philosopher's proofs might be disproven.[50] Moreover, ibn Ḥabib differentiated among various sectors of the Jewish community in a manner quite distinct from what Maimonidean philosophy proposed. Intellection was not the basis on which the hierarchy that distinguished the elite from the masses was constructed for ibn Ḥabib. Rather, what distinguished one individual from another was the nature of his faith.

Indeed, the notion that one should worship God without any expectation of reward was not a new concept for ibn Ḥabib. It had its roots in the Mishnah and Talmud. In *m. Abot* 1:3, for example, it states, "Antigonus Ish Sokho used to say: 'Be not like servants who serve their master on the condition of receiving a reward; but be like servants who serve their master without the condition of receiving a reward.'"[51] It was also the case that Maimonides, in his commentary on the Mishnah, quoted *m. Abot* 1:3 to make the same point: one's relationship with God should not depend on recompense.[52] Ibn Ḥabib drew from both these contexts. Rabbinic concepts played a central role in his commentary, but he also freely embraced Maimonidean ideas when they supported his theological vision. More often than not, these were ideas that surfaced in Maimonides' *Commentary on the Mishnah* and in his *Mishne Torah*. In stark contrast, however, ibn Ḥabib continuously distanced himself from the Maimonidean stance found in the *Guide for the Perplexed*. Bothered by the idea that halakhic Jews were somehow less valued if they lacked philosophic knowledge of God and were, therefore, unable to achieve immortality,[53] as noted by Maimonides in the *Guide,* ibn Ḥabib displayed both a commitment to aggadic exegesis and a desire to take a stance against Maimonides in the controversy that had pitted reason against faith.[54] He latched on to an aggadic passage that mentioned reward (specifically the reward of the World to Come), and then he devised a construct that did not even appear in the original pericope (*b. Ber.* 4b)—"person of intellect" (*ish hamaskil*) and "common person" (*ish hahamoni*)—in order to tackle his concerns about the role of intellection. Indeed, while the word *maskil* suggested a philosophical agenda, ibn Ḥabib preferred to redefine the concept so that it would fit into his overall theological agenda.

Ibn Ḥabib also found other opportunities to grapple with the meanings of words that had often signified "philosophic knowledge."[55] Aggadot that mentioned terms such as "wisdom" (*ḥokhmah*) became perfect textual fodder for ibn Ḥabib to redirect his readers' attention away from a theological ideal that was rooted in a rationalist curriculum. For example, the aggadic passage in *b. Ber.* 10a that attributes Ps. 31:26, "She opens her mouth in wisdom, and the Torah of kindness is on her mouth," to King David, provided just such an exegetical opportunity.[56] Although ibn Ḥabib made no reference to Maimonides in his commentary to *b. Ber.* 10a, his polemical stance jumps out at the reader, who encounters a type of "wisdom" (*ḥokhmah*) that claims no resemblance to knowledge in the philosophic sense. In his commentary, ibn Ḥabib defined David's wisdom as a pure and constant devotion to God. For ibn Ḥabib, "wisdom" did not connote that David possessed "knowledge" of any sort, either philosophic or even Toraitic.

To drive home his point, ibn Ḥabib made clear that the aggadic pericope not only claims Solomon as the author of Ps. 31:26 but also maintains that Solomon had authored the verse to describe his father, David. This gave ibn Ḥabib the exegetical opportunity to contrast the biblical persona of Solomon, who was labeled in 1Kgs. 5:11 as the "wisest of all men," with that of David. The moment was opportunistic: ibn Ḥabib could thereby take a biblical character who was known for his supreme wisdom and renegotiate his image. In this way Solomon became, for ibn Ḥabib, a king who exhibited a lower form of wisdom than that of David.[57] Solomon's wisdom was rooted in his knowledge of natural science. In the Aristotelian sense of the term, naturalism included the investigation of the attributes and causes of all natural objects (minerals, plants, and animals) as well as that which contained all of these objects, namely time, space, and motion. Maimonides conceived of natural science as the study of the world insofar as no human being interfered with it.[58] Natural science was one of the preliminary components of the philosophic curriculum. For ibn Ḥabib, Solomon's commitment to natural science was conveyed through 1Kgs. 5:9–13, which described Solomon as a man with knowledge of the trees, beasts, fowl, creeping things, and fishes.[59] However, this association was a mere attempt on ibn Ḥabib's part to associate Solomon's wisdom with the study of philosophy and to position Solomon's wisdom as inferior to that of David's.[60]

Ibn Ḥabib's belief that Solomon had also authored Ecclesiastes enabled him to add an additional polemical layer to his argument. Certainly, the description of wisdom offered by Ecclesiastes further supported ibn Ḥabib's position that intellection was an inferior means to developing a close relationship with God. Ibn Ḥabib quoted Solomon saying, "My mind has zealously absorbed wisdom and learning . . . but as wisdom grows, vexation grows" (Eccl. 1:16–18). This meant, in ibn Ḥabib's mind, that wisdom was a futile pursuit for Solomon. Fearing God and observing His commandments was what "made every man" (Eccl. 12:13).

Ibn Ḥabib thus used Ecclesiastes to show that Solomon diminished the value of his own wisdom. It was an interpretive setup that enabled ibn Ḥabib to embrace an entirely different and new definition of the term "wisdom," which he believed was best exemplified not by Solomon but by David. In so doing, ibn Ḥabib replaced the Maimonidean ideal of human knowledge, which was to know God's attributes,[61] with a dogmatic commitment to "becom[ing] aware of God's acts and wonders, specifically [the fact that He] created the world."[62] In a manner that recalled the Naḥmanidean link between miracles and faith, ibn Ḥabib argued that David's "higher form of wisdom" was tied to believing in God's ability to bring about a change in the natural order which, in turn, proved that the world had a God who created it.[63] A person who possessed this higher form of wisdom was a person who was also able to devote himself to God day and night, and to commit himself to the idea of repentance wholeheartedly.[64]

In addition, ibn Ḥabib made a point about the role of mitsvot and their relationship to wisdom. Echoing the end of the book of Ecclesiastes, ibn Ḥabib argued that "when all was said and done" (Eccl. 12:13), one needed to fear God in order to observe His commandments. This meant that, for ibn Ḥabib, practice was an outgrowth of faith. Whereas Naḥmanides argued that the performance of the commandments—for example, placing the mezuzah on the doorpost—was a testimony or a reminder of God's miraculous intervention in the world,[65] ibn Ḥabib saw observance as an expression of one's faith. The performance of commandments was not a means through which one achieved an intellectual-philosophical ideal, as Maimonides argued,[66] but a response to a preexisting faith. Therefore in ibn Ḥabib's attempt to carve out his own theological stance, the aggadic statement (*b. Ber.* 10a) in which David "opened his mouth in wisdom" and "spoke songs of praise" of God (Prov. 31:26) conveyed that philosophic inquiry was not a necessary precondition for faith; fearing God was not a by-product of intellection, as Maimonides had argued.[67] Rather, as ibn Ḥabib postulated, one needed to begin one's religious journey as a person of pure faith in order to become "wise," like David.[68]

This discourse put forth an important logical distinction between "paths" to God, but the primary role that ibn Ḥabib gave to fearing God, along with its relationship to wisdom and the performance of mitsvot, surfaces in a clearer way in response to an aggadic passage where ibn Ḥabib finds another opportunity to define wisdom (*ḥokhmah*). In an aggadic state-ment attributed to Rava, "the purpose of wisdom [*ḥokhmah*] is repentance and good deeds" (*b. Ber.* 17a), which centers on Ps. 111:10 ("The beginning of wisdom is the fear of God"), ibn Ḥabib equates wisdom with Torah study through his description of the "wise person" (*ḥakham*).[69] Without dwelling on the exact content of "wisdom" or the curricular requirements necessary for amassing it, ibn Ḥabib points out that individuals do not achieve the final objective of wisdom until they become utterly devoted to performing good deeds with great immediacy.[70] Moreover, in committing oneself to this religious path of mitsvah performance, which encapsulated both ethi-cal and ritual commandments, one was required to execute them without any ulterior motive. Failing to carry out such deeds was a sign that one had faltered in the attainment of true wisdom. In contrast to Maimonides, who had argued in his *Guide for the Perplexed* that the performance of mitsvot aided one in his pursuit of the intellectual-philosophical ideal, ibn Ḥabib believed that the performance of good deeds was proof that an individual had acquired true wisdom, that is, the wisdom of Torah. For Maimonides, the performance of deeds was to accompany philosophic inquiry concern-ing the fundamental principles of religion, whereas for ibn Ḥabib the per-formance of deeds was the final objective.[71]

More significant, however, to understanding ibn Ḥabib's theological viewpoint is the fact that in his comment on *b. Ber.* 17a, he embraces Ps. 111:10, "The beginning of wisdom is the fear of God." In ibn Ḥabib's read-ing, one's fear of God becomes the starting point for one's spiritual journey. Ibn Ḥabib stresses this idea by turning to another aggadic statement found in *b. Shabbat* 31b, integrating this passage into his commentary on *b. Ber.* 17a. In so doing, he roots himself in what he believes to be a rabbinic per-spective on the matter at hand, reinforcing his position that wisdom is con-tingent on one's fear of God. The aggadic statement *b. Shabbat* 31b points ibn Ḥabib to the words of Rabbi Yannai, who bemoans the person who fails to make his fear of God primary. Rabbi Yannai states,[72] "Woe to the one who does not own a house, but he, nevertheless, makes himself a gate [to surround the area where the house might stand]."[73] This Talmudic image concretizes for ibn Ḥabib the dependency of wisdom on fearing God. Wis-dom, which is symbolized by the gate, yields nothing if it is not built to en-close something of value, such as the house. The house represents one's fear of God. In other words, a person needs to fear God before he can acquire wisdom—that is, before he can engage in the study of Torah. Wisdom is not defined as the achievement of an intellectual perception of God, which according to Maimonides was what led an individual to fear God. Rather, in order to engage in Torah study in an effective way, a person needed first to fear Him.[74]

Ibn Ḥabib sharpened this point in his comment on *b. Ber.* 33a, where he argued that one's fear of God must, on the one hand, precede wisdom (or Torah study) and, on the other hand, be an outgrowth of that wisdom. An individual was to "worship God with all his heart and all his might and to be fearful of sin" before and after engaging in his study of Torah.[75] In his introduction to the *En Yaaqov,* ibn Ḥabib relied on *m. Abot* 3:10 to make a similar point that Torah study "sustains, even enhances, one's fear of God." If one studies to enhance his own honor or does so for monetary gain, his wisdom does not endure.[76]

But what prompted ibn Ḥabib to think about an individual's spiritual path in this step-by-step way? What was so attractive to ibn Ḥabib about this rabbinic understanding regarding the primacy of fearing God? In addition, why did he see the performance of mitsvot as a final goal rather than as the starting point in cultivating a relationship with God? And, finally, why did wisdom represent an intermediate stage in the spiritual path he defines, taking its place between the objective of fearing God and the final goal of worshiping God through righteous conduct? Why wasn't wisdom the ultimate goal, as Maimonides proposed?

Without being explicit about his own historical experiences in his commentary, ibn Ḥabib promoted a theological perspective that made fearing God a spiritual starting point, over and above wisdom or even mitsvot, in his desire to construct a community of Jews who, no matter the situation, feared God. He knew from firsthand experience that Jews could not always study Torah freely or perform a set of commandments. Events ranging from expulsions to forced conversions had surely proven this to be the case. Thus it is not surprising that ibn Ḥabib chose to embrace a theology that began with an internal, emotional relationship with God. In fact, ibn Ḥabib's contemporary Isaac Caro supposed that Jews who had converted would be forgiven because they believed in the principles of faith in their hearts.[77] In the face of external threats, fear of God, if strong enough, was sustainable in moments when one could not observe mitsvot or study Torah, and it was accessible to all. Thus ibn Ḥabib's primary goal was to teach his readers the value of fearing God. It was also what made Maimonides' position on intellectual perfection—where the fear of God was a byproduct rather than a starting point in the attainment of a final religious ideal—less spiritually compelling for ibn Ḥabib. His theological position did not emerge in a vacuum; it was a reaction to both historical and intellectual forces. It was the way he convinced himself and, he hoped, his generation that they could all be linked to God in the same manner.

Despite ibn Ḥabib's concerns about the importance of fearing God as a primary step in the path toward religious perfection, the significance of study and mitsvot remained central throughout his commentary. In most cases, ibn Ḥabib failed to define what he meant by study, simply noting that one should engage in "Torah and good deeds." However, in grappling with the definition of yet another term commonly used to signify philosophical pursuits, *iyyun,* ibn Ḥabib insisted on a certain type of study that was disconnected from rationalism. He defined *iyyun* both as the attainment of the knowledge of the "religious principles of faith,"[78] meaning Jewish dogma, as well as the worldly ideas that were necessary for running one's home and one's country.[79]

The base text for this definition was an aggadic passage (*b. Ber.* 33a) attributed to Rabbi Eleazar, who argued that any person who had acquired "understanding" (*deah*) had symbolically constructed the sanctuary (the Temple) in Jerusalem in his day.[80] Biblical proof for this idea came from the fact that the word "sanctuary" (*miqdash*) mentioned in Ex. 15:17 was placed between two divine names: "The Place You made to dwell in, O Lord, the sanctuary, O Lord, which Your hands established." In the same way, the word "understanding" (*deah*) also appeared between two divine names in 1Sam. 2:3: "For the Lord is an understanding God." This parallelism prompted the aggadist of *b. Ber.* 33a, in a manner typical of midrashic exegesis, to draw a connection between "sanctuary" and "understanding." Ibn Ḥabib, however, in noting this equation between the two concepts, feared that his readers might "turn the association on its head" and argue the opposite. They might be led to conclude one day that anyone who worshiped in God's rebuilt sanctuary or Temple in Jerusalem would automatically consider himself to be a person who had achieved an "understanding" (*deah*) of God. This is what propelled ibn Ḥabib to comment. He argued that if the Temple was rebuilt, one needed to understand that study, or *iyyun,* would continue to be more significant than bringing sacrifices. In other words, if the Temple was restored, *iyyun* would still be necessary. The physical act of offering sacrifices would simply not be enough.[81]

In this regard, *iyyun* had a religious and a practical goal. Through *iyyun* a person was to become a faithful individual, knowledgeable in the principles that defined his faith. It would also prepare him to govern his community and construct a stable home. *Iyyun* offered a person practical insight into constructing a relationship with God without ignoring the importance of navigating the challenges of everyday life. It was not a synonym for philosophical investigation or for an in-depth approach to the study of Torah. Nor was it an analytical process that ultimately removed an individual from everyday life when he achieved some higher intellectual status through speculation.[82]

That said, ibn Ḥabib understood that not everyone could engage in *iyyun* effectively. Therefore, in his comment on *b. Ber.* 33a, he also addressed the person who might not be able to engage in *iyyun*. He advised such a person to have a commitment to "think[ing] and possess[ing] good and true intentions in [one's] heart [that are] desired by God."[83] In other words, he asked such individuals to develop at the very least an emotional connection to God. But ibn Ḥabib did not stop there. In a comment on another aggadic passage (*b. Ber.* 12a), he also stated that one did not need to rely on *iyyun* to understand the principles of faith. Instead, faith alone could "gird one's loins."[84] Faith without study was sufficient in defining one's relationship with God.

And yet ibn Ḥabib's desire to offer an alternative form of spirituality to that of Maimonidean intellectualism emerges even more clearly in the way he ties *iyyun* to the study of the expertise required to run one's home and one's country. Engaging in *iyyun* would not only yield an understanding of the principles of faith but also have practical designs. Faith, like the spirituality it would construct, was not an end in and of itself.[85] Individual relationships with God, developed through *iyyun,* led to the construction of Jewish communities better able to sustain themselves in the wake of day-to-day challenges, or so ibn Ḥabib wanted to believe. In his mind, philosophical inquiry would not accomplish this objective.[86] In fact, rationalist intellection might even generate a greater sense of self-doubt and insecurity given that not everyone could engage in it or achieve the goals set by it.[87] Theology, for ibn Ḥabib, needed to be practical. This meant not only that God and His rewards would be accessible to each member of the Jewish community, whether they could engage in *iyyun* or not, but also that the community as a whole would be better off because of it.

Toward a Practical Theology: The Question of Audience

To be sure, ibn Ḥabib's theological interests cannot be separated from his deep concern for practical matters, as noted in the preceding section. This becomes even more apparent when one observes the method ibn Ḥabib uses to inspire both the religious leader and the average Jew. Neither one was to be left behind for the sake of the other. Each had as much of an ability to achieve the reward of immortality as the other.

As an aggadic exegete ibn Ḥabib embraced a cast of biblical figures in his comment explicating *b. Ber.* 3b, including Noah, Abraham, and most prominently David, the central figure in the aggadic passage. Not surprisingly, his goal was to provide religious leaders with appropriate models. King David became the uncontested leader *par excellence,* while Noah became his negative counterpart due to the narrowness of his religious vision. Ibn Ḥabib portrayed Noah as a biblical character who had focused on achieving a sense of individual religious completion (*shelemut; b. Ber.* 3b). He had, according to ibn Ḥabib, earned the biblical description of a man who "walked with God."[88] However, Noah focused entirely on his own personal relationship with God to the detriment of his people, and he failed to offer them spiritual and political direction. Noah was not preoccupied with the issues of his generation; he did not warn his people that their sinful behavior would have negative consequences. In ibn Ḥabib's eyes, Noah's deficient leadership meant that his personal commitment to religious perfection was not as valuable as, for example, that of Abraham.

It was Abraham, not Noah, who would stand out for ibn Ḥabib.[89] In the continuation of his comment on *b. Ber.* 3b, ibn Ḥabib lauded Abraham for actively ensuring that "the people of his land and his family rejected idol worship and became familiar with the ways of faith." In this manner, ibn Ḥabib transformed the biblical Abraham into a leader who reached beyond himself to inspire others, leading them away from sin and toward God.

But even Abraham was no match for King David, whose leadership projected a concern for both the spiritual and the practical. David never allowed his spiritual needs to prevent him from caring for the daily material needs of his people. His interest in Torah study, for example, did not overshadow his commitment to guiding his people in managing their everyday matters. The aggadic passage *b. Ber.* 3b, which describes David as a man who studied Torah all night until the appearance of "the light of dawn," contains an exchange between David and the sages of Israel. They confront David with their pleas saying, "Our master, the king! We need sustenance!" David advises them, "Go and support each other." Ibn Ḥabib used this portion of the aggadic passage to accentuate the need for Jewish leaders to nurture both the spiritual and physical needs of their people.[90]

That ibn Ḥabib embraced David, a Jewish king, to a greater degree than Noah and Abraham, was also a strategic interpretive move. Through David he was able to convey that a leader was not "religiously complete" until he "[caused] the people of his country to benefit." Religious perfection was not a personal matter but, rather, directly connected to one's contribution to the maintenance of the Jewish community as a whole. Even during times when the Jews were not in control of themselves, they were responsible for aiding the "[non-Jewish] king and the inhabitants of his kingdom."[91]

Not surprisingly, ibn Ḥabib ignored the continuation of the aggadic passage (*b. Ber.* 3b), where the sages dismiss David's advice ("Go and support each other") by replying: "A handful [of food] does not satisfy a lion, and a pit cannot be filled from its own earth," implying that they had no resources to sustain one another. In response, David advised the sages to prepare for war against their enemies. Although ibn Ḥabib quoted this portion of the aggadah in his anthology, he completely disregarded the image of David as a military leader in his interpretive remarks. Rather, ibn Ḥabib cautioned, one should strive to benefit "the [non-Jewish] king and the inhabitants of his kingdom." In this regard, ibn Ḥabib made selective use of his aggadic sources in order to express a particular message. When the aggadic material disagreed with that message, he ignored those sections so that he could make his point without conflict.

Implicit in ibn Ḥabib's portrayal of the biblical figures Noah, Abraham, and especially David (*b. Ber.* 3b) was a desire to ensure that the quest for faith did not remove individuals from the world at large. The cultivation of faith was not to become a personal mission detached from communal concerns. Each was to serve the other; each was to thrive because of the other.

In addition, the community was to work within the framework set up by its non-Jewish leaders. Ibn Ḥabib was well aware of the need for Jewish leaders to endear themselves to non-Jewish monarchs. Indeed, one can read between the lines of ibn Ḥabib's commentary in the *En Yaaqov* and find a man with a survivor's instinct. In the process of thinking about a way to restore his community's faith in God, he reflected on the fact that faith and communal solvency were connected. But the shift away from intellectualism and the connection of this shift to the construction of a self-sufficient and cohesive Jewish community are nowhere more evident than in ibn Ḥabib's comment on an aggadic passage found on *b. Ber.* 8a, where he argues that the reward of the World to Come is not necessarily dependent on a wholehearted commitment to Torah study or wisdom. Speaking to average Jews rather than communal leaders, he argues that one can value earning a livelihood more than study and not sacrifice the potential for achieving immortality.

Ibn Ḥabib believed that all people were born with the ability to develop a fear of God, even without devoting their energies to a rationalist program or even to Torah study, but what were the guideposts for this life? Where should such an individual spend his time? Should a person study halakhah for the sake of arriving at legal resolutions? Or is it preferable to occupy one's time in the academy, studying for the sake of studying? Should one pray in the synagogue or simply in the place where one has chosen to study Torah? Which takes precedence? Is it one's home, the academy, or the synagogue? Reverberating throughout a lengthy aggadic section on *b. Ber.* 8a is a concern that addresses, in principle, where an individual should focus his energies. The following section of the larger aggadic pericope caught ibn Ḥabib's attention as he reflected on what enabled individuals to achieve the reward of immortality:

> Rabbi Ḥiyya bar Ami said in the name of Ulla: Greater is the one who derives benefit from his own labor than the one who fears Heaven. For, with regard to the one who fears Heaven [alone] and does not [bother to] derive benefit from his own labor, it is written: "Praiseworthy is the man who fears God" (Ps. 112:1). Whereas with regard to the one who fears Heaven and derives benefit from his own labor, it is written: "When you consume the labor of your hands, you are praiseworthy, and it is well with you" (Ps. 128:2). [You get double reward.] "You are praiseworthy," [means you will get reward] in this world. "It is well with you," [means who will get reward] in the World to Come. With respect to the one who fears Heaven but does not benefit from his own labor, [the words], "it is well you with," are not written. (*b. Ber.* 8a)

This aggadic piece allowed ibn Ḥabib to support an individual's personal choices when he committed himself both to fearing God and to being concerned for his livelihood. Ibn Ḥabib's decision to ignore the questions set up by the larger aggadic context is telling. He was less concerned with entering the Talmudic conversation regarding which institution was more central—the home, the academy, or the synagogue—and more interested in defining the parameters of what was acceptable behavior for an individual who was committed to developing a relationship with God. Ultimately, he preferred that an individual participate in daily life by earning a living to support himself rather than by devoting all his daily energies to cultivating this relationship. He wrote in his commentary regarding this passage:

> The intention of Rabbi Ḥiyya was to teach that . . . there are two people who fear God . . . [but] there is a difference between them. It is the practice of one of them to sit on a consistent basis all day [studying] and refraining from working and to be de-

lighted and happy because [of his ability to] fear God. But [the other] one also fears God. And this is his first priority to fear God. But he has another intention, which is his commitment to removing all obstacles [that get in his way] in order to feed and sustain himself from the labor of his hands. And possibly someone might say that what takes precedence is [the approach of the person] who is devoted to God alone and does not concern himself with deriving benefit from his own labor, because [he thinks that] there is nothing in comparison to the value of fearing God. To overturn this deficient idea Rabbi Ḥiyya instructed us that "greater is the one who benefits from the labor of his hands," that is to say, . . . his reward is greater than the one who fears God alone and does not derive benefit from his labor, because it is possible that [the person who fears God alone] will need to rely on others [for his sustenance].[92]

While ibn Ḥabib was clear in his commentary that the one who focused all his attention on his relationship with God, to the exclusion of supporting himself, was still worthy of the World to Come, he was more desirous of encouraging individuals not to rely on others. As ibn Ḥabib pointed out in his comment on *b. Ber.* 8a, anyone could fear God as long as he performed God's commandments without any expectation of reward, despite his preoccupation with his livelihood. This type of person was worthy of immortality; he did not need, as Maimonides had argued, to acquire an apprehension of God.[93] Instead he needed to become a stable member of the community, that is, one who contributed to it and not someone who drew resources from it.

Ibn Ḥabib even went one step further, offering a similar caveat to the one he offered when he discussed *iyyun*. After all, what of those who were unable to fear God? Were they valued members of the Jewish community? In another aggadic passage (*b. Ber.* 6b), which explores the meaning of Eccl. 12:13, "When all is said and done, fear God and observe His commandments, for this is all of [what makes up] a man," ibn Ḥabib highlights the interdependence between those who fear God and those who do not make their fear of God central with respect to the construction of strong communities. Relying on the opinion of Rabbi Simon ben Azzai, who states, "The entire world was created only [so that the] community [could gather] to support this [God-fearing person]" (*b. Ber.* 6b), ibn Ḥabib argues that some individuals have the valuable role of merely assisting those who fear God.[94] God-fearing individuals devoted to Torah study need people to attend to their daily needs, to bake and to sew their clothes. These daily responsibilities should not be discredited. There is great value in performing them so as to best support those who can achieve a connection with God. Arguably, it is still preferable to fear God and to be able to support oneself in the process. However, as ibn Ḥabib points out, individuals who sustain those who fear God deserve to know that they are the reason God created the world.[95]

In this way ibn Ḥabib strove to link a wide range of Jews to God, enabling even those who did no more than support the more spiritually inclined to feel as though they were acceptable to God and deserving of God's rewards. His practical concerns and desire for the cultivation of a type of spirituality that was more emotional than intellectual, more communal than individualist, and that appealed to a more diverse audience than Maimonidean philosophy, comprised a strategy of hope. In reappropriating terms such as *sekhel, ḥokhmah,* and *iyyun,* he hoped that a broader populace would be inspired by his messages; that they would all see themselves as integral members of the Jewish community.

The remainder of this chapter will focus more directly on the confluence between the categories and ideas of the Talmud that engaged ibn Ḥabib and the medieval intellectual culture to which he was exposed. Taken together, the sections that follow on prayer, reward and punishment, messianism, the World to Come, and God present an image of a postexpulsion rabbi struggling to create a spiritual guide that would lead individuals closer to God. Given that ibn Ḥabib wrote the majority of his commentary on the aggadic passages in tractate *Berakhot,* many of his exegeses dealt with subjects related to the nature of prayer. It was also prayer more than any other subject that brought the issue of God's existence to the fore. In fact, a belief in God's existence had been the first dogmatic principle on the lists of many fifteenth-century Spanish Jewish thinkers. Viewing ibn Ḥabib through the lens of prayer offers a clear picture of what he believed the aggadot of the Talmud conveyed.

God's Existence and the Power of Prayer: The Image of Rabbi Ḥanina ben Dosa

Dogmatists had argued for centuries that one of the fundamental principles of faith was the belief that God exists.[96] For ibn Ḥabib, the fact of God's existence generated a practical set of questions focused on how his readers would go about forming a relationship with God on the basis of their acceptance of a mere principle of faith. He was more concerned with speaking to a readership that was struggling to find evidence of God's presence in the world than with proving God's existence. The aggadic passages that filled the Talmud were perfect launching pads for discussing how one was to cultivate a relationship with God. Whereas the genre of the running commentary prevented ibn Ḥabib from unveiling a systematic theology, it gave him the ability to address everyday questions and concerns that arose among his readers about the connection between their actions and God's.

One of the most difficult issues that needed to be addressed by ibn Ḥabib was what role prayer played in the drama of building a relationship with God. When individuals turned to God in supplication, pleading for Him to respond to their requests, did God listen and respond? How was one's relationship with God affected if it appeared that God did not answer his prayers?

In searching for a way to respond, ibn Ḥabib found himself caught between the more conventional understanding of a God who acted in history, as presented throughout the Bible and rabbinic literature, and the philosophical position held by many medieval thinkers that God was not affected by an individual's petitions. Biblical and rabbinic texts had conveyed that God heard the supplications of His people and responded to them directly. But given that most of his readership had not experienced God directly answering their prayer requests, ibn Ḥabib also considered the philosophical view. Maimonides, for example, had argued that because God was "nonexistent," God did not resemble human beings and, therefore, could not possibly change His intentions in response to individuals' petitionary prayers.[97] Maimonides denied God any corporeality that would compromise the notion of divine unity and insisted that God was not subject to any external causes or human affections.[98] However, ibn Ḥabib was well aware that, if God could not be affected by any force outside Himself, human petitionary prayer had no object. It was pointless.[99] Ibn Ḥabib also understood that people needed to pray in order to establish a relationship with God. They also needed a language of communication with the divine. But mostly, they needed to believe that their prayers were somehow being heard.

Aware of both the philosophical position of Maimonides regarding God's inability to change and the practical needs of his readership, who needed to believe in the power of prayer, ibn Ḥabib turned to an aggadic story about a rabbi who managed to change God's decree through the strength of his prayer. Rabbi Ḥanina ben Dosa successfully prayed on behalf of the sons of Rabban Gamaliel and Rabban Yoḥanan ben Zakkai. His prayers healed them (*b. Ber.* 34b). The aggadic story reads as follows:[100]

Mishnah: They said about Rabbi Ḥanina ben Dosa that he would pray for the sick and would then say: "This one will live and this one will die." They said to him, "How do you know?" He answered them, "If my prayer is fluent in my mouth, then I know that it has been well received. But if it is not, then I know that my prayer has been rejected."

Gemara: The Rabbis taught in a baraita: It once happened that Rabban Gamaliel's son fell ill. Rabban Gamaliel sent two scholars to Rabbi Ḥanina ben Dosa requesting that he seek divine mercy for him. As soon as Rabbi Ḥanina ben Dosa saw them approaching, he went up to the attic and sought divine mercy for him. On coming down [from the attic] he said to them: "Go [back to Rabban Gamaliel], for the fever has left him." They asked him, "From where do you know this?"[101] He said to them, "And so I have a tradition from my father's house[102] that if prayer is fluent in my mouth then I know that it has been well received [and the sick person will recover]. But if not then I know that [my prayer] has been rejected." . . .

And another thing happened concerning Rabbi Ḥanina ben Dosa, who went to study Torah from Rabban Yoḥanan ben Zakkai, and Rabban Yoḥanan ben Zakkai's son fell ill. [Rabban Yoḥanan ben Zakkai] said to him: "Ḥanina, my son, seek divine mercy for him that he may live." Rabbi Ḥanina laid his head between his knees and sought divine mercy for him, and he lived. At that point, Rabban Yoḥanan ben Zakkai said: "Had ben Zakkai [that is, I myself] placed my head on the ground[103] all day long [and prayed], they would not have paid attention [to my son in heaven]." His wife said to him: "Is Ḥanina greater than you?" He said to her: "No, rather he is like a servant before the king, whereas I am like an officer before the king." (*b. Ber.* 34b)

In his comment on this passage, ibn Ḥabib begins with the presumption that prayer can change God's decrees. After all, Rabbi Ḥanina ben Dosa prayed, and God answered his prayers. He healed the sons of Rabban Gamaliel and Rabban Yoḥanan ben Zakkai. However, ibn Ḥabib also asks the question, "Under what circumstances does God hear one's prayer?"[104] The nature of the question is significant. Ibn Ḥabib is interested in the conditions that prompted God to act as He did when Rabbi Ḥanina ben Dosa prayed. What was it about Rabbi Ḥanina ben Dosa that led God to perform a miracle and heal the sons of Rabban Gamaliel and Rabban Yoḥanan ben Zakkai? Surely, if He answered one's prayers, the great rabbinic scholars Rabban Gamaliel and Rabban Yoḥanan ben Zakkai would not have needed to turn to Rabbi Ḥanina ben Dosa. So in what way was Ḥanina ben Dosa exceptional? Can his behavior be emulated? What was the nature of his belief in, and relationship with, God that made his prayers effective?

In response, ibn Ḥabib distinguishes Ḥanina ben Dosa from Rabban Yoḥanan ben Zakkai and Rabban Gamaliel by describing him as a man who "separated himself and worshiped [God] with utter devotion. Because of this, God answered his prayers." The political and religious authority that Rabban Yoḥanan ben Zakkai and Rabban Gamaliel commanded as leaders of the Jewish community was due, in contrast, to the strength of their wisdom (*ḥokhmah*), that is, to their scholarship.[105] Their wisdom, while of great value, did not grant them the same kind of power as that of Rabbi Ḥanina ben Dosa. From such a statement, it seems that ibn Ḥabib believed that God was influenced by human prayer when the worshiper was like ben Dosa—that is, when the worshiper exhibited an extraordinary type of spiritual devotion not necessarily connected to Torah scholarship.

Yet the issue was not wholly simple for ibn Ḥabib. He moved quickly in his comment to dismiss the idea that God could change His mind all of a sudden. To think in such a way would be to consider God as a "flesh and blood king," one who changed his mind simply because his subjects ventured forth to supplicate him. Echoing the position held by medieval philosophers, ibn Ḥabib wrote, "But God is not like that, because His thoughts are not ours." God is "not a master of change who retracts his position." God is not "like a human being who in his nature is found to be one who changes [his mind] and sets [a different course of events] in motion."[106]

Implicit in ibn Ḥabib's comment is the same struggle that many of his predecessors had experienced in their attempts to understand God's ways. People needed to believe that prayer was effective and could save them from their suffering. However, God operated in accordance with a set of laws that never changed.[107] Ibn Ḥabib's reference to a "flesh and blood" king was his way of setting up the conflict between these two positions. The "flesh and blood king" represented the biblical God ibn Ḥabib chose to reject in favor of a philosophical position quite distinct from the conceptualization of God found within the very rabbinic source on Rabbi Ḥanina ben Dosa that he was trying to explicate. No doubt Rabbi Ḥanina prays to God. God sends him a sign. His prayers become fluent within his mouth, and he instantly knows that God has changed His initial decree. The children live.

In an attempt to resolve the dilemma he exposed, ibn Ḥabib adopted an opinion similar to that of the philosopher Joseph Albo. According to Albo, when a decree was made with regard to an evil person, it was based on the expectation that such a person would maintain his unacceptable behaviors. However, if he took it upon himself to change by repenting for his sins, he transformed into another person entirely from the one on whom the decree had been issued. In this regard, a person could save himself from a negative decree. He merely needed to transform himself.[108] Ibn Ḥabib agreed. He recommended that, through the process of repentance, which he vaguely described as a change in "one's thoughts, one's speech, and one's deeds," a person could save himself from punishment. The onus, however, rested on the individual. It was up to a person to transform himself so that God would act upon him as if he were an entirely different individual with a different fate. In such a system God never changes, individuals do.

And so it was with Rabbi Ḥanina ben Dosa. As ibn Ḥabib understood the aggadic passage, it was not God who was responsible for making Ḥanina's prayers fluent in his mouth as a sign that He would heal Rabban Yoḥanan ben Zakkai's and Rabban Gamaliel's sons. Rather, it was Rabbi Ḥanina ben Dosa who sent a sign to God regarding which sick people to heal and which not. Rabbi Ḥanina's fluency in prayer came from within him. His utter devotion to God and his single-minded fidelity to Him enabled him to pray in a fluent manner when he wanted an individual to be healed. Everything depended on the kind of spiritual persona Ḥanina presented before God. And his persona was subject to change. When Ḥanina changed, God responded to that change by looking at him as a different person with a different fate. God Himself did not change.

Ibn Ḥabib did his utmost to advocate for individual control. It was within the power of every individual to become utterly devoted to God to the extent that his prayers became "fluent in his mouth." This was the worshiper whom God would recognize; this was the worshiper who would have his prayers answered. But it was only because this individual had changed and not because God had changed him or his circumstances.

This was ibn Ḥabib's way of presenting an image of God that was, to some extent, in keeping with his philosophically minded predecessors, but which at the same time did not entirely undermine the rabbinic conception, presented in the aggadic passage, of a God who hears individual prayers and responds to them. There were circumstances when prayer supplication was, indeed, effective. That the image belongs to Rabbi Ḥanina ben Dosa and not to the great scholarly leaders Rabban Gamaliel and Rabban Yoḥanan ben Zakkai also sets the stage for spiritual devotion to supersede great Toraitic knowledge. According to ibn Ḥabib devotion to God entails improving one's "speech," which probably means prayer, one's "thoughts," presumably about God, and one's deeds. Study is not one of the requirements for achieving the type of devotion that made Ḥanina capable of healing sick individuals. And so while ibn Ḥabib inches closer to advocating for a philosophical conception of a God who does not change, he maintains a comfortable distance from the idea that somehow knowledge, whether philosophical or Toraitic, advances an individual's relationship with God.

In fact, the desire to develop a model of spiritual perfection that was not dependent on achieving the highest levels of Talmudic mastery and scholarly expertise, along the lines represented by Rabbi Ḥanina ben Dosa, prompted ibn Ḥabib to speak directly to those who made Torah study their primary occupation. In commenting on an aggadic passage (*b. Ber.* 17a) that compares those who work in the field and those who work in the city, presumably to study Torah, "provided they direct [their] heart[s] toward heaven," ibn Ḥabib wrote:

> Perhaps [the person who works in the city and who chooses to study Torah as an occupation][109] will say that the person who works in the field has a great advantage [over him] because [the fieldworker] does not have to advance in his craft [whereas] the Torah scholar must advance with respect to Torah, and if he does not do so, his reward decreases. In order to overturn this [idea], "we [the rabbis of Yavne] learned that both the one who does much and the one who does little [are equally rewarded], provided that each directs his heart toward heaven (*b. Ber.* 17a)." [This was] in order to express that even if a Torah scholar engages in his craft minimally, his reward will be great if he devotes his heart to heaven. And it follows from this that he has a great advantage over the one who works in the field, [despite the fact] that he [the Torah scholar] is a human being like [the one who works in the field]. His craft [however] is more praiseworthy, specifically because there is nothing of value [that is greater] than the value of the Torah.[110]

While ibn Ḥabib lauded the value of devoting oneself to Torah study, placing it above any other occupation that one might choose, it is clear from his comments that as long as a person (even a person whose sole occupation was Torah study) dedicated his heart toward God, the degree to which he achieved Torah mastery was inconsequential. Ibn Ḥabib did not believe that the scholarly erudition symbolized by the Talmudic figures Rabban Yoḥanan ben Zakkai and Rabban Gamaliel was a requirement in the quest for spiritual perfection. He preferred the model espoused by Rabbi Ḥanina ben Dosa, who was committed to studying Torah, but who focused more intently on cultivating a type of devotion to God that enabled him to communicate with Him.

Blessing God and the Image of Rabbi Yishmael ben Elisha

Ibn Ḥabib was attentive to the issue of prayer throughout his commentary, approaching it from a number of different angles. In fact, in another aggadic passage (*b. Ber.* 7a) that describes the famous encounter between Rabbi Yishmael ben Elisha and Akatriel, ibn Ḥabib embarks on another lengthy excursus on the meaning of the word "blessing" (*berakhah*), in an attempt to approach the issue of supplication from a vantage point different from that of Rabbi Ḥanina ben Dosa. In this aggadic passage Akatriel, who was identified by some as God, physically appeared to Rabbi Yishmael in the innermost chambers of the Temple and requested, "Yishmael, my son, bless me."

Not surprisingly, this aggadic source became the locus of much discussion among Spanish Jewish scholars of medieval Kabbalah, who struggled to make sense of what appeared to be a divine manifestation in the presence of a human being, Rabbi Yishmael. One of the first known Kabbalists in Spain, Ezra of Gerona (early thirteenth century), who composed a commentary on the aggadot of the *Bavli,* believed that Akatriel was the tenth *sefirah,* that is, God's attribute of judgment. For the Spanish Kabbalist Todros ben Joseph Halevi Abulafia, Akatriel became a symbol of the entire "emanative and theurgic act" that was set in motion through prayer.[111]

Disinterested in the Kabbalistic debate over what Akatriel represented, ibn Ḥabib worked from the presumption that Rabbi Yishmael had simply met God directly. He then molded an aggadic passage that had been so much a part of the Kabbalistic mystical tradition of his time into a text that focused on the type of relationship God forms with those who worship Him, as signified by Akatriel/God's words to Yishmael, "Bless me." At the same time ibn Ḥabib also discussed the relationship that one forms with God through prayer, specifically through the words, "Blessed are you, God" (*barukh attah adonai*).[112] His comment represented his attempt to define the liturgical term *berakhah.*

Such an interpretive choice was intentional. A range of questions had prompted ibn Ḥabib to comment on Rabbi Yishmael's encounter with God. After all, one had to wonder why God had asked Rabbi Yishmael to bless him at all. Did God have any need for human blessing? How could a human being like Rabbi Yishmael enhance God's existence? Wasn't God a self-sufficient being?

In grappling with the relationship between God's existence and a person's role in blessing Him through prayer, ibn Ḥabib relied on several medieval thinkers to define the term *berakhah*. He focused on this central component of rabbinic liturgy to present a theological point of view regarding the relationship formed with God in the moment when one uttered, "Blessed are you, God" (*barukh attah adonai*). In so doing, ibn Ḥabib entered into a conversation that was centuries old, as many Kabbalists and philosophers had ventured to define the meaning of this liturgical term in the context of *b. Ber.* 7a.[113] Thus ibn Ḥabib in his commentary was able to reference the opinions of Solomon ben Abraham ibn Adret (Rashba, as found in his thirteenth-century Talmud commentaries), Joseph Gikatilla (as found in *Sefer Shaare Orah,* a thirteenth-century Kabbalistic work on the *sefirot*), Baḥya ben Asher (as found in his thirteenth-century commentary on the Torah), Joshua ibn Shu'eib (as found in his fourteenth-century collection of sermons), and the fifteenth-century philosopher Joseph Albo. In referring to these rabbis, ibn Ḥabib was careful not to coopt or dismiss outright the philosophical and Kabbalistic opinions that he cited. His comment on *b. Ber.* 7a clearly shows that he was familiar with many medieval Spanish Jewish works but also that he was not dependent on them. Instead, he presented various perspectives on the issue of the *berakhah,* interweaving them with a theological perspective all his own and linking the idea of blessing God to the concept of faith.

Key to ibn Ḥabib's understanding of the *berakhah* was the fact that it appeared to be an acknowledgment of God's ability to bestow additional benefits on individuals and was not merely a term of praise and thanksgiving. Joseph Albo captured this sense of the term when he wrote the following, to which ibn Ḥabib referred in his commentary:

> *Blessing* is a term applied to addition and increase of benefit and favor. Hence when the word *barukh* is applied to the recipient, it is a passive participle . . . meaning receiving abundance of benefits. When the word is applied to the giver, it is an adjective, like merciful and gracious, which are adjectives applied to God, indicating that the act which emanates from Him is blessing, for example, an increase of influence and goodness. Just as curse means lack of goodness, as all commentators agree, so blessing means an increase in goodness. The word *barukh,* therefore, is

an attribute describing the one who bestows an abundance of goodness. The term blessing [*berakhah*] is applied to the abundance of various kinds of prosperity and success.[114]

For Albo, as for ibn Ḥabib, the term *barukh* described God's goodness. But ibn Ḥabib pushed Albo's view one step further. He wanted to make sense of what effect human blessing had on God. Why had God asked Rabbi Yishmael to bless Him, and why had Rabbi Yishmael responded to His request? "*Barukh*" had to be about more than the mere acknowledgment of God's goodness. Somehow, as the aggadic source conveyed, the *berakhah* had to have an effect on God. For this reason ibn Ḥabib argued, using the opinions of Rashba and Baḥya, that the act of uttering the *berakhah* added a dimension to God; it magnified Him. According to Rashba and, more specifically, to Baḥya, the *berakhah* not only conveyed that God was "blessed" but also elevated God to the level of King.[115]

Within the same comment ibn Ḥabib went still further by including an image present in a fourteenth-century sermon authored by Joshua ibn Shu'eib. Ibn Shu'eib had noted that the word *berakhah* was a cognate of the word *berekhah,* or pool. Just as water flows into the pool from an original source, so too do blessings magnify God who, in turn, overflows with blessings for all.[116] While ibn Ḥabib did not embrace the full Kabbalistic force of the comment made by ibn Shu'eib, who maintained that blessings magnify the *sefirah* of *malkhut* (Kingdom),[117] he did cite Joseph Gikatilla's remark in *Sefer Shaare Orah* that blessing affects not only human beings but the *sefirot*.[118] Yet as soon as ibn Ḥabib made this reference to the *sefirot,* he abandoned it; a carefully developed Kabbalistic excurses on the role of the *berakhah* never surfaces. It seems more likely that ibn Ḥabib wished to emphasize that the *berakhah* had an effect on God and, to some extent, had the power to generate a type of divine influx that brought about material blessings. However, ibn Ḥabib had little interest in situating this idea within the context of a discussion about the system of *sefirot* and the ways in which prayer could activate them.[119] The remainder of this comment, and certainly his commentary more generally, attest to his lack of interest in the role that individuals play in influencing the *sefirot*.

And yet although ibn Ḥabib relied on his predecessors to accentuate that the *berakhah* not only influenced God but was a spiritual act that magnified Him, he went even further in describing how this was to be achieved. Ibn Ḥabib writes:

We bless God and God is blessed through us, because we need everything from Him, and He does not need anything from us except what His perfection requires in order to impart goodness to us. And this benefit [of goodness] will not come to us unless we have the proper preparation, which was referred to above, that is, that we should be steadfast in this [type of] faith [in God] and [in our] knowledge [of Him], and [we] also [need] to recall this in our mouths, for through its means [God's] wonderful desire [to impart goodness] will be perpetuated. . . . And, if one were allowed to say so, we have the power to confer the title "Blessed" on Him with our mouths, though surely He is blessed independently, in and of Himself. . . .[120]

It is fitting to give the name of *berakhah* to all of our prayers before Him, may He be blessed, for on their account, He, may He be blessed, increases and magnifies the benefits to us. And through this [use of the word *berakhah*] His wonderful desire is fulfilled, to shower us with His beneficence which is called *ḥesheq* [or desire] in accord with His high dignity.[121]

Prayer, according to ibn Ḥabib, was a process through which individuals could move God to bestow goodness on them. But the cycle was dependent on, or began with, one's faith. Without a depth of faith that was "inscribed in one's heart,"[122] whereby one depended only on God and no other being, this process could not be initiated. To be sure, the *berakhah* was a means of praising God's creative and protective powers. However, for ibn Ḥabib there was an element of reciprocation; there was a cycle in which both human beings and God participated. Individuals bring God's blessings into their world through their faith in Him, which underlies their blessings.

But the questions still remained: Did God need human prayer at all? How was the individual worshiper to conceive of God when he prayed "*Barukh attah adonai*"? Ibn Ḥabib looked to the relationship between Abraham and Isaac, characterizing it as that of a son who consistently turned to his father, blessing him for "all the good in store for him." As ibn Ḥabib argued, surely Abraham blessed his son, "meaning that he added and increased his beneficences." But Isaac also blessed his father, "meaning that he increased and magnified his [father's] exalted desire" to impart goodness to him.

To elaborate further on this image of God, ibn Ḥabib introduced the nursing mother. He wrote, "More than the calf wishes to suckle, the cow wants to nurse [the calf]." Through this metaphor ibn Ḥabib conveyed his sense of a God who had more desire to impart goodness to His people than His people's desire for it. Therefore, when an individual blessed God with the words *barukh attah adonai,* it was more than a description of God's goodness or even an acknowledgment of one's faith in God. The worshiper was offering God what God desired. These words set a process into motion that pleased God and, in turn, moved God to bestow blessings of goodness on him.

Through an aggadic pericope (*b. Ber.* 7a) that raised significant theological questions regarding the relationship between God and human beings in prayer, ibn Ḥabib offered practical spiritual guidance. He informed his readers, from the most righteous to those who needed to repent for past indiscretions, that each individual could achieve the level of faith that was essential to making their prayers effective and, in so doing, create a relationship with God that God desired. Ibn Ḥabib offered his readers a way to understand "how" God existed in the world, that is, how God interacted with them through prayer.

And yet, for all this attention to the role of faith in making prayer effective, one can also detect a degree of slippage in ibn Ḥabib's theological message. His theology was not entirely consistent throughout his commentary. He had also argued that one's faith was not to be dependent on the rewards (or lack thereof) that God bestowed.[123] One was to have faith irrespective of reward. By comparison, in his comment on *b. Ber.* 7a, ibn Ḥabib seemed to argue the opposite: blessing God enhanced God's goodness which, in turn, caused Him to overflow with blessings for all. This suggested that those who worshiped Him received reward.

Ibn Ḥabib did not synthesize these comments to explain away the contradiction. But this discrepancy discloses something about the honest approach of a rabbi struggling to develop a workable theology. On the one hand, he did not want individuals to develop a sense of faith that was contingent on what God would provide for them. He feared that this type of faith could be threatened too easily. On the other hand, he understood the human condition. He knew that it was difficult for individuals, from the most intellectual to the common person, to live without the hope that they had control in the world. They wanted to have a relationship with a God who answered their prayers and brought them material blessing.[124] And just as they needed God, they also wanted God to need them. Ibn Ḥabib understood that even the most faithful possessed both instincts in their attempts to grapple with God's existence. For this reason, he failed to present a synthetic view.[125] But the tension ibn Ḥabib felt regarding the issue of reward did not prevent him from trying to explain how God's system of retribution operated. In the next section I will explore how ibn Ḥabib attempted to accomplish this through another aggadic passage found on *b. Ber.* 7a.

Reward and Punishment

As with prayer, ibn Ḥabib entered the discussion regarding reward and punishment interested in appealing to his community on a personal level. He sought to address those struggling to understand God's retributive process amid their own tumultuous histories. The righteous had suffered, and no one could comprehend why this was so. How could one maintain his faith in God while questioning the ways in which He exacted judgment? In an effort to resolve these difficulties, ibn Ḥabib focused on the individual's role in reward and punishment.

As noted earlier, however, ibn Ḥabib was not interested in cultivating individuals who worshiped God out of a fear of punishment and a desire for reward. Echoing Maimonides' position in his commentary on the Mishnah, where he quotes from *m. Abot* 4:7, "Do not make the Torah a crown for self-glorification or a spade with which to dig,"[126] ibn Ḥabib reiterated that one was not to perform mitsvot in response to the fear of God's retributive power or even for the sake of recompense.[127] Although ibn Ḥabib did not make specific mention of the historical circumstances that had brought his community to the shores of the Ottoman empire, the relationship between his experiences and his position on reward and punishment cannot be readily dismissed. Within this context his desire to shift theological attention away from the concept of exact retribution makes sense. Better to worship God believing that there is no understandable correlation between catastrophe and one's daily actions. For ibn Ḥabib, the "fear of God," which was the necessary byproduct of faith, was to be cultivated outside the realm of any theological equation made between one's deeds and God's providence.[128]

But how was ibn Ḥabib to break the direct link between deeds and the expectation of exact recompense? How would he accomplish this while upholding the dogmatic principle that God rewarded and punished fairly? How would he speak to a community of people who continued to question God's retributive system?

To be sure, there is no shortage of Talmudic passages that describe a God who metes out judgment fairly. The wicked are punished, and the righteous are rewarded.[129] However, the rabbis also struggled to understand God's approach to reward and punishment.[130] For example, an aggadic passage (*b. Ber.* 7a) cast Moses in the role of challenging God on just this issue:

> Rabbi Yoḥanan said in the name of Rabbi Yose: . . . [Moses]
> requested that God make known to him the ways of the Holy
> One, Blessed is He, and God granted him this request, as it
> is stated: "Make your ways known to me" (Ex. 33:13). Moses
> said before God: "Master of the Universe, what is the reason
> why there is a righteous person for whom things are good and a
> righteous person for whom things are bad? [Equally so], there is
> a wicked person for whom things are good and there is a wicked
> person for whom things are bad.[131]

As the aggadic passage continues, it becomes clear that not everyone agreed
that God had granted Moses's requests, and that He had informed Moses
as to why the righteous suffer. This is evident in the words of Rabbi Meir:

> [The request that God should make known to Moses His ways]
> was not granted to him, as it was stated: "I [God] shall show
> favor to whomever I shall choose to favor," despite the fact that
> he is unfit. [And the verse continues]: "And I shall show mercy
> to whomever I shall choose to show mercy," despite the fact that
> he is unfit. (Ex. 33:19)[132]

In his commentary ibn Ḥabib attacked Rabbi Meir because of his feeble
attempt to explain the reasons why God rewards the righteous and punishes
the wicked. Ibn Ḥabib argued, "God save us from thinking," that God is
gracious without any reason for acting this way. By invoking the philosophical conception of an unchanging God, as he did in his earlier discussion of
Rabbi Ḥanina ben Dosa, ibn Ḥabib reasoned, "God forbid there is a change
in the will of God in accordance with the hour, without a reason." Ibn
Ḥabib did not believe that God changed His mind at whim, without any
reason other than His desire to show compassion.[133]

Furthermore, to embrace Rabbi Meir's view of reward and punishment
also undermined a "fundamental principle of faith," namely that God rewards and punishes in accordance with the actual deeds of man.[134] Apparently, ibn Ḥabib had no intention of dismissing this dogmatic principle; it
was, after all, a core principle of faith. Through his exegesis of *b. Ber.* 7a, ibn
Ḥabib searched for a way to uphold the dogmatic principle of reward and
punishment while attempting to find a more suitable way to explain God's
retributive actions.

Toward this end, ibn Ḥabib turned to Job, the biblical figure who epitomized the ineffectiveness of God's system of reward and punishment. Ibn

Ḥabib recounts Job's encounter with his friend Tsofar:

> [Tsofar said to Job]: "If God would speak and talk to you him-
> self, he would tell you the secret of his wisdom for there are
> many sides to sagacity. And know that God has overlooked
> some of your iniquity" (Job 11:6).
>
> It was [Tsofar's] intention to say to Job, "If God would have
> spoken to you, He would have told you that you are not as righ-
> teous as you thought. This is because the uprightness and the
> justness of your essence are dependent on speculative beliefs
> [*emunot iyyuniyyot*],[135] and you have not achieved a perfect un-
> derstanding of them because 'they are the secrets of wisdom
> and there are many sides to sagacity.'" This is to say that what
> is revealed and what is hidden operate in a many-sided fashion
> and knowledge of what is hidden is not apparent to you.[136]

To some extent, ibn Ḥabib reintroduced Rabbi Meir's position into the
conversation, even after taking him to task for his misleading position on
reward and punishment. At the root of Rabbi Meir's comment lay the idea
that human beings were unable to understand the way God worked in the
universe. Reward and punishment would never be clearly understood, and
therefore Job's attempt to do so was futile. However, ibn Ḥabib's point is not
exactly parallel to Rabbi Meir's. Ibn Ḥabib, through Tsofar, lambastes Job
more directly for relying on speculation to understand God. As ibn Ḥabib
cautions, His ways remain hidden even to those who, like Job, are capable
of employing their knowledge of rational speculation in an attempt to understand Him.

But what should Job have done? How was he to have gone about bet-
tering himself? How could he seize control of the system of reward and
punishment? Ibn Ḥabib continued:

> With regard to the righteousness of one's deeds, it is fitting to
> differentiate between people in accordance with their innate
> abilities [to perform these deeds] and also in accordance with
> their temperaments. And Job had a great degree of innate po-
> tential to do good deeds and also a fitting temperament. He, of
> his own accord, was a decent and upright man, and he had the
> wherewithal to contribute much to the performance of good
> deeds, and all the more so he was in possession of great wealth.
> "And know that God has overlooked some of your iniquity"

(Job 11:6) . . . that is to say, that the good with which God has favored you has been the cause of your forgetting your sin, for when you see that God has given you riches and honor, you presumed [on that basis] that you were righteous, not bearing in mind that considering what a favorable temperament and legacy of wealth you were blessed with, you have not performed the amount of good deeds that would have been expected.[137]

Job, in ibn Ḥabib's opinion, had not lived up to his potential. He had misread the riches that God initially had bestowed on him as a reward for his good deeds. Instead he needed to strive in a far greater way to achieve religious perfection in God's eyes. Job's mistake was that he focused on God and not on the fact that he had underestimated himself. He did not understand that he had a greater potential to serve God in a more perfect way. Ibn Ḥabib wanted to emphasize through Job that individuals have a degree of control in this system of reward and punishment, but this control is rooted in their ability to understand their inner selves. In an interesting theological twist, ibn Ḥabib required that individuals understand themselves and their different personal spiritual potentials rather than focus on achieving a perfect understanding of God through rational inquiry. God's ways were hidden, but a person's own behaviors as well as his own faith were elements of his religious self that were within his grasp. In a world where it was easy to blame an imperfect God for the tragic circumstances that had forced the Jewish community out of their homes and destroyed their livelihoods, ibn Ḥabib attempted to refocus his community's attention on those elements of their religious existence over which they had power. This was the means by which ibn Ḥabib hoped to develop a sense of self-sufficiency and security in his readers and in his community.

In this way ibn Ḥabib upheld the dogmatic principle of reward and punishment. In response to Moses's question regarding the reasons why God rewards some righteous people and punishes others, ibn Ḥabib protected the fairness of God's retributive actions. The answer was not, as Rabbi Meir had argued, that God simply shows mercy to whomever He wishes. There was a pattern of reward and punishment that was not beyond human comprehension. Two individuals could exhibit similar righteous behaviors on the outside and have different experiences with reward and punishment. This was because only one of them had lived up to his innate spiritual potential. The other, like Job, had not. This spiritual failure made one individual less righteous and less deserving of reward. Accordingly, ibn Ḥabib cautioned against labeling the members of one's community as either righteous or wicked based on their external conduct. External behavior, unfortunately, was no measure of whether one had lived up to his spiritual potential.

Taking this point one step further, ibn Ḥabib concluded his comment on *b. Ber.* 7a by referring to the rise of political circumstances that could rob individuals of the opportunity to cultivate their innate spiritualities, despite the best of intentions.[138] In keeping with his sense of pragmatism, ibn Ḥabib did not ignore the question of how God's retributive system functioned during times of crisis when individuals could not cultivate their innate spiritual potentials. Although he does not mention forced converts here and could cite an example from his own life experience, one can sense that he is referring to a phenomenon that was familiar to him. Did everyone who did not live up to their spiritual potentials deserve God's punishment? Was Job a fitting exemplar for all situations?

In the midrashic selection from *Shemot Rabbah* (quoted by ibn Ḥabib in his commentary on *b. Ber.* 7a, as discussed in chapter 1), Moses points to an unknown treasure and asks God, "To whom does this great treasure belong?" God replies, "This is the treasure that I have set aside for those who have no credit in order to dispense reward to those who may not necessarily have earned it." Based on this midrash, ibn Ḥabib concludes his exegesis of *b. Ber.* 7a:

> [And this text from *Shemot Rabbah*] alludes to [the case of] the man who desires in his soul to better his understanding and his deeds. [But] this man doesn't have the preparation [so as to] fulfill his desire due to the many external obstacles which confront him and prevent him from acting as he wishes. And because of this he does not have the means [by which] he can become [a] gracious servant. But God knows [the true] thoughts [that people possess], [and He] prepares a large treasure for the person [who is in this challenging situation]. And from this [treasure] He gives [this person] a free reward and [God] does so with righteousness, justice, graciousness, and mercifulness.[139]

According to ibn Ḥabib, God knows the "thoughts" people possess, that is, God knows their internal spiritual potentials as they confront obstacles beyond their control. While it might look to an outsider that such individuals had sinned, it was more often the case that they did not have the opportunity to act in accordance with their own spiritual wishes. Ibn Ḥabib suggests that their external actions were no reflection of the level of their true faith. At times it appeared as though God was handing out free rewards to such individuals, and to some extent that was true.[140] But in reality such rewards were given to those who possessed a particular internal spiritual potential that pleased God. These were individuals who did what they could under their given circumstances to maintain their commitments to God and Judaism. Thus it was incumbent on individuals to recognize their innate potentials and, in so doing, to develop a strong internal faith that did not involve questioning God's role in the universe or God's judgments. If individuals faced barriers that impeded their ability to serve God, ibn Ḥabib hoped they would be able to fall back on an internal spiritual strength, believing that this might even earn them reward.

God's retributive system made sense to ibn Ḥabib once he established that it was difficult to know who was righteous and who was not based solely on their external actions. Indeed, he understood that what continuously challenged a person's belief in the dogmatic principle of reward and punishment was the person's inability to make sense of the internal spiritual dispositions of his neighbors. To his credit, ibn Ḥabib focused here on the individual rather than on trying to understand reward and punishment from a communal perspective. He never wrestled in his commentary with the reasons God meted out communal punishments, such as the expulsion of Iberian Jewry. Without offering any theological answers, ibn Ḥabib preferred to think more pragmatically about building a faithful community one person at a time.

The following two sections focus on the reward of messianism and the reward of the World to Come. These were among the forces that generated a high level of anxiety for ibn Ḥabib, given his concern over the extent to which faith could be destabilized by failed messianic claims. Moreover, just as he did with respect to the issue of reward and punishment, ibn Ḥabib had to take into consideration that messianism and the reward of the World to Come were not only central Talmudic concepts but also core principles of faith. Paralleling his treatment of prayer and reward and punishment, ibn Ḥabib's comments regarding messianism exhibit a keen sense of spiritual pragmatism. Indeed, he hoped to find a way to protect Jewish faith from the possibility that the messiah might never arrive to usher in a new era.

Messianism

For generations Jews produced no unified theology of redemption.[141] Even the Talmud offered a variety of messianic visions, reflecting ambivalence regarding the nature of the messiah and the character of the biblical "end of days." Isaac Abarbanel, ibn Ḥabib's contemporary, had noted in his work on messianism, *Yeshuot Meshiḥo,* that rabbinic messianic dicta were "strange" and contradictory to any "intelligent believer."[142] One example that baffled medievalists was the pronouncement of Rabbi Hillel that "there [would] be no messiah for Israel, since they ha[d] already enjoyed/consumed him during the reign of Hezekiah" in the very same passage where the Talmud argued that the messiah had not yet come (*b. San.* 98b–99a).[143] The question of messianism was particularly confounding in ibn Ḥabib's time, as despairing Jews yearned for spiritual redemption amid existential turmoil.[144] For ibn Ḥabib the issue of greatest concern was how messianism, while possessing the potential to instill hope in a generation of exiles, also fueled feelings of disappointment. Why had God continued to withhold the messianic age? Why hadn't the biblical promise come true in his time?

In his introductory remarks to the *En Yaaqov,* ibn Ḥabib brought up the difficult aggadic text containing Rabbi Hillel's remarks.[145] Did Rabbi Hillel really believe that the messiah had already come (*b. San.* 99a)?[146] Not surprisingly, the statement had provided Christian opponents with a means to attack Judaism: they possessed a text in the name of the rabbinic sage Rabbi Hillel suggesting that Jesus had come. No doubt it was also a disturbing text to Jews, who could not make sense of it in the wake of their present circumstances, which bore no resemblance to the messianic age. To quell the controversial nature of the passage, ibn Ḥabib invoked Rashi who, in explaining the statement, argued that "Israel has no messiah except God, who will rule over them Himself and redeem them alone."[147] Relying on Rashi, ibn Ḥabib rejected the notion of a human king who would usher in the messianic age; God would be Israel's only king.[148] He thus reinterpreted Rabbi Hillel's statement: Rabbi Hillel had not denied that there would be a messianic age; he merely pointed out that there would be no human king appointed by God to usher it in. Ibn Ḥabib writes regarding *b. San.* 99a:

> It appears that [Rabbi Hillel's] dictum is shameful [because it] negates a true principle [of faith][149] that is ancient to us; that is, the coming of the messiah.
>
> And Rashi wrote in his commentary [on *b. San.* 99a] a short passage that was [rich in] quality, and this was what he stated: Israel has no messiah except God, who will rule over them Himself and redeem them alone. And [Rashi's] intention in [stating] this was to remove [accusations of] heresy that the words of Rabbi Hillel [might warrant] regarding [his negation of] the ingathering of exiles, the growth of the nation of Israel, and the Torah of Moshe Rabbenu. . . . But Rabbi Hillel's intention

was to say that the truth is that Israel will be redeemed from [their] exil[ic circumstances] and from all [their] other troubles. And all the idol worshipers will worship them. . . . Rabbi Hillel agreed with all [the prophecies in the Torah and in the Prophetic books of the Bible] and therefore holds that the messiah [that is, a human savior] will not come to obligate all of the idolaters to worship God and His Torah, only that God with all His glory will Himself place [His glory] in the hearts [of the idolaters]. [And God will bring] success to all who help Him and will support each Jew, and He will subdue all those who rise up against Him. And what need is there to appoint a king to redeem Israel, because all the kings and officers and all the 70 nations who worship idols will [invoke God's glory] because they desire to [do so].[150]

In his comment ibn Ḥabib defends the sacredness of the Talmud, protects Rabbi Hillel from accusations that he is a heretic, and embraces the concept of a future messianic age. However, he argues, there will be no Davidic king-messiah. God, and only God, will usher in this new era. Although the rejection of the notion of a human messianic savior was not a new idea,[151] ibn Ḥabib's decision to align himself with this position is significant. It reflects ibn Ḥabib's concerns about the dangers of false messianism, specifically the risks of the appearance of influential personalities capable of swaying individuals into believing in something that might not come to fruition. At an opportune moment such as the one in which he was living, messianic fervor could be unleashed, provoking individuals to detach themselves from mundane Jewish life and to embrace alternative religious norms.[152] During his time ibn Ḥabib witnessed an escalating interest in an interpretation of religious life that was connected to hastening the messianic era and calculating the messiah's coming, especially by Kabbalists.[153] The apocalyptic writings of the Kabbalist Abraham ben Eliezer Halevi and his circle exemplified the attempts to produce messianic propaganda in the Ottoman empire during the early sixteenth century.[154] In fact, as Rachel Elior argues, it was Kabbalah, in conjunction with messianic longings, that invoked a process of spiritualization among mystics who hoped to create a fundamental change in popular religious life through mystical thought.[155] This is not to say that the expulsion unleashed messianic tendencies unseen during the preexpulsion age in Spain. In every generation there were those who desired to usher in a transcendent existence through a messiah. However, as Hava Tirosh-Samuelson argues, historical crises often intensify messianic longings,[156] yearnings about which ibn Ḥabib exhibited concern. As an assault on such messianic heresies, he argued that God alone would bring about the messianic age, not a human agent.

For many fifteenth-century philosophers who had occupied themselves with defining Jewish faith, a belief in messianic redemption was a central dogmatic principle.[157] Ibn Ḥabib certainly followed suit. Therefore, in addition to dissociating the messiah concept from the biblical idea of a human savior, ibn Ḥabib, in an effort to maintain the verity of the principle, also offered his readers guidance regarding how they should wait for the messianic age which, as of that time, had not come. Ibn Ḥabib's intention here was to inject a pragmatic spirit into an obscure idea that continuously threatened to undermine the faith of his readers. By speaking through an aggadic exchange on *b. Ber.* 3a between Rabbi Yose and the prophet Elijah, himself a harbinger of the messiah, ibn Ḥabib offered his community advice regarding how to live out their days in a premessianic age:

> Rabbi Yose said: I was once traveling on a road, and I entered one of the ruins of Jerusalem to pray. Elijah [the prophet], who is remembered for good, came and waited for me at the entrance [of the ruin] until I finished my prayer. Elijah said to me: "Peace to you, my teacher." And I responded, "Peace to you, my teacher and master." And he said to me, "My son, for what [reason] did you enter this [ruin]?" I said to him, "To pray." And he said to me, "You should have prayed on the road." And I said to him, "I was afraid that people passing by would interrupt me." And he said to me, "[In that case,] you should have prayed an abridged prayer." And Elijah said to me: "My son, what sound did you hear [when you were] in this ruin?" And I said to him: "I heard a heavenly voice cooing like a dove and saying, 'Woe to the sons because of whose sins I destroyed my house and burned my temple and exiled them among the nations [of the world].'" (*b. Ber.* 3a)[158]

The appearance of the prophet Elijah in this passage recalled for ibn Ḥabib the biblical association made by the prophet Malachi between Elijah and the "the coming of the great and terrible day of the Lord" (Mal. 3:23). Malachi indicates that God will send Elijah as the forerunner of the messianic age.[159] It was Elijah, therefore, who led ibn Ḥabib to turn this aggadic passage into an instructive piece on messianism, despite the fact that, on the surface, it disclosed nothing about the subject.

More specifically, Elijah and his concern for the fact that Rabbi Yose prayed in a ruin rather than outside of it caught ibn Ḥabib's attention. He wondered why Elijah cautioned Rabbi Yose against praying in the ruin and tried to make sense of why Elijah waited for Rabbi Yose outside. Elijah's advice seemed odd. Rabbi Yose's decision to pray in a more secluded spot appears to be a sound decision. Surely the individual who prays in an open area draws attention to himself, whereas a man who tries to hide himself behind a ruin hopes to pray in safety. In an attempt to uncover the reason for Elijah's advice, ibn Ḥabib used Rabbi Yose's place of prayer as a symbol to instruct his readers about messianism. Ibn Ḥabib writes:

In interpreting [the aggadic passage where Elijah asks], "What did you hear in the ruin," I [ibn Ḥabib] think that there is a hidden idea included in this passage, written in symbolic language. [This idea] is that, when Rabbi Yose saw that many days had passed since the destruction [of the Temple] and still the messiah had not come, he dedicated his heart and his thoughts to prayer regarding this issue, as Daniel had done. . . .[160]

And the truth is that the generation of Rabbi Yose followed the generation of Rabbi Akiva, who despaired over the delay in the coming of the messiah and erred in the counting of the days and thought that Ben Kosibah was the messiah. This [Talmudic] passage was constructed against the backdrop [of these events], when it says, "And once [Rabbi Yose] entered a ruin," that is to say, [Rabbi Yose entered the ruin] to inquire of God regarding the desolation of Jerusalem.

And because of the great devotion of his [Rabbi Yose's] soul to this thought [the desolation of Jerusalem], what came to him was a perception, in the image of a small prophecy that was not even [delivered to him] by an angel, but rather [by a being] lower than this,[161] that is, by the living being, Elijah. And [Elijah] said to him: "Why did you enter the ruin?" In other words, "Why are you preoccupied with this thought [about the destruction of Jerusalem and the coming of the messiah]? God forbid [you should be thinking this way], because perhaps . . . you are like the one who lodges a complaint against the qualities of God. . . ."

[Therefore,] it is possible that [Elijah] was hinting to [Rabbi Yose] that the time [of the messiah's coming] had still not arrived. And in symbolic language, [Elijah] hinted to [Rabbi

Yose] that it is fitting and necessary for him to pray on the path [outside the ruin] for the existence and the establishment of Israel during all the lengthy days of their exile, [because it] parallels the path [that one is on during the premessianic age]. . . . Many days are coming before [the arrival of the messiah], and therefore it is necessary to pray on the path. . . .

To this Rabbi Yose responded that he feared those who would pass [him] by [on the road]. [This] is parabolic language for the many oppressions that happen over and over again when we are exiles among the nations, from the perspective of the difficult decrees [these nations invoke] against God's nation[162] and also [from the fact that such nations] stand in the way of our desire [to take care of our daily] physical needs. But all this will go away at the time of redemption in the ways that were spoken of [by the rabbis of the Talmud who said], "The future of the land of Israel is that we will draw from it fine cakes and woolen garments" (*b. Shabbat* 30b).[163] And this is not exactly the literal meaning [of *b. Shabbat* 30b]. It is only [that I want to] say that in the coming days [when the messiah comes] the inhabitants of the land of Israel will get bread to eat and clothing to wear without depending upon their hands or toil. And the land will be filled with the knowledge of God.[164]

According to ibn Ḥabib, Rabbi Yose's reason for entering the ruin to pray was to inquire regarding the coming of the messiah. His decision to pray specifically in a ruin symbolized his desire to gain information about the messianic age, when Jerusalem's ruins would finally be rebuilt. In this way ibn Ḥabib transformed *b. Ber.* 3a from a passage about an encounter between a prophet and rabbi concerning prayer into a passage about messianic inquiry.

Indeed Rabbi Yose's decision to pray in hiding was particularly bothersome to ibn Ḥabib. He even agreed with Elijah's reprimand, "You should have prayed on the road [outside of the ruin]." For ibn Ḥabib Elijah's words were those of warning; they were words of instruction. One should not inquire into the reasons why the messiah had not yet come. To address God about the coming of the messiah was to complain about the qualities of God and to question the way He worked in the universe. A faithful individual did not challenge God in this manner. He never calculated the date of the messiah's coming. He waited patiently and trusted that God would ultimately bring about a new era.

To be sure, the reason Elijah was bothered by Rabbi Yose's choice to pray inside the ruin was not made clear in the aggadic text. Why did prayer need to take place on a "path"? Why did Rabbi Yose pray in a ruin? According to ibn Ḥabib, Elijah conveyed symbolically that praying for "the establishment of Israel during all the lengthy days of their exile" had to be done in an open space, rather than in a place that was presumably hidden from public view, so as to mirror their present-day experience. The Jews were still on a journey that would eventually lead them out of exile when the messiah arrived. But in the meantime they needed to acknowledge that they were still on a "path," always progressing forward in a manner that would bring them closer to exile.

Ibn Ḥabib also used Elijah's warning about praying inside ruins to convey that hidden prayer represents a desire to flee not only from one's present predicament or one's regular path but also from one's identity. According to ibn Ḥabib, one cannot hide or run away from the circumstances that are on one's "path," that is, from "the many oppressions that happen over and over again when we are exiles among the nations." This was symbolized by Rabbi Yose's reference to his fear of whom he might meet outside the ruin. Praying on the "path" for the establishment of Israel, despite the dangers that one might encounter, suggests that Jewish identity is expressed when one conveys that he is different from the "other." Hiding is about loss; it is about negating one's identity. In fact, it is precisely what the conversos had done; they had concealed their Jewish identities. By entering the ruin Rabbi Yose attempted to mask his identity, and this weakened the power of his prayer. Had he prayed on the "path," albeit in potential danger, Rabbi Yose would have conveyed that he was engaged in confronting life's obstacles and, no doubt, that he was putting his trust in God. Prayer was not the mechanism by which a person removed himself from the world; it was, instead, how he confronted it.

At the same time, ibn Ḥabib added, a person's messianic expectations while on the "path" were not to dissuade anyone from turning away from daily life, hoping for an alternate (possibly safer) spiritual reality. In fact, when the messiah finally arrived, one's daily routine would not be altered. There would be no metahistorical transformation. The messianic age would not generate a complete rupture with the present, as others had argued; instead, things would continue much as they had for generations. As in Maimonides' vision of the messianic age, found in his commentary on the Mishnah, ibn Ḥabib argued that, during the time of the messiah, one's everyday existence would become easier; one's sustenance would no longer require toil. Quoting from *b. Shabb.* 30b, just as Maimonides had done, ibn

Ḥabib argued that there would be sowing and reaping in messianic times. Individuals would continue to earn livelihoods. However, only minimal labor would be required to produce great benefits.[165]

Curiously, ibn Ḥabib did not elaborate on what he meant by his prediction that the messianic age would bring with it a world full of the knowledge (*deah*) of God (Is. 11:9) in his comment on *b. Ber.* 3a. But when describing what life would be like in the World to Come, as presented in greater detail in the next section, ibn Ḥabib made it clear that this knowledge had nothing to do with achieving a philosophic ideal. Instead, righteous individuals would become aware of the interpretations of the Torah with which they had struggled during their lifetimes and would come to understand the reasons for performing the mitsvot.[166]

For ibn Ḥabib, as for many of his predecessors, messianism was intimately tied to Jewish faith. Jews were to believe that God would one day bring about a messianic age. In the meantime, they were not to question God or to calculate when the messiah would come. Ibn Ḥabib encouraged them to continue living their lives and to face whatever travail came their way. If it meant that the "troubles of exile" did not allow for lengthy prayer, for example, one could even pray using a more concise form.[167] Above all Jews should remain on the "path," he argued, assured that at some unknown time the journey out of exile would end and a new era would begin.

Although ibn Ḥabib upheld the dogmatic belief in the resurrection of the dead, and even hoped for a national redemption that would be accompanied by a return to the Land of Israel (as discussed below), his pragmatic perspective on the messianic age surfaces here. He rejected more lofty notions such as a belief in a messiah figure who would wreak vengeance against the nations of the world and/or who would bring about the return of prophecy and miracles.[168] This fit with his overall desire to create a practical religious theology for a broad populace. Ultimately he hoped that his community would not opt for a life removed from everyday reality in the wake of false messianic claims and that they would maintain their faith in messianism.

The matter of the World to Come also proved to be a challenge for ibn Ḥabib. If messianism carried with it the ultimate reward of immortal life, how was such a reward to be achieved? Furthermore, what would life be like in this alternative world? How was one to envision life in the World to Come? In the following two sections on the World to Come, I will explore ibn Ḥabib's position and show that he not only grappled with the practical matter of how one earned such a reward but also participated in the controversy that had preoccupied generations of Jews surrounding the Talmud's corporeal description of it in *b. Ber.* 17a.

The Path toward the Ultimate Reward of Immortality

In keeping with the Mishnaic promise that "all Israel has a right to the World to Come," ibn Ḥabib devoted his energies to figuring out the formula for achieving this reward. His primary objective was to describe how one developed a relationship with God that earned him a place in the World to Come. Oddly, the clearest statement that ibn Ḥabib made on this issue appeared in his response to an aggadic passage in *y. Berakhot*[169] that did not mention immortality. Rather, it was the association that this aggadic source drew between the Torah and the Land of Israel that prompted ibn Ḥabib to contend with whether the reward of the World to Come was dependent on one's return to Israel. Ibn Ḥabib was a rabbi who lived out his life in exile, thus a firm connection between immortality and one's presence in the Land of Israel threatened to undercut his and his community's ability to achieve this ultimate reward. The basis for ibn Ḥabib's comments was the following Talmudic passage:

> Rabbi Simon said in the name of Rabbi Joshua ben Levi, "If one did not mention the Torah [in the second blessing recited after meals, *birkat hamazon,* whose theme is the] Land [of Israel], we require him to repeat it." What is the reason [for this requirement]? [Because it is stated in Ps. 105:44], "He gave them the lands of nations." And what is the reason [He gave the Israelites the lands of nations]? [So] "that they [the Israelites] might keep His laws and observe His teachings" (Ps. 105:45).[170]

In commenting on this passage, ibn Ḥabib insists that God's ultimate purpose in designating for the Israelite people a land that once belonged to the nations of the world was for them to study Torah and observe the commandments. Individuals cultivated their observance, in particular, through their presence in the land itself. In other words, as ibn Ḥabib pointed out, it was not as Deut. 8:1 had described, "You shall faithfully observe all of the instructions that I enjoin upon you today, so that you may thrive and increase and be able to possess the Land that the Lord promised in an oath to your fathers." Instead, ibn Ḥabib argued, "The true belief that is inscribed in our souls is that the land . . . is a preliminary means of [achieving] knowledge of Torah and the observance of its commandments." That is, the final reward is not the Land of Israel but "something far more lofty and praise-worthy." That reward is "the lengthening of one's days and the days of one's children in the form of the eternity of the soul by meriting life in the World to Come."[171] Observance and the study of Torah assured one the ultimate reward of immortality and not the reward of the Land of Israel. Observance and the study of Torah were the means through which one achieved religious perfection.

Ibn Ḥabib's central objective was to caution his readers against upholding the belief that their observance automatically led to inheriting the Land of Israel. For this reason, he positioned the role of the Land of Israel as primary to that of observance; it was the place where individuals observed mitsvot, not their reward for doing so. Once the Land of Israel was detached from the ultimate goal of achieving immortality, ibn Ḥabib could make the argument that, by observing God's commandments with the proper intention, that is, with the proper "duties of the heart," immortality could be achieved even outside the Land of Israel. All those who had lived in exile and observed God's commandments, "to the extent that it was possible to do so," were, in fact, worthy of the reward of the World to Come.[172] In making an argument for diaspora life, ibn Ḥabib wrote:

> And, specifically, the precise intention of the language of the [aggadic passage found in] the *Yerushalmi* provided me with a great opportunity with respect to what I could write about it, and that is to strengthen the discouraged among God's people, may He be Blessed. These are [the people] for whom the lands of the [foreign] nations are our birthplaces. And our fathers and grandfathers were buried there. And [it is true of] them [and about] us that we never tried with all of our strength to live in the holy land. And this shall be our consolation, that the observance of the Torah and its commandments in all of the lands of our dispersion, in accordance with our ability [to uphold them], was what sustained our fathers and [therefore will sustain] us [as well]. This applies to our fundamental teaching of the understanding and practice of all the commandments, which are obligations of the body, and of matters of faith, [which are] obligations of the heart; of positive and negative commandments; and, above all, to our hope regarding the salvation of our souls, which shall come about through the advent of the messiah, [as] our vindicator said: [one of the six things one is asked on entry

to the next world is:] "Did you hope for salvation?" [in *b. Shabb.* 31a].[173]

Undoubtedly, ibn Ḥabib's desire to weaken the link between the Land of Israel and the notion of an ultimate reward was the product of a Jewish experience lived outside it. How was ibn Ḥabib to convince a community of Jews that their commitment to the observance of Torah and its commandments was valued in the eyes of God if the final reward was one that was either difficult to achieve or even, for some, undesirable? How could he make sense of his readers' Jewish lives in exile if the final goal of religious spirituality was rooted in an idea that was not part of the political reality in which they lived? Their lives, like those of their ancestors, ibn Ḥabib argued, were religiously meaningful outside the Land of Israel. Indeed, they too had an ability to form a strong relationship with God beyond its borders. That such a message emerged out of a Talmudic text authored in the Land of Israel only intensifies ibn Ḥabib's message. Even the *Yerushalmi,* as ibn Ḥabib saw it, supported communal life in the diaspora.

It was in this comment more than any other authored by ibn Ḥabib that his exilic circumstance surfaced in a direct way. His words could resonate with a community of Jews, many of whom had no intention of migrating to the Land of Israel. He conveyed that one went home to the texts of the Talmud, both to the *Bavli* and the *Yerushalmi,* but not necessarily to the physical home of Israel. And yet ibn Ḥabib concluded his comment by echoing the words of the prophet Isaiah, who spoke of the redemption of Jerusalem and of God's return to Israel. Leaving his interpretive voice aside, ibn Ḥabib embraced the supplicatory words of the biblical figure, Isaiah: "Our Father, the Father of mercy, hasten [to bring about] the prophecies of [Your] prophets, may they rest in peace, [so] that 'every eye will behold the Lord's return to Zion' [Is. 52:8]."[174]

Ibn Ḥabib did not encourage his community to return to the Land of Israel and resettle there to be assured of life in the World to Come. Rather, he hoped that at some point in the future God would return those who had merited immortal life to Zion in the form of a national redemption. As part of this redemptive spirit, God would resurrect those who died in exile, bringing them to the land where they would resume their everyday lives, as noted earlier.[175] People's faith, despite their presence in the lands of their dispersion, would set the stage for this post-historical messianic drama. Such a time would include, according to the prediction of Isaiah, the experience of God in Jerusalem. God would return to the Land of Israel along with His people, as ibn Ḥabib hoped.[176]

In keeping with the pattern in evidence throughout ibn Ḥabib's commentary, he did not embrace philosophic conceptions of immortality rooted in intellectual perfection or Kabbalistic presumptions that encouraged human beings to observe God's commandments in order to restore the world to a perfect state.[177] Instead, ibn Ḥabib preached a more straightforward path of faith, of Torah study, and of observance so that one could earn the reward of the World to Come.

Descriptions of the World to Come

Despite ibn Ḥabib's pronounced interest in charting a practical religious journey for the members of his community, he also took sides in several longstanding theological debates on issues that emerged from the Talmud, including the World to Come. One such controversy ensued over how to understand the description of the World to Come found in *b. Ber.* 17a.[178] At the heart of the debate was a struggle over how to interpret Talmudic aggadah, although the discussion was every bit as much about how to portray the World to Come. Straddling his desire to make a statement about aggadic exegesis and the nature of the World to Come, ibn Ḥabib navigated through the discussions of philosophers, Kabbalists, and Talmudists. Despite his far more pronounced interest in reaching a broad spectrum of the Jewish community with a pragmatic religious message, he widened the scope of his mission in special cases like *b. Ber.* 17a, where the texts had served as launching pads for addressing weighty intellectual issues.

Ibn Ḥabib's entry point into the discussion about the World to Come was the aggadic passage found in *b. Ber.* 17a, which compared the World to Come with this world:

> [It was] a habitual saying in the mouth of Rav: The World to Come is not like this world. [In] the World to Come, there is no eating, no drinking, no procreation, no business, no jealousy, no hatred, and no rivalry. Rather, the righteous sit with crowns on their heads and enjoy the splendor of the Divine Presence, as it is stated, "They gazed at God, and they ate and drank" (Ex. 24:11). (*b. Ber.* 17a)[179]

This passage set off a flood of debate as medieval thinkers, beginning from the time of Saadya Gaon, argued about what it meant to receive the reward of the World to Come. The controversy was rooted in the question of whether one should read aggadic texts literally—and thus envision a corporeal understanding of the World to Come—or symbolically. Maimonides in particular, in his attempt to differentiate "this world" and "the World to Come," identified the World to Come with the perfection of the intellect and immortal existence with the idea of a disembodied soul.[180] For Maimonides the words of the aggadot signified concepts that belonged to his philosophical system rather than ideas that were present at the literal level of the passages. Such nonliteralist readings provoked strong negative reactions with respect to his reading of Talmudic aggadah.

Equally problematic was the fact that a spiritual conception of immortality based on *b. Ber.* 17a did not dovetail with a belief in the resurrection of the dead, that is, with the dogmatic principle that even Maimonides himself espoused in his list of thirteen principles of faith.[181] If Maimonides, for example, was correct that only the intellect came to know God and, as a result, only the soul gained eternal life, this dashed any promise that one could triumph over death via resurrection. Many had taken comfort in the idea of an afterlife where body and soul were rejoined in the process of God's resurrection of the dead.[182] For Maimonides, the World to Come was premised on a body-soul dualism and therefore on a disembodied eternity.[183] Furthermore, Maimonides' conception of the World to Come limited immortal bliss to those who could perceive God intellectually. It was this conception of the World to Come, embraced by Maimonides in his *Mishne Torah* and in his *Commentary on the Mishnah,* which unnerved many of his contemporaries and successors,[184] including ibn Ḥabib.

In fact, ibn Ḥabib enjoined his readers to "inscribe in [their] hearts a belief in the resurrection of the dead." He saw Rabbi Yoḥanan's midrashic exegesis of the words from Ps. 32:6 in *b. Ber.* 8a, "'At the time of finding'; this [refers to] the need for a proper burial," as an allusion (*remez*) to the idea that the body was the dwelling place of the soul (*mishkan neshamah*). For this reason, one's relatives were to take care with respect to burial, that is, they had to bury the body in a suitable place to prepare appropriately for the resurrection of the dead.[185]

Ibn Ḥabib also used his commentary on *b. Ber.* 17a to critique Maimonides. He charged him with upholding a forced view of the World to Come that did not make sense within the context of the Talmudic presentation. If Maimonides had argued accurately that only the soul achieved immortality, *b. Ber.* 17a would not have needed to point out that the World to Come was different in character from this world (*olam haze*); Rav would not have needed to describe the difference between the two worlds, noting that in the World to Come one did not eat, drink, procreate, and so forth. It would have been automatically understood that there was something drastically different about the World to Come. The fact that the aggadah made such a point of describing the World to Come as a state where individuals no longer performed regular bodily functions, ibn Ḥabib argued, could only mean that the body and the soul remained intact. The aggadic source intended to convey that immortality brought with it something different about the body, that is, the body no longer ate or drank. Thus the body existed in the World to Come in an entirely different manner than it did in this world—it did not drink, eat, procreate, or argue.

Taking his argument one step further, ibn Ḥabib then chose to align himself with the thirteenth-century Spanish halakhic scholar Aharon Halevi, who presented his argument about *b. Ber.* 17a in his commentary on Alfasi's *Hilkhot Harif.* Halevi took a position resembling that of his teacher, Naḥmanides, without fully embracing his Kabbalistic nuances. Naḥmanides had also opposed Maimonides' conception of the World to Come and instead viewed it as a state where God resurrected both the body and soul of the deceased.[186]

In ibn Ḥabib's understanding, which took the form of a direct quote from Aharon Halevi, immortality entailed that individuals would maintain a form of corporeal existence in the World to Come that was different from their existence in this world. Instead of being composed of corruptible matter, the bodies of those who achieved immortality would be composed of a higher form of matter—the incorruptible matter of which the spheres were composed—while never becoming completely incorporeal, as Maimonides had believed. Halevi's dismissal of the body-soul dualism captured ibn Ḥabib's attention because it challenged the notion that only the perfection of the soul and, therefore, only the perfection of the intellect, counted. It bothered ibn Ḥabib that somehow the physical body that performed God's commandments was dismissed in favor of the soul. The physical body merited reward as well.[187]

Intent on tying the reward of the World to Come to praxis, ibn Ḥabib imagined the righteous in *b. Ber.* 17a as individuals who had studied the Torah and performed good deeds, who were sitting "with crowns on their heads and enjoy[ing] the splendor of the Divine Presence." The "crowns," according to ibn Ḥabib, symbolized the fact that in the World to Come these righteous individuals would become aware of the "truth of the faithful interpretations that they had struggled with while they were alive." In addition, they would gain "knowledge of the reasons for the mitsvot they had performed in their lifetimes." Only after the righteous became "clothed in radiant bodies," in accordance with the words of Aharon Halevi, would they "merit attaining the truth" on these two levels. In this way, they would enjoy the "radiance of God's presence [the *shekhinah*] like the ministering angels, who revel[ed] in the attainment of the ideas that influenc[ed] them from the radiance of the *shekhinah,* from which they became glorified."[188]

Given that the World to Come was among the most ambiguous concepts in rabbinic Judaism, ibn Ḥabib felt compelled to enter the conversation surrounding the search for its definition. Navigating through centuries of material that ranged from philosophers to Kabbalists and even to the more halakhically minded, like Aharon Halevi, ibn Ḥabib took sides in the controversy. In so doing, he chose a position that was peppered with the same sense of spiritual pragmatism in evidence throughout his commentary on other subjects. His viewpoint preserved the hope in a future resurrection of the deceased. It encouraged the performance of mitsvot and supported a life of study in this world that did not necessarily produce firm truths until one reached the World to Come. It also deemphasized the Maimonidean notion of a disembodied eternality so that, once again, a spirituality that was not rooted in intellectual perfection would emerge.

The Aggadic Conception of God: Taking the Middle Road

In comparison to ibn Ḥabib's viewpoint regarding the World to Come, his comments on the Talmud's anthropomorphic references to God reflect a greater sense of anxiety related to the need to defend the credibility of aggadah as well as a strong desire to take sides in the centuries-old debate regarding how to approach texts that described God in human form. These texts posed a great risk to the success of his interpretive endeavor. On the one hand, if he did not take aggadic references to God at face value, he endangered his ability to reach an audience that needed to conceive of a God with human characteristics. On the other hand, if he argued that aggadic descriptions of God should not be taken literally, he jeopardized his own credibility in an intellectual arena where philosophers had long dismissed the Talmud's anthropomorphic references to God. The stakes were high. Thus ibn Ḥabib attempted to find a middle road that would appeal to a wide readership. He straddled an interpretive spectrum in an attempt to generate comments on those aggadic texts that preserved the unity of God and His transcendent nature but also spoke to a broad audience that he believed was striving to find and form a simple connection with God.

The Talmud's fanciful aggadic references to God couched in anthropomorphic terms had been the bane of medieval philosophy. Maimonides, for example, on finding a supportive aggadic dictum on divine attributes, conveyed his wish that "all dicta . . . be like it."[189] Could God nod His head, wear tefillin, or coo like a dove? Unquestionably, the dogmatic principle regarding God's unity, which ibn Ḥabib upheld, did not allow for references to God's plurality. Ibn Ḥabib's discomfort with accepting the literal sense of the aggadic texts that referred to God in anthropomorphic terms led him to adopt the pervasive belief that the Torah (including Talmudic texts) "spoke in the language of human beings." In fact, ibn Ḥabib imparted this dictum numerous times in his commentary, finding underlying meanings for the Talmud's anthropomorphic statements. The attribution of human characteristics to God became for him a metaphor for something more palatable to those struggling with the integrity of aggadah and of the Talmud.[190]

For example, *b. Ber.* 7a, the text where God shows Moses the knot of His tefillin, within the context of a midrashic passage based on Ex. 32–33, had generated much debate. The aggadah reads: "[Scripture states]: 'Then I [God] shall remove My hand and you [Moses] will see My back (Ex. 33:23).' Rav Ḥama bar Bizna said in the name of Rabbi Simon Ḥasida, 'This teaches that the Holy One, Blessed be He, showed Moses the knot of tefillin [which is worn at the back of His head].'"[191] In the case of this aggadic passage, ibn Ḥabib took sides in the debate by embracing the more conservative position of Hai Gaon (as quoted by Rashba).[192] Clear about his desire to reject the philosophic viewpoint that completely allegorized the original aggadic text, ibn Ḥabib lauded Hai Gaon and his cohort for trying to stay as close to the literal sense of the aggadot in their midrashic/aggadic interpretations without stating that the events occurred precisely as the aggadic dictum narrated them.[193] Ibn Ḥabib relied on Hai Gaon to describe God's relationship with Moses. The image that emerged was straightforward: God was Moses's teacher. Just as God instructed Moses how to build His sanctuary, the tabernacle (*mishkan*),[194] so God instructed Moses how to wear tefillin. However, God did not, as a matter of course, wear His own set of tefillin.[195]

In presenting Hai Gaon's perspective, ibn Ḥabib took the opportunity to express his dissatisfaction that so many of his predecessors had chosen to interpret the aggadic passage regarding the knot of God's tefillin in a figurative way. For them it was merely an allusion (*remez*) to the deeper message that, in fact, God exposed Moses to the chain of existents set in motion by God, as Jewish philosophers had argued in their attempt to prove God's existence. They had embraced the Aristotelian idea that there had to be one cause whose existence was necessary and who was the ultimate cause of the chain. That cause was God.[196] Ibn Ḥabib chose to reject this perception in a manner that dovetailed with his desire to keep philosophical interpretations of God at a distance.

In another example, where ibn Ḥabib struggles with the notion that God nodded his head in response to the praises heaped on Him by individuals engaged in worshiping Him (*b. Ber.* 3a), he argued vehemently that "God [should] save us from perceiving these things according to their plain sense [that is, to believe that] God [actually] . . . nods his head. . . . These actions are those of mortals, and He, may He be exalted, is distinct from all of this in a greatly exalted way."[197] Indeed, as ibn Ḥabib argued, the aggadah was rendered to "speak in the language of human beings," and therefore God had not actually nodded His head. The action described in the aggadic dictum was instead a way of communicating something about God. It was an allusion (*remez*) that was designed to symbolize how God felt about the destruction of the Temple and the exile of the Jewish people from Jerusalem. The nodding motion represented God's anger that, in response to the sinful behavior of His people, He had to punish them. It upset God that, in meting out divine retribution, His people suffered. Because God experiences great joy when His people praise Him, He felt much sadness over the loss that He brought on them, which meant that they could no longer praise Him in the Temple.

Ibn Ḥabib concluded his comment by explaining why the anthropomorphic reference to God's nodding His head was used in the aggadic passage instead of a more straightforward explanation of this action. Why did the aggadah use this more cryptic and humanlike manner of describing God rather than stating outright what this nodding represented? For ibn Ḥabib, the answer lay in the fact that God was too inexpressible to be described in any manner other than through the guise of metaphorical language. The essence of God could never be fully captured and, therefore, "the language of human beings" became the means by which the aggadot of the Talmud referred to God. In this regard, ibn Ḥabib aligned himself with Maimonides' commentary on the Mishnah. There, in the introduction to *Pereq Ḥeleq,* Maimonides had argued that anthropomorphic aggadot should be interpreted metaphorically so that they would be consistent with divine notions of incorporeality.[198]

While ibn Ḥabib resolved the dilemma of how to handle anthropomorphic references that threatened to undermine the credibility of an aggadic passage, he unfortunately committed the same offense as the framers of the aggadah. To be sure, God did not actually nod His head. But, according to ibn Ḥabib, God did express humanlike emotions. In his comment on *b. Ber.* 3a, he described God as "upset" over the destruction of the Temple and as "happy" to receive the prayers of His people. Physical actions, when ascribed to God, were bothersome to ibn Ḥabib, but not emotions.[199] God, according to ibn Ḥabib, allowed His goodness to overflow because He loved His people. More than His people desired Him, God desired His people.[200]

Arguably, ibn Ḥabib's familiarity with the work of Ḥasdai Crescas informed his perception of God. Although ibn Ḥabib did not specifically refer to Crescas in his comment on *b. Ber.* 3a, it was Crescas's rejection of Maimonidean philosophy on the grounds that divine bliss was not to be connected to knowledge that resonated with ibn Ḥabib. According to Crescas, bliss could not be attributed to a God whose essence consisted only in thinking or was dependent on an individual's continuous acquisition of knowledge. God's happiness did not come from the intellect, but from feeling. Divine bliss was, therefore, not born out of a relationship with God that was conceived of in an exclusively intellectual way. God was a "feeling" God, or a joyous God; He was subject to emotions. His essence was supreme goodness in that He allowed His goodness to overflow and create, continually maintaining the world's existence. His creative acts were a sign of His love and a response to the good deeds performed by human beings. More than human beings loved God, He loved them.[201] For this reason, it is not surprising to find ibn Ḥabib embracing a conception of an emotive God. Certainly, his conception of a God who could express emotion but who did not possess a physical human form enabled him to steer through the various positions on the issue of anthropomorphism, opting for a middle course.

Furthermore, ibn Ḥabib's decision to align himself with Crescas's conception of an emotive God emerged from his view of what his community needed at the time. The perception of a God who had emotions and who therefore could love His people more than they loved Him must have been a soothing thought in ibn Ḥabib's mind. It was one that enabled him to encourage a wide spectrum of individuals, whether they could study philosophy or not, to emulate God and develop an emotional relationship with Him, rooted in love above all else.

The humanlike descriptions of God found in the Talmud gave ibn Ḥabib one more opportunity to function as an exegete while tackling some of the issues that had been on the agenda of medieval Jewish thinkers. Within this context he considered his audience, hoping to offer them an impression of a God who loved them. That ibn Ḥabib did not systematically integrate Crescas's position into his commentary on *b. Ber.* 3a, or anywhere for that matter, merely reflects a sense of interpretive freedom. As a reader of a library of philosophical and Kabbalistic texts, ibn Ḥabib embraced the more general themes in them, taking sides in the debates that were connected to the aggadic texts he anthologized. He referenced various thinkers haphazardly, feeling no need to be explicit about his relationship to each thinker. This was all in the name of building a theology rooted in the aggadot of the Talmud for an audience who, he believed, needed the kind of spiritual sustenance that only the texts of the Talmudic corpus could provide. Without ignoring historical and intellectual developments, he centered his theological journey on a return home to the security of the texts of the Talmud.

The Final Theological Objective:
Having Faith, Achieving Happiness

Although ibn Ḥabib repeated many times throughout his commentary that it was necessary for individuals to have faith in God, he was also concerned with guiding his community toward felicitous lives. His interest in aggadah and in faith did not diminish his interest in molding believing individuals for whom the observance of mitsvot both required and generated a disposition of happiness.

The aggadic passage in *b. Ber.* 30b provided the perfect context for ibn Ḥabib, because of its concern for excessive cheerfulness. Quoting from Ps. 2:11, which enjoins individuals "to worship God with fear" and "to rejoice with trembling," the aggadah expressed concern that an overly joyful disposition endangered the seriousness of one's devotion to the performance of commandments. The amora Rabbah, the aggadah indicates, criticized Abbaye for his exuberance and cautioned him to "rejoice with trembling." Abbaye responded, "[But] I am wearing tefillin."[202] Rabbah must have expressed concern over the fact that Abbaye's disposition seemed irreverent or lacking in solemnity. Abbaye, however, informed him that his cheerfulness was connected to his observance of the commandment of tefillin. In other words, one can rejoice and "tremble" in fear of God all at once.

Ibn Ḥabib relied on this passage to make the point that spiritual perfection was contingent on the manner in which one approached observance. His reference to Ps. 119:111, "Your decrees are my eternal legacy; they are my heart's delight," led him to state the following:

> When will your decrees be to me [God] as an eternal legacy? [That will occur] when my heart delights in them, that is to say, when my heart is happy and much strengthened in the fulfillment of your decrees. And for this reason [Abbaye] responded, "I am wearing tefillin," as if to say, even though [excessive] happiness is a discreditable act with respect to worldly (secular)

matters, this is not so with respect to the person who fulfills the commandments with much happiness.[203]

Ibn Ḥabib concluded this comment by defining what he believed the psalmist in Ps. 2:11 meant when he stated that one should "rejoice with trembling." After an individual inscribes in his heart a fear of God, he can "rejoice with trembling" before God. Rejoicing begins with fear. From one's fear of God, one comes to rejoice "with fear" in his performance of mitsvot. Mitsvah performance is not a habitual act, in ibn Ḥabib's opinion. Instead it requires a deliberate disposition toward God and then toward mitsvot, that is, an emotional disposition of joyousness that begins with fearing Him.

That mitsvah performance needed to be an act of happiness for ibn Ḥabib is also not surprising for a rabbi interested in enlivening a community of Jews in the aftermath of traumatic historical events. The idea of prompting Jews to think about mitsvah observance as a joyous act within a culture where Jews had converted and were now returning to Judaism or where Jews may have been questioning whether their deeds had brought past tragedy on them makes sense for a postexpulsion Spanish rabbi. Ibn Ḥabib was making a case not only for performing mitsvot but also for cultivating a sense of joy in the lives of the people in his community through their attachment to them. Ibn Ḥabib wanted to believe that with a fear of God that developed from one's faith in Him came happiness and a joyful desire to perform mitsvot.

Conclusion: Thinking Theologically with Aggadic Texts

Ibn Ḥabib's interest in theological matters diverted him from the more common interpersonal concerns that emanated naturally from many of the aggadic texts found in the Talmud. He devoted little interpretive space to exploring the aggadot that offered insight into the political affairs of the academy or those that dealt with relationships between rabbis or even relationships between rabbis and their students. Advice on how best to assume leadership roles in the Jewish community, while present, did not figure greatly in his commentary. For example, an aggadic story in which one student mocks a fellow student for having recited the wrong blessing provoked no more than a cursory reaction on the part of ibn Ḥabib, where he does little more than reiterate the main message presented in the aggadic text (*b. Ber.* 39a). Even the role of the master rabbinic scholar Bar Kappara, who disapproves of the behavior of both the student who recited a blessing before consulting him and the student who mocked his fellow, does not yield a lengthy interpretive analysis.[204]

More surprising is the absence of any extensive analysis of the well-known aggadic story about Rabban Gamaliel's public humiliation of Rabbi Joshua and the rabbinic academy's decision to oust Rabban Gamaliel from his post as the patriarch (*b. Ber.* 27b–28a). Given ibn Ḥabib's position as the head of an academy in Salonika, it is surprising that he chose not to confront the dangers of rabbinic leadership head on. Instead, when ibn Ḥabib comments on *b. Ber.* 27b–28a, he first highlights the character transformation of Rabban Gamaliel and then notes the changes made in the rules of the academy that would prevent further disrespect between rabbinic authorities. In addition, rather than exploring four significant parallel aggadic passages about rabbinic figures who were also challenged and even excommunicated, ibn Ḥabib chose merely to list them. He did not bother to summarize their contents or integrate their messages into his overall comment. Instead, he did no more than offer the reader references to them as a reminder to search out these aggadot and to analyze them.[205] His brevity is telling. Given ibn Ḥabib's otherwise consistent verbose style and tendency not only toward lengthy comments but also toward explicating extensively the parallel Talmudic sources that he cites within his comments, his conciseness is surprising. It would seem that rabbinic leadership as related to the structure of the Torah academies in Salonika was not his chief concern in compiling and composing the *En Yaaqov.*

Ibn Ḥabib was more interested in utilizing the classic categories of rabbinic theology to address matters pertaining to faith for an audience far wider than the rabbinic elite of the academy. His interest in the theological lessons of the aggadic texts was directly related to a desire to speak to all men and women who were in need of the theological messages that the aggadot could bring to the fore.[206] The faith of members of the rabbinic elite and of the populace had been challenged by similar theological questions that were directly tied to being human, not necessarily to whether one was a rabbinic scholar. Questions as to why the messiah had not come, who would get the reward of the World to Come, whether one should live in the Land of Israel, why the righteous were punished, and how one should think about his relationship with God were far higher on ibn Ḥabib's agenda because they were issues that affected the entire Jewish community.

In this regard, ibn Ḥabib was not merely an aggadic commentator interested in a broad interpretive sweep of all that the aggadic material of the Talmud had to offer. Rather, he had a specific agenda. He wished to address rabbinic theological categories in the name of remaking the Talmud of the academy into a central theological text for a larger, literate constituency who could study the contents of the *En Yaaqov*. He devoted his energies to unearthing the Talmud's underlying meanings to persuade his community that it contained a practical spiritual path. Along the way ibn Ḥabib confronted historical factors and intellectual trends that defined his era, communicating that the Talmud was a timeless text with messages for any age. In his hands the Talmud became, for the first time in printed form, a text that preached a pragmatic spirituality of faith and mitsvot capable of speaking to a postexpulsion Spanish community through the medium of the commentary. It was ibn Ḥabib's way of finding security not in the physical place where he lived but in the words of the Talmud themselves. It was the means by which he found home.

5

THE SUCCESS AND THE FAILURE
OF IBN ḤABIB'S *EN YAAQOV*

Shulamit Soloveitchik Meiselman describes how the people of her father's East European shtetl took pleasure in a nightly group class studying the "tales of ibn Ḥabib."[1] Rayna Batya, the first wife of Naftali Tsvi Judah Berlin (Netsiv) and the granddaughter of Ḥayyim of Volozhin, pored over the *En Yaaqov* as she sat each day focused entirely on her books, to the exclusion of household matters.[2] The Baal Shem Tov would predict people's futures by assessing the way they read holy books like the *En Yaaqov*.[3] And for many children the *En Yaaqov* was an integral part of their elementary education.[4] Remarkably, even the briefest of surveys conveys that not everyone "read" the *En Yaaqov* in the same way. Ibn Ḥabib's work appeared to suit different situations and intentions. Evening synagogue-goers did not approach the *En Yaaqov* as Rayna Batya did in her attempt to live up to her grandfather's ideal of studying Torah for the sake of study (*torah lishmah*) and in her desire to reverse gender expectations regarding study and home life. The Baal Shem Tov had a mystical agenda, using the *En Yaaqov* as a means for "reading" the divine will. And rabbinic teachers viewed the *En Yaaqov* as a significant component in the early childhood education of males.

Like many authors, Jacob ibn Ḥabib compiled the *En Yaaqov* intending that it would have an impact on his own society and culture. He hoped that it would be a new vehicle for bringing rabbinic theology to a constituency that had long overlooked its potential for conveying messages about faith. He also anticipated that his work, designed as it was to resemble the Talmudic corpus, would change the way people viewed Talmudic aggadah and transform the manner in which individuals approached the study of the Talmud. The question is: In what ways did he succeed? It does not appear that all the individuals noted in the previous paragraph studied the *En Yaaqov* as ibn Ḥabib intended. In this regard, there appears to be no direct relationship between the author's original intentions and the later history of the *En Yaaqov*.[5] Indeed, the work took on a life of its own. But how and why did this occur?

In an era when Hebrew book printing enabled the pages of the Talmud to become increasingly more standardized, the *En Yaaqov* exhibited a large degree of fluidity that defied this trend. In this regard, the *En Yaaqov* became a very different kind of book from the Talmud, with an entirely different printing history. Efforts to standardize its contents continuously met with resistance, and so it remained throughout its long history a book that exhibited a great deal of flexibility—that is, a propensity for change. Such resistance may have been due to the nonlegal nature of aggadah; those who studied it thus felt comfortable approaching it with a greater degree of interpretive freedom than they did the halakhic material of the Talmud.

Prior to the appearance of the *En Yaaqov*, the authorship of running commentaries on Talmudic aggadah was not a prominent intellectual interest for Spanish Jewry. But following the printing of this work in cities throughout Europe, interest in Talmudic aggadah grew. Different intellectual, social, political, and economic contexts drove individuals to rethink the purpose of Talmudic aggadah and, therefore, of the *En Yaaqov*. Like ibn Ḥabib, they used it to reveal new religious agendas. They wrote new essays on aggadah and new commentaries with new introductions explaining their objectives. They even changed ibn Ḥabib's anthology of Talmudic aggadah by adding more passages from the Talmud to their new editions. This pushed printers to maintain the *En Yaaqov*'s fluidity in response to a perceived demand for an adaptable document. Every modification that printers embraced reflected characteristics of the audience they wished to target rather than aspects of the power of the original author to produce a work that would outlive him. While the commitment of printers to the fluidity of the *En Yaaqov* meant that ibn Ḥabib undoubtedly lost control over what happened to his collection,[6] the *En Yaaqov* successfully enabled Jews through the ensuing centuries, from Damascus[7] to New York,[8] to think about "what is" Talmudic aggadah. It provided the framework whereby generations could freely disagree about the purpose of aggadah, its messages, and even its audience.

Arguably, a successful book is a well-read one. But standardization was not the only means of ensuring that people read a given book. The *En*

Yaaqov testifies to the fact that some books flourished because Jews continually reshaped them. In the case of the *En Yaaqov,* in particular, Jews participated in clear acts of interweaving aggadah with the changing needs of their communities. Ibn Ḥabib unwittingly gave birth to a book genre that thrived for centuries, rather than to a set text or set book. More than the mere title of a standard collection, the title "*En Yaaqov*" became a descriptive term for a genre of work on Talmudic aggadah that documented a changing cultural history of the Jews different from that of works like the Talmud.

To be sure, the reception of a book is a passive thing, especially since it is often difficult to find a thorough record of a community's reactions to a book over centuries.[9] However, the unique and extensive printing history of the *En Yaaqov* tells the story not only of its survival but also of the way the collection endured. Because it is the form of the book that ultimately makes texts like those contained in the *En Yaaqov* readable,[10] the modifications made to its printed editions throughout the generations offer valuable insight into ibn Ḥabib's success and failure. It was the printers' efforts, responding as they were to the perceived needs of their readers, that preserved the unstable relationship between ibn Ḥabib's version of the *En Yaaqov* and the Jews who inherited it. It was these printers, in conjunction with compositors, copyeditors, proofreaders, and even censors, who turned the *En Yaaqov* into a vital touchstone of Talmudic aggadah. Indeed, revealing this printing history sets the stage for the next phase of research on the *En Yaaqov,* which includes analyses of the subsequent introductions, essays, and commentaries that appeared in later editions. It is my hope that this book, *The* En Yaaqov: *Jacob ibn Ḥabib's Search for Faith in the Talmudic Corpus,* will serve as a model for contending with later "authored" editions in an attempt to further scholarly understandings not only of the role of aggadah in the intellectual culture of the Jews in the years following ibn Ḥabib's death but also of the people who continually took an interest in it. In much the same way that this book exposed the intentions of Jacob ibn Ḥabib in creating the *En Yaaqov* and revealed a response to late fifteenth- and early sixteenth-century Spanish history and culture, later editions—that is, their compilers and the authors of their commentaries—can be consulted to peer into the cultures of different times and places.

Surveying the Printing History of the En Yaaqov

Following the completion of ibn Ḥabib's work on the first *seder* (order) of the Talmud, *Zeraim,* he reflected on his own sense of failure. As he began to contemplate further work in *Seder Moed,* he bemoaned the fact that his contributions to the remainder of the *En Yaaqov* project would be sorely lacking due to the limits of time, money, page space, and even the sheer enormity of his objectives. His hopes for the collection ultimately were unrealized in his lifetime, as he died before seeing his life's work to its fitting completion.[11]

Upon Jacob ibn Habib's death in the middle of the *En Yaaqov* project, his son, Levi ibn Habib, took on the role of author to complete what his father had begun. Whether this was a gesture to memorialize his father or a sign that the collection was in demand is less relevant than the fact that Levi ibn Habib solidified its future. Despite his less than enthusiastic commitment to anthologizing Talmudic aggadah and to explicating its contents,[12] Levi ibn Habib took an incomplete work on two *sedarim* of the Talmud and turned it into one that embodied the image of an aggadic work on the entire Talmudic corpus. Whatever his reasons, Levi ibn Habib's decision to complete the *En Yaaqov* ensured that his father's dream of elevating the value of Talmudic aggadah would be realized.

Levi ibn Habib's second volume of the *En Yaaqov,* titled *Bet Yaaqov,* rolled off the presses in Salonika in 1522, when the Venetian printer Daniel Bomberg printed the first full edition of the multivolume *Talmud Bavli.* Interestingly, while the collections were published at virtually the same time, their printing histories tell radically different stories about the Jews' attitude toward the role of the printed book in Jewish culture. While Bomberg was responsible for initiating a printing trajectory that was defined by a commitment to standardizing the Talmud's texts, folio numbers, and commentaries, Levi ibn Habib and the printer of *Bet Yaaqov,* Judah Gedaliah, supported a different printing model that sanctioned greater fluidity when it came to the texts of the Talmud and its commentaries. Indeed, Levi ibn Habib's anthology of and commentary on aggadah were far less comprehensive than his father's, and he showed little concern for the theological program that characterized his father's work on Talmudic aggadah.[13] Although Judah Gedaliah printed the second volume of the *En Yaaqov* well aware of its divergence from the model set by Levi's father, he nonetheless chose to consider both volumes as one work, titling the first volume *En Yaaqov* and the second *Bet Yaaqov,* despite their discrepancies.

For the next four centuries, printers, editors, and authors made various modifications to the *En Yaaqov.* The more than one hundred editions that bore the title *En Yaaqov/Bet Yaaqov* (or *En Yisrael/Bet Yisrael*)[14] were printed in almost every city that had a printing press, including Venice, Verona, Amsterdam, Hamburg, Frankfurt, Berlin, Sulzberg, Furth, Königsburg, Leipzig, Prague, Cracow, Minsk, Kopys, Zhitomir, Lemberg, Korzec, Ostrog, Hrubieszow, Mezhirich, Vilna, Slobuta, Shklov, Izmir, Warsaw, Calcutta, Jerusalem, and New York, and each exhibited a comfort level with change.[15] There were new authors and printers who freely embraced the literary license to reshape the *En Yaaqov,* producing new editions that did not entirely resemble ibn Ḥabib's original work. More than a book devised by a single author to have a particular impact on a given society, the *En Yaaqov* found a readership that had more influence on it than its original author had on future generations. While early printings of the *En Yaaqov* in Venice (1546, 1566) and Cracow (1587) proved to be, for the most part, "mechanical multiplication[s]"[16] of this book of aggadah (see appendix, figures 2, 3, 4, 5), by the end of the seventeenth century, editions printed in Amsterdam began to exhibit far greater modifications (see appendix, figures 6, 7, 8, 9, 10, 11). What came off the presses were copies of different forms of the *En Yaaqov* (for comparison, see appendix, figure 1).

By the middle of the sixteenth century, printers outside the Ottoman empire began to realize the value and potential popularity of the *En Yaaqov.* Its marketability led printers in Venice, the center of the Hebrew book industry in Italy, to prepare editions of it.[17] By 1546 the prominent non-Jewish printer Marco Antonio Giustiniani had taken an interest in reprinting the *En Yaaqov,* publishing in the same year an edition of tractate *Berakhot* of the *Talmud Bavli.*[18] Both were in demand. The 1546 edition of the *En Yaaqov* was a reproduction of the first printed edition (Salonika, 1516/1522). By creating a clearer and more readable copy, its printer wished to reproduce the *En Yaaqov* for a readership that was anxious to purchase it. Ironically, it was this level of popularity that led the Church's papal committee to place the *En Yaaqov* on its list of banned books (*Escutori contro la bestemmia*) in 1553.[19] This committee was responsible for making determinations as to which compendiums and books were to be confiscated and burned in the wake of anti-Jewish legislation regarding Hebrew books.[20] Books that were well known and studied often, like the *En Yaaqov,*[21] were included on this list, especially those that bore a resemblance to the Talmud and were thought to contain anti-Christian polemics.

By 1563–64 the papal ban to burn the Talmud and other books in Italy was lifted for a short period. This granted printers the opportunity to return to printing Hebrew books. In fact, five independent Christian houses began to print such books, each competing with the other. One of these printing houses, that of Giorgio di Cavalli, successfully printed several seminal books, including an edition of the *En Yaaqov* in 1566 (see appendix, figures 2 and 3) that was also modeled very closely on the two-volume work of Jacob ibn Ḥabib and his son, Levi (Salonika, 1516/1522).[22] Ibn Ḥabib's anthology of aggadot drawn from the Talmud remained the same. Cavalli also made sure that all the section numbers used to introduce each aggadic passage and interpretive comment correlated with ibn Ḥabib's section numbers (despite the fact that the page numbers varied). The quotations from Rashi and Tosafot were virtually the same as well. Ibn Ḥabib's commentary also flanked the pages just as it had in the first edition, and each volume contained indexes designed in accordance with the same thematic principles used by ibn Ḥabib.[23] Like the 1546 edition, this was in every way an attempt to reprint the work of Jacob and Levi ibn Ḥabib in a manner that seemed to parallel Daniel Bomberg's plan to systematize the texts of the Talmud.

Cavalli, however, did make one significant change that had an effect on the history of the *En Yaaqov* for centuries—he changed the title of the collection. The *En Yaaqov/Bet Yaaqov* became the *En Yisrael/Bet Yisrael* (see appendix, figure 2).[24] For the remainder of the sixteenth century, all editions of the *En Yaaqov* bore this new title, and for years afterward editions continued to be titled *En Yisrael* (see appendix, figures 4, 6, 7, and 8).[25] As each modification in the printing of a collection communicates something about the history of the period and the potential impact of that history on the future reception or even survival of the collection, these changes should not be overlooked. This is especially true in the case of the *En Yaaqov,* where a title change was only the first of many modifications in its five-century history.

Cavalli's title change, in particular, was a direct reaction to the strong hand the Church continued to exert in the printing of Hebrew books, even as it lifted the papal ban in 1563.[26] For example, in addition to imposing strict requirements regarding the censorship of potentially anti-Christian statements,[27] the Church demanded that titles such as "Talmud"[28] and "*En Yaaqov*"[29] be changed, presumably to thwart their sale and confuse buyers. If book titles were unknown, the market for them disappeared. However, what began as a papal anti-Jewish decree actually enhanced the value of the *En Yaaqov,* attesting further to its demand. In later years, when the Church reinstituted its ban, the *En Yaaqov* circumvented its decree under a different title, *En Yisrael.* Indeed, it was the *En Yaaqov* that remained on the *Index librorum prohibitorum* until 1948 and not the *En Yisrael.*[30]

Throughout the sixteenth and early seventeenth centuries, the *En Yaaqov/En Yisrael* continued to be printed in Italy. It would take approximately eighty years after its first publication for another edition of the *En Yaaqov* to be printed in Salonika.[31] However, during these years the collection was still available to Salonikan Jews through booksellers who brought editions from Italy to the Ottoman empire. Surely the fact that the later

Salonika edition was titled *En Yisrael* (Salonika, 1595–1601) attests not only to the influence that the Italian editions had on presses elsewhere but also to the market for this collection outside of Salonika. But despite the fact that printers in Salonika,[32] Cracow,[33] and Prostitz[34] published markedly similar editions of the *En Yaaqov/En Yisrael* at the end of the sixteenth and early seventeenth centuries, Italian Jews continued to make inroads in its study and, more generally, in the study of Talmudic aggadah. Not only did Italian printing houses, particularly in Venice, maintain a commitment to publishing the *En Yaaqov/En Yisrael*,[35] they also began to publish separate indexes that were intended to compensate further for the fact that ibn Ḥabib's collection followed the format of the Talmud. Working off the *En Yisrael/Bet Yisrael* edition of 1566 (Venice), which already contained an index modeled after ibn Ḥabib's indexes,[36] these alphabetical and thematic indexes further broadened the collection's accessibility.[37] Those who created such indexes also presumed that the text of the *En Yaaqov* had reached some level of standardization. In other words, they must have worked under the presumption that reprintings would continue to be in line with the 1566 edition, displaying the same page and section numbers, since printing changes would quickly render the indexes obsolete.[38] Within twenty-five years, at least three indexes were produced: the index of Yedidyah ben Moshe, titled *Liqqute Aggadah Misefer En Yaaqov* (1602–3 [manuscript]); that of Eliezer Reiti, titled *Luaḥ Maamare En Yisrael* (Venice, 1612), which was printed as a separate index and then added to later collections of the *En Yaaqov*, such as an edition printed in Amsterdam in 1684–85; and that of Judah Aryeh (Leone) Modena, titled *Bet Leḥem Yehudah* (Venice, 1625).[39]

The index, however, is also a powerful tool, which does far more than make the material found within a given collection like the *En Yaaqov* more accessible. The insertion of different types of indexes also sends the message that communities did not study Talmudic aggadah in the same way. In fact, one of the earliest modifications made to editions of the *En Yaaqov* occurred in the index of the Cracow edition printed in 1587. The printer, Isaac ben Aharon of Prostitz, appended a markedly different index to the editions of the *En Yaaqov/En Yisrael*,[40] suggesting that Jews in this community studied aggadah differently from the Jews of Venice. Despite efforts to maintain the same page and section numbers as those found in the Venice printings of the *En Yaaqov/En Yisrael* (1546, 1566), this printer included an index that cited a vast array of external sources where references to the aggadot mentioned in the *En Yaaqov* could be found. The index, titled *"Simanim limtso divre ḥefets,"* included references to Baḥya ben Asher's thirteenth-century commentary on the Torah; the responsa of Solomon ibn Adret (Rashba);

Jacob ben Asher's (d. 1340) halakhic code, *Arbaah Turim;* Menaḥem Recanati's early fourteenth-century Kabbalistic work, *Taamei Hamitsvot* (Constantinople, 1544); Joshua ibn Shu'ieb's fourteenth-century *Sefer Derashot al Hatorah* (Cracow, 1573); Abraham Saba's (d. 1508) commentary on the Torah, *Tseror Ḥamor* (Venice, 1522); Joseph Albo's fifteenth-century philosophical work on dogmatics, *Sefer Haiqqarim;* Joseph Caro's early sixteenth-century halakhic commentary on the *Arbaah Turim, Bet Yosef;* and many other works. No longer the self-contained book that ibn Ḥabib had designed and subsequent Venetian printers embraced, the *En Yaaqov* became the jumping-off point for the study of aggadah more generally. The range of philosophical, homiletical, and halakhic works listed in the index was so vast that the *En Yaaqov* could now point its readership to discussions of Talmudic aggadot found throughout medieval Jewish literature. It presumed an audience actively seeking the ability to study Talmudic aggadah in other contexts, reversing the initial objectives of ibn Ḥabib. It was ibn Ḥabib who had gathered together passages of Talmudic aggadah and situated them alongside commentaries so that individuals could study aggadah as if they were studying the Talmud. Through the index alone, the printer Isaac ben Aharon directed his readership beyond the Talmud and the *En Yaaqov,* reshaping ibn Ḥabib's objectives.[41]

Efforts to remold the image of the *En Yaaqov* are no more evident than in the role which the Italian rabbi Judah Modena played in its history during the early seventeenth century. His commitment to making Talmudic aggadah more accessible began with the composition of a topical, alphabetical index. But he did not stop there. As he was preparing his index for publication, he also collected and published a sample of aggadic texts drawn from the Talmud, along with parallel comments made by Rashi, compiling them into another collection. According to Modena, these were aggadot that ibn Ḥabib had unfortunately left out of the *En Yaaqov,* and Modena wished to rectify his error. With no intention of supplanting ibn Ḥabib's *En Yaaqov,* Modena became the author of a new collection of Talmudic aggadah, *Bet Yehudah* (Venice, 1635), through which he intended to complement the work of ibn Ḥabib.[42] The books were to be studied side by side, one an augmentation of the other. In fact, Modena writes in his autobiography that he never desired anything more in his life than to see the *Bet Yehudah* "printed and disseminated among the dispersion of Israel." He was certain that from it he would "earn merit and honor and an everlasting reputation, which would never be lost."[43]

Like ibn Ḥabib, Modena also authored a commentary interpreting the aggadot, titled *Habone.*[44] However, this work bore a greater likeness to

Rashi's commentary on the Talmud than it did to ibn Ḥabib's interpretive approach to aggadah. Indeed, in writing his commentary Modena felt no allegiance to ibn Ḥabib's *Hakotev;* he virtually ignored ibn Ḥabib's theological interests and commitment to the principles of faith. Modena thus exerted a great degree of editorial/authorial freedom. He was in no way bound by ibn Ḥabib's anthological choices or by his approach to aggadah. At the same time he viewed his contributions as a necessary corrective integral to his desire to enhance ibn Ḥabib's *En Yaaqov.*

At around the same time that Modena was working on the *En Yaaqov,* two other rabbis devoted themselves to writing new commentaries on the aggadot of the *En Yaaqov.* They were Josiah Pinto (Harif) (1565–1648) of Damascus,[45] who wrote *Meor Enayim,* and the Polish rabbi Samuel Eliezer ben Judah Halevi Edels (Maharsha) (1555–1631), who wrote *Ḥiddushe Aggadah.*[46] That each had an edition of the *En Yaaqov* available to him, despite the fact that editions of it had yet to be printed in the cities they inhabited when they wrote their commentaries, is further proof of its popularity and accessibility. Like Modena, each of these rabbis departed from ibn Ḥabib's style of commentary. Edels (Maharsha), in contrast to ibn Ḥabib, used philosophy in his interpretations of aggadah. He even encouraged the knowledge of secular sciences, considering it significant for a proper understanding of Torah and vital for disputes with non-Jews.[47] Pinto integrated Kabbalah into his lengthy excurses, despite ibn Ḥabib's desire to distance the study of aggadah from Kabbalah.[48]

With respect to the authorship of subsequent commentaries, the contents of ibn Ḥabib's commentary did not seem to have a strong impact on later scholars. Although ibn Ḥabib respected the approaches of others to the study of aggadah, compiling as he did the comments of Rashi, Tosafot, and ibn Adret (Rashba) in his original edition of the *En Yaaqov,* it is interesting that later rabbinic scholars did not readily embrace his view of rabbinic theology. He had a far greater impact on cultivating scholarly and nonscholarly interest in Talmudic aggadah more generally.

By the end of the seventeenth century, when the center of Hebrew printing had shifted to Amsterdam, editors and printers began to generate more editions of the *En Yaaqov.* It was so popular throughout the late seventeenth and eighteenth centuries that many of the printers in Amsterdam who produced Hebrew books published an edition of it. Remarkably, these collections were far more fluid than their Italian and Polish counterparts of the sixteenth and early seventeenth centuries. Editors and printers added the commentaries of Pinto and Edels to the pages of the *En Yaaqov,* placing them and their introductory remarks alongside ibn Ḥabib's (see appendix, figures 6, 7, 10, 11). To some extent, this was not all that surprising, given that ibn Ḥabib had set up a template; the *En Yaaqov* was already an anthology of commentaries. However, in some editions the commentaries that ibn Ḥabib anthologized fell by the wayside in favor of other commentaries. Rashba's commentary, for example, was rarely reprinted. In 1698, the printer Caspar Steen printed a small-sized edition that contained only an abridged commentary, similar to Rashi's Talmud commentary (see appendix, figures 8 and 9). It did not contain ibn Habib's *Hakotev.* But its small size saved costs on paper and made it easier to transport to other cities for sale.[49]

What is more surprising, however, is that editors took the liberty to change ibn Ḥabib's anthology of aggadic passages. Not only did they add Modena's missing passages as found in the *Bet Yehudah,* using the symbol of a flower to signify what he had added, but they also added more Talmudic material to the pages of editions of the *En Yaaqov.*[50] For example, the first Mishnah in tractate *Berakhot,* which dealt with the legal question of when one was to say the *Shema* prayer in the morning, became a permanent addition, appearing in the vast majority of later printed editions of the *En Yaaqov.* Arguably, this insertion contains a brief story about Rabban Gamaliel that may have been considered aggadic. However, the editors also added the Talmudic material that followed this Mishnah found in the Gemara, which was not aggadic. This inclusion of additional Talmudic material of a legal nature begs the question as to whether there was a desire to further ibn Ḥabib's mission of creating a new version of the Talmud. From a printer's perspective, a more concise one- or two-volume Talmud might sell far better, to a wider audience, than a multivolume Talmudic corpus.[51] More interesting, however, is the fact that editors and printers assumed the freedom to reshape the *En Yaaqov,* transforming it into a work that its original author would not have recognized as his own. Jacob ibn Ḥabib's status as "the" author was usurped over time by a host of individuals whose names were added to the title pages of subsequent editions of the *En Yaaqov* in a manner that completely overshadowed him and his role as the author.[52]

During the nineteenth century, while many printers of the *En Yaaqov* pushed for greater fluidity in their production of new editions, others made less than successful efforts to standardize the collection.[53] A brief look at three editions published in one of the many East European cities where the *En Yaaqov* was printed highlights the tension printers experienced as they struggled with the advantages and limitations of stasis and change in the printing of the Hebrew book.

In 1869 the printers Samuel Joseph Fuen and Abraham Hirsch (Tsvi) Rosenkranz published an edition of the *En Yaaqov* in Vilna with a new commentary authored by Elijah Shik (see appendix, figures 13 and 14). Shik was a leading rabbi with a great interest in aggadah, most especially for the purpose of the rabbinic sermon.[54] As a result, his running commentary on the *En Yaaqov* contained many Talmudic cross-references and additional sources, including references to ibn Ḥabib's commentary. But, oddly, the edition contained just a brief reference to Jacob ibn Ḥabib on the title page. The intentional placement of a bolder citation of both the title, *En Yaaqov,* and the name of Shik's commentary, *En Eliyahu,* overshadowed any reference to ibn Ḥabib. And while one can find Edels's (Maharsha's) commentary *Hiddushe Aggadah* situated next to Shik's in this edition of the *En Yaaqov,* the absence of ibn Ḥabib's introduction and his commentary is glaring. Why did Shik's introduction take the place of ibn Ḥabib's? Why did these printers promote editorial decisions that pushed the original author to the margins of the history of his own collection?[55]

Only seven years later ibn Ḥabib was neglected once again. In an edition of the *En Yaaqov* published by the Romm family's press in Vilna in 1876, ibn Ḥabib's commentary was left out. This omission, however, is more notable because of the press's stated commitment to produce a standard text to rectify the fact that there were too many different editions of the *En Yaaqov* available to their readership. In their words, no two editions contained the same texts of the aggadot or drew from the same versions of the Talmud. This, they argued, confused rather than properly instructed their readership.[56] But why did the Romm printers choose to leave out ibn Ḥabib's introduction and his commentary? If there was a desire to push the collection toward a greater degree of standardization, why did they ignore the collection's original author?

More surprising, however, is that this edition (Vilna, 1876) contained a selection of commentaries that differed entirely from editions published before and after it, even by the Romm family press itself. In addition to leaving out ibn Ḥabib's commentary, these printers also did not include Elijah Shik's commentary in this edition or in any later editions they published. Instead, they incorporated Rashi's commentary; the commentary of Ḥayyim Yosef David Azulai, *Petaḥ Enayim;* a condensed form of Edels's (Maharsha's) *Hiddushe Aggadah;* the commentary of Zvi Hirsch Chajes, referred to as his *Hiddushim;* and a new commentary on the *Yerushalmi, Or Hadash,* which was drawn from earlier commentaries on the *Yerushalmi, Korban Haedah,* and *Pnai Moshe.*[57] Why did these commentaries stand out as those that should define the *En Yaaqov* collection, being as they were commentaries that had never appeared together in earlier editions of the *En Yaaqov*? In what ways did they reshape ibn Ḥabib's overall purpose and transform the *En Yaaqov* into a different work?

Another seven years would pass before the Romm family press fell into the hands of David Romm's widow and his brothers.[58] They published yet another edition of the *En Yaaqov* in 1883 (see appendix, figures 15, 16, 17). Continued concern over the vast number of editions of the *En Yaaqov* containing different texts of the aggadot and the commentaries led the Romm printers to make another attempt to standardize the collection. Taking great care to synthesize different versions of the *En Yaaqov* into one edition, they used brackets and parentheses to distinguish among the texts drawn from older versus more recent editions. They also generated an entirely different and far larger anthology of introductions, commentaries, and essays on aggadah[59] from that of the edition printed in 1876. Although they left out both Azulai's and Chajes's commentaries, they displayed ibn Ḥabib's commentary prominently. Once again, the Romm family molded the *En Yaaqov* into another type of collection, raising questions as to its nature. They hoped this edition would mark a turning point in the history of the *En Yaaqov* and that it would be reprinted over and over again, becoming a standard edition in a fashion similar to the editions of the *Talmud Bavli* that rolled off their presses. They even chose a print layout that matched the design of their Talmud editions, placing the texts drawn from the Talmud in the center of each page with the commentaries surrounding them. Although the Romm editions of the Talmud were quickly becoming the standard editions in Vilna at the time, the Romm family did not succeed with the *En Yaaqov* in quite the same way. Different editions of the *En Yaaqov* continued to be produced with different layouts, anthologies of Talmudic material, commentaries, and introductions, despite the fact that some looked to the Romm edition (Vilna, 1883) as the standard edition.[60]

Printers continued to encourage and to protect the fluidity of the *En Yaaqov*, ultimately enabling the single-authored original 1516 edition of the *En Yaaqov* to become the work of many. They allowed different historical contexts, varied intellectual cultures, and diverse audiences to govern the very nature of the *En Yaaqov*, passing down a legacy rather than a book. By the end of the nineteenth century, the *En Yaaqov* had become a title that connoted a discipline of study centered on Talmudic aggadah. In fact, the title *En Yaaqov* figured more prominently in the minds of those who studied it than the name of its author, the place of its inception, and the community it had been originally designed to address. But its printing history also highlights the fact that an ideological change had taken place during the years since the printing of the first edition of the *En Yaaqov* in 1516. The debate that ibn Ḥabib entered into at the end of the fifteenth century had, in part, centered on determining which texts defined rabbinic Judaism and the curriculum of Jewish study. Ibn Ḥabib produced the *En Yaaqov* in the hope that the aggadic texts of the Talmud would be considered as significant as its legal texts. He hoped that through the *En Yaaqov* he would draw more people to the study of Talmud. However, following ibn Ḥabib's death, the printing history of the *En Yaaqov* suggests that for authors, editors, and printers of this work, the debate had widened to query the very nature of the Jewish "book." With the success of the Hebrew printing press and the ability of Jews to publish and repeatedly reprint the Talmud and the *En Yaaqov,* the question became whether printing should be employed to standardize sacred books like the Talmud or whether it should allow for greater fluidity. The *En Yaaqov* served as one medium through which Jews questioned the boundaries of what constituted "the book" or "the canon," and explored the potential advantages and limitations of standardizing sacred texts.

Indeed, the printing history of the *En Yaaqov* suggests that there is no clear link between the success of a book and the efforts made to standardize it. Fluidity also ensured that a "book" was read and reread. In this way, the history of the printing of the *En Yaaqov* indicates that there is no single Jewish cultural definition of the "book." Jews did not "receive" their canonical texts from an earlier generation in a monolithic fashion. Although they desired stasis, they also embraced change and variation. And, just as efforts to standardize the texts of the Talmud communicate something about the Jewish community in its desire for set folios surrounded by the same commentaries of Rashi and Tosafot,[61] the fluidity of the *En Yaaqov* enables scholars to ask about the motivations for each modification and addition and thereby to come to understand other aspects of Jewish life and culture.[62] For example, in the next stage of research on the *En Yaaqov,* scholars must consider how later commentators created new "rounds of reception." How did later commentators read Talmudic aggadah in contrast to ibn Ḥabib? In what ways did their agendas differ? How did they change the image of the *En Yaaqov?*[63]

Books like the *En Yaaqov* are protected from obscurity by those who continue to write about them.[64] In this book, *The* En Yaaqov: *Jacob ibn Ḥabib's Search for Faith in the Talmudic Corpus,* I have called attention to the man and the collection that inspired generations to focus on the study of the aggadot of the Talmud. The printing of ibn Ḥabib's *En Yaaqov* was a turning point in the history of aggadah that led a greater number of Jews to become interested in the aggadot of the Talmud than had been interested before its publication in the early sixteenth century. That its rich history unraveled in its own way should not obscure the accomplishments of its original author. But it is precisely this history that should evoke the need for further research on the role that Talmudic aggadah and the *En Yaaqov* played in later centuries, if not today. Who was interested in the study of Talmudic aggadah through the lens of the *En Yaaqov* and why? What prompted their interests? What religious agendas did they bring to the fore through their commentaries on the aggadot of the Talmud? Just as ibn Ḥabib spurred his successors to study Talmudic aggadah with increased vigor, it is my hope that this book will encourage scholars to study its later editions with greater interest and offer increased insight into the nature of Talmudic aggadah. I have laid out the origins of the *En Yaaqov* in this book, but there remain many more pieces to unravel before a complete history of this work unfolds.

Appendix:

Pages from Editions of the *En Yaaqov*/ *En Yisrael*, 1516–1923

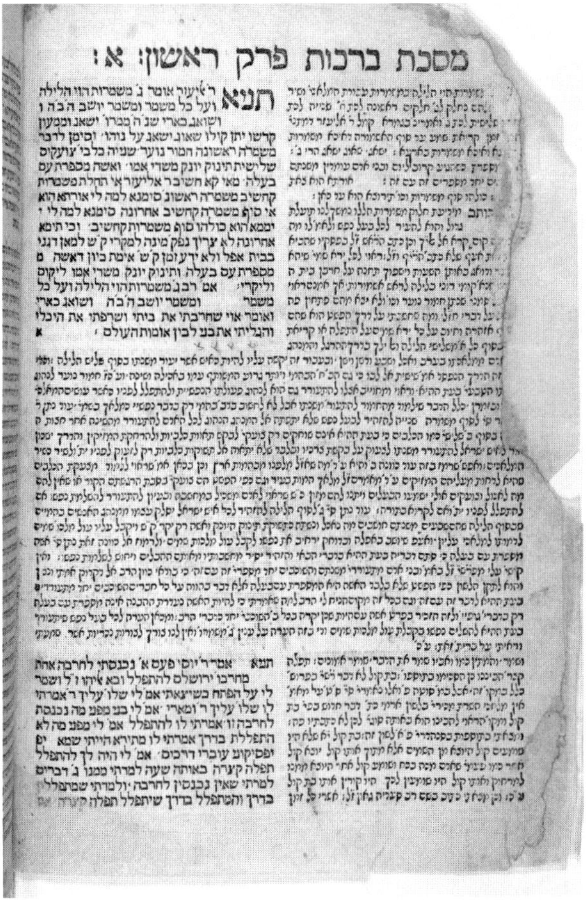
מסכת ברכות פרק ראשון: א:

תנא ר׳ אליעזר אומר ג׳ משמרות הוי הלילה ועל כל משמר ומשמר יושב הקב״ה ושואג כארי שנ׳ ה׳ ממרום ישאג וממעון קדשו יתן קולו שאוג ישאג על נוהו׳ וסימן לדבר משמרה ראשונה חמור נוער׳ שניה כלבי׳ צועקים שלישית תינוק יונק משדי אמו׳ ואשה מספרת עם בעלה׳ מאי קא חשיב ר׳ אליעזר אי תחלת משמרות קחשיב משמרה ראשונ׳ סימנא למה לי אורתא הוא אי סוף משמרה קחשיב אחרונה סימנא למה לי יממא הוא כולהו סוף משמרות קחשיב׳ וכי תימא אחרונה לא צריך נפק׳ מינה למקרי ק״ש למאן דגני בבית אפל ולא ידע זמן ק״ש אימת כיון דאשה מספרת עם בעלה ותינוק יונק משדי אמו ליקום וליקרי׳ אמ׳ רב ג׳ משמרות הוי הלילה ועל כל משמר ומשמר יושב הקב״ה ושואג כארי ואומר אוי שחרבתי את ביתי ושרפתי את היכלי והגליתי את בני לבין אומות העולם׳ א

תנא אמ׳ ר׳ יוסי פעם א׳ נכנסתי לחרבה אחת מחרבו׳ ירושלם להתפלל ובא אליהו ז״ל ושמר לי על הפתח כשיצאתי אמ׳ לי שלו׳ עליך ר׳ אמרתי לו שלו׳ עליך ר׳ ומורי׳ אמ׳ לי בני מפני מה נכנסת לחרבה זו׳ אמרתי לו להתפלל אמ׳ לי מפני מה לא התפללת בדרך אמרתי לו מתירא הייתי שמא יפסיקונו עוברי דרכים׳ אמ׳ לי היה לך להתפלל תפלה קצרה באותה שעה למדתי ממנו ג׳ דברים למדתי שאין נכנסין לחרבה׳ ולמדתי שמתפללין בדרך והמתפלל בדרך שיתפלל תפלה קצרה

Figure 1. *En Yaaqov* (Salonika: Judah Gedaliah, 1516), first printed edition, tractate *Berakhot*. Courtesy of the Jewish Theological Seminary Library, New York.

Figure 2. *En Yisrael* (Venice: Giorgio di Cavalli, 1566), title page. Courtesy of the Jewish Theological Seminary Library, New York.

Figure 3. *En Yisrael* (Venice: Giorgio di Cavalli, 1566), tractate *Berakhot.* Courtesy of the Jewish Theological Seminary Library, New York.

Figure 4. *En Yisrael* (Cracow: Isaac ben Aharon of Prostitz, 1587), title page. Courtesy of the Jewish Theological Seminary Library, New York.

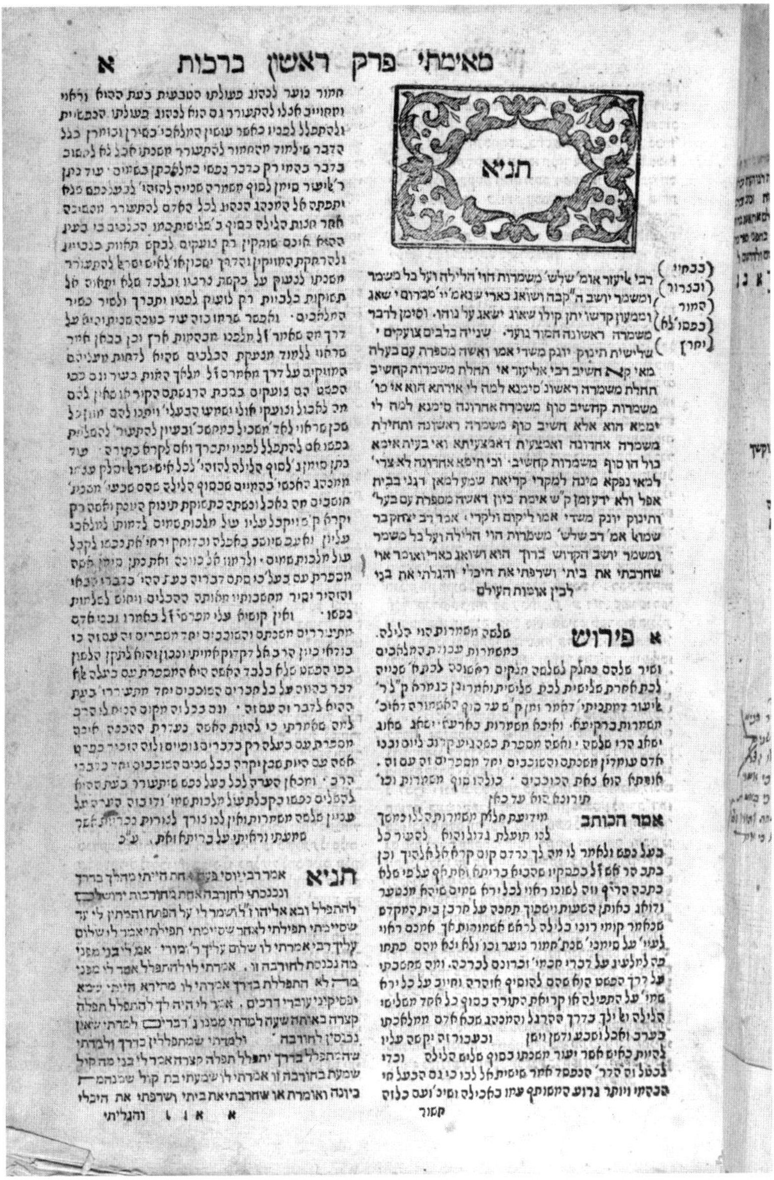

מאימתי פרק ראשון ברכות א

תניא

רבי אליעזר אומ' שלש' משמרות הוי הלילה ועל כל משמר ומשמר יושב ה"קבה ושואג כארי שנאמ' י"י ממרום ישאג וכו' וסימן לדבר משמרה ראשונה חמור גוער. שנייה כלבים צועקים שלישית תינוק יונק משדי אמו ואשה מספרת עם בעלה...

א פירוש

אמר הכותב

תניא אמר רבי יוסי פעם אחת הייתי מהלך בדרך ונכנסתי לחורבה אחת מחורבות ירושלם להתפלל ובא אליהו ז"ל ושמר לי על הפתח והמתין לי עד שסיימתי תפילתי לאחר שסיימתי תפילתי אמר לי שלום עליך רבי ואמרתי לו שלום עליך ר' ומורי...

Figure 5. *En Yisrael* (Cracow: Isaac ben Aharon of Prostitz, 1587), tractate *Berakhot.* Courtesy of the Jewish Theological Seminary Library, New York.

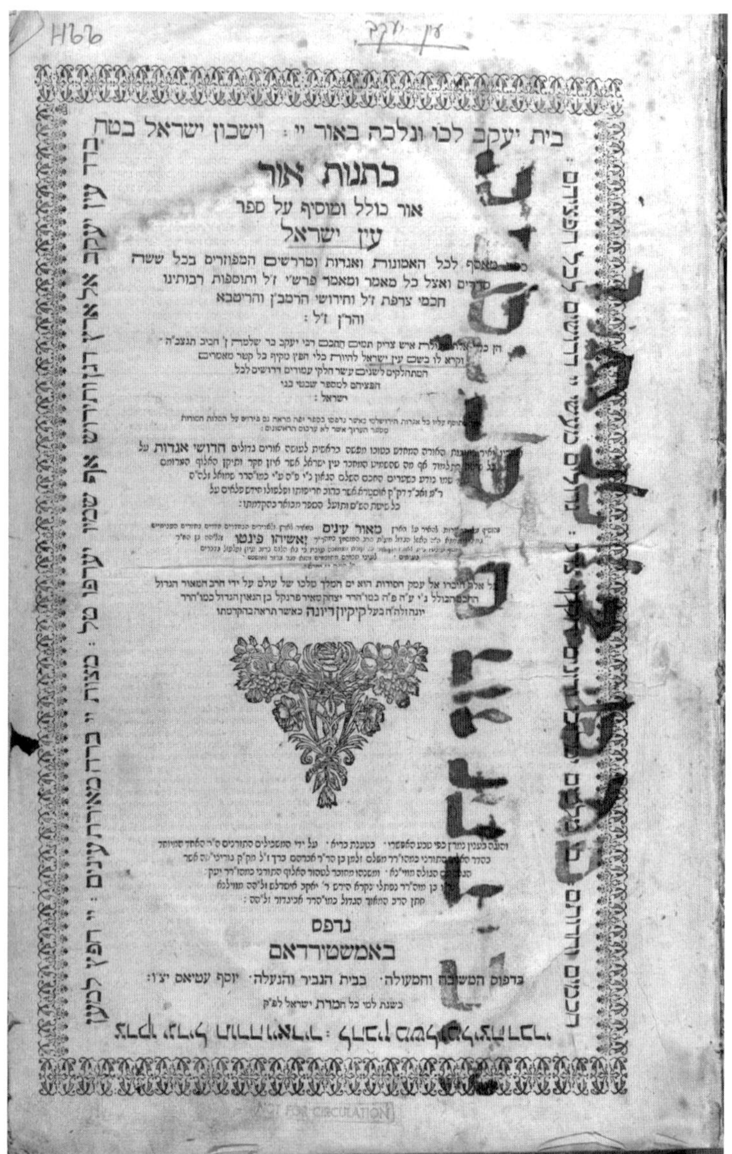

Figure 6. *Qotnot Or [En Yisrael]* (Amsterdam: Joseph Athias, 1684), vol. 1, title page. Courtesy of the Jewish Theological Seminary, New York.

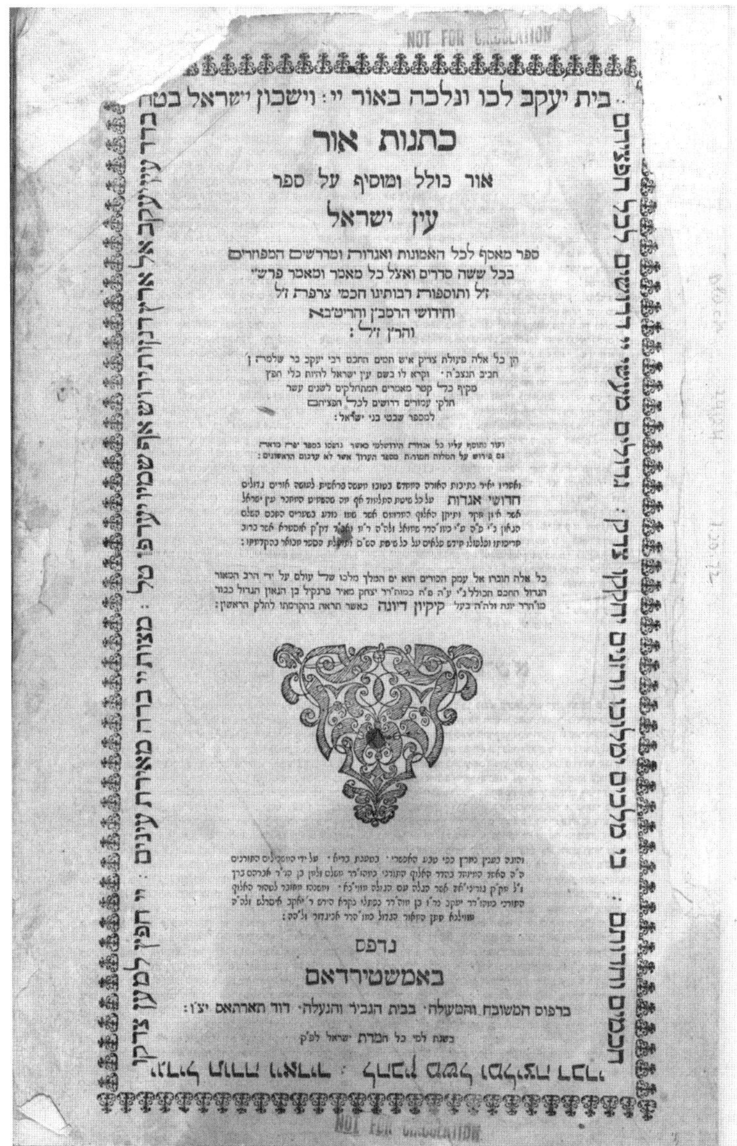

Figure 7. *Qotnot Or [En Yisrael]* (Amsterdam: David de Castro Tartas, 1684), title page. Courtesy of the Jewish Theological Seminary Library, New York.

Right: Figure 8. *En Yisrael* (Amsterdam: Caspar Steen, 1698), title page. Courtesy of the Jewish National University Library, Jerusalem.
Left: Figure 9. *En Yisrael* (Amsterdam: Caspar Steen, 1698), tractate *Berakhot.* Courtesy of the Jewish National University Library, Jerusalem.

Figure 10. *Qohelet Shlomo [En Yaaqov im Qotnot Or]* (Amsterdam: Herts Levi Rofe, 1740), title page (on blue paper). Courtesy of the Jewish Theological Seminary Library, New York.

מאימתי פרק ראשון ברכות   א

מאימתי

א ב **קורין** את שמע בערבית• משעה שהכהנים נכנסין לאכול בתרומתן עד סוף האשמורה הראשונה דברי רבי אליעזר• וחכמים אומרים עד חצות• רבן גמליאל אומר עד שיעלה עמוד השחר• מעשה שבאו בניו מבית המשתה אמרו לו לא קרינו את שמע• אמר להם אם לא עלה עמוד השחר חייבין אתם לקרות ולא זו בלבד אמרו אלא כל מה שאמרו חכמים

Figure 11. *Qohelet Shlomo [En Yaaqov im Qotnot Or]* (Amsterdam: Herts Levi Rofe, 1740), tractate *Berakhot* (on blue paper). Courtesy of the Jewish Theological Seminary Library, New York.

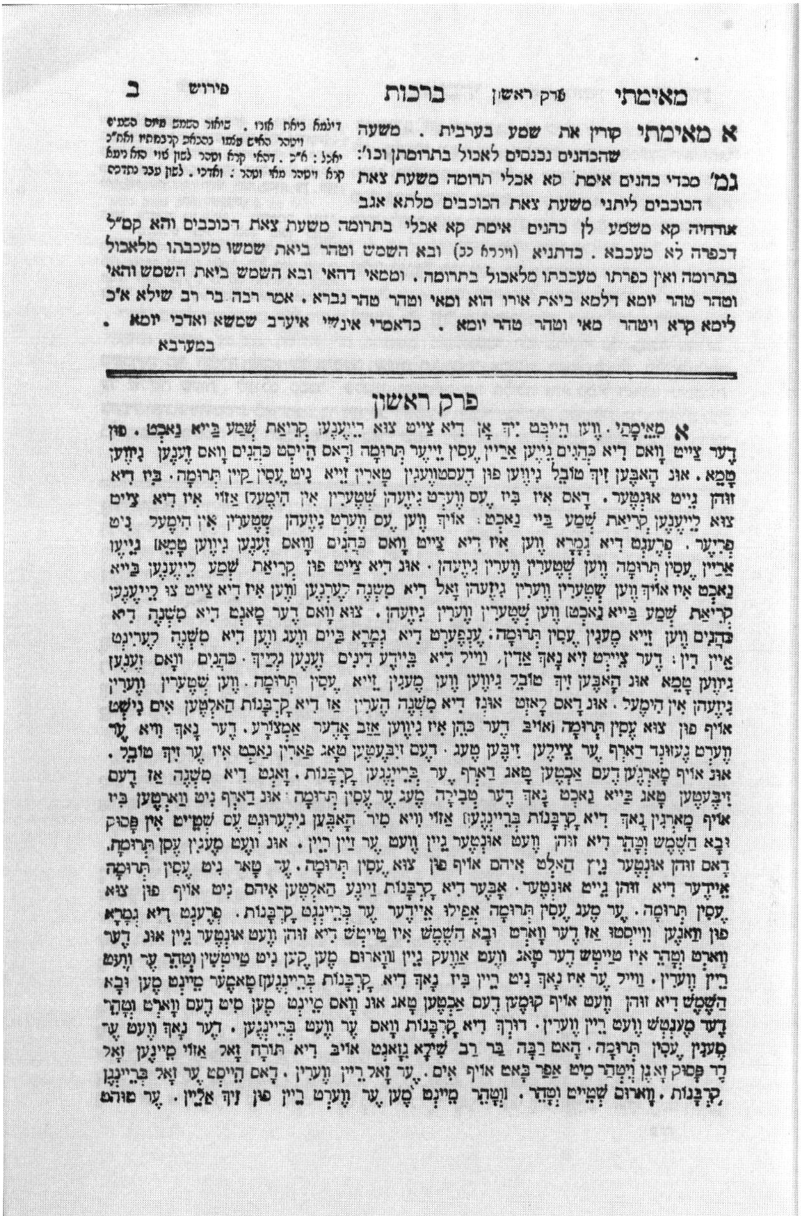

ב   פירוש   מאימתי   פרק ראשון   ברכות

א **מאימתי** קורין את שמע בערבית . משעה שהכהנים נכנסים לאכול בתרומתן וכו':

גמ' מכדי כהנים אימת קא אכלי תרומה משעת צאת הכוכבים ליתני משעת צאת הכוכבים מלתא אגב אורחיה קא משמע לן כהנים אימת קא אכלי בתרומה משעת צאת הכוכבים והא קמ"ל דכפרה לא מעכבא . כדתניא (ויקרא כב) ובא השמש וטהר ביאת שמשו מעכבתו מלאכול בתרומה ואין כפרתו מעכבתו מלאכול בתרומה . וממאי דהאי ובא השמש ביאת השמש והאי וטהר טהר יומא דלמא ביאת אירו הוא ומאי וטהר טהר נברא . אמר רבה בר רב שילא א"כ לימא קרא ויטהר מאי וטהר טהר יומא . כדאמרי אינשי איערב שמשא ואדכי יומא במערבא

פרק ראשון

א **מאימתי** . ווען הייבט זיך אן דיא צייט צוא רייענען קריאת שמע בייא נאכט . **פון** דער צייט וואס דיא כהנים גייען אריין עסין זייער תרומה (דאס הייסט כהנים וואס זענען נימא . אונ האבען זיך טובל געוועזן פון העסטוועניגין מארין זייא ניט עסן קיין תרומה . ביז דיא זוהן גייט אונטער . דאס איז ביז עס ווערט נייטהן זייעהן שטערין אין הימעל) אזוי איז דיא צייט צוא רייענען קריאת שמע בייא נאכט . אויך ווען עס ווערט נייטהן שטערין אין הימעל גיט פריער . פרעגט דיא גמרא ווען איז דיא צייט וואס כהנים וואס זענען נימא ניועזן אריין עסין תרומה ווען שטערין ווערין גיזעהן . אונ דיא צייט פון קריאת שמע בייא נאכט איז אויך ווען שטערין ווערין גיזעהן ואל דיא משנה לערנען ווען איז דיא צייט צו רייענען קריאת שמע בייא נאכט ווען שטערין ווערין גיזעהן . צוא וואס דער מאנט דיא משנה דיא כהנים ווען זייא מעגין עסין תרומה . ענטפערט דיא גמרא בייים וועג וואס איז משנה לערינט אין רין : דער צייט דיא נאך אדין . וייל דיא בייהע דינים זענען גלייך כהנים וואס זענען גיוועזן טמא אונ האבען זיך טובל גיוועזן ווען מענין זייא עסין תרומה . ווען שטערין ווערין גיזעהן אין הימעל . אונ דאס וואס לאזט אונ: דיא משנה הערין אז דיא קרבנות האלטמען אים נישט אויף פון צוא עסן תרומה ואויב דער כהן איז גיוען אב אדער אמצורע . דער נאך ווא ער ערט גענוונד דארף ער ציילען דעם זיבעמען מאג פארין נאכט איז ער זיך טובל . אונ אויף מארינגט דעם אכטמן טאג דארף ער ברייינגען קרבנות . זאגט דיא משנה אז דעם זיבעמען מאן בייא נאכט נאך דער טביריה מעג ער עסין תרומה אונ דארף ניט ווארטען ביז אויף מארגין נאך דיא קרבנות ברייינגען אזוי ווא מיר האבען גיערונט עם שטיים אן פסוק ובא השמש וטהר דיא זוהן וועט אונטער ביין וועט ער זיין ריין . אונ ווען מענין עסן תרומה . דאס זוהן אונטער נען גין האלט איהם אויף פון צוא עסן תרומה . ער טאר ניט עסן תרומה איידער דיא זוהן גייט אונטער . אבער דיא קרבנות ווינע האלטען איהם נישט אויף פון צוא עסין תרומה . ער מעג עסן תרומה אפילו איידער ער ברייינגט קרבנות . פרעגט דיא גמרא פון וואנען וויימסו אז דער ווארם יובא השמש איז מיימש דיא זוהן וועט אונטער גיין אונ דער ווארט וטהר איז מיימש דער טאג וועט אווענק גיין ווארום מען קען ניט מיימשן וטהר ער וועט ריין ווערין . וייל ער איז נאך ביז ניט ריין ביז דיא נאך דיא קרבנות ברייינגען דאסער טיינט וואס זאגט דיא זוהן וועט אויף קומען דעם אבכמען טאג אונ ווא סיינט זען ווא דעם וואריט וטהר דער ריין ווען ווערין . דורך דיא קרבנות וואס ער וועט ברייינגען . דער נאך וועט ער מעניין עסן תרומה . האם רבה בר רב שילא ניאנט אויב דיא תורה זאל אזוי מיינען ואל דער פסוק זאגן ויטהר מים אפר כאם אויף אים . ער זאל רעין ווערין . דאם הייסט ער זאל ברייינגען קרבנות . ווארום שמיים וטהר . וויטהר מיינט זען ער וועט בין ויך זיך אליין . ער שורה

Figure 12. *En Yaaqov* (Warsaw, 1895), tractate *Berakhot* (with Yiddish paraphrase of the Talmudic passages). Courtesy of the Jewish Theological Seminary Library, New York.

Figure 13. *En Yaaqov* (Vilna: Samuel Joseph Fuen and Abraham Hirsch [Tsvi] Rosenkranz, 1869), title page. Courtesy of the Jewish Theological Seminary Library, New York.

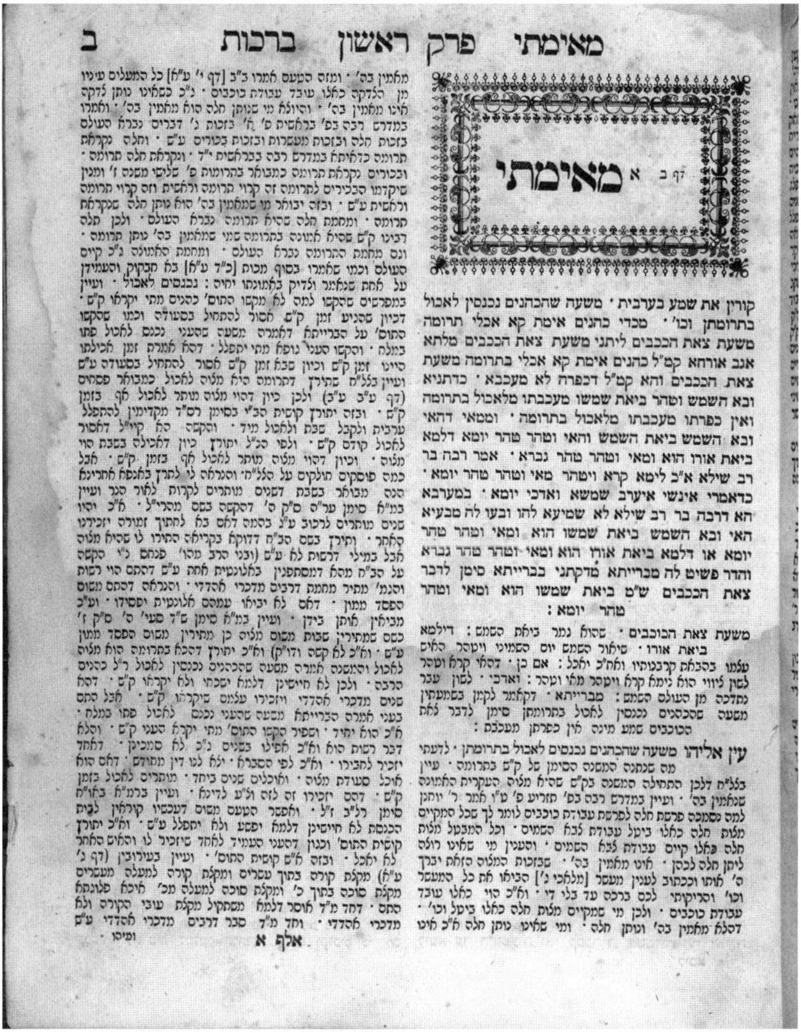
מאימתי פרק ראשון ברכות ב

דף ב א מאימתי

קורין את שמע בערבית · משעה שהכהנים נכנסין לאכול בתרומתן וכו׳ · מכדי כהנים אימת קא אכלי תרומה משעת צאת הככבים ליתני משעת צאת הככבים מלתא אגב אורחא קמ״ל כהנים אימת קא אכלי בתרומה משעת צאת הככבים והא קמ״ל דכפרה לא מעכבא · כדתניא ובא השמש וטהר ביאת שמשו מעכבתו מלאכול בתרומה ואין כפרתו מעכבתו מלאכול בתרומה · וממאי דהאי ובא השמש ביאת השמש והאי וטהר טהר יומא דלמא ביאת אורו הוא ומאי וטהר טהר גברא · אמר רבה בר רב שילא א״כ לימא קרא ויטהר מאי וטהר טהר יומא · כדאמרי אינשי איערב שמשא ואדכי יומא · במערבא הא דרבה בר רב שילא לא שמיעא להו ובעו לה מבעיא האי ובא השמש ביאת שמשו הוא ומאי וטהר טהר יומא או דלמא ביאת אורו הוא ומאי וטהר טהר גברא והדר פשיט לה מברייתא מדקתני בברייתא סימן לדבר צאת הככבים ש״מ ביאת שמשו הוא ומאי וטהר טהר יומא :

Figure 14. *En Yaaqov* (Vilna: Samuel Joseph Fuen and Abraham Hirsch [Tsvi] Rosenkranz, 1869), tractate *Berakhot*. Courtesy of the Jewish Theological Seminary Library, New York.

Figure 15. *En Yaaqov* (Vilna: Romm, 1923), reprint of *En Yaaqov* (Vilna: Romm, 1883), first title page. Courtesy of the Jewish Theological Seminary Library, New York.

Figure 16. *En Yaaqov* (Vilna: Romm, 1923), reprint of *En Yaaqov* (Vilna, 1883), second title page. Courtesy of the Jewish Theological Seminary Library, New York.

Figure 17. *En Yaaqov* (Vilna: Romm, 1923), reprint of *En Yaaqov* (Vilna, 1883), tractate *Berakhot.* Courtesy of the Jewish Theological Seminary Library, New York.

NOTES

Throughout these notes I make reference to two editions of the *En Yaaqov.* The citation listed first refers to ibn Ḥabib's first printed edition of 1516, and is abbreviated *EY* (Salonika, 1516). Each of these citations is followed by its corresponding reference in the Jerusalem edition of the *En Yaaqov* published in 1961, and notated parenthetically as (= Jerusalem, 1961). This latter edition, an exact reprint of the traditional Romm (Vilna, 1883) text, is currently among the most widely available and commonly used modern editions of the *En Yaaqov.* Also note that the *Bavli* pagination postdates ibn Ḥabib and follows the standard editions of the *Bavli* published by Romm. Ibn Ḥabib did not have access to an edition of the Talmud with standardized page numbers.

All primary sources are capitalized using "headline style"; secondary sources follow the standard Society of Biblical Literature format, which uses "sentence style" capitalization.

Introduction

1. Isadore Twersky, "Talmudists, Philosophers, Kabbalists: The Quest for Spirituality in the Sixteenth Century," in *Jewish Thought in the Sixteenth Century,* ed. Bernard Dov Cooperman (Cambridge, MA: Harvard University Press, 1983), 432, and Moshe Halbertal, *People of the Book: Canon, Meaning, and Authority* (Cambridge, MA: Harvard University Press, 1997), 101–3.

2. Note that in the twelfth century, when Maimonides produced his legal code, the *Mishne Torah,* he wrote in his introduction that when a person reads "the written Torah and then reads this book, [he] knows from it the whole Oral Torah and needs no other book besides them." Such a statement suggests that the direct study of the Talmud was unnecessary. In addition, he describes the *Mishne Torah* as a successful and comprehensive summary of the Talmud that renders the study of the Talmud "a waste of time and of very little usage." See Halbertal, *People of the Book,* 104–5, where he cites letters drawn from *Iggerot Harambam,* 2 vols., ed. Y. Shailat (Jerusalem: Hotsaat Maaliyot, 1987), 1:257–59, 312–13, and 438–39. Also see Maimonides, *Mishnah im Perush Rabbenu Moshe ben Maimon,* 6 vols., trans. Joseph Kafiḥ (Jerusalem: Mossad Harav Kook, 1963), introduction.

3. Isaac Alfasi, *Hilkhot Rav Alfas [Hilkhot Harif],* ed. Nissan Zaks (Jerusalem: Mossad Harav Kook), 1969, 2 vols. This edition is based on the first printed edition

(Constantinople, 1509). *Hilkhot Harif* can be found in the back of standard printed editions of the Babylonian Talmud. See Leonard Robert Levy, "R. Yitzhaq Alfasi's Application of Principles of Adjudication in 'Halakhot Rabbati'" (Ph.D. diss., Jewish Theological Seminary, 2002), iv, for additional bibliographic information. For Asher ben Yeḥiel's *Piskei Harosh [Hilkhot Harosh]*, see the back of standard editions of the Babylonian Talmud. Also see Jacob ben Asher, *Tur* (Jerusalem, 1957–1960).

4. Halbertal, *People of the Book*, 105 (including n41), where he states that even if one argues that Maimonides did not view the *Mishne Torah* as a complete replacement for the Talmud, he believed that viewing the Talmud as the only document worthy of study was an error.

5. Menachem Kellner points to another aspect of Maimonides' critique of the Judaism of his day, sharing with Moshe Idel the notion that Maimonides' views developed in response to "proto-Kabbalistic" trends. Within this context, Kellner characterizes Maimonides as a reformer seeking to promote a new vision of Judaism. See Kellner, "Maimonides' Critique of the Rabbinic Culture of His Day," in *Rabbinic Culture and Its Critics: Jewish Authority, Dissent, and Heresy in Medieval and Early Modern Times*, ed. Daniel Frank and Matt Goldish (Detroit: Wayne State University Press, 2008), 84–85, 90. See also Moshe Idel, "Maimonides and Kabbalah," in *Studies in Maimonides*, ed. Isadore Twersky (Cambridge, MA: Harvard University Press, 1990), 34.

6. Menachem Kellner, *Maimonides' Confrontation with Mysticism* (Oxford: Littman Library of Jewish Civilization, 2006), 1.

7. See Moses Maimonides, *Guide for the Perplexed*, trans. Shlomo Pines (Chicago: University of Chicago Press, 1963), 3:51, regarding the idea that those who have studied the Talmud and not philosophy "make it" only as far as the courtyard in the parable of the palace and not to the palace itself. Also see Maimonides, *Mishne Torah, Yesode Hatorah*, 4:13, as referred to by Halbertal, *People of the Book*, 105–6.

8. See both Halbertal, *People of the Book*, 119–22, and Rachel Elior, "Messianic Expectations and Spiritualization of Religious Life in the Sixteenth Century," *Revue des Études Juives* 145 (1986): 37–41, for discussions of the development of Kabbalah in the aftermath of the expulsion and its attempt to negate the idea that the literal interpretation of the Torah and Mishnah had sufficient spiritual meaning.

9. See, for example, *EY Berakhot* (Salonika, 1516), vol. 1, 21b (= Jerusalem, 1961, vol. 1, 28a).

10. *EY* (Salonika, 1516), vol. 1, introduction (= Jerusalem, 1961, vol. 1, introduction).

11. The compiler of the anthology of Talmudic aggadah, *Haggadot Hatalmud* (Constantinople, 1511), which was published in Constantinople a few years prior to the *En Yaaqov*, did not make the same claims as ibn Ḥabib regarding the need for a work of aggadic material equivalent to that of Alfasi's code. The anthology was also a far more modest attempt to compile Talmudic aggadah than ibn Ḥabib's *En Yaaqov*. Ibn Ḥabib notes in his introduction that he intends to make a more substantive contribution to the study of aggadah than the compiler of *Haggadot*

Hatalmud. Its printing does, however, support the notion that others also believed a collection focused on Talmudic aggadah was necessary for the curriculum of Jewish study.

12. Marc Saperstein, *Decoding the Rabbis: A Thirteenth-Century Commentary on the Aggadah* (Cambridge, MA: Harvard University Press, 1980), vii.

13. See chapter 2, "The *En Yaaqov:* A Response to the Problems and Challenges of Aggadah," where I discuss this phenomenon in more detail.

14. Twersky, "Talmudists, Philosophers, Kabbalists," 437.

15. Jacob Neusner, *Judaism in Society: The Evidence of the Yerushalmi* (Chicago: University of Chicago Press, 1983), 25; Peter Brown, *Religion and Society in the Age of Saint Augustine* (New York: Harper & Row, 1972), 16.

16. Neusner, *Judaism in Society,* 25.

17. See Elior, "Messianic Expectations and Spiritualization," 35nn1–3, where she bases her observations on the research of Yitzhak Baer, A. Z. Aescoli, Haim Hillel Ben-Sasson, and Gershom Scholem. She also points to the postexpulsion writings of Isaac Caro, Joseph Hayon, and Isaac Abarbanel as examples of this phenomenon.

18. See Yosef Hayim Yerushalmi, "Exile and Expulsion in Jewish History," in *Crisis and Creativity in the Spanish World: 1391–1648,* ed. Benjamin R. Gampel (New York: Columbia University Press, 1997), 21, and Hava Tirosh-Samuelson, "The Ultimate End of Human Life in Postexpulsion Philosophic Literature," in *Crisis and Creativity in the Spanish World: 1391–1648,* ed. Benjamin R. Gampel (New York: Columbia University Press, 1997), 225, 354–55n10.

19. Yosef Hayim Yerushalmi, *Zakhor: Jewish History and Jewish Memory* (Seattle: University of Washington Press, 1982), 60.

20. Yerushalmi, "Exile and Expulsion," 21.

21. Yerushalmi, "Exile and Expulsion," 21 (note that Abarbanel was commenting on Is. 43); Yerushalmi, *Zakhor,* 59. The sense of inconsolable despair felt by many of the exiles is also clearly expressed by Abarbanel's son, Judah, who preferred to speak through the genre of poetry in "The Travails of Time." See Judah Abarbanel, *Sefer Havikkuaḥ* (Lyck, 1871), 6–11 (repr. in *Mivḥar hashirah haivrit beitalyah,* ed. Jefim Hayim Schirman [Berlin, 1934], 216–22); Raymond P. Scheindlin, "Judah Abarbanel to His Son," *Judaism* 41 (1992): 190–99; Hava Tirosh-Samuelson, "The Ultimate End of Human Life," 223–25 (who quotes this poem as well).

22. Neusner, *Judaism and Society,* 26.

23. See chapter 1, "From Spain to the Ottoman Empire: The Life and Contexts of Jacob ibn Ḥabib," for a larger discussion of ibn Ḥabib's role as a community rabbi in Salonika.

24. Yerushalmi, "Exile and Expulsion," 21.

25. Yerushalmi, *Zakhor,* 59, in his discussion about the interest Jews took in writing historiographies following the Spanish expulsion, makes the argument that there was a "highly articulated consciousness among the generations following the expulsion from Spain that something unprecedented had taken place, not just that an abrupt end had come to a great and venerable Jewry, but something beyond that."

26. See chapter 4, "From Talmudic Text to Theology: The Search for God, the Search for Home," for a larger discussion of this matter. More specifically, see ibn Ḥabib's discussion of Rabbi Ḥanina ben Dosa and the role individuals play in ensuring that God does not punish them for wrongdoing in *b. Ber.* 34b; *EY Berakhot* (Salonika, 1516), vol. 1, section 89, 38a–b (= Jerusalem, 1961, vol. 1, section 98, 69b–71a).

27. *EY* (Salonika, 1516), vol. 1, introduction (= Jerusalem, 1961, vol. 1, introduction).

28. *EY Berakhot* (Salonika, 1516), vol. 1, section 1, 7a (= Jerusalem, 1961, vol. 1, section 3, 2a–b).

29. *EY Berakhot* (Salonika, 1516), vol. 1, section 4, 9b–10a (= Jerusalem, 1961, vol. 1, section 8, 7a).

30. See, for example, ibn Ḥabib's comment on the Talmud's discussion of the inclusion of Ps. 145 (*b. Ber.* 4b) in one's daily prayers: *EY Berakhot* (Salonika, 1516), vol. 1, section 4, 9b–10a (= Jerusalem, 1961, vol. 1, section 8, 7a).

31. Hava Tirosh-Rothschild, *Between Worlds: The Life and Thought of Rabbi David ben Judah Messer Leon* (Albany: State University of New York Press, 1991), 88.

32. See Haim Hillel Ben-Sasson, "*Dor gole sefarad al atsmo,*" *Zion* 26 (1961): 59, and Yitzhak Baer, *A History of the Jews in Christian Spain,* 2 vols. (Philadelphia: Jewish Publication Society, 1992), 2:115, 131. Also see Warren Zev Harvey, "Hasdai Crescas's Critique of the Theory of the Acquired Intellect" (Ph.D. diss., Columbia University, 1973), 18–19, where he notes that following the travail of 1391 in Spain, Ḥasdai Crescas blamed "the Greek (Aristotle)" for "darken[ing] the eyes of Israel" and thereby weakening the Jews' commitment to Judaism.

33. See *EY Berakhot* (Salonika, 1516), vol. 1, section 68, 32b (= Jerusalem, 1961, vol. 1, section 77, 55a–b).

34. See Elior, "Messianic Expectations and Spiritualization," 37, 41, where she argues that Kabbalah, in the aftermath of the expulsion, represented a commitment to the spiritualization of religion and a rejection of the reliance on rationalism to interpret the Torah. Ibn Ḥabib, who was also committed to the spiritualization of Judaism, chose a different approach; he was not drawn to Kabbalah.

35. See chapter 4, "From Talmudic Text to Theology: The Search for God, the Search for Home," where I discuss the texts drawn from ibn Ḥabib's commentary that deal with these issues in detail.

36. Menachem Kellner, *Dogma in Medieval Jewish Thought: From Maimonides to Abravanel* (Oxford: Littman Library of Jewish Civilization, 1986), 1–9; Kellner, *Must a Jew Believe Anything?* (Oxford: Littman Library of Jewish Civilization, 1999), 13n2; Kenneth Seeskin, "Judaism and the Linguistic Interpretation of Jewish Faith," in *Studies in Jewish Philosophy: Collected Essays of the Academy for Jewish Philosophy, 1980–1985,* ed. Norbert Samuelson (Lanham, MD: University Press of America, 1987), 215–34.

37. Hava Tirosh-Rothschild, "Jewish Philosophy on the Eve of Modernity," in *Routledge History of World Philosophies: History of Jewish Philosophy,* ed. Daniel H. Frank and Oliver Leaman (London: Routledge, 1996), 509–10.

38. See, for example, the following texts, where ibn Ḥabib stresses the impor-

tance of believing in these principles of faith: that God exists, *EY Berakhot* (Salonika, 1516), vol. 1, section 79, 35a–b (note that two pages are numbered 36; this is the first of the two pages and should be marked 35) (= Jerusalem, 1961, vol. 1, 63b); that one must believe that God is one without relying on philosophical proofs, *EY Berakhot* (Salonika, 1516), vol. 1, section 52, 25a–b (= Jerusalem, 1961, vol. 1, section 56, 38b); that God has no intervening helpers, *EY Berakhot* (Salonika, 1516), vol. 1, section 110, 45a (= Jerusalem, 1961, vol. 1, section 123, 89a); that the Torah is from heaven, *EY Shabbat* (Salonika, 1516), vol. 1, section 2, 61a–b (note that this page is numbered 61 but should be page 63, due to some extra pages that are not numbered) (= Jerusalem, 1961, vol. 1, section 2, 2b), and *EY Megillah* (Salonika 1516), vol. 1, 152a (=Jerusalem, 1961, vol. 2, 2a); that God punishes transgressors and rewards the righteous, *EY Berakhot* (Salonika, 1516), vol. 1, section 127, 48b (= Jerusalem, 1961, vol. 1, section 139, 103a); that the messiah will come, *EY Berakhot* (Salonika, 1516), vol. 1, section 5, 54b–55a (*Yerushalmi* section) (= Jerusalem, 1961, vol. 1, section 5, 5a); that one will be resurrected, *EY Berakhot* (Salonika, 1516), vol. 1, section 35, 21a–b (= Jerusalem, 1961, vol. 1, section 39, 28a); that God created the world *ex-nihilo*, *EY Berakhot* (Salonika, 1516), vol. 1, section 1, 7b (= Jerusalem, 1961, vol. 1, section, 3, 3b), and *EY Shabbat* (Salonika, 1516), section 4, 61b (= Jerusalem, 1961, vol. 1, section 3, 5a); that God performs miracles, *EY Shabbat* (Salonika, 1516), vol. 1, section 4, 61b (note that this page is numbered 61 but should be page 63, due to some extra pages that are not numbered) (= Jerusalem, 1961, vol. 1, section 3, 5a).

39. For example, in *EY Berakhot* (Salonika, 1516), vol. 1, section 59, 27b–28a (= Jerusalem, 1961, vol. 1, section 68, 45b), ibn Ḥabib mentions the importance of performing mitsvot simply for the sake of doing them. Note also that folio 27 is mistakenly marked as folio 28. I am referring to it here as 27, despite this error.

40. See Tirosh-Rothschild, *Between Worlds*, 145.

41. Abraham Shalom, *Neve Shalom* (Venice, 1525), is one exception, as it was arranged as a commentary to the aggadot of the Talmud. The nature of Shalom's commentary, however, differs from that of ibn Ḥabib. Shalom was committed to harmonizing the Arabic-Aristotelian philosophical school with traditional Jewish beliefs, whereas Ibn Ḥabib did not focus on this type of synthesis. Rather, he chose to move away from the rationalist program of his predecessors. See Herbert A. Davidson, *The Philosophy of Abraham Shalom: A Fifteenth-Century Exposition and Defense of Maimonides* (Berkeley: University of California Press, 1964), and Kellner, *Dogma*, 157–59.

42. *EY* (Salonika, 1516), vol. 1, introduction (= Jerusalem, 1961, vol. 1, introduction).

43. See, for example, *EY Berakhot* (Salonika, 1516), vol. 1, section 52, 25a–b (= Jerusalem, 1961, vol. 1, section 56, 37b–38b).

44. Hava Tirosh-Samuelson, "The Ultimate End of Human Life," 227–28.

45. Joseph Hacker, "The Intellectual Activity of the Jews of the Ottoman Empire during the Sixteenth and Seventeenth Centuries," in *Jewish Thought in the Seventeenth Century,* ed. Isadore Twersky and Bernard Septimus (Cambridge, MA: Harvard University Press, 1987), 102–10.

46. Hacker, "Intellectual Activity," 107–9.

47. At the end of his work on *Seder Zeraim*, Ibn Ḥabib states that many people have purchased quires and desire a similar work on *Seder Moed*. They do not want to purchase a full volume unless it contains the aggadic material from *Seder Moed*, and ibn Ḥabib regrets that he has not been able to provide a work similar in scope on the aggadot found within *Seder Moed*. See *EY* (Salonika, 1516), vol. 1, 63b (after the last citation from and commentary on the *Yerushalmi*) (= Jerusalem, 1961, vol. 1, 15a) (second pagination after the last citation from and commentary on the end of *Seder Zeraim*).

48. Joseph Hacker, "Intellectual Activity," 11–114. Note that the following books were published prior to the production of the *En Yaaqov* in Salonika: a holiday prayer book (*Maḥzor*) (Salonika, 1500); the Torah (Salonika, 1510); a midrashic commentary on the book of Psalms, *Midrash Tehillim* (Salonika, 1515); *Ketuvim*, with Rashi's commentary (Salonika, 1515); and Solomon Almoli, *Pitron Ḥalomot* (Salonika, 1515). Interestingly, tractate *Berakhot* was not published in Salonika until after the printing of the *En Yaaqov* in 1521; see Yeshayahu Vinograd, *Otsar hasefer haivri*, 2 vols. (Jerusalem: Institute for Computerized Hebrew Bibliography, 1993–95), 2:666. A printing of the Babylonian Talmud in its entirety was not completed until 1520–23 in Venice. In keeping with the surge of interest in aggadic commentary that occurred during the sixteenth century, after the death of Jacob ibn Ḥabib, Samuel Jaffee Ashkenazi wrote commentaries on *Midrash Rabbah* (*Yefe Toar* [Venice, 1597–1606, on Genesis and Exodus; Constantinople, 1648, on Leviticus], *Yefe Anaf* [Frankfurt, 1696, on the *megillot*], and *Yefe Qol* [Smyrna, 1739, also on the megillot]), as well as a commentary on the aggadot of the *Yerushalmi* (*Yefe Mare* [Constantinople, 1587]).

49. A collection of Talmudic aggadah titled *Haggadot Hatalmud*, which was also arranged in accordance with the order of the aggadot found in the Talmud, was printed in Constantinople in 1511. It never achieved the kind of popularity attained by the *En Yaaqov*. In fact, I have not been able to locate any reprinting of *Haggadot Hatalmud*, whereas the *En Yaaqov* was reprinted more than one hundred times.

50. Hacker, "Intellectual Activity," 113–14.

51. The second volume of the *En Yaaqov* was published in 1522. The next printed edition was not produced until 1595 in Salonika. Another edition was printed in 1620. See Marvin Heller, *The Printing of the Talmud* (Brooklyn: Im Hasefer, 1992), 244.

52. See Hans-Jürgen Becker, "Die Yerushalmi-Midrashim der Ordnung Zeraim in Ya'akov ibn Ḥabib's *En Ya'aqov*," *Frankfurter Judaistische Beiträge* 18 (1990): 77, who also notes that manuscripts of the *En Yaaqov* dating to the period prior to its first printed edition are not available presently.

53. Note that there are some minor differences in pagination between the *En Yaaqov* (Salonika, 1516) printed edition that I used in the Rare Book Room at the Jewish Theological Seminary Library and the digitized edition that can be found on the website of the Jewish National Library Digitized Book Depository. I cite from the 1516 edition found in the Rare Book Room at JTS.

54. See *En Yaaqov* (Vilna, 1883; repr. Jerusalem, 1961; repr. Jerusalem, 2000), *"Haqdamat hamadpisim."*

55. It seems that ibn Ḥabib had another collection of Talmudic aggadah, which he does not name. I am assuming this was a manuscript collection. Ibn Ḥabib relies on it to draw aggadic material from the *Yerushalmi* due to his inability to find editions of this Talmud. See ibn Ḥabib's comments at the end of *Seder Zeraim, EY* (Salonika, 1516), vol. 1, 60b (= Jerusalem, 1961, vol. 1, 15a).

56. See Shamma Friedman, *"Sippur rav kahana verabbi yohanan* (b. B. Qam. *117a–b) veanaf nusah genizah hamburg,"* *Bar-Ilan* 30–31 (2006): 409–90 (refer specifically to the appendix). Also see Stephen Wald, "Bavli pesaḥim pereq elu overin: Mahadurah madait uviur meqif" (Ph.D. diss., Hebrew University, 1994), 418–20.

57. Ibn Ḥabib began to compile the *En Yaaqov* late in his life, as he notes in his introduction. See *EY* (Salonika, 1516), introduction.

58. In his introduction to the *En Yaaqov,* ibn Ḥabib describes his access to the library of the Ben Banvanest family of Salonika. This family figured prominently among wealthy scholars in this city. They not only collected books and manuscripts but also hired scribes to copy some of Judaism's seminal works. Ibn Ḥabib writes: "For a long time I thought to perform such a deed [compile the *En Yaaqov*], but only now do I do so, because I have not had access to all six orders of the Mishnah and the Talmud with all of the commentaries, and it was almost impossible for me to collect all of the necessary books until God led me to this place, Salonika, and I found this multitude of books when I arrived at the home of the honorable scholar, Don Judah, the son of the pious and exalted prince, Don Abraham Ben Banvenest of blessed memory, who was honored in the courts and palaces of kings, but distinguished himself in the service of the Lord." See Hacker, "Intellectual Activity," 104–5, and *"Hamidrash hasefardi: Sifriyah tsiburit yehudit,"* in *Rishonim veaharonim: Mehkarim betoldot yisrael mugashim leavraham grossman,* ed. Joseph R. Hacker, Yosef Kaplan, and B. Z. Kedar, 281–83 (Jerusalem: Zalman Shazar Center, 2010). Also see M. Molcho, *"Bate eqed sefarim,"* *Maḥberet 2* (1954), nos. 23–24.

59. Wald also argues that when ibn Ḥabib worked on tractate *EY Pesaḥim,* he drew from the Oxford manuscript of the *Bavli.* Wald, *Bavli pesaḥim,* 420.

60. Ibn Ḥabib writes that he was working directly with the printer, carefully checking his work for errors. See *EY* (Salonika, 1516), vol. 1, 203 (this page can be found immediately before the first index at the end of volume 1). According to Joseph Hacker, ibn Ḥabib corrected mistakes in printed quires, and Gedaliah republished them with corrections. This is why, as Hacker has observed, 1516 editions of the *En Yaaqov* exhibit minor textual discrepancies. Hacker has not yet published these observations. (Note that Hacker spoke about these observations at the Manfred R. Lehmann Memorial Master Workshop in the History of the Jewish Book, 2006, which took place at the Herbert D. Katz Center for Advanced Judaic Studies, University of Pennsylvania.)

61. Ibn Ḥabib's work includes a limited amount of aggadic material drawn from the *Yerushalmi* on the following tractates: *Berakhot, Peah, Kilayim, Shabbat, Pesaḥim, Sheqalim, Yoma, Rosh Hashanah, Taanit,* and *Ḥagigah.* He invites his readers to correct the texts he drew from the *Yerushalmi,* in the event that they were to

come across manuscripts or printed editions better than the ones available to him. Ibn Ḥabib admits to being in possession of faulty texts of the *Yerushalmi* and to his inability to find a better version of it. He only had one tractate of the *Yerushalmi* and relied on another work, which he does not name, that contained a collection of "midrashim" from both the *Bavli* and the *Yerushalmi*. This enabled him to cull some aggadic texts from the *Yerushalmi* that were found in *Seder Zeraim* and *Seder Moed*. See ibn Ḥabib's comments at the end of *Seder Zeraim, EY* (Salonika, 1516), vol. 1, 60b (= Jerusalem, 1961, vol. 1, 15a [top]). Also note that this page is erroneously numbered as page 60, but it is actually page 62, due to some extra pages that were not numbered correctly. Also see Samuel Jaffe Ashkenazi, *Yefe Toar,* introduction, 2a, where he complains about the inadequate anthology of material that ibn Ḥabib drew from the *Yerushalmi* (cited by Jacob Elbaum, "*Yalqut Shim'oni* and the Medieval Midrashic Anthology," *Prooftexts* 17 [1997]: 133–47, repr. in *The Anthology in Jewish Literature,* ed. David Stern [Oxford: Oxford University Press, 2004], 173n16). In addition, see Becker, "Die Yerushalmi-Midrashim der Ordnung Zeraim in Ya'akov ibn Ḥabib's *En Ya'aqov,*" 71–83, where he discusses the influence ibn Ḥabib had on Solomon Sirillo (d. 1558), who wrote a seminal commentary on the *Yerushalmi.* Becker highlights the difficulties of ibn Ḥabib's endeavor as the community was not studying the *Yerushalmi* seriously in Salonika during ibn Ḥabib's day, which, he notes, accounts for the lack of manuscripts. Sirillo relied on the texts that ibn Ḥabib drew from the *Yerushalmi* and which appeared in the *En Yaaqov.* He also claimed ibn Ḥabib as his teacher (73–75).

62. Before ibn Ḥabib's anthology of aggadot found in tractate *Megillah,* his section numbers virtually end. The last tractate in which one finds carefully ordered section numbers is tractate *Taanit.* This is the mark of a compiler who, nearing the end of his life, could not work fast enough to complete the work he had begun. See ibn Ḥabib's comments at the end of *Seder Zeraim, EY* (Salonika, 1516), vol. 1, 60b (= Jerusalem, 1961, vol. 1, 15a), where he informs his readers that his work on the tractates of *Seder Moed* will not measure up to the work that he did on tractate *Berakhot.* Also note that this page is erroneously numbered as page 60 but should be page 62, due to some extra pages that were not numbered correctly. *Yerushalmi* passages have section numbers.

63. See ibn Ḥabib's comments at the end of *Seder Zeraim, EY* (Salonika, 1516), vol. 1, 60b (= Jerusalem, 1961, vol. 1, 15a, second pagination). Also note that this page is mistakenly numbered as page 60, but is actually page 62, due to some extra pages that were not numbered correctly.

64. See Levi ibn Ḥabib, *Sheelot Uteshuvot* (Venice, 1565), #126, where he states that there are many things in the aggadot that are not fitting to speak about and should not be written down. Presenting *b. B. Metsia* 54a as an example, he notes that such aggadot have little purpose and that few delight in those similar to it. Also see Jacob Elbaum, *Lehavin divre ḥakhamim: Mivḥar divre mavo laaggadah ulemidrash mishel ḥakhame yeme habenayim* (Jerusalem: Bialik Institute, 2000), 21n13.

65. Joseph Hacker, *"Rabbi yaaqov ibn ḥabib: Lidmutah shel hahanhagah hayehudit besaloniqi bereshit hameah ha-16," Proceedings of the Sixth Congress of Jewish Studies* 2 (1975): 117–26.

66. See Susan Handelman, "The 'Torah' of Criticism and the Criticism of Torah: Recuperating the Pedagogical Moment," in *Interpreting Judaism in a Postmodern Age,* ed. Steven Kepnes (New York: New York University Press, 1996), 228–32; George Steiner, *Real Presences* (Chicago: University of Chicago Press, 1989), 30.

Chapter 1

1. Note that the definition of the term "converso" has been the subject of debate. Some argue for a more limited definition, claiming that the term refers only to those who were coerced to convert to Christianity and who, in spite of this, maintained their connections to Judaism in secret. This definition is rooted in the Hebrew word *anus,* which means "forced." Others claim that the term refers in a broader sense to anyone forced to adopt another religion and does not imlpy that these converts practiced Judaism. See Shaul Regev, "The Attitude Towards the Conversos in Fifteenth and Sixteenth Century Jewish Thought," *Revue des Études Juives* 156:1–2 (1997): 118–19. Jose Faur notes that the converso population can be divided into four classes: Jews who wanted to be Christian and converted voluntarily, converts who wanted to be Jewish in secret with no sincere relationship to Christianity, those who wanted to be both Jewish and Christian, and those who wanted to be neither. See Faur, "Four Classes of Conversos: A Typological Study," *Revue des Études Juives* 149:1–3 (1990): 113. Also see Jose Faur, *In the Shadow of History* (Albany: State University of New York Press, 1992), 9–40. For the purposes of this discussion, I have adopted a broad definition of the term *converso* that includes those who converted voluntarily and those who converted by force. I also assume that the commitments of the conversos to Judaism ran the gamut from sincere attachments to Judaism to full-fledged conversions to Christianity.

2. See Joseph Hacker, "The Sephardim in the Ottoman Empire in the Sixteenth Century," in *Moreshet Sepharad: The Sephardi Legacy,* 2 vols., ed. Haim Beinart (Jerusalem: Magnes Press, 1992), 2:109–13. Also see Hacker, "*Rabbi yaaqov ibn ḥabib,*" 117

3. Haim Beinart, "The Judaizing Movement in the Order of San Jeronimo in Castile," *Scripta Hierosolymitana* 7 (1961): 183–88.

4. Yirmiyahu Yovel, *The Other Within: The Marranos—Split Identity and Emerging Modernity* (Princeton, NJ: Princeton University Press, 2009), 141. See Miriam Bodian, "'Men of the Nation': The Shaping of Converso Identity in Early Modern Europe," *Past and Present* 143 (1994): 53. See Haim Beinart, "The Great Conversion and the Converso Problem," in *Moreshet Sepharad: The Sephardi Legacy,* 2 vols., ed. Haim Beinart (Jerusalem: Magnes Press, 1992), 1:352–53, and Beinart, "The Conversos and Their Fate," in *Spain and the Jews: The Sephardi Experience 1492 and After,* ed. Elie Kedourie (London: Thames & Hudson, 1992), 92. Beinart argues that mass conversions did not "open society's gates to the converted." Spanish Christian society did not create the means to assimilate these converts; they were not accepted as equals. Converts, therefore, resorted to writing treatises in an attempt to combat an "anti-converso ideology" promoted by Christians who held prominent positions in the Iberian political and religious hierarchy. Also see David Nirenberg, "Enmity and Assimilation: Jews, Christians, and Converts in Medieval

Spain," *Common Knowledge* 9:1 (2003): 138, who questions why Spain struggled, at first, to assimilate their minorities only to resist that assimilation once they succeeded. Also see the Spanish historian Carlos Carrete Parrondo, for a different view of the conversos: "Jews, Castilian Conversos, and the Inquisition: 1482–1492," in *The Jews of Spain and the Expulsion of 1492*, ed. Moshe Lazar and Stephen Haliczer (Lancaster, CA: Labyrinthos, 1997), 147–51.

5. There is no unified position in contemporary scholarship regarding the extent to which conversos maintained their Jewish identities. In *A History of the Marranos* (New York: Hermon Press, 1974), Cecil Roth describes the inner religious life of the conversos, noting that they were markedly Jewish. In addition, basing his conclusions on inquisitorial files, Haim Beinart argues that Jews regretted their adherence to Christianity and wished to return to Judaism. See Beinart, *The Expulsion of the Jews from Spain,* trans. Jeffrey Green (Oxford: Oxford University Press, 2002), 19. On the other hand, Jane Gerber notes that "like any group, the New Christians included people with a variety of motives, beliefs and approaches to life." See Jane Gerber, *The Jews of Spain: A History of the Sephardic Experience* (New York: Free Press, 1992), 123. Miriam Bodian argues that converso self-perception and loyalties to Judaism were far more complex due to the "mobilization of general human strategies in dealing with conflict, stigma, and survival." See Bodian, " 'Men of the Nation,' " 50. Also see David Graizbord, "Religion and Ethnicity among 'Men of the Nation': Toward a Realistic Interpretation," *Jewish Social Studies* 15:1 (2008): 33–37, for another review of the scholarship on the conversos.

6. See Richard Popkin, "Marranos, New Christians and the Beginnings of Modern Anti-Trinitarianism," in *Jews and Conversos at the Time of the Expulsion,* ed. Yom Tov Assis and Yosef Kaplan (Jerusalem: Zalman Shazar Center for Jewish History, 1999), 152–53.

7. For example, when a converso was put on trial in Valencia in 1486, he informed his inquisitors that he believed "firmly and completely" in both Judaism and Christianity. In fact, this was true for many conversos. They developed an alternative type of faith whereby Judaism was mingled with Christianity, blurring the boundaries between these two religions. Roberto Bonfil, "Dubious Crimes in Sixteenth-Century Italy: Rethinking the Relations between Jews, Christians, and *Conversos* in Pre-modern Europe," in *The Jews of Spain and the Expulsion of 1492,* ed. Moshe Lazar and Stephen Haliczer (Lancaster, CA: Labyrinthos, 1997), 307–8. Also see Bodian, " 'Men of the Nation,' " 49–51.

8. Bodian, " 'Men of the Nation,' " 52–53.

9. According to Roberto Bonfil, "The more we dig through the numberless archival dossiers of trials related to the conversos, such as those published by Haim Beinart for fifteenth-century Spain or by P. D. Ioly Zorattrini for sixteenth-century Venice, the more we realize how ambiguous their condition was." The rich diversity of converso portraits indicates how distinct the conversos were both from one another and from Jews who claimed to represent "normative Judaism" of the time. They offered different solutions to the question of self-definition by introducing the right of choice, thereby breaking conventional models of religious affiliation. See

Bonfil, "Dubious Crimes," 305, 308. See Yovel, *The Other Within,* 126–36, for accounts of the lives of specific male as well as female conversos.

10. Yosef Hayim Yerushalmi, *From Spanish Court to Italian Ghetto: Isaac Cardoso, A Study in Seventeenth-Century Marranism and Jewish Apologetics* (Seattle: University of Washington Press, 1981), 28.

11. David Nirenberg, "Mass Conversion and Genealogical Mentalities: Jews and Christians in Fifteenth-Century Spain," *Past and Present* 174 (2002): 6–7. In the face of this destabilization, Nirenberg argues, the conversos created new forms of communal identity by "rereading their own traditions and those of their rivals." Also see Nirenberg, "Enmity and Assimilation," 140.

12. Graizbord, "Religion and Ethnicity," 49.

13. Nirenberg, "Mass Conversion," 13.

14. David Graizbord, *Souls in Dispute: Converso Identities in Iberia and the Jewish Diaspora, 1580–1700* (Philadelphia: University of Pennsylvania Press, 2004), 2.

15. See Rashi's responsum regarding the marital status of women whose husbands were converted during the Crusades in Jacob Rader Marcus, *The Jew in the Medieval World* (New York: Athenuem, 1938), 301–2. Also see Jacob Katz, "*Af al pi sheḥata yisrael hu,*" *Tarbiz* 27 (1958): 203–17.

16. See Abraham Halkin and David Hartman, *Crisis and Leadership: Epistles of Maimonides* (Philadelphia: Jewish Publication Society, 1985), 29, for a translation of Maimonides' "Epistle on Martyrdom." Also see Nirenberg, "Mass Conversion," 19–20.

17. See Solomon ibn Adret, *Sheelot Uteshuvot* (Ashdod and Jerusalem: Mir, 2004), 1:162, 5:66. See David Novak, *The Election of Israel: The Idea of a Chosen People* (Cambridge: Cambridge University Press, 1995), 196–97; Nirenberg, "Mass Conversion," 8.

18. Graizbord, "Religion and Ethnicity," 35.

19. Ibn Adret, *Sheelot Uteshuvot,* 1:162.

20. Solomon ben Simon Duran (1400–1467) of Algiers, the son of the Spanish refugee Simon ben Tsemaḥ Duran, ruled that even the uncircumcised sons of converts (or second- and third-generation converts) who did not know anything about Judaism were still Jews. Simon ben Tsemaḥ's grandson followed suit, arguing that "uncircumcised is circumcised." Nirenberg, "Mass Conversion," 19–21 (including nn46–48).

21. Nirenberg, "Mass Conversion," 21.

22. Nirenberg, "Mass Conversion," 37–38.

23. Nirenberg, "Mass Conversion," 38.

24. See Simha Assaf, "*Anuse sefarad ufortugal besifrut hateshuvot,*" *Zion* 5 (1932–33): 19–60; Hirsch Jakob Zimmels, *Die Marranen in der rabbinischen Literatur: Forschungen und Quellen zur Geschichte und Kulturgeschichte der Anussim* (Berlin: R. Mass, 1932); Ben-Sasson, "*Dor gole sefarad al atsmo,*" 23–64; and see Benzion Netanyahu, *The Marranos of Spain: From the Late Fifteenth to the Early Sixteenth Century* (New York: American Academy of Jewish Research, 1966), for a more extensive discussion regarding the attitudes of Spanish rabbis toward the conversos.

25. Joel ibn Shu'eib, *Nora Tehillot* (Salonika, 1568), 155a–158a; Joseph Jabetz, *Magen Avot* (Leipzig, 1855), 72b; Isaac Caro, *Toledot Yitshaq* (Mantua, 1558; repr. Amsterdam, 1708, and Jerusalem: H. Vagshal, 1993–94), introduction and 118b; Isaac Abarbanel, *Perush al Neviim Aharonim* (Jerusalem: Torah Vedaat, 1956), Is. 44:5, 211a–213a. See specifically Netanyahu, *Marranos,* 157–80.

26. See Abraham Saba, *Tseror Hamor* (Warsaw, 1879; repr. Bene Beraq: Hekhal Hasefer, 1989–90), on Deut. 6:4–5. In the Warsaw edition of *Tseror Hamor* (1879), this comment can be found on 15a–b. Indeed, in Saba's commentary on these biblical verses that form the prayer *Shema,* he notes that Jews should look to the image of the Hasmoneans and, like the woman and her seven sons in 2 Macc. 7, sacrifice their lives rather than transgress God's precepts. In addition, see Caro, *Toledot Yitshaq,* 118b, who also argues that Jews should choose to martyr themselves. See Netanyahu's discussion, *Marranos,* 157–58; see Joseph Hacker, "'Im shakhahnu shem elohenu venifros kappenu leel zar': Gilgulah shel parshanut al reqa hametsiut bisfarad biyme habenayim," *Zion* 57 (1992): 264–72. See Miriam Bodian, *Dying in the Law of Moses: Crypto-Jewish Martyrdom in the Iberian World* (Bloomington: Indiana University Press, 2007).

27. See Ben-Sasson, *"Dor gole sefarad al atsmo,"* 38 (regarding ibn Shu'eib) and 40–41 (regarding Isaac Caro). See Hacker, "'Im shakhahnu,'" 265–68. In this article Hacker indicates that, beginning in the 1480s, there was a recognizable shift in Spanish Jewish attitudes toward martyrdom. Scriptural passages such as Ps. 44:19–23, which had been used in the past to invoke Jews' loyalty to God even to the point of martyrdom, were now used to reflect on their failure to resist conversion and to embrace God's covenant. See Bodian, *Dying in the Law of Moses,* 9.

28. Regev, "Attitude Towards the Conversos," 117–34. Also see Nirenberg, "Mass Conversion," 13.

29. See Ben-Sasson's references to the idea that Jews worshiped God in their hearts, *"Dor gole sefarad al atsmo,"* 36. See Hacker, "'Im shakhahnu,'" 265–66, and his discussion of the perspective of Isaac Arama found in *Aqedat Yitshaq* (Venice, 1547), 73, 215a. At an earlier point, Simon ben Tsemah Duran, who fled from Spain in the wake of the massacres of 1391 and resettled in Majorca, noted in a responsum that it was impossible to know the secrets of the human heart, and because of this the conversos should not be judged harshly for refusing to leave Spain when faced with decrees of forced conversion. See Nirenberg, "Mass Conversion," 20–21 (including nn46–48).

30. Ben-Sasson, *"Dor gole sefarad al atsmo,"* 37–38.

31. Isaac Abarbanel, *Mashmia Yeshuah* (Offenbach, 1767), 54r (repr. Tel Aviv, 1960), 434, as discussed by Regev, "Attitude Towards the Conversos," 120–27. Also note that even those who regretted their transgressions at a later time and returned to God in a devoted manner could be redeemed. Also see Yerushalmi, *From Spanish Court to Italian Ghetto,* 29, especially n41. Yerushalmi cites Abarbanel's statement in *Mashmia Yeshuah,* where Abarbanel argues that no outward signs of Jewish observance were to be expected from conversos; instead they fulfilled their commitment to God through worshiping him "with all their heart and all their

soul" (Deut. 6:2).

32. Yerushalmi, *From Spanish Court to Italian Ghetto*, 1, who quotes ibn Verga.

33. Viktor Gecas, "Value Identities, Self-Motives, and Social Movements," in *Self, Identity, and Social Movements,* ed. Sheldon Stryker, Timothy J. Owens, and Robert W. White (Minneapolis: University of Minnesota Press, 2000), 94–95. Also see Ram Ben-Shalom, "The Typology of the Converso in Isaac Abravanel's Biblical Exegesis," *Jewish History* 23:3 (2009): 281–92.

34. This is Ben-Sasson's descriptive term, *"Dor gole sefarad al atsmo,"* 42.

35. In keeping with the Kabbalistic notion that each divine commandment performed by a Jew generates a cloth that covers a Jew's soul in the afterworld, Saba argued that circumcision could generate the entire cloth, thereby elevating that one mitsvah to the level of the performance of all of them. See Abraham Gross, *Iberian Jewry, from Twilight to Dawn: The World of Rabbi Abraham Saba* (Leiden: E. J. Brill, 1995), 108–9.

36. See Abraham Saba, *Eshkol Hakofer* (Venice, 1567; repr. Bartfeld, 1907), 23a. Also see Ben-Sasson, *"Dor gole sefarad al atsmo,"* 42; Revel, "Attitude Towards the Conversos," 129; Gerson D. Cohen, "[On] Ben Zion Netanyahu, *The Marranos of Spain* (1966)," *Jewish Social Studies* 29 (1967): 184; and Abraham Gross, *Iberian Jewry,* 108–9.

37. See Gross, *Iberian Jewry,* 109–14, for a discussion regarding Saba and his attitude toward the conversos, which Gross argues was not entirely positive.

38. See, for example, Hacker, "'*Im shakhahnu,*'" 247–74; Gross, *Iberian Jewry,* 109–14.

39. See Natan Ophir, *"Qeriah hadashah beor hashem lerabbi hasdai crescas uveayat haanusim,"* *Proceedings of the Eleventh World Congress of Jewish Studies* (Jerusalem: World Union of Jewish Studies, 1994), 3:2, 41–47; Natan Ophir, *"Harav hasdai crescas kefarshan filosofi lemaamare hazal"* (Ph.D. diss., Hebrew University, 1993), 227–34, 251.

40. Ophir, *"Harav hasdai crescas,"* 244–56.

41. Ibn Ḥabib mentions that he relocated to the city of Lisbon in his introduction to the *En Yaaqov* (Salonika, 1516), when he recalls the beginnings of his relationship with the Hebrew printer who published the *En Yaaqov,* Judah Gedaliah.

42. See Yovel, *The Other Within,* 189–91.

43. Maria José Pimenta Ferro Tavares, "Expulsion or Integration? The Portuguese Jewish Problem," in *Crisis and Creativity in the Sephardic World,* ed. Benjamin Gampel (New York: Columbia University Press, 1997), 98.

44. Tavares, "Expulsion or Integration?" 98–99.

45. Tavares, "Expulsion or Integration?" 99–100.

46. Yosef Hayim Yerushalmi, *The Lisbon Massacre of 1506 and the Royal Image of Shevet Yehudah* (HUCA Supplements 1; Cincinnati: Hebrew Union College Press, 1976), 6. See also Yerushalmi, *From Spanish Court to Italian Ghetto,* 4–12; Alexandre Herculano, *History of the Origin and Establishment of the Inquisition in Portugal* (New York: Ktav, 1972), 121–24/253–56 (there are two paginations), and also see Yosef Hayim Yerushalmi's "Prolegomenon," 7–55, to this edition where

he discusses Herculano's contributions; Joseph Hacker, "*Lidemutam haruḥanit shel yehude sefarad besof hameah ha-15*," *Sefunot* n.s. 2 (1983): 29–38.

47. For a copy of Manuel's edict, see Meyer Kayserling, *Geschichte der Juden in Spanien und Portugal* (Berlin, 1861; repr., Hildesheim: Gerstenberg, 1978), 347–49. Also see Yovel, *The Other Within*, 193–94.

48. Tavares, "Expulsion or Integration?" 100.

49. Herculano, *History*, 123/255.

50. Yosef Hayim Yerushalmi, "A Jewish Classic in Portuguese Language," introduction to Samuel Usque, *Consolação às Tribulações de Israel*, 2 vols. (Lisbon: Fundação Calouste Gulbenkian, 1989), 1:19–28; Yerushalmi, *Lisbon Massacre*, 6; Hacker, "*Lidemutam haruḥanit*," 38; see Isaiah Tishby, "*Dape genizah miḥibbur meshiḥi-misti al gerushe sefarad ufortugal*," *Zion* 48 (1983): 90–93.

51. Abraham Saba, *Eshkol Hakofer* (Warsaw, 1879), Esther, introduction, 22. This translation is drawn from Gross, *Iberian Jewry*. There he notes that the additions found in the Parma manuscript are those of a scribe. (All parenthetical notes and bracketed interpolations here are according to Gross's text. Unless otherwise noted, all other interpolations throughout this book are my own.) Although this translation is based on the Warsaw printed edition (1879), Gross notes there are several extant manuscripts. They are listed in his appendix A, 179. There is also an earlier printed edition (Venice, 1567) on which Ben-Sasson relied in his article "*Dor gole sefarad al atsmo*." It is also interesting that in *Tseror Ḥamor*, Saba mentions that he believes his eventual release was a reward for the merit bestowed on the Jews through the martyrdom of Rabbi Simon Meme, who sacrificed himself in Lisbon in the wake of the events of 1497. See *Tseror Ḥamor* (Warsaw, 1879), Leviticus, 35a. See also Gross, *Iberian Jewry*, 31n49. For a more extensive discussion of this event, whereby a group of Jews were allowed to leave Lisbon in 1497, see Herculano, *History*, 124/256, who bases his conclusions on "Manuscript Memoirs of the Ajuda Library," folio 220, and also see Tishby, "*Dape genizah*," 90–93.

52. See Tishby, "*Dape genizah*," 90–93.

53. See Tishby, "*Dape genizah*," 91. Also see Abraham Gross, *Iberian Jewry*, 9–10, who points out, from documents written by ibn Ḥabib's contemporary, Abraham Saba, that Saba resisted conversion, was jailed, and was released six months later. The Portuguese king granted a boat to him and several others, and they traveled to El Kasar el Kabir. Tishby believes that ibn Ḥabib, like Saba, may have also traveled to North Africa; see Tishby, "*Dape genizah*," 93.

54. This source authored by ibn Ḥabib can be found in a collection of *teshuvot* written by Elijah Mizraḥi. See Mizraḥi, *Sheelot Uteshuvot* (Jerusalem: Darom, 1937), #47. This version of Mizraḥi's responsa is based on a collection published in Constantinople in 1560. Also see Tishby, "*Dape genizah*," 90–93.

55. Also see Hacker, "*Lidemutam haruḥanit*," 24, for his comments regarding Joseph Garson, a Castilian rabbinic scholar, who left Lisbon in 1497 and whose whereabouts were also unknown until he reached Salonika in 1500. It appears that there were Jews who found avenues of escape in 1497 despite attempts by the Portuguese monarch to prevent Jews from leaving. Also note that Tishby concurs with Herculano, *History*, 124/256.

56. Joseph Hacker, *"Lidemutam haruḥanit,"* 30; Shlomo Rosanes, *Divre yeme yisrael betogarmah,* 4 vols. (Tel Aviv: Dvir, 1930), 1:84 and Herculano, *History,* 121/252.

57. See Tishby, *"Dape genizah,"* 89, where he notes that Jacob ibn Ḥabib may have been able to escape with his son to Salonika following his son's conversion. He notes that it is also possible that they left separately.

58. Some argue that when Levi ibn Ḥabib writes that he was "not yet [of age to] deserve punishment in His [God's] court of law," he was referring to the fact that he was younger than thirteen. See Levi ibn Ḥabib, *Sheelot Uteshuvot* (esp. the section at the end of his collection of responsa titled *"Semikhat zeqenim o quntres hasemikhah"*), and Tishby, *"Dape genizah,"* 89–90. However, Levi ibn Ḥabib could have been even as old as nineteen, as sources indicate that one is not liable for one's actions in "God's heavenly court" until the age of twenty. This might explain how Levi ibn Ḥabib was able to teach as soon as he arrived in Salonika, as he may have been about nineteen or twenty (Tishby, *"Dape genizah,"* 89–90).

59. See Tishby, *"Dape genizah,"* 89–90, for his reading of Levi ibn Ḥabib's admission that he converted to Christianity, as found in Levi ibn Ḥabib, *Sheelot Uteshuvot,* 298a–299a.

60. Regarding those Jews who chose death in order to sanctify God's name rather than convert to Christianity, see Baer, *History,* 2:96. See also Bodian, *Dying in the Law of Moses,* 14–22.

61. Levi ibn Ḥabib, *Sheelot Uteshuvot,* 298a–299a (see the section at the end of his collection of responsa titled *"Semikhat zeqenim o quntres hasemikhah"*). Also see Rosanes, *Divre yeme yisrael betogarmah,* 1:84.

62. For a more extensive discussion on the controversy of restoring the Sanhedrin (Jewish court) and its authority not only to punish individuals for wrongdoings but also to ordain rabbis, see Jacob Katz, *"Maḥloket hasemikhah ben rabbi yaaqov berav veharalbaḥ (levi ibn Ḥabib),"* Zion 17 (1959): 28–45.

63. See Abraham Gross, *Iberian Jewry,* 8, where he discusses the mournful state of Abraham Saba following the forced conversion of his children and his ultimate separation from them.

64. See Mark Mazower, *Salonika: City of Ghosts* (New York: Alfred A. Knopf, 2004), 66–68. Also note that one could find conversos who returned to Judaism and then converted back to Christianity or who converted to Isalm. See Brian Pullan, *"'A Ship with Two Rudders': Righetto Marrano and the Inquisition in Venice,"* Historical Journal 20:1 (1977): 25–58. See Marc Baer, "Islamic Conversion Narratives on Women: Social Change and Gendered Religious Hierarchy in Early Modern Istanbul," *Gender and History* 16:2 (2004): 425–58. Although Graizbord, *Souls in Dispute,* 143–78, discusses a period following the death of ibn Ḥabib, he also underscores that conversos converted and then reconverted.

65. See Mizraḥi, *Sheelot Uteshuvot,* #66. In this responsum Mizraḥi notes that the Jewish community of Candia rejected Algazi because he discredited Jews before the Ottoman authorities. Whether he deserved this or not is unclear. However, in the minds of the Jews of his community, Algazi had performed an evil act. His

name was to be publicly defamed. In response, Mizraḥi warned against slandering one's fellow Jews, including his own son.

66. See Aryeh Shmuelevitz, "The Responsa as a Source for the History of the Ottoman Empire," in *Ottoman History and Society,* ed. Aryeh Shmuelevitz (Istanbul: Isis Press, 1999), 25–26.

67. *b. B. Metsia* 58b.

68. Mizraḥi, *Sheelot Uteshuvot,* #66 and #87.

69. Shmuelevitz, "Responsa as a Source," 8.

70. That apostasy was a topic of discussion during the tannaitic period indicates that conversion was a reality even in earlier periods. See for example *b. Yebam.* 47b, where Rabbi Ḥelbo casts aspersions on converts, referring to them as the "scab[s] of Israel." See Edward Fram, "Perception and Reception of Repentant Apostates in Medieval Ashkenaz and Premodern Poland," *Association for Jewish Studies Review* 21:2 (1996): 299–339 (esp. 299n2), for a more extensive discussion of apostasy. See Jacob Katz, *"Af al pi sheḥata,"* 203–17. Also see Marc Baer, "Islamic Conversion Narratives on Women," 425–58 (esp. 432).

71. For example, Muslims rewarded Jews and Christians who converted. Not only were converts considered full-fledged Muslims, but they also had greater economic advantages. They could be freed from prison, women could rid themselves of recalcitrant husbands who refused to offer them divorces (in these cases children were awarded to the mother), and women were not required to perform Levirate marriage. For this reason, some Jews were attracted to Islam and converted to improve the unfortunate circumstances in which they found themselves. See Baer, "Islamic Conversion Narratives on Women," 434–51.

72. See Miriam Bodian, *Hebrews of the Portuguese Nation: Conversos and Community in Early Modern Amsterdam* (Bloomington: Indiana University Press, 1999), 155–56. Also see Talya Fishman, *Shaking the Pillars of Exile: "Voice of a Fool," an Early Modern Jewish Critique of Rabbinic Culture* (Stanford, CA: Stanford University Press, 1997), 10. There she notes that while only a few converso attacks on rabbinic culture survive, others can be found embedded in early modern apologia and rabbinic responsa. She carefully describes one such attack in her analysis and translation of *Kol Sakhal,* written by Judah Aryeh Modena in Venice in 1623 (43–66).

73. See n64.

74. Jacob Berav, *Sheelot Uteshuvot,* #39. Also see Assaf, *"Anuse sefarad,"* 45n4. Regarding the ancient punishment of lashes, see *"Semikhat zeqenim o quntres hasemikhah,"* printed as an appendix at the end of Levi ibn Ḥabib, *Sheelot Uteshuvot.*

75. Assaf, *"Anuse sefarad,"* 57. Also see Rivka Cohen, *"Lisheelat qelitatam shel anusim lisheavar biyehadut haotomanit beferuts hahagirah haportugezit leaḥar 1536,"* in *Milisbon lesaloniqi vequshta,* ed. Zvi Ankori (Jerusalem: Geref Ḥen, 1988), 15, for her discussion of the sharpness of the critique against the conversos that continued into the years following ibn Ḥabib's death in 1516.

76. These rabbis were Jacob ibn Ḥabib, Solomon Taitazek, Meir Arama, Joseph Fasi, Moses Arobis, and Eliezer Hashimoni. See Assaf, *"Anuse sefarad,"* 56.

77. Samuel de Medina, *Sheelot Uteshuvot* (Salonika, 1598; repr. Lemberg,

1862), *Even Haezer,* #10 (end); Assaf, *"Anuse sefarad,"* 56. Also see Joseph Hacker, "Sephardim in the Ottoman Empire," 2:125–26, where Hacker discusses how the expulsion broke families apart. Many lost family members along their journeys. Wives left husbands who had converted or had been forcibly baptized, and husbands left wives behind in Spain and Portugal. Many saw marriage as part of beginning life anew and, in those early years in the Ottoman empire, often overlooked lineage and status in the rush to remarry. No doubt ibn Ḥabib composed his legal rulings against this dramatic and chaotic societal backdrop.

78. Assaf, *"Anuse sefarad,"* 56.

79. See, for example, *b. San.* 27a, for a discussion of what disqualifies witnesses; Maimonides, *Mishne Torah, Edut* 12:2, 5–10; Joseph Caro, *Shulhan Arukh, Hoshen Mishpat* 34:25. See *Shulhan Arukh, Hoshen Mishpat* 34:29–35, which provides details regarding what qualifies as repentance for those transgressions that disqualified a witness. Indeed, one could repent for one's sins and then be reinstated as a qualified witness.

80. See the *haskamah* signed by Jacob ibn Ḥabib, Solomon Taitezek, and Eliezer Hashimoni in 1515 in D. Frenkel, ed., *Zera Anashim* (Husiyatin, 1902), #53, 45a. Note that my citations refer to this printed edition of *Zera Anashim.* Also see the manuscript at the National Library in Jerusalem, 8° 2001. See de Medina, *Sheelot Uteshuvot, Even Haezer* #10 (the end of the responsum).

81. In the wake of signing the *haskamah* of 1515, ibn Ḥabib authored a lengthy responsum surveying the history of the debate, where he brought geonic support for his own position and that of Mizrahi. It can be found in a collection of responsa authored by Elijah Mizrahi, *Sheelot Uteshuvot,* #47. See Assaf, *"Anuse sefarad,"* 57.

82. Mizrahi, *Sheelot Uteshuvot,* #48.

83. In one case, a forty-five-year-old woman had been widowed for the second time and did not have any children with her prior two husbands. Her brother-in-law was anxious to marry her, but she did not want to marry him and was not able to bear children any longer. She pointed out to Mizrahi that her brother-in-law was more interested in her husband's assets. Upon marrying her, he would be freed from paying her the value of her *ketubbah* and be released from returning any of the assets she had brought into the marriage. Mizrahi required her to marry her brother-in-law stating, "She is equal to all other widows who need Levirate marriage; if he [the brother] wants, he divorces, if he does not want, he marries [her]." See Mizrahi, *Sheelot Uteshuvot,* #22; and *t. Yebam.* 2:5. Also see Minna Rozen, *A History of the Jewish Community in Istanbul: The Formative Years, 1453–1566* (Leiden: E. J. Brill, 2002), 157–62, on Levirate marriages that were not done in good faith. Brothers-in-law sought fiscal gain and extorted women.

84. Mizrahi, *Sheelot Uteshuvot,* #48, 66, and 87.

85. Mizrahi, *Sheelot Uteshuvot,* #87.

86. Bodian, *Hebrews of the Portuguese Nation,* 14.

87. Yovel, *The Other Within,* 338–77. Yovel believes that the "marranos served as catalysts in modernizing trends that had already begun without them, or joined the process as a contributing factor, or helped prepare the ground by undermining the solidity of the existing state of affairs and pointing to its possible mutation."

He points out that historical transformations are so intricate that it is important to consider many participating agents, including the marranos; Yovel, *The Other Within,* 339.

88. Mizraḥi, *Sheelot Uteshuvot,* #66. Joseph Hacker makes note of this in his article "Elijah Mizraḥi," in *Encyclopedia Judaica* 8:1176–78. Also see Mizraḥi, *Sheelot Uteshuvot,* #21, where he cleared a woman who had decided to return to Judaism of charges in the death of her first husband.

89. Mizraḥi, *Sheelot Uteshuvot,* #88.

90. Mizraḥi, *Sheelot Uteshuvot,* #47. See Assaf, *"Anuse sefarad,"* 57.

91. Katz, *"Af al pi shehata,"* 203. Also see Rozen, *History,* 93–95.

92. Mizraḥi, *Sheelot Uteshuvot,* #47.

93. Katz, *"Af al pi shehata,"* 205, 215.

94. Mizraḥi, *Sheelot Uteshuvot,* #47. Joseph Hacker, *"Rabbi yaaqov ibn ḥabib,"* 118; Katz, *"Af al pi shehata,"* 216.

95. See page 39 where I treat ibn Ḥabib's discussion regarding the issue of judging others in more detail: *EY Berakhot* (Salonika, 1516), vol. 1, section 26, 18a–b (= Jerusalem, 1961, vol. 1, 23a). Also see Rivka Cohen, *"Lisheelat qelitatam shel anusim lisheavar,"* 15–17, where she discusses the sharpness of the critique against the conversos and the difficulty this caused in reintegrating conversos into the Jewish community.

96. See Joseph Hacker, *"Haḥevrah hayehudit besaloniqi veagapeha bemeot ha-15 veha-16"* (Ph.D. diss., Hebrew University, 1978), 192, where he discusses the fact that Jews were expelled from countries other than Spain and that many arrived in the Ottoman empire seeking an opportunity to rebuild their lives.

97. Bodian, *Hebrews of the Portuguese Nation,* xii, notes that the study of conversos contributes to topics that have been researched in contemporary scholarship, including "responses to stigma, responses to the suppression of ethnic or religious experience, conceptions of ethnic difference, strategies among immigrants and refugees to adapt to a new environment, the social control of dissent, and the maintenance of coherent diaspora societies." She views the study of the conversos as a way to analyze these issues while considering how such concerns induced strategies of religious adaptation. Ibn Ḥabib, however, while not a converso, was responding to many of the same questions that these converts and their Ottoman Jewish neighbors brought to the fore. He too offers a strategy of religious adaptation in his creation of the *En Yaaqov.* I will discuss this in greater detail in chapter 4.

98. See, for example, *EY Berakhot* (Salonika, 1516), vol. 1, section 5 (*Yerushalmi* section), 54b–55b (= Jerusalem, 1961, vol. 1, 4b). In fact, Yosef Hayim Yerushalmi points out that the phenomenon of Jews envisioning their present crisis through the paradigm of the destruction of the Temple was common among medieval Jews. He sees a shift in this phenomenon, however, in postexpulsion historiography, a shift to which the third chapter of his book, *Zakhor,* is devoted.

99. See page 21, including note 20 (regarding Simon ben Tsemaḥ Duran).

100. See *EY* (Salonika, 1516), vol. 1, section 26, 18ab (= Jerusalem 1961, section 94, 66b–67b). And see Perez Zagorin, *Ways of Lying: Dissimulation, Persecution, and Conformity in Early Modern Europe* (Cambridge, MA: Harvard University

Press, 1990), 3. In this book Zagorin points to the conversos as one example of individuals who used lying to conform and thereby to protect themselves.

101. *Shemot Rabbah* 45:6 (Vilna, 1878).

102. *EY Berakhot* (Salonika, 1516), vol. 1, section 26, 18a–b (= Jerusalem, 1961, vol. 1, 23a). For another example see *EY Berakhot* (Salonika, 1516), vol. 1, section 85, 36b–37b (specifically 37b) (= Jerusalem, 1961, vol. 1, section 94, 67a–b, specifically 67b). In this source ibn Ḥabib communicates that the attainment of *iyyun* (knowledge) and the performance of deeds play central roles in his spiritual vision. However, according to this passage, individuals are encouraged to pursue *iyyun* and perform deeds to the extent that it is possible given the circumstances of the day.

103. For a more extensive discussion regarding the faith of many of the conversos, see Ben-Sasson, *"Dor gole sefarad al atsmo."* Also see Yosef Hayim Yerushalmi, *From Spanish Court to Italian Ghetto,* 38n56, where he makes reference to a later work of responsa, *Devar Yisrael* (Venice, 1702), #45, written by the Venetian rabbi Samuel Aboab (1610–94). While Aboab lived after ibn Ḥabib, his comments reflect sentiments that underscore the extent to which rabbis continued to grapple with conversion for many decades. Aboab writes: "The conversos hold Christianity to be forbidden only as belief, but when one believes in one's heart that this idolatry is nothing, there is no divine punishment for the external observance of its rituals." Also see Shalom Rosenberg, "The Concept of *Emunah* in Post-Maimonidean Philosophy," in *Studies in Medieval Jewish History and Literature,* 2 vols., ed. Isadore Twersky (Cambridge, MA: Harvard University Press, 1984), 2:305.

104. *EY Berakhot* (Salonika, 1516), vol. 1, section 15, 13b (= Jerusalem, 1961, vol. 1, section 19, 16a).

105. Even the Talmudic passage is committed to clearing David of his transgressions.

106. This is a paraphrase of the following phrase: "*hu ḥasid ledavar kolel lo.*"

107. Note that earlier in this comment, ibn Ḥabib describes David as one who, like a drunk man, briefly "meddled with wine for an hour." In this regard, he was judged in accordance with the majority of his deeds.

108. See Ps. 26:1, where David wonders why he has not been vindicated.

109. See *b. Ber.* 28a.

110. The term that ibn Ḥabib uses here is *deot emuniyyot,* which literally means "faithful ideas" or "faithful opinions." However, if we take into consideration the larger context of ibn Ḥabib's commentary and his continued preoccupation with knowing the principles of faith (see chapter 4), it would seem more likely that the upshot of this statement is that David had a perfect understanding of faith—that is, a perfect relationship with God that allowed him to "always walk in [God's] true path."

111. *EY Berakhot* (Salonika, 1516), vol. 1, section 3, 8b–9b (= Jerusalem, 1961, vol. 1, section 7, 5a–7a).

112. Throughout ibn Ḥabib's discussion, he refers to David as someone who is "perfect" (*shalem*) and as one who achieved spiritual perfection. See Twersky, "Talmudists, Philosophers, Kabbalists," 440, who discusses this term in light of the vocabulary of spirituality and religiosity used during the sixteenth century.

113. Mazower, *Salonika,* 50–51; Yerushalmi, "Exile and Expulsion in Jewish History," 8–14. Also see Martin A. Cohen, *Samuel Usque's Consolation for the Tribulations of Israel* (Philadelphia: Jewish Publication Society, 1965), 211–12. Usque, in his description of Salonika, added that it is "established on the very deep foundations of the Law. And it is filled with the choicest plants and the most fruitful trees presently known anywhere on the face of the globe. These fruits are divine, because they are watered by an abundant stream of charities. The city's walls are made of holy deeds of the greatest worth." Also see Abraham Danon, "La Communauté Juive de Salonique au XVIe siècle," *Revue des Études Juives* 40 (1900): 207, where he refers to de Medina's description of Salonika as a place where the majority of the population is Jewish and notes that the elders of the city referred to it as "*yerushalayim haqetanah*" (the miniature Jerusalem).

114. See Hacker, "*Haḥevrah hayehudit besaloniqi,*" 92–98, 161–66, 221–22, and Tirosh-Rothschild, *Between Worlds,* 81, who emphasize that the Romaniot community was not a sizable force in Salonika during the period when ibn Ḥabib lived there. Sultan Mehmet II had transplanted Romaniot Jews to Constantinople during the fifteenth century in an effort to rebuild the city. That said, despite ibn Ḥabib's position in a city that lacked Romaniot Jews, he had to contend with their desire for hegemony throughout the Ottoman empire. See Hacker, "*Rabbi yaaqov ibn ḥabib,*" 120, where he discusses ibn Ḥabib's ability to maintain Sephardic custom in Salonika while conceding to Romaniot custom outside of Salonika.

115. Yerushalmi, "Exile and Expulsion in Jewish History," 19–21. Also see Danon, "La Communauté Juive de Salonique," 209–16, where he draws from various responsa on the nature of the Jewish community in Salonika (see especially his notes there). Also see Hacker, "*Haḥevrah hayehudit besaloniqi,*" 192. And see Hacker, "Sephardim in the Ottoman Empire," 2:109–18.

116. Hacker, "*Rabbi yaaqov ibn ḥabib,*" 120, where he discusses the strength of the Romaniot influence throughout the Ottoman empire and ibn Ḥabib's resistance to it. See also Aron Rodrigue, "The Sephardim in the Ottoman Empire," in *Spain and the Jews: The Sephardi Experience 1492 and After,* ed. Elie Kedourie (London: Thames & Hudson, 1992), 165. For a further discussion, see Mark A. Epstein, "The Leadership of the Ottoman Jews in the Fifteenth and Sixteenth Centuries," in *Christians and Jews in the Ottoman Empire: The Functioning of a Plural Society,* 2 vols., ed. Benjamin Braude and Bernard Lewis (New York: Holmes & Meier, 1982): 1:101–16.

117. Rozen, *History,* 80.

118. Eyal Ginio, "The Administration of Criminal Justice in Ottoman Selanik," *Turcia* 30 (1998): 185–209; also see Mazower, *Salonika,* 57. See a more recent responsum authored by Moshe Feinstein regarding a similar debate over the kashrut of fish containing scales that were not readily apparent to the naked eye. In the responsum Feinstein refers to the opinion of Jacob ibn Ḥabib, who spoke out frequently in matters related to dietary concerns in Salonika. See Feinstein, *Iggerot Moshe* (New York, 1959–1973), *Yoreh Deah* 3:8.

119. Nirenberg, "Mass Conversion," 3–4, 22, discusses the fact that Sephardim exerted a sense of genealogical superiority over other Jews. He points to the Italian

rabbi David ben Judah Messer Leon, who ridiculed Isaac Abarbanel's claims to an Iberian royal pedigree.

120. Minna Rozen, "Individual and Community in the Jewish Society of the Ottoman Empire: Salonika in the Sixteenth Century," in *The Jews of the Ottoman Empire,* ed. Avigdor Levy (Princeton, NJ: Darwin Press, 1994), 218. Also see Frenkel, ed., *Zera Anashim, Even Haezer,* #44, and Hannah Davidson's discussion of this responsum in "Communal Pride and Feminine Virtue: 'Suspecting *Sivlonot*' in the Jewish Communities of the Ottoman Empire in the Early Sixteenth Century," in *Sephardi Family Life in the Early Modern Diaspora*, ed. Julia R. Lieberman (Waltham, MA: Brandeis University Press, 2011), 36–37. For an overview of life in Salonika during the sixteenth century, see Tirosh-Rothschild, *Between Worlds,* 81–83.

121. It is interesting that, after the death of the Romaniot chief rabbi Elijah Mizraḥi in 1526, no one replaced him. Due to the power struggles between the Romaniot Jews and the Jews from Spain, no Romaniot Jew was able to assume this position after 1526, and it remained vacant until the nineteenth century. The main task of tax gathering fell into the hands of a Spanish Jew. See Rodrigue, "Sephardim in the Ottoman Empire," 165.

122. Despite the new freedoms and opportunities granted to the Jews when they arrived in the Ottoman empire after 1492, they continued to meet with challenges. Ibn Ḥabib described his own experience: "We are not permitted to obtain permanent quarters for a synagogue let alone build one. We are compelled to hide underground, and our prayers must not be heard because of the danger." This is quoted by Joseph Caro, *Bet Yosef, Oraḥ Ḥayyim,* #154.

123. Joseph ibn Lev (1505–1580), *Sheelot Uteshuvot* (Bene Beraq, 1988), vol. 2, #72 (first printed edition, Kuru Tshesme, 1597). In this responsum ibn Lev describes the segregated life in Salonika, in which each group of Jews lived among other Jews who came from the same countries. See Mazower, *Salonika,* 59. Also see Rozen, "Individual and Community," 218. Also note that social and cultural struggles led to the proliferation of distinct congregations in Constantinople (Istanbul), where Mizraḥi led the Romaniot Jewish community. In the early sixteenth century, the Cordoba community, for example, established a *haskamah* preventing Jews from joining other congregations. Several Iberian congregations that developed in those early years issued similar decrees. See Rozen, *History,* 81. Indeed, the multicongregational structure that developed enabled Iberian Jews to maintain their own communal identity, but it also stood in the way of the proliferation of Romaniot hegemony.

124. See Hacker, "*Haḥevra hayehudit besaloniqi,*" 223–76, for an extensive discussion of the community framework in Salonika. Also see Rozen, "Individual and Community," 216–17; de Medina, *Sheelot Uteshuvot, Yoreh Deah,* #97, 125, 189; *Ḥoshen Mishpat,* #12, 398; L. Borenstein-Makovetzki, "Tendencies of Separation and Unification in Greek-Jewish Communities during the Sixteenth and Seventeenth Centuries," *Annual of Bar-Ilan Studies in Judaica and Humanities* 20–21 (1983): 243–45nn3–15.

125. Morris S. Goodblatt, *Jewish Life in Turkey in the Sixteenth Century as Re-*

flected in the Legal Writings of Samuel de Medina (New York: Jewish Theological Seminary, 1952), 72. Also see Rozen, "Individual and Community," 230, where she discusses how wealthier members of the Jewish community who had more clout moved freely from one community to another.

126. Mazower, *Salonika,* 61.

127. According to Rozen, there were a large number of mixed Romaniot-Iberian marriages, which forced Spanish Jews to accept certain Romaniot customs in Constantinople (Istanbul). See Rozen, *History,* 138.

128. See Rozen, "Individual and Community," 219. Also see 267n21, where she notes that Solomon of the House of Levi, despite his Sephardic origin, served as the *marbits torah* (rabbinic leader) of the Provence congregation. Mordekhai Kalai served as the head of the Portugal Yahiya congregation in Salonika even though he was not Portuguese.

129. See David Pipano, *Sefer Shalshelet Rabbane Saloniq Verabbane Sofia,* published with *Ḥagor Efod* (Sofia, 1925), 4a; Mizraḥi, *Sheelot Uteshuvot,* #48.

130. Rozen, "Individual and Community," 217.

131. See Meir Benayahu, *"Rav yosef taitazak misaloniqi: Rosh golat sefarad,"* in *Meaz vead ata,* ed. Zvi Ankori (Tel Aviv: Tel Aviv University Press, 1984), 27. Also see Rivka Cohen, *Yehude yavan ledorotam* (Tel Aviv: Tel Aviv University Press, 1984), 97. It appears that the board was first made up of Sephardic rabbis, including Meir Arama, Jacob ibn Ḥabib, and Solomon Taitazak. By 1514 the name Eliezer Hashimoni appears as one of the three signatures placed at the bottom of the *haskamot.* Some have argued that Hashimoni was an Ashkenazic rabbi from Frankfurt and that his signature indicates an attempt to create intercommunal unity. Others argue that in fact he was a Sephardic rabbi with origins in Catalonia. See Simḥa Assaf, *"Mikhtavim meet gedole saloniqi,"* in *Meqorot umeḥqarim betoledot yisrael* (Jerusalem, 1946), 209–10, and Rivka Cohen, *Yehude yavan,* 127n113, who believe Hashimoni was from Frankfurt. Yitzḥak Emmanuel, *Matsevot saloniqi betseruf toledot ḥayyehem shel gedole haqehillah,* 2 vols. (Jerusalem: Ben Tzvi Institute, 1963), 1:51, argues that Hashimoni was from Catalonia. See *Zera Anashim,* #53.

132. When Jacob ibn Ḥabib arrived in Salonika, each community had its own yeshiva. Centralization with respect to Torah learning did not occur until two generations after the arrival of the Jews from Spain. See Avraham Shaul Amarillo, *"Hevrat hatalmud torah hagadol besaloniqi,"* *Sefunot* 13 (1971–8): 275–308.

133. Tirosh-Rothschild, *Between Worlds,* 82.

134. Goodblatt, *Jewish Life in Turkey,* 101.

135. See de Medina, *Sheelot Uteshuvot, Oraḥ Ḥayim,* #35, where he notes that "all Jews in Salonika or [at least the] majority abandoned their [prayer] customs and followed the customs of Spain." Also see Rozen, "Individual and Community," 217–18, and Danon, "La Communauté Juive de Salonique," 212n1. A communal yeshiva was also set up.

136. Joseph Hacker, *"Gaon vedikkaon: Ketavim behavayatam haruḥanit vehaḥevratit shel yotse sefarad ufortugal baimperyah haotomanit,"* in *Tarbut vehevrah betoldot yisrael biyeme habenayim,* ed. Reuven Bonfil, Menaḥem Ben-Sasson, and Joseph Hacker (Jerusalem: Zalman Shazar Center for Jewish History, 1989), 571–72.

137. Hava Tirosh-Rothschild, *Between Worlds,* 83. See also Rozen, *History,* 88n6, who cites a responsum written by Mizraḥi where he writes that Sephardim could not be compelled to obey his legal decisions (Mizraḥi, *Sheelot Uteshuvot* [Jerusalem, 1959], 57:192, and in Rozen, document 12 [appendix]). Sephardim did approach Mizraḥi regarding their legal questions. At times, they held by their own Sephardic customs, but also in many cases accepted local rule. See Mizraḥi, *Sheelot Uteshuvot,* 28:77, as cited by Rozen, *History,* 88n6 (also 84–85, 163, 165).

138. See Hacker, *"Rabbi yaaqov ibn ḥabib,"* 119–20, esp. n7, where he discusses ibn Ḥabib's position on *nefiḥah* which appeared in a responsum authored by Samuel de Medina, *Sheelot Uteshuvot, Yoreh Deah,* #40 and #42.

139. Hacker, *"Rabbi yaaqov ibn ḥabib,"* 119, esp. n7, where Hacker discusses ibn Ḥabib's position as found in a responsum authored by de Medina (see the preceding note).

140. See Joseph Caro, *Avqat Rokhel,* #209, where Caro reports that a certain rabbi found a treatise containing ibn Ḥabib's stringency with respect to animals whose lungs were attached to their chest walls. However, this rabbi was to learn that those who supervised kashrut procedures followed the more lenient procedure of Sephardic Jews. Caro discusses the problem whereby an earlier non-Sephardic practice adopted by prominent Sephardic rabbis was later overturned in favor of the Sephardic position.

141. *Zera Anashim,* #43. For a more extensive discussion on the issue of *sivlonot* and ibn Ḥabib's position, see Hacker, *"Rabbi yaaqov ibn ḥabib,"* 119–20; Rozen, *History,* 132–38; and Hannah Davidson, "Communal Pride and Feminine Virtue," 24–35.

142. Note that for Romaniot Jews *qiddushin* and *nissuin* remained separate ceremonies. This meant that during the period between *qiddushin* and *nissuin,* if a bride-to-be accepted *sivlonot* she was considered unavailable to another man, even though her marriage had not yet been finalized. Romaniot Jews encouraged the bride and groom to spend time together during this interim period and even allowed sexual relations. This ran counter to the customs of Iberian Jews, who did not recognize the couple as fully married until *qiddushin* and *nissuin* had both been performed, and therefore created tension between the two communities. See Rozen, *History,* 132–38.

143. Hacker, "Rabbi yaaqov ibn ḥabib," 119–20; Davidson, "Communal Pride and Feminine Virtue," 24.

144. *Zera Anashim,* #43. See Davidson, "Communal Pride and Feminine Virtue," 33–34.

145. *Zera Anashim,* #43.

146. See Samuel de Medina, *Sheelot Uteshuvot, Yoreh Deah,* #40 and #41, where ibn Ḥabib relies on Deut. 14:1, *"lo titgodedu"* (you shall not cut yourselves), as discussed in *b. Yebam.* 14a. According to *b. Yebam.* 14a, this phrase implies that one should not create separate groups or sects. Also see Hacker, *"Rabbi yaaqov ibn ḥabib,"* 119n7, where he cites this source and discusses it.

147. *Zera Anashim,* #43.

148. This translation is based on the version of *y. Sheqalim* that appears in the *EY*

Sheqalim (*Yerushalmi*) (Salonika, 1516), vol. 1, 192a. Also see the parallel Talmudic version in *b. Shabb.* 112b. Hacker, "*Rabbi yaaqov ibn ḥabib*," 122, also n11.

149. *EY Sheqalim* (*Yerushalmi*) (Salonika, 1516), vol. 1, 192a (= Jerusalem, 1961, *Sheqalim* [*Yerushalmi*], vol. 1, section 17, 7a–b). Hacker, "*Rabbi yaaqov ibn ḥabib*," 122, also n11.

150. *EY* (Salonika, 1516), vol. 1, introduction (= Jerusalem, 1961, vol. 1, introduction).

151. Joseph Hacker, "*Rabbi yaaqov ibn ḥabib*," 123–26.

152. See Caro, *Avqat Rokhel,* #209. In this responsum he informs us of an incident in which a treatise on kashrut law authored by ibn Ḥabib was uncovered. Also see Joseph ibn Lev, *Sheelot Uteshuvot,* 3:94, where he also notes his awareness of a treatise on kashrut authored by Jacob ibn Ḥabib.

153. See previous note.

154. Moshe Feinstein, *Iggerot Moshe, Yoreh Deah* 3:8. Also see, for example, Joseph Caro, *Bet Yosef, Oraḥ Ḥayyim* 25, 27, 142, 154, 162; *Yoreh Deah* (on kashrut), 6, 14, 18, 22, 30, 35, 37, 39, 43–44, 46, 48, 56, 57, 64–65, 67, 86, 90, 92–93, 275 (which also mentions Isaac Canpanton); *Even Haezer* (on *sivlonot*), 45; Caro, *Avqat Rokhel,* #122 (on the sanctity of synagogues), 200 (on kashrut).

155. Hacker, "*Rabbi yaaqov ibn Ḥabib*," 117.

Chapter 2

1. Both Israel Ta-Shma and Jacob Elbaum have recognized the absence of literary productivity with respect to Talmudic aggadah. See Ta-Shma, "The Study of Aggadah and Its Interpretation in Early Rabbinic Literature," in *Creativity and Tradition: Studies in Medieval Rabbinic Scholarship, Literature, and Thought* (Cambridge, MA: Harvard University Press, 2006), 205; and Jacob Elbaum, *Lehavin divre ḥakhamim,* 41.

2. Elbaum correctly points to this absence of commentaries on the aggadot of the Talmud. Although he detects a change in this phenomenon beginning in the fifteenth century in Spain, the extent of this change is very limited in comparison to what occurs in the early sixteenth and seventeenth centuries. See Elbaum, *Lehavin divre ḥakhamim,* 41, and *Petiḥut vehistagrut: Hayetsirah hasifrutit befolin uveartsot ashkenaz beshilhe hameah ha-16* (Jerusalem: Magnes Press, 1990). Joseph Hacker points to a flowering of interest in Talmudic aggadah beginning in the early sixteenth century in the Ottoman empire. See Hacker, "Intellectual Activity," 114–16.

3. Ibn Ḥabib's anthology of passages from the *Bavli* is more comprehensive than his work on the *Yerushalmi.* See my introduction, where I discuss ibn Ḥabib's work on the *Yerushalmi.*

4. See, for example, Jehuda Theodor and Hanokh Albeck, eds., *Midrash Bereshit Rabbah: Critical Edition with Notes and Commentary,* 3 vols. (Berlin, 1929; repr. Jerusalem: Wahrmann Books, 1965). Also see *Bereshit Rabbah,* which can be found in *Midrash Rabbah* (Vilna, 1878).

5. Mordecai Margulies, ed., *Midrash Vayiqra Rabbah* (New York: Jewish Theological Seminary, 1956–58, as well as *Vayiqra Rabbah,* which can be found

in *Midrash Rabbah* (Vilna, 1878); and the two editions of *Devarim Rabbah:* Saul Lieberman, ed., *Devarim Rabbah* (Jerusalem, 1940), and *Devarim Rabbah,* found in *Midrash Rabbah* (Vilna, 1878), which are examples of homiletical midrashim. See Joseph Heinemann, "*Hapetiḥtot bemidrashe haaggadah: Meqoran vetafqidan,*" *Proceedings of the Fourth World Congress of Jewish Studies* (1969): 2:43–47, and "The Proem in the Aggadic Midrashim: A Form-Critical Study," *Scripta Hierosolymitana* 22 (1971): 100–122, where he discusses the structure of the proem, which scholars believe was an ancient form used in sermonizing. In this sermonic form a verse from the weekly Torah reading was explicated via its juxtaposition with a verse from the non-Toraitic books of the Bible. Often the homily ended on a note of consolation. Also see Norman Cohen, "Leviticus Rabbah, Parashah 3: An Example of a Classic Rabbinic Homily," *Jewish Quarterly Review* 72:1 (1981): 18–31; David Stern, "Midrash and the Language of Exegesis: A Study of *Vayikra Rabbah* Chapter 1," in *Midrash and Literature,* ed. Geoffrey H. Hartman and Sanford Budick (New Haven, CT: Yale University Press, 1986), 105–24; and Burton L. Visotzky, *Golden Bells and Pomegranates: Studies in Midrash Leviticus Rabbah* (Tübingen: Mohr Siebeck, 2003), 23–30.

6. See Wilhelm Bacher, *Erkhe midrash* (Tel Aviv, 1922/1923), 24, who argues that the word *aggadah* is derived from the expression "*higgid hakatuv,*" which for him means "Scripture related [or relates]," because these were the words with which many aggadic discourses opened. I am arguing that when "Scripture relates" something, the genre is midrash aggadah and not aggadah per se.

7. See Louis Finkelstein, ed., *Sifre Devarim* (Berlin, 1939; repr. New York: Jewish Theological Seminary, 1969), 48, 306; see *b. Moed Qatan* 15a and *b. Ber.* 22a, where a baraita about those who have sexual relations with their menstruant wives makes allowances for husbands to "read from the Torah, the Prophets, and the Writings, and to study Mishnah, midrash, gemara, halakhah, and aggadah." In *b. Git.* 67a, within a discussion about the merits of various sages, Rabbi Akiva is described as a "storehouse with compartments." Rashi, who draws from a tradition about Rabbi Akiva that is found in *Abot Rab. Nat.,* interprets this phrase to mean that Rabbi Akiva is someone who learned Scripture, midrash, halakhah, and aggadah as separate disciplines and then taught each one separately. See also *b. Taan.* 16a, where Rabbi Judah describes the person who leads prayer as someone who has a thorough knowledge of the Torah, the Prophets, the Writings (Hagiographa), midrash, halakhot, aggadot, and all the benedictions. A baraita found on *b. Taan.* 30a notes that one fasting on the ninth of Av or one in mourning is prohibited from reciting passages from the Torah, the Prophets, and the Writings (Hagiographa), and from learning Mishnah, Talmud, midrash, halakhot, and aggadot; *b. Moed Qatan* 21a makes a similar point about the mourner, distinguishing aggadah from midrash. And *m. Ned.* 4:3 makes a similar distinction: "He may teach him midrash, halakhot, and aggadot." Also see *y. B. Qam.* 4:1, 4b; *y. Ḥag.* 1:8, 76d; *y. Ned.* 3:9, 38b; *Vayiqra Rab.* 3:7 (ed. Margulies). *Abot Rab. Nat.* A, 8, notes that when one puts aside his study of Bible, his teacher should teach him Mishnah. When one puts aside his study of Mishnah, his teacher should instruct him in midrash. When one puts aside his study of midrash, his teacher should teach him halakhot,

and after halakhot his teacher should teach him aggadah. Also see *Abot Rab. Nat.* A, 14, where Rabban Yoḥanan is described as a rabbi who never put aside "Bible, Mishnah, Gemara, halakhot, aggadot. . . ." And see *Abot Rab. Nat.* A, 28, and 40; B, 12 and 18; *Soferim* 16:4; and *Shemot Rab.,* which can be found in *Midrash Rabbah* (Vilna, 1878) 30:14; 46:1; 47:7.

8. And yet the categories are far from foolproof. No doubt we also find instances where aggadah, not midrash, is listed as part of the proposed curriculum of study. For example, *Shemot Rab.* (Vilna, 1878) 47:1, claims that "oral Torah" (in comparison to written Torah) is defined by Mishnah, Talmud, and aggadah. In another case in *Shemot Rab.* (Vilna, 1878) 15:2, aggadah is listed alongside Scripture, Mishnah, and Talmud without mention of midrash. Such a case may suggest that "aggadah" is a larger category that includes midrash aggadah and that "halakhah" is a larger category that includes midrash halakhah.

9. While the early collections produced prior to approximately 600 CE were collections of midrash aggadah, following this period we find a few rare examples of aggadic collections that were not organized around a verse or book of the Bible. For example, *Eliyahu Rabbah* and *Eliyahu Zuta,* also known as *Tanna Deve Eliyahu Rabbah* and *Tanna Deve Eliyahu Zuta,* were unique in that they incorporated material from the *Bavli* using the form of a narrative written in the first person. These works are not tied to any scriptural book. Instead, they move from topic to topic in the name of making an ethical or didactic point. *Abot Rab. Nat.* is a commentary on *m. Abot* and is not arranged in accordance with a set of biblical verses. Although the early core of the work is from an earlier period, its redaction was completed in the geonic period. See Burton L. Visotzky, "The Literature of the Rabbis," in *From Mesopotamia to Modernity,* ed. Burton L. Visotzky and David E. Fishman (Boulder, CO: Westview Press, 1999), 83–92.

10. The fact that there is disagreement among scholars as to the definition of the term *aggadah* reflects its inexact nature. Moshe David Herr and editors ("Aggadah," in *Encyclopedia Judaica* 2:354–64) view midrash aggadah as a subset of the larger category of aggadah. See also Isadore Epstein, "Haggadah," in *Interpreter's Dictionary of the Bible* 2:509, who defines aggadah as "scriptural interpretation which is non-legal or narrative in character." Leopold Zunz hedges a bit when he argues that, on the one hand, not all comments on scripture (midrash) can be considered aggadah, and that, on the other hand, aggadot can function to explain the texts of the Bible. See Zunz, *Haderashot beyisrael* (Jerusalem: Mossad Bialik, 1974), 32–33. Note that Margulies, *Midrash Vayiqra Rabbah,* introduction, xxvi–xxvii, argues that the responsa literature of the geonim refers to the midrashic work *Vayiqra Rabbah* as "*haggadah devayiqra.*" This suggests that some used the terms *midrash* and *aggadah* interchangeably. On the other hand, scholars such as Ofra Meir distinguish between aggadah and midrash aggadah more carefully by attributing the *Bavli* and *Yerushalmi* to the category of aggadah and works like *Bereshit Rabbah* and *Midrash Tanḥuma* (Genesis) to the category of midrash aggadah. See Meir, "Hademuyot hapoalot besippure hatalmud vehamidrash" (Ph.D. diss., Hebrew University, 1976), 46–78, and her book, *Hasippur hadarshani bivereshit rabbah* (Tel Aviv: Hakibbuts Hameuḥad, 1987). See Judah Goldin, "The Freedom and

Restraint of Haggadah," in *Studies in Midrash and Related Literature,* ed. Barry L. Eichler and Jeffrey Tigay (Philadelphia: Jewish Publication Society, 1988), 254–55, who upholds the distinction for which I am arguing here, whereby midrash aggadah and aggadah are distinct genres. On the other hand, Goldin does admit to the inexactness of the term *aggadah* and points to the infrequent instances where the word *aggadah* stands for an interpretation of a verse. Louis Finkelstein's discussion about the term *aggadah* ("*Midrash halakhah veaggadot,*" in *Yitzhak F. Baer Jubilee Volume on the Occasion of His Seventieth Birthday,* ed. Salo W. Baron [Jerusalem: Historical Society of Israel, 1960], 31–32), and the discussion in Bacher, *Erkhe midrash,* 24, make reference to this interpretation of the word *aggadah.*

11. See my discussion in Marjorie Lehman, "The Ein Ya'akov: A Collection of Aggadah in Transition," *Prooftexts* 19 (1999): 21–40.

12. Note the one rare exception in *EY Berakhot* (Salonika, 1516), vol. 1, section 27, 19a (= Jerusalem, 1961, vol. 1, section 31, 23a), where ibn Ḥabib quotes a passage from *Shemot Rab.* (Vilna, 1878), 3:1 and integrates it with his citation from the *Bavli.* Ibn Ḥabib also rarely quotes lengthy passages from midrashic works in his commentary on the *En Yaaqov.* However, ibn Ḥabib's commentary on *b. Ber.* 7a is one of the few examples where ibn Ḥabib quotes a lengthy passage from *Shemot Rab.* 45:5.

13. During the early years of the printing press in the Ottoman empire (early sixteenth century), Hebrew printers in Constantinople and in Salonika took a great interest in publishing aggadic collections as well as collections of midrash aggadah. Their goal was to transfer much of the midrashic and aggadic literature from manuscript to print to meet the needs of a Jewish community interested in this material. For a list of printed works produced in Constantinople and Salonika, see Vinograd, *Otsar hasefer haivri,* 2:666. Also see Joseph Hacker, "Intellectual Activity," 114–15 and nn39–40.

14. During the medieval period most of the collections of aggadah were midrashic. Between the tenth and thirteenth centuries, *Shemot Rabbah* (a midrashic work on Exodus), *Bamidbar Rabbah* (a midrashic work on Numbers), and *Devarim Rabbah* (a midrashic work on Deutermonomy) were produced. Moshe Hadarshan, an eleventh-century French rabbi, composed the medieval midrashic collection *Bereshit Rabbati* on the book of Genesis. *Leqaḥ Tov* (a late eleventh-century commentary on the Torah and the five megillot), *Aggadat Shir Hashirim* and *Midrash Shir Hashirim* (on Song of Songs), *Ruth Zuta, Talmud Torah* (Jacob Sikili's fourteenth-century Spanish anthology of material arranged around the verses of the Torah), and others surfaced during the medieval period. That said, there were a few aggadic collections, such as that of Rabbenu Nissim Gaon (Nissim ibn Shahin of Kairawan, 990–1062). He composed a collection of aggadic stories in Arabic, *Ḥibbur Yefe Mehayeshuah,* ed. H. Z. Hirschberg (Jerusalem: Mossad Harav Kook, 1954). For a more extensive discussion of medieval collections of midrash aggadah, see Jacob Elbaum, "*Yalqut Shim'oni* and the Medieval Midrashic Anthology," *Prooftexts* 17 (1997): 133–47, repr. in *The Anthology in Jewish Literature,* ed. David Stern (Oxford: Oxford University Press, 2004), 159–75. Also see Visotzky, "Literature of the Rabbis," 98–100.

15. For example, the thirteenth-century collection *Yalqut Shim'oni* is a *summa* of midrashic tradition. It includes quotations from the sages' midrashim on all the books of the Bible by following the order of the verses of the Bible and draws from more than fifty rabbinic works. It is similar to (although far more comprehensive than) Makhir ben Abba Mari's *Yalqut Hamakhiri* on Psalms, which was composed at the same time. The thirteenth-century *Midrash Hagadol,* which was produced in Yemen, is also representative of this genre. Its author, David Haadani, described it as "the midrash of the five books of the Torah." But rather than merely quoting his sources or abridging them, as one finds in *Yalqut Shimoni,* Haadani expanded his sources and added his own words. Indeed, some anthologizers made more extensive changes, even adding commentary into the midrashim themselves. And yet despite their differences, all of these collections belong to the same anthological genre. See Elbaum, "*Yalqut Shim'oni,*" 162. In addition, Marc Bregman points out that the phenomenon of the anthology that so characterized the medieval period can be concretized in another way. A medieval variant of *m. Abot* 4:1, "Who is wise? He who learns from every person," describes the archetypal wise person as "he who collects (*measef*) from every place." See Bregman, "Midrash Rabbah and the Medieval Collector Mentality," *Prooftexts* 17 (1997): 67–68, repr. in *The Anthology in Jewish Literature,* ed. David Stern (Oxford: Oxford University Press, 2004), 196–208, esp. 200; and Alexander Kohut, ed., *Notes on a Hitherto Unknown Exegetical, Theological and Philosophical Commentary to the Pentateuch Composed by Aboo Manzur Al-Dhamari* (New York: A. Ginsberg, 1892), 47.

16. Bregman describes the medieval period as marked by a type of "anthological avidity" and notes a parallel interest in the compilation of anthologies among Muslims and Christians. The Muslims produced legal anthologies of Hadith (legal traditions) and the Tafsir commentaries on the Quran, beginning in the ninth century. The Christians produced the great *summae* and other *florilegia*. See Bregman, "Midrash Rabbah and the Medieval Collector Mentality," 67. Also see Joseph R. Strayer, "Anthologies," in *Dictionary of the Middle Ages* 1:317–20.

17. See Jacob Elbaum's discussion of the difficulties involved in demarcating terminological boundaries between midrashic literature and medieval anthologies in "*Yalqut Shim'oni,*" 135, 138, 149n16 (160, Stern ed.). See Moshe David Herr, "Midrash," in *Encyclopedia Judaica* 11:1507–14.

18. See Elbaum, "*Yalqut Shim'oni,*" 140 (165, Stern ed.).

19. See *EY* (Salonika, 1516), vol. 1, introduction (= Jerusalem, 1961, vol. 1, introduction). In addition, when ibn Ḥabib refers to the thirteenth-century Provencal rabbi Isaac ben Yedayah, who wrote a running commentary on the aggadot of the Talmud, he describes him as someone who "elaborated in a midrashic interpretation on this tractate [*Berakhot*]," despite the fact that ben Yedayah's work is an aggadic commentary on the aggadic passages of the *Bavli*. See later editions of the *En Yaaqov,* because this passage is missing from the first printed edition. See, for example, *EY Berakhot* (Jerusalem, 1961), vol. 1, 109a and the note on 108a claiming that this passage can be found in *EY* (Venice, 1566). Unfortunately, I could not find this passage quoted in *EY* (Venice, 1566). Yet the language of the passage

reflects ibn Ḥabib's style of writing and the perspective conveyed suggests that the comment was authored by him. Therefore I chose to speak about it as if it was original to ibn Ḥabib, in keeping with the observations of the editors of *En Yaaqov* (Vilna, 1883). Also see Marc Saperstein's article, "R. Isaac b. Yeda'ya: A Forgotten Commentator on the Aggada," *Revue des Études Juives* 138 (1979): 38, who quotes this source.

20. See *EY* (Salonika, 1516), vol. 1, introduction (= Jerusalem, 1961, vol. 1, introduction).

21. See *EY* (Salonika, 1516), vol. 1, introduction (= Jerusalem, 1961, vol. 1, introduction).

22. Elbaum, "*Yalqut Shim'oni,*" 137 and 149n13 (163 and 172n13, Stern ed).

23. Elbaum, "*Yalqut Shim'oni,*" 137 and 149n13 (163 and 172n13, Stern ed.), where Elbaum discusses other terms used during the medieval period.

24. See Dov Noy, "*Tippusim ben-leumiyyim viyehudiyyim bemidrash aseret hadibberot,*" *Proceedings of the Fourth World Congress of Jewish Studies* (1968): 2:353–55, and Joseph Dan, "Midrash Aseret Hadibberot," in *Encyclopedia Judaica* 11:1514–15. Dan dates the composition of this collection to a time between the seventh and eleventh centuries. Also see Anat Shapira, *Midrash aseret hadibberot* (Jerusalem: Mossad Bialik, 2005).

25. Elbaum, "*Yalqut Shim'oni,*" 137–38 (163, Stern ed.).

26. *Sifre Devarim* (ed. Finkelstein), 48.

27. See *b. Sot.* 40a and Rashi *ad loc.* Also see Jacob Z. Lauterbach, ed., *Mekhilta Derabbi Yishmael* (New York: Jewish Theological Seminary, 1976), *Shirah* 9, 2:95 *ad* Ex. 15:26; *Bereshit Rab.* 58:3; and *Shir Hashirim Rab.* 4:2 for sources that underscore the stimulating appeal of aggadah.

28. Indeed, contemporary scholars remain at odds regarding the independence from or interdependence of aggadic passages in the *Bavli* in regard to their surrounding textual context in Talmudic *sugyot.* Jonah Fraenkel believes that one should look at aggadic passages as closed units detached from their literary contexts. He ignores the legal discussions in which these aggadic sources are embedded and finds the seams that distinguish one genre from the other. Fraenkel's perspective on the Talmudic *sugya* regards the Talmud as containing a variety of sources that might have been designed to instruct different constituencies. Jeffrey Rubenstein disagrees with Fraenkel and argues that the literary context is essential for reaching a proper understanding of the aggadot. In this regard, he sees aggadah and halakhah as interdependent genres. See Jonah Fraenkel, *Darkhe haaggadah vehamidrash* (Masada: Yad Letalmud, 1991), and most especially his article "*Sheelot hermeneutiyot beheqer sippur haaggadah,*" *Tarbiz* 47 (1978): 139–72, which introduces his approach to aggadic stories and his rejection of historical and contextual analyses. See Jeffrey M. Rubenstein, *Talmudic Stories: Narrative Art, Composition, and Culture* (Baltimore, MD: Johns Hopkins University Press, 1999), 11–21.

29. The third-generation amora Rabbi Simon bar Yehotsadak poses a question before Rabbi Samuel bar Naḥman, because he is considered a *baal aggadah,* an aggadic master (*Bereshit Rab.* 3: 4). Rabbi Yoḥanan ben Zakkai was known to have mastered all portions of the rabbinic curriculum, including Scripture, Mishnah,

Talmud, halakhah, and aggadah (*b. Sukkah* 28a). In this source, his knowledge of fox fables is lauded. See Goldin, "Freedom and Restraint," 255.

30. *b. Shabb.* 89a. Also note that Rabbi Yoḥanan advised that whenever one hears the words of aggadah of Rabbi Eleazar, the son of Rabbi Yose the Galilean, he should "make [his] ear like a funnel" to hear these words more clearly (*b. Ḥul.* 89a).

31. See *b. B. Bat.* 9b–10a. Also see *b. B. Bat.* 145b, where wealth is equated with knowing aggadah.

32. See *b. Ber.* 23ab, *b. Git.* 60a, *b. B. Metsia* 116a, *b. B. Bat.* 52a, and *y. Ber.* 5:1, 9a. According to *b. Git.* 60a and *b. Tem.* 14b, Rabbi Yoḥanan and Rabbi Simon ben Lakish would read from a book of aggadah on the Sabbath. The fact that they were rabbis who lived during the third century suggests that, prior to the completion of the Talmud, there was a collection of aggadah that circulated among Palestinian rabbis. See Jay M. Harris, *Nachman Krochmal: Guiding the Perplexed of the Modern Age* (New York: New York University Press, 1991), 305n26.

33. It is beyond the scope of this presentation to discuss the differences in overall attitude toward aggadah reflected in the *Bavli* and the *Yerushalmi* corpora, and the extent to which geographical location influenced such attitudes. However, the fact that each Talmud possesses both positive and negative statements toward aggadah suggests that it was, at the very least, the subject of controversy and that not everyone agreed regarding its value and purpose.

34. See *b. Taan.* 7a. Also see Goldin, "Freedom and Restraint," 259n36.

35. *b. Ber.* 11b; *b. Git.* 60a.

36. For example, in *Bereshit Rab.* 81:2 (Vilna, 1878), when Levi, the son of Sisi, is considered for a rabbinical post in the city of Simonia, the inhabitants of the town first ask him a set of legal questions, presumably to test his knowledge base. When he cannot answer the questions, they then turn to ask him aggadic questions, suggesting that aggadah is somehow less complex than halakhah. Parallel versions of this story appear in *y. Yebam.* 12:6, 13a and in *b. Yebam.* 60b–61a. Also note that in *Vayiqra Rab.* 9:3, when Rabbi Yannai tests a man who offers him hospitality, the text found in the Margulies edition indicates that first he inquired as to his knowledge of Mishnah, then of Talmud, and then finally of aggadah. And yet the parallel version of *Vayiqra Rab.* 9:3 found in the Vilna edition presents a different order of disciplines (that is, Rabbi Yannai tested the man who approached him first with regard to Scripture, then Mishnah, then aggadah, and then Talmud). Possibly, when aggadah is mentioned last in texts that deal with a list of subjects that define the curriculum, this indicates that it was valued less. However, the fact that there exists a rare text that lists "Talmud" after "aggadah" may reflect that, within certain circles, aggadah had a different status or was valued differently. And yet, given how rare it is to find aggadah listed before Talmud, it is possible that the text is corrupt.

37. Edward Breuer, "Maimonides and the Authority of Aggadah," in *Be'erot Yitzhak: Studies in Memory of Isadore Twersky,* ed. Jay Harris (Cambridge, MA: Harvard University Press, 2005), 27.

38. Breuer, "Maimonides and the Authority of Aggadah," 25, who cites Isadore Twersky, "Joesph ibn Kaspi: Portrait of a Medieval Jewish Intellectual," in *Studies*

in Medieval Jewish History and Literature, ed. Isadore Twersky (Cambridge, MA: Harvard University Press, 1979), 234–35.

39. See Neil Danzig, *Mavo lesefer halakhot pesuqot* (New York: Jewish Theological Seminary, 1999).

40. In some cases, however, an aggadic text was quoted to make a halakhic point. For example, see Isaac Alfasi, *Hilkhot Harif,* on *b. Pesah.* 100a.

41. See Saperstein, *Decoding,* 1. To protect rabbinism from the attacks heaped on it by Karaitic Jews, in particular, and to uphold the sacredness of halakhic discourse, the geonim opted to reduce the authority of aggadic sources. And while, from the fifth to the ninth century, there was great literary productivity in the area of aggadah, as several important aggadic collections were written during this time, the geonim were responsible for driving a wedge between the two genres of halakhah and aggadah.

42. Benjamin M. Lewin, ed., *Otsar Hageonim: Teshuvot Geone Bavel Uferusham al pi Seder Hatalmud,* 13 vols. (Haifa: 1928–62), 4:60 (on *b. Hag.* 14a). Also see Goldin, "Freedom and Restraint," 257.

43. See Israel M. Ta-Shma, *Hasifrut haparshanit latalmud beeropah uvitsfon Africa,* 2 vols. (Jerusalem: Magnes Press, 1999–2000), 2:191, where he points out that Rabbenu Hananel, Nissim Gaon, and Hai Gaon were not devoted to the study of aggadah. They often skipped over aggadic passages or glossed over them quickly, merely paraphrasing their contents.

44. Avraham Grossman, "Legislation and Responsa Literature," in *Moreshet Sepharad: The Sephardi Legacy,* 2 vols., ed. Haim Beinart (Jerusalem: Magnes Press, 1992), 1: 203.

45. I will refer to Isaac Alfasi's code as *Hilkhot Harif* from here onward. Leonard Levy discusses the different names used to refer to Alfasi's code, including *Halakhot Rabbati* and the *Halakhot.* See Leonard Robert Levy, "R. Yitzhaq Alfasi's Application of Principles of Adjudication in 'Halakhot Rabbati,'" 1n1.

46. *Olelot* are small, incompletely formed clusters of grapes that lack a central stalk. They can also be clusters where the grapes do not hang down upon each other, as in a normal cluster. Lev. 19:20 and Deut. 24:21 prohibit one from harvesting these undeveloped clusters. They must be left for the poor. See *m. Peah* 7:4 and Adin Steinsalz, *The Talmud: A Reference Guide* (New York: Random House, 1989), 238.

47. Ibn Habib uses the word *parperaot,* which refers to "appetizers," "desserts," or "side dishes" served at a meal, to describe the peripheral quality Alfasi attached to the aggadot of the Talmud.

48. See *EY* (Salonika, 1516), vol. 1, introduction (= Jerusalem, 1961, vol. 1, introduction), where he notes the first reason for titling his collection *En Yaaqov.* There he indicates that his collection reflects twelve pillars, paralleling the twelve sons born to the biblical figure Jacob. Citing Onqelos, the Aramaic translator and interpreter of the Bible, he claims that his collection, the *En Yaaqov,* "is like the *berakhot* that Jacob gave his twelve sons."

49. See Is. 41:14, where the phrase *tolaat yaaqov* is used. God says, "Fear not, O worm Jacob, O men of Israel, I will help you." Also see *EY* (Salonika, 1516), vol.

1, introduction (= Jerusalem, 1961, vol. 1, introduction), the locus for the quote.

50. Codifiers relied to a far larger extent on examining the Talmud's legal intricacies. See Carmi Horowitz, *"Al perush haaggadot shel harashba: Ben kabbalah lefilosofia,"* *Daat* 18 (1987): 15. Also see Elbaum, *Lehavin divre ḥakhamim,* 20n12, where Elbaum makes the point that aggadah was, at times, used as an aid in the explication of a halakhic point. However, it was generally not the case that scholars explicated halakhic issues through the lens of the aggadic passages.

51. *EY* (Salonika, 1516), vol. 1, introduction (= Jerusalem, 1961, vol. 1, introduction).

52. See *EY* (Salonika, 1516), vol. 1, introduction (= Jerusalem, 1961, vol. 1, introduction).

53. This is a paraphrase of Prov. 4:24.

54. *EY* (Salonika, 1516), vol. 1, introduction (= Jerusalem, 1961, vol. 1, introduction).

55. Saperstein, *Decoding the Rabbis,* 1. Note also that the Karaite Salmon ben Yeruḥim (tenth century) was outraged by the way rabbinic texts referred to God. The fact that these sources described God as binding tefillin around His head, or as one who would come and rejoice as well as drink and dance with His people in the Garden of Eden, was to offer a "brute" description of God. See Israel Davidson, *Sefer Milḥamot Hashem* (New York: Jewish Theological Seminary, 1934), 110–11, which includes ben Yeruḥim's attack on Saadya Gaon. See Goldin, "Freedom and Restraint," 258.

56. See, for example, Lewin, ed., *Otsar Hageonim, Berakhot,* 1:16, which represents one geonic response to anthropomorphic references to God made in Toraitic narratives.

57. Saperstein, *Decoding the Rabbis,* 3. Also see the original source, Petrus Alfonsi, *Dialogu, PL,* ed. J. P. Migne (Paris, 1854), 535–72 (esp. ch. 1, cols. 541–67).

58. Saperstein, *Decoding the Rabbis,* 3, and Alfonsi, *Dialogi,* col. 551.

59. Saperstein, *Decoding the Rabbis,* 4.

60. Charles Ber Chavel, *Rabbenu moshe ben naḥman* (Jerusalem: Mossad Harav Kook, 1973), 308. Also see Robert Chazan, *Barcelona and Beyond: The Disputation of 1263 and Its Aftermath* (Berkeley: University of California Press, 1992), 149.

61. See for example the work of Saul Lieberman, who, in the closing pages of his monograph *Sheqiin,* argues that the position regarding aggadah presented by Naḥmanides made sense, given the attitudes toward aggadah conveyed in both rabbinic and geonic sources. These sources also negated the authority of aggadah. Lieberman, *Sheqiin: Midrashe teman* (Jerusalem: Wahrmann, 1970), 81–83. For a scholarly overview of Naḥmanides' opinion as conveyed during the disputation of 1263, see Martin A. Cohen, "Reflections on the Text and Context of the Disputation of Barcelona," *Hebrew Union College Annual* 35 (1964): 170–71; Jeremy Cohen, *The Friars and the Jews: The Evolution of Medieval Anti-Judaism* (Ithaca, NY: Cornell University Press, 1982), 119; Bernard Septimus, " 'Open Rebuke and Concealed Love': Naḥmanides and the Andalusian Tradition," in *Rabbi Moses Naḥmanides (Ramban): Explorations in His Religious and Literary Virtuosity,* ed. Isadore Twer-

sky (Cambridge, MA: Harvard University Press, 1983), 20; Marvin Fox, "Naḥmanides on the Status of Aggadot: Perspectives on the Disputation at Barcelona, 1263," *Journal of Jewish Studies* 40 (1989): 98; Robert Chazan, *Daggers of Faith: Thirteenth-Century Missionizing and the Jewish Response* (Berkeley: University of California Press, 1989), 170–73; Elliot R. Wolfson, "'By Way of Truth': Aspects of Naḥmanides' Kabbalistic Hermeneutic," *Association for Jewish Studies Review* 14 (1989): 103–78; and Chazan, *Barcelona and Beyond,* 142–57.

62. Disputations between Jews and converts continued to involve attacks on and defenses of aggadic material. In 1412 a convert to Christianity, Joshua Halorki, used aggadic texts to prove to the Jews the truth of Christian prophecies regarding the messiah. See Benjamin Gampel, "A Letter to a Wayward Teacher: The Transformation of Sephardic Culture in Christian Iberia," in *Cultures of the Jews: A History,* ed. David Biale (New York: Schocken Books, 2002), 426–27. Also see Moisés Orfali, "Jeronimo de Santa Fe y la Polémica Cristiana Contra el Talmud," *Annuario Di Studi Ebraici* 10 (1984): 177–78.

63. King James, royal officials, barons, ecclesiastical dignitaries, leading burghers, and Catalan Jews were all present at this disputation. Friar Paul relied on rabbinic texts to prove to the Jews that their Talmudic tradition sanctioned the truths of Christianity. When the Jews were confronted with the texts of their tradition, they were expected to recognize that they had sinned and, in turn, to convert to Chrsitianity. See Chazan, *Barcelona and Beyond,* 1.

64. Lewin, ed., *Otsar Hageonim, Berakhot,* 1:131. Also see Ta-Shma, "*Hasifrut haparshanit,*" 191.

65. See Sherira Gaon's comment in Lewin, ed., *Otsar Hageonim, Ḥagigah,* 4:59–60.

66. Saperstein, *Decoding the Rabbis,* 13.

67. Saperstein, *Decoding the Rabbis,* 12.

68. See Breuer, "Maimonides and the Authority of Aggadah," 25–45, and Yair Lorberbaum, "*Temurot beyaḥaso shel harambam lemidreshot ḥazal,*" *Tarbiz* 78:1 (2009): 81–122, for more extensive analyses of Maimonides' approach to aggadah.

69. Maimonides writes that "subtle notions that very clearly elude the mind cannot be considered through the instrumentality of the customary words . . . for the bounds of expression in all languages are very narrow indeed, so that we cannot represent this notion to ourselves except through a certain looseness of expression." Maimonides, *Guide for the Perplexed,* 1:57. Also see Arthur Hyman, "Maimonides on Religious Language," in *Studies in Jewish Philosophy,* ed. Norbert Samuelson (New York: University Press of America, 1987), 351–67.

70. See Maimonides, *Guide for the Perplexed,* 3:43–45, and Frank Talmage, "Apples of Gold: The Inner Meaning of Sacred Texts in Medieval Judaism," in *Jewish Spirituality: From the Bible through the Middle Ages,* ed. Arthur Green (New York: Crossroad, 1987), 335; repr. in *Apples of Gold in Settings of Silver: Studies in Medieval Jewish Exegesis and Polemics,* ed. Barry Dov Walfish (Toronto: Pontifical Institute of Mediaeval Studies, 1999), 130. Hereafter references to this article will be to the 1999 reprint.

71. Maimonides, *Mishnah im Perush Rabbenu Moshe ben Maimon, Seder Zeraim,* 20 (ed. Kafiḥ). Also see Breuer, "Maimonides and the Authority of Aggadah," 31.

72. See Maimonides, *Guide for the Perplexed,* introduction (ed. Pines), 9–10; 3:43–5 (573). Also see Talmage, "Apples of Gold," 130.

73. Note also the comment made by Shem Tov ben Isaac Shaprut in his work, *Pardes Rimonim* (Zhitomir, 1866), 22–23: "Now reader, see how all of these aggadot explain great secrets and awesome matters hidden from the eyes of the sages. Praised be God who revealed their intention to us so we could understand their inner meaning." See Talmage's discussion in "Apples of Gold" for a translation of this source (129–31) as well as Isadore Twersky's inclusion of it in "*R. yedayah hapenini uferusho laaggadah,*" in *Studies in Jewish Religion and Intellectual History Presented to A. Altman,* ed. Siegfried Stein and Raphael Loewe (Tuscaloosa: University of Alabama Press, 1979), 71.

74. Maimonides, *Mishnah im Perush Rabbenu Moshe ben Maimon,* introduction to *Pereq Ḥeleq,* 4:209

75. See Lorberbaum, "*Temurot,*" 88. And see Talmage, "Apples of Gold," 131.

76. Note that when Maimonides' son, Abraham, approached the medium of aggadah, he reflected a concern for the importance of defining "aggadah" rather than for producing an interpretive treatise. In his essay "*Maamar al Odot Derashot Ḥazal,*" which was eventually printed in later editions of the *En Yaaqov,* Abraham upholds the distinction between aggadot that are exegetical (midrash aggadah) and those that are narrative in nature, with no connection to scriptural verses. Within these two categories he describes different types of aggadot, including those that have a clear meaning and can be understood in accordance with their literal sense, those that have a hidden meaning, those that have both a literal meaning and an underlying meaning, and those that have a poetic form. There are also narrative aggadot that are literally true, symbolically true, or didactic fictions. See Carmi Horowitz, *The Jewish Sermon in Fourteenth-Century Spain: The Derashot of Rabbi Joshua ibn Shu'eib* (Cambridge, MA: Harvard University Press, 1989), 135. See later editions of the *En Yaaqov* that contain this essay, such as *EY* (Jerusalem, 1961), and see Abraham Maimonides, "*Maamar al Odot Derashot Ḥazal,*" in *Milḥamot Hashem* (Jerusalem, 1953). The first printed edition of the *En Yaaqov/Bet Yaaqov* (Salonika 1516, 1522) did not contain Abraham Maimonides' essay on aggadah. Oddly, editors placed this essay at the beginning of the first English translation of the *En Yaaqov* (New York: Glick, 1917), vol. 1, instead of ibn Ḥabib's original introduction to the collection. Ibn Ḥabib's introduction was left out altogether.

77. Saperstein, *Decoding the Rabbis,* 12.

78. Even anti-philosophers responded by gravitating to the same aggadot, and they used them as loci in the defense of their own views.

79. Elbaum, *Lehavin divre ḥakhamim,* 22–23.

80. Breuer, "Maimonides and the Authority of the Aggadah," 44–45. Also see Lorberbaum, "*Temurot,*" 82–95.

81. Hava Tirosh-Rothschild, "Jewish Philosophy on the Eve of Modernity," 2:549–50n3. Also see Alexander Broadie, "The Nature of Medieval Jewish Phi-

losophy," in *Routledge History of World Philosophies: History of Jewish Philosophy,* ed. Daniel H. Frank and Oliver Leaman, 2 vols. (London: Routledge, 1996), 2:88–89.

82. Broadie, "The Nature of Medieval Jewish Philosophy," 2:88–89.

83. Broadie, "The Nature of Medieval Jewish Philosophy," 2:89.

84. Tirosh-Rothschild, "Jewish Philosophy on the Eve of Modernity," 2:550n3.

85. See *m. Ḥag* 2:1. Also note Saadya Gaon's discussion of this passage in his *Sefer Emunot Vedeot,* where he states that the sages of the Talmud would never have forbidden one to speculate about matters noted in *m. Ḥag.* The comment made in *m. Ḥag.* is, according to Saadya, merely aimed against those who engage in the type of philosophical speculation that is entirely independent of and not guided by the prophetic works of Scripture. And yet, despite Saadya's desire to dissuade his constituency from independent speculative activity and to root such activity in biblical texts, *Sefer Emunot Vedeot* is not arranged as a running commentary on the books of the Bible. It is a philosophical treatise that integrates biblical and rabbinic passages where needed. See Saadya Gaon, *Emunot Vedeot,* trans. Samuel Rosenblatt (New Haven, CT: Yale University Press, 1948), 27. Also see Broadie, "The Nature of Medieval Jewish Philosophy," 2:89–90.

86. Marc Saperstein, "The Social and Cultural Context: Thirteenth–Fifteenth Centuries," in *Routledge History of World Philosophies: History of Jewish Philosophy,* ed. Daniel H. Frank and Oliver Leaman, 2 vols. (London: Routledge, 1996), 2:312–13n125.

87. Eric Lawee, *Isaac Abarbanel's Stance toward Tradition: Defense, Dissent, and Dialogue* (Albany: State University of New York Press, 2001), 85–86.

88. Lawee, *Abarbanel,* 86. See Maimonides, *Guide for the Perplexed,* 1:59 (140), and Maimonides, *Iggerot Harambam,* ed. Yitzhak Shailat (Jerusalem: Maaliyot Press, 1987–88), 2:488.

89. Talmage, "Apples of Gold," 131.

90. Saperstein, *Decoding the Rabbis,* 7.

91. Bernard Septimus, "Piety and Power in Thirteenth-Century Catalonia," in *Studies in Medieval Jewish History and Literature,* ed. Isadore Twersky (Cambridge, MA: Harvard University Press, 1979), 201–5, where he discusses the nature of the battle over rationalism that erupted between the communities of France and Germany.

92. See Meir Halevi Abulafia, *Kitab al-rasa'il,* ed. J. Brill (Paris, 1871), 14. Also see Julius Guttmann, *Philosophies of Judaism: A History of Jewish Philosophy from Biblical Times to Franz Rosenzweig* (New York: Schocken Books, 1964), 209–11, where he also makes reference to the oppositions of Judah Alfakar.

93. Bernard Septimus, *Hispano-Jewish Culture in Transition: The Career and Controversies of Ramah* (Cambridge, MA: Harvard University Press, 1982), 5, 11, 16–17.

94. Septimus, *Hispano-Jewish Culture in Transition,* 84–85.

95. See Horowitz, *"Al perush haaggadot,"* 16, where he notes that Rabbi Solomon ben Abraham ibn Adret's compilation of interpretations on the aggadot of the Talmud was widely read. It was known to the following rabbinic figures: Shem Tov ibn Gaon, Joshua ibn Shu'eib, Baḥya ben Asher, Meir Aldabi, Shem Tov ibn

Shaprut, Isaac Abarbanel, Meir ibn Gabbai, Joseph Jabetz, Joseph Ashkenazi, and Azariah de Rossi.

96. See Shalom Meshulam Weinberger, ed., *Ḥiddushe Harashba al Aggadot Hashas* (Jerusalem, 1966). Note that not all the material attributed to ibn Adret found in this collection was actually written by him, as Horowitz notes, "*Al perush haaggadot*," 16–17. Leon A. Feldman has attempted to develop a critical edition of this work and has published portions of ibn Adret's commentary, including work on the following tractates: *Baba Batra:* "*Perush haaggadot larashba lemasekhet baba batra,*" *Bar Ilan University Studies in Judaica* 7–8 (1969–70): 138–53; *Megillah:* "R. Solomon ibn Adret: Commentary on the Legends in the Talmud, Tractate Megillah," in *Rabbi Joseph H. Lookstein Memorial Volume,* ed. Leo Landman (New York: Ktav, 1980), 119–24; *Nedarim:* "*Perush haagadot lerashba lemasekhet nedarim,*" in *Hagut ivrit beamerika,* ed. Menaḥem Zohari, Aryeh Tartakover, and Haim Ormian (Tel Aviv: Yavne, 1972), 1: 421–25; and *Hullin:* "*Perush haaggadot lerashba lemasekhet ḥullin,*" *Sinai* 64:5–6 (1969): 243–47. Although Feldman claims that ibn Adret wrote a much larger work on the aggadot of the Talmud (see "Rabbi Solomon ibn Adret," 119), Horowitz argues that this work consisted of only fifty-seven comments ("*Al perush haaggadot,*" 21). It is most interesting that ibn Adret's work remained in manuscript until ibn Ḥabib incorporated the material that he had into the first printed edition of the *En Yaaqov* in 1516. Printed editions of ibn Adret's aggadic commentary were not published until the twentieth century, as noted by Feldman in "Rabbi Solomon ibn Adret," 19–120.

97. Marc Saperstein, "The Conflict over the Rashba's Herem on Philosophical Study: A Political Perspective," *Jewish History* 1:2 (1986): 28. Also see Ram Ben-Shalom, "The Ban Placed by the Community of Barcelona on the Study of Philosophy and Allegorical Preaching: A New Study," *Revue des Études Juives* 3:4 (2000): 387–404, and his earlier article, "Communication and Propaganda between Provence and Spain: The Controversy over Extreme Allegorization (1303–1306)," in *Communication in the Jewish Diaspora,* ed. Sophia Menache (Leiden: Brill, 1996), 171–224.

98. Note that in Sirat's discussion of ibn Adret's letter, she indicates that he lodged his attack against the philosophy of Levi ben Abraham. By this point, she argues, no one dared to attack Maimonides outright. Instead they targeted other adversaries who supported Maimonides. See Colette Sirat, *A History of Jewish Philosophy in the Middle Ages* (Cambridge: Cambridge University Press, 1985), 243–44.

99. F. Kobler, *Letters of the Jews through the Ages* (Philadelphia: Jewish Publication Society, 1978), 256–57, as quoted by Sirat, *A History of Jewish Philosophy,* 244–45.

100. Catalonia had strong political, cultural, and linguistic ties with southern France. Barcelona's rabbinic scholars had been in close contact with their contemporaries in Provence since the beginning of the twelfth century. See Septimus, *Hispano-Jewish Culture in Transition,* 28–30.

101. Saperstein, *Decoding the Rabbis,* 206.

102. Note that Yedayah Bedersi (or Yedayah Hapenini) has often been confused with Isaac ben Yedayah. See Isadore Twersky, "*R. yedayah hapenini uferusho laagga-*

dah," 63–82. See Marc Saperstein, "R. Isaac b. Yeda'ya: A Forgotten Commentator on the Aggada," *Revue des Études Juives* 138:1–2 (1979): 17–45, where he argues that Twersky mistakenly attributed Isaac ben Yedayah's commentary on the aggadot of the Talmud to Yedayah Hapenini Bedersi. Also see Saperstein, "Selected Passages from Yedayah Bedersi's Commentary on the Midrashim," in *Studies in Medieval Jewish History II,* ed. Isadore Twersky (Cambridge, MA: Harvard University Press, 1984), 423–40. See Horowitz, *The Jewish Sermon,* 136.

103. See Saperstein's discussion in *Decoding the Rabbis,* 207, 273–75nn17–20. There, he refers to the fourth part of Meir ben Simon's *Milḥemet Mitsvah,* where the discussion is devoted to the aggadot being used by Christians and Kabbalists for their own purposes. He notes that Meir ben Simon discussed aggadot that the geonim had found difficult and which had been exploited by Christians for their own polemical purposes (273n17). Also see Frank Talmage, *David Kimhi: The Man and His Commentaries* (Cambridge, MA: Harvard University Press, 1975), 81 (as cited by Saperstein). As part of the same genre, Saperstein also makes reference to Moses ibn Tibbon's *Sefer Peah;* Levi ben Abraham's section titled "*Shaar Haaggadah,*" in his work *Livyat Ḥen;* and Yedayah Bedersi's philosophical commentary on the midrashim. Other works, including commentaries written on aggadic passages, have been cited in various treatises but have been lost, such as Shem Tov Falaquera's thirteenth-century *Sefer Haderush* (see Saperstein, *Decoding the Rabbis,* 207). Falaquera, who lived in the border provinces between Spain and France, cites this work in his commentary on Maimonides' *Guide, Moreh Hamoreh.*

104. That ibn Adret and Hapenini were in communication with each other is clear from the fact that Hapenini wrote to ibn Adret directly imploring him to understand the value of studying the books of Maimonides. He informed ibn Adret that his ban would yield no profit, and therefore he should abandon his mission by making peace with the scholars of Provence. See Yedayah Hapenini, *Ketav Hahitnatslut,* folios 120v and 125v. *Ketav Hahitnatslut* was printed in Solomon ibn Adret, *Sheelot Uteshuvot* (Hanover, 1610), 65d–67a (416–18). And see Sirat's translation in *A History of Jewish Philosophy,* 274–75, 440.

105. Saperstein notes that there were some exceptions. The Spanish philosopher Shem Tov Falaquera wrote a philosophic exposition of aggadic passages from the Talmud titled *Sefer Haderush.* The collection is no longer extant. See Marc Saperstein, *Decoding the Rabbis,* 207, and Horowitz, *The Jewish Sermon,* 136.

106. Israel M. Ta-Shma, "The Study of Aggadah and Its Interpretation in Early Rabbinic Literature," 202.

107. Isadore Twersky describes this moment in Jewish cultural history as a time when "Hebrew literature became . . . the repository of the whole Aristotelian heritage of Greek philosophy." So exact were the translations, claims Twersky, that Jews were able to achieve an "exactness in philosophical comprehension." Indeed, the desire to be "wise in the eyes of the nations" proved to be a powerful catalyst in the decision to embrace the rationalist agenda. See Twersky, "Aspects of the Social and Cultural History of Provencal Jewry," in *Jewish Society through the Ages,* ed. H. H. Ben-Sasson and S. Ettinger (London: Vallentine, 1971), 190–202. Also see Colette Sirat's discussion regarding the renewal of urban life that prompted this dissemi-

nation of philosophic study beyond the elite sectors of the Jewish communities in Provence and in Catalonia. Sirat, *A History of Jewish Philosophy,* 212–14.

108. Marc Saperstein dismisses the commonly held perception of Jewish philosophy as "the privileged possession of the intellectual elite." In his description of French philosophers, he notes that philosophically minded Jews, such as David Kimḥi, were not members of the aristocracy. Referring also to the works of the French medieval philosopher Gersonides (1288–1344), Saperstein notes that this philosopher wrote on three different levels. Gersonides wrote technical supercommentaries on Averroës, an independent theological treatise, and biblical commentaries for a broad readership. See Saperstein, "Social and Cultural Context," 306–14.

109. For example, the Provencal rabbi Yedayah Hepenini Bedersi's works reflect a presentation of philosophy on varying levels of difficulty. Some of his works were quite technical, such as his commentaries on Averroës' *Physics* and Avicenna's *Canon,* as well as his independent treatises that display an interest in both Islamic and Scholastic philosophy. Other works were of a more popular nature, in which he wedded his philosophical interests to reflections about more traditional forms of Jewish piety. See Saperstein, "Social and Cultural Context," 307–8. Also see Saperstein's *Decoding the Rabbis* (205) regarding Isaac ben Yedayah's desire to spread philosophy to more popular circles of Jews.

110. See Ta-Shma, "The Study of Aggadah," 210, where he notes that ibn Adret was so intrigued by Maimonides' aggadic interpretations from the *Guide* that he quoted them with a great degree of admiration. Also see Saperstein, "The Conflict over the Rashba's Herem," 37n22.

111. Weinberger, ed., *Ḥiddushe Harashba al Aggadot Hashas.* According to Horowitz, Weinberger drew material from other places and, therefore, not all the texts contained therein were authored by ibn Adret. Horowitz, *"Al perush haaggadot,"* 16–17.

112. See Elbaum, *Lehavin divre ḥakhamim,* 183.

113. Leon A. Feldman, *"Perush haaggadot lerashba lemasekhet baba batra,"* 140–44. Ibn Adret's understanding of the World to Come is quite different from that of Maimonides, who argues for a purely spiritual interpretation. According to Maimonides, the Talmudic notion of a feast in the World to Come is an allusion to spiritual bliss. See Maimonides, *Mishne Torah, Hilkhot Teshuva* 8:2. For a larger discussion of Maimonides' views on immortality, see Harry Blumberg, "The Problem of Immortality in Avicenna, Maimonides, and St. Thomas Aquinas," in *Essays in Medieval Jewish and Islamic Philosophy,* ed. Arthur Hyman (New York: Ktav, 1977), 104.

114. Horowitz, *"Al perush haaggadot,"* 21–24. Here Horowitz relies on observations made by Isadore Twersky, *Rabad of Posquieres* (Philadelphia: Jewish Publication Society, 1980), 359, and Abraham Halkin, "Yedayah Bedershi's Apology," in *Jewish Medieval and Renaissance Studies,* ed. Alexander Altmann (Cambridge, MA: Harvard University Press, 1967), 176–79.

115. See Elbaum, *Lehavin divre ḥakhamim,* 22n16. See Lawee, *Abarbanel,* 86, 131–32, and Isaac Abarbanel, *Yeshuot Meshiḥo* (Königsberg, 1861), 5r.

116. See Lawee, *Abarbanel,* 131; Abarbanel, *Yeshuot Meshiḥo,* 5r.

117. Lawee, *Abarbanel,* 53. See also Saperstein, "R. Isaac b. Yeda'ya," 37. Both Lawee and Saperstein agree that Abarbanel lauded ibn Adret because he was particularly bothered by the fact that his predecessors did not explore the aggadot which contained messianic content often used in disputations against Christians. Abarbanel's work, *Yeshuot Meshiḥo,* was devoted to a discussion of messianism, and therefore this aggadic material was most relevant to him in completing his work.

118. In his introduction to the *En Yaaqov,* ibn Ḥabib notes that his ability to compile the *En Yaaqov* while living in Salonika was due to the fact that he had access to the library of the Ben Banvanest family. They not only collected books and manuscripts but hired scribes to copy some of Judaism's seminal works. See Joseph Hacker, "Intellectual Activity," 104–5. Also see M. Molcho, *"Bate eqed sefarim,"* *Maḥberet 2* (1954): 23–24 (on libraries in sixteenth-century Salonika).

119. See ibn Ḥabib's commentary on *b. Ber.* 55b: *EY Berakhot* (Salonika, 1516), vol. 1, section 110, 42b–43b (= Jerusalem, 1961, vol. 1, section 123 [middle], 86b), where he discusses ben Yedayah's understanding of dreams, specifically with respect to a question posed by Rava about whether dreams speak truths or lies. Also see *EY Berakhot* (Jerusalem, 1961), vol. 1, 108b–109b, where ibn Ḥabib writes that he intends to copy only a small part of Isaac ben Yedayah's work on aggadah. He continues to point out that the reason for drawing on only a small portion of the material is because ben Yedayah's aggadic commentary contains philosophical homilies that are not essential to understanding the true roots of faith, and that some of his interpretive comments do not capture the original intent of the aggadic passage. Within the same comment, ibn Ḥabib lambastes his Spanish contemporary Abraham Bibago, who was overly focused on providing his students with desired philosophic interpretations. Note that this comment is missing from *EY* (Salonika, 1516). The editors of *En Yaaqov* (Vilna: Romm, 1883) claim that this statement can be found in *En Yisrael* (Venice, 1566) and they printed it based on what they saw in this collection. Later editions also contain this text—specifically *EY* (Jerusalem, 1961), because it is an exact reprint of *EY* (Vilna, 1883). Although I did not locate the text in *EY* (Venice, 1566), the language of the passage reflects ibn Ḥabib's style of writing and the perspective conveyed suggests that the comment was authored by him. Therefore I chose to speak about it as if it was original to ibn Ḥabib, in keeping with the observations of the editors of *En Yaaqov* (Vilna, 1883). Also see Saperstein, "R. Isaac b. Yeda'ya," 38.

120. Ibn Ḥabib incorporates many of the comments made by ibn Adret into his anthology, distinguishing them clearly from his own. At times ibn Ḥabib discusses ibn Adret's ideas within his own commentary, even admitting to his inability to understand passages better through them. For example, in response to the aggadic passage on *b. Ber.* 7a, where Rabbi Yishmael enters the Holy of Holies to burn incense and sees either a form of God named Akatriel or an angel, who asks Rabbi Yishmael to bless him, ibn Ḥabib writes: "And also [despite] all that ibn Adret [wrote in his] interpretation [of this passage,] I still have not merited to understand the full [sense] of the passage." See *EY Berakhot* (Salonika, 1516), section 23, 15a–b, where ibn Ḥabib's remarks are found following a lengthy quotation from ibn Ad-

ret's commentary on an earlier section of this aggadic passage (= Jerusalem, 1961, vol. 1, section 27, 19b).

121. Regarding ibn Adret and his relationship to Kabbalah, Carmi Horowitz notes that, of the fifty-seven passages that he commented on, sixteen were passages on which Azriel of Gerona commented and twenty-six were passages that Todros ben Joseph Halevi Abulafia explicated in his commentary on Talmudic aggadah, *Otsar Hakavod* (Warsaw, 1879). With respect to these passages, ibn Adret either argues against the methods of interpretation used by these Kabbalists in their study of aggadah or avoids Kabbalistic explanations altogether (Horowitz, "*Al perush haaggadot*," 21–22). Ibn Adret was also known to decline public and literary discussion of esoteric matters (Horowitz, *The Jewish Sermon*, 7–9). This is not to say, however, that ibn Adret isolated himself entirely from Kabbalah; indeed, he was well aware of the intellectual developments occurring in Barcelona regarding Kabbalah. He was also influenced by his teacher Naḥmanides. See Elbaum, *Lehavin divre ḥakhamim*, 183.

122. See Wolfson, "'By Way of Truth,'" 161–76, on Naḥmanides' approach to rabbinic aggadah.

123. Wolfson, "'By Way of Truth,'" 161. Wolfson argues that Naḥmanides would interpret Talmudic aggadah in light of the symbolism found in *Sefer Habahir* 166–69.

124. Such a commitment to aggadah also explains why Kabbalah could emerge in rabbinic centers and be studied by mainstream rabbis instead of in marginal areas of rabbinic culture. See Michael A. Fishbane, *Biblical Myth and Rabbinic Mythmaking* (Oxford: Oxford University Press, 2003), 11.

125. Matt Goldish, "Rabbinic Culture and Dissent," in *Rabbinic Culture and Its Critics: Jewish Authority, Dissent, and Heresy in Medieval and Early Modern Times,* ed. Daniel Frank and Matt Goldish (Detroit: Wayne State University Press, 2008), 20.

126. See *EY Shabbat* (Salonika, 1516), vol. 1, section 3, 61b (= Jerusalem, 1961, vol. 1, section 3, 4a–b). And see Joseph Gikatilla, *Sefer Shaare Orah* (Warsaw, 1883), 23a.

127. *b. Ḥag.* 14b.

128. See Moshe Idel's reference to A. Kohut, ed., *Arukh Hashalem* (Vienna, 1878), 1:14 (*s.v. "avne shayish tahor"*), as noted in his article, "From Italy to Ashkenaz and Back: On the Circulation of Jewish Mystical Traditions," *Kabbalah* 14 (2006): 49.

129. See *EY Ḥagigah* (Salonika, 1516), vol. 1, 180b–181a (note there are no section numbers in tractate *Ḥagigah* as there are in earlier tractates of the 1516 edition) (= Jerusalem, 1961, vol. 3, section 11, 33b–34a). Ibn Ḥabib's remarks in the first printed edition of the *En Yaaqov* attest to the fact that he discovered both these passages in a "book that was found" in the house of a great rabbinic scholar from the kingdom of Catalonia. This book was presumably brought to Salonika, where ibn Ḥabib was able to view it and cite from it. It is also interesting that ibn Ḥabib ends this comment nostalgically. With memories of Spain on his mind, he reminds his readers of the greatness of the Catalonian Jewish community "of blessed memory."

130. Scholars believe that the original version of *b. Ḥag.* 15b (which elaborates on the baraita on *b. Ḥag.* 14b regarding the experience in paradise) originally read, "Rabbi Akiva descended and ascended in peace," instead of "Rabbi Akiva ascended and descended in peace." If Hai Gaon had a text that described Rabbi Akiva as descending and then ascending, it makes sense that he would describe him as having descended into a contemplative state, where he had a vision of the Divine Throne, and then ascending from it in peace. For a more detailed discussion of the textual issues, see Maria E. Subtelny, "The Tale of the Four Sages Who Entered Pardes: A Talmudic Enigma from a Persian Perspective," *Jewish Studies Quarterly* 11 (2004): 31–32.

131. Idel, "From Italy to Ashkenaz and Back," 50–51.

132. See *EY Ḥagigah* (Salonika, 1516), 180b–81a (= Jerusalem, 1961, vol. 3, section 11, 33b–34a).

133. Tirosh-Rothschild, "Jewish Philosophy on the Eve of Modernity," 500; Maud Kozodoy, "A Study of the Life and Works of Profiat Duran" (Ph.D. diss., Jewish Theological Seminary, 2006), 3.

134. Tirosh-Rothschild, "Jewish Philosophy on the Eve of Modernity," 500.

135. Tirosh-Rothschild, "Jewish Philosophy on the Eve of Modernity," 500–501.

136. Tirosh-Rothschild, "Jewish Philosophy on the Eve of Modernity," 500–502.

137. Tirosh-Rothschold, "Jewish Philosophy on the Eve of Modernity," 502.

138. Tirosh-Rothschild and Eliezer Schweid attribute the limited impact of Crescas' thought on other philosophers to the fact that he never replaced the Aristotelian system with his own cosmology. Tirosh-Rothschild, "Jewish Philosophy on the Eve of Modernity," 502–3; Eliezer Schweid, *The Classic Jewish Philosophers: From Saadia through the Renaissance,* trans. Leonard Levin (Leiden: E. J. Brill, 2008), 358.

139. Kellner, *Dogma,* 108–9.

140. Schweid, *The Classical Jewish Philosophers,* 421.

141. Marc Saperstein, *"Your Voice Like a Ram's Horn": Themes and Texts in Traditional Jewish Preaching* (Cincinnati: Hebrew Union College Press, 1996), 75.

142. See Ari Ackerman, "Jewish Philosophy and the Jewish-Christian Philosophical Dialogue in Fifteenth-Century Spain," in *The Cambridge Companion to Medieval Jewish Philosophy,* ed. Daniel H. Frank and Oliver Leaman (Cambridge: Cambridge University Press, 2003), 382.

143. See Saperstein, *"Your Voice,"* 78.

144. Saperstein, *"Your Voice,"* 77, summarizes the difficulties incurred by a scholar studying Jewish preaching, given the oral nature of the genre.

145. Saperstein, *"Your Voice,"* 87.

146. See Saperstein, *"Your Voice,"* 78–84.

147. According to Saperstein, this sermon on the binding of Isaac was found in the manuscripts of two collections: Shem Tov ben Joseph ibn Shem Tov, *Derashot Hatorah* (Cambridge University MS Dd. 10.46, fols. 34r–36r and Cambridge Trinity College MS 140 [F12 49], folios 48r–52v). See Saperstein, *"Your Voice,"* 252–53, 257.

148. For example, Shalom discusses *b. Ber.* 2a, regarding the creation of the

world (*Neve Shalom* 1:1, 1a); *b. Ber.* 33a, on the divine attributes (*Neve Shalom* 12:1:1, 198a); and *b. Ber.* 33b, on free will (*Neve Shalom* 10:2:1, 208a). See Davidson, *The Philosophy of Abraham Shalom,* 3n21.

149. Davidson also makes the point that Shalom's homilies often digressed from their aggadic locus in the name of another objective. Shalom was devoted to reviewing the philosophic statements of his predecessors in order to evaluate which ones were in harmony with Scripture—that is, which ones were correct. Davidson suggests that these sections may have been composed independently by Shalom and that he, at a later point, incorporated them into his homilies. Davidson, *The Philosophy of Abraham Shalom,* 3.

150. In fact, Jews were forced to attend synagogues where clerics like Vincente Ferrer preached with great fervor against Judaism. Kellner, *Dogma,* 80–81, writes, "The traditional communal/halakhic leadership, despite their pronounced interest in halakhic matters, was forced by the circumstances in which it found itself to embark upon a clearly theological endeavor despite the fact that it had little innate interest in purely theological questions."

151. Kellner, *Dogma,* 3.

152. See Daniel J. Lasker, *Jewish Philosophical Polemics against Christianity in the Middle Ages* (New York: Ktav, 1977).

153. The degree to which the conversos participated in or became interested in the intricacies of the philosophical debate over dogma remains unclear. After all, was the average crypto-Jew invested in what emerged from these intellectual conversations which, at times, came to be about challenging Maimonides' intellectualist view of faith rather than about expanding the discussion of his thirteen principles? Was the average Jew concerned about internalizing a set of theological principles? Tirosh-Rothschild, *Between Worlds,* 146, has argued that the conversation surrounding dogmatics had little practical import. Jews were not excommunicated for failing to uphold a set of dogmatic principles, as communities were far too localized and fragmented to put such a system into place. Indeed, this was a conversation that took place among the intellectual elite in an attempt to develop an imagined sense of identity in a world where the security of that identity was being challenged by Christianity at every turn.

154. See, for example, Haim Hillel Ben-Sasson, *"Dor gole sefarad al atsmo,"* 36–37.

155. Tirosh-Rothschild, *Between Worlds,* 141.

156. Tirosh-Rothschild, *Between Worlds,* 144.

157. Kellner, *Dogma,* 81.

158. This would explain why so many of the dogmatists during the fifteenth century spent their time writing polemical anti-Chrisitan tracts or recording contentious dialogues with Christians. See Lasker, *Jewish Philosophical Polemics.*

159. Tirosh-Samuelson, "The Ultimate End of Human Life," 227–28.

160. See ibn Ḥabib's comments at the end of *Seder Zeraim* in the *EY* (Salonika, 1516), vol. 1, 60b (= Jerusalem, 1961, vol. 1, 15a [middle of the page]), where he specifically refers to the demands made on him for interpretations of Talmudic aggadah. Also note that this page is mistakenly numbered as page 60, but is actu-

ally page 62, due to some extra pages that were not numbered correctly.

161. As noted earlier, the *Bet Yaaqov* (Salonika, 1522) was the second volume of the *En Yaaqov,* compiled by Jacob ibn Ḥabib's son, Levi ibn Ḥabib, after his father died.

162. Also see Hacker, "Intellectual Activity," 114–15n39–40, where he mentions other collections of midrash aggadah and of aggadah that were printed in the Ottoman empire during the period 1510–25.

163. See ibn Ḥabib's comments at the end of *Seder Zeraim* in the *EY* (Salonika, 1516), vol. 1, 60b (= Jerusalem, 1961, vol. 1, 15a [top of the page]). Also note that this page is erroneously numbered as page 60 but is in fact page 62, due to some extra pages that were not numbered correctly.

164. See Hacker, "Intellectual Activity," 114–15; Tirosh-Rothschild, "The Ultimate End of Human Life," 231.

165. *EY* (Salonika, 1516), vol. 1, introduction (= Jerusalem, 1961, vol. 1, introduction).

166. *EY* (Salonika, 1516), vol. 1, introduction (= Jerusalem, 1961, vol. 1, introduction).

167. The best printed examples reflecting the decision to focus on writing commentaries on the texts of the Bible and Talmud can be found in the late sixteenth-century commentary on *Midrash Rabbah, Yefe Toar,* written by Samuel Jaffe Ashkenazi, as well as his commentary on the aggadot of the *Yerushalmi, Yefe Mare.* Solomon Levet Halevi's sixteenth-century work on the aggadot of the Talmud is another example. Both rabbis were living in the Ottoman empire during the sixteenth century, and their works were published in Venice at the end of the sixteenth century. See Hacker, "Intellectual Activity," 115. Note that many commentaries were never printed.

168. *EY* (Salonika, 1516), vol. 1, introduction (= Jerusalem, 1961, vol. 1, introduction).

169. *EY Berakhot* (Salonika, 1516), vol. 1, section 26, 18a–b (= Jerusalem, 1961, vol. 1, section 30, 22a–23a). Also see chapter 4, where I discuss this passage in greater detail.

170. *EY Berakhot* (Salonika, 1516), vol. 1, section 1, 6b–7a (= Jerusalem, 1961, vol. 1, section 3, 2a–4a). Also see chapter 4, where I discuss this passage in detail.

171. *EY Berakhot* (Salonika, 1516), vol. 1, section 4, 9b (= Jerusalem, 1961, vol. 1, section 8, 7a).

172. Jacob Elbaum correctly points to this absence of commentaries on the aggadot of the Talmud. Although he detects a change in this phenomenon beginning in the fifteenth century in Spain, I have not been able to locate a pronounced flowering of commentaries on the aggadot of the Talmud until the beginning of the seventeenth century. See Elbaum, *Lehavin divre ḥakhamim,* 41, and *Petiḥut vehistagrut.*

173. Tirosh-Samuelson, "The Ultimate End of Human Life," 228. The *En Yaaqov* supports the notion that sixteenth-century Ottoman Jewish culture was represented by a variety of literary forms, values, and ideas. It was part of a comprehensive increase in the literary productivity that was taking place during the

postexpulsion period in the Ottoman empire in the areas of halakhah, biblical and rabbinic hermeneutics, homiletics, poetry and prose, Kabbalah, philosophy, and theology. In fact, Yosef Yahalom refers to the first decades of the sixteenth century in the Ottoman empire as a "Hebrew Renaissance." See Yosef Yahalom, "A Hebrew Renaissance in the Sephardi Diaspora," *Peamim* 26 (1986): 10.

174. See *EY* (Salonika, 1516), vol. 1, introduction (= Jerusalem, 1961, vol. 1, introduction).

Chapter 3

1. George Steiner, "Our Homeland, the Text," *Salmagundi* 66 (1985): 7. This is Steiner's phrase.

2. David Stern, *The Anthology in Jewish Literature* (Oxford: Oxford University Press, 2004), 6–7.

3. See Lee S. Shulman, *The Wisdom of Practice: Essays on Teaching, Learning, and Learning to Teach* (San Francisco: Jossey-Bass, 2004), 421, where Shulman discusses Joseph Schwab's strategy of critical reading in approaching the works of Aristotle. Shulman notes that it was the discovery of what Aristotle was "doing" and not merely what he was "saying" that yielded a better understanding of Aristotle's work.

4. Stern, *The Anthology in Jewish Literature,* 10.

5. Halbertal, *People of the Book,* 126.

6. *EY* (Salonika, 1516), introduction (= Jerusalem, 1961, introduction).

7. Not surprisingly, *Haggadot Hatalmud* never achieved the same level of prominence as the *En Yaaqov.* It was not reprinted in the years after the first printed edition appeared in Constantinople in 1511. Printers took a greater interest in producing the *En Yaaqov.*

8. For example, see tractate *Ḥagigah* (Gaudalajara, 1480) and the Spanish printing of tractate *Eruvin,* in Haim Z. Dimitrovsky, *Seride bavli* (New York: Jewish Theological Seminary, 1979). While it is not clear that ibn Ḥabib had these exact printed works at his disposal when he thought about how to arrange the *En Yaaqov,* nor is it clear that the Salonikan printer of the *En Yaaqov,* Judah Gedaliah, used them as templates, it is well known that Spanish Jews created libraries in Salonika, which made a large number of classical materials more available than they had ever been in the past. See *EY* (Salonika, 1516), vol. 1, introduction, and Hacker, "Intellectual Activity," 104–5.

9. Baḥya ben Asher, *Kad Haqemaḥ,* in *Kitve Rabbenu Baḥya,* ed. Charles Ber Chavel (Jerusalem: Mossad Harav Kook, 1969), 18 (introduction).

10. There are two different works titled *Menorat Hamaor.* See Israel ibn al-Nakawa, *Menorat Hamaor,* 2 vols., ed. Hyman Gerson Enelow (New York: Bloch, 1929), and Isaac Aboab, *Menorat Hamaor* (Jerusalem: Mossad Harav Kook, 1961).

11. It is not clear from ibn Ḥabib's introduction whether he was referring to the edition of *Menorat Hamaor* compiled by ibn al-Nakawa or by Aboab. However, it is possible that he was familiar with both. Indeed, when noting that he intends to break from the template set by the "compiler of *Menorat Hamaor* and *Kad Haqemaḥ,*" he adds, "and [I also intend to break from] those [collections] that are

like them." Here ibn Ḥabib intimates that he knows of several collections that follow a topical editorial structure, like *Menorat Hamaor* and *Kad Haqemaḥ*. One of these collections could have been the second collection titled *Menorat Hamaor*. See *EY* (Salonika, 1516), introduction, vol. 1 (= Jerusalem, 1961, introduction, vol. 1).

12. See Aboab, *Menorat Hamaor,* 18 (introduction), where he discusses his editorial plan not only to draw material from the Talmud but also to include aggadic passages from other collections of midrash.

13. See *Kitve Rabbenu Baḥya* (ed. Chavel), 21. Also see Israel Bettan, *Studies in Jewish Preaching, Middle Ages* (Cincinnati: Hebrew Union College, 1939), 89–129, and Carmi Horowitz, *The Jewish Sermon,* 26–27. The extent to which *Kad Haqemaḥ* was studied by the populace, not necessarily by preachers, is not known.

14. See ibn al-Nakawa, *Menorat Hamaor,* 1:9–37 (the introduction authored by Hyman Gerson Enelow discusses ibn al-Nakawa's goals).

15. During the tumultuous events of the fourteenth century, which included the burning of Jewish books in the hope of converting Jews to Christianity, Israel ibn al-Nakawa was able to preserve various rare and unknown aggadic texts. See ibn al-Nakawa, *Menorat Hamaor,* 1:24 (Enelow's introduction).

16. Ta-Shma, "The Study of Aggadah and Its Interpretation in Early Rabbinic Literature," 211.

17. See ibn al-Nakawa, *Menorat Hamaor,* 2:23 (Enelow's introduction), and the section written by ibn al-Nakawa on prayer.

18. Ta-Shma, "The Study of Aggadah and Its Interpretation in Early Rabbinic Literature," 205. Also note that the topic headings for each of the chapters in *Menorat Hamaor* reflect ibn al-Nakawa's concern for cultivating the moral and religious Jew. The subjects of the twenty chapters he edited are charity, prayer, repentance, humility, fixed hours of study, the commandments and their fulfillment, acts of mercy, the observance of the Sabbath and holy days, honoring one's parents, marriage, the education of children, the upright conduct one must have in business, the proper administration of justice, contentment, equanimity, avoidance of flattery and deception, love of friends and the treatment of them, cleanness of speech, keeping a friend's secret, and good manners.

19. See ibn al-Nakawa, *Menorat Hamaor,* 1:23 (Enelow's introduction), and the poem at the beginning of ibn al-Nakawa's introduction in Hebrew. Also see Ta-Shma, "The Study of Aggadah and Its Interpretation in Early Rabbinic Literature," 205, where he attributes the lack of interest in aggadah to a general sense that it was intrinsically "unimportant" because it had no practical consequences in real life. Ibn al-Nakawa was trying to change this image of aggadah.

20. Ibn al-Nakawa writes of his lack of worthiness in assuming the role as the compiler of *Menorat Hamaor* (see *Menorat Hamaor,* vol. 1, 13 [Hebrew introduction]). It was not until "an angelic being inspired the necessary trembling and resolution" that he was able to begin work on the project (see the poem at the beginning of ibn al-Nakawa's introduction, vol. 1). See Goldin, "The Freedom and Restraint of Aggadah," 257n19, who quotes this source.

21. Aboab, *Menorat Hamaor,* 11–19.

22. In the middle of *EY* (Salonika, 1516), vol. 1, the section numbers end (be-

ginning with tractate *Megillah* there are virtually no section numbers). This is the mark of a compiler who, nearing the end of his life, could not labor fast enough to complete the work he had begun. See ibn Ḥabib's concluding remarks, found at the end of his anthology of aggadic texts drawn from the *Yerushalmi, Seder Zeraim: EY* (Salonika, 1516), vol. 1, 60b (= Jerusalem, 1961, vol. 1, 15a [second pagination]). There, ibn Ḥabib informs his audience that his work on the tractates of *Seder Moed* will not be on par with his work on tractate *Berakhot.* Also note that a few pages are not numbered. Therefore this page, although marked as 60, is in fact page 62.

23. Also see Aboab, *Menorat Hamaor,* 19, where he refers to the various themes in his aggadic collection as those that support the world—that is, as the foundations (*yesodot*) of the world. When ibn Ḥabib prepared his index, he relied on Aboab's conceptualization.

24. The index found in *Haggadot Hatalmud* also has sections with topic headings that include the biblical books found in the Prophets and the Writings.

25. See ibn Ḥabib, *EY* (Salonika, 1516), vol. 1, introduction, where he outlines his conceptual index. Also see *EY* (Salonika, 1516), vol. 1 (end), where both indexes can be found. See Ann Blair, "Reading Strategies for Coping with Information Overload, ca. 1550–1700," *Journal of the History of Ideas* 64:1 (2003): 11–28. Although Blair writes of the anxiety felt by authors over the ever-increasing production of books made possible by the printing press, her work points to the great efforts undertaken by compilers to categorize the large amounts of material that were thus made more readily available. In ibn Ḥabib's case, he had great plans to compose a helpful index. However, the index found at the end of the first printed edition of the *En Yaaqov* is incomplete and unusable. References to pages and section numbers do not align with the material in the collection itself. It makes sense that the index may have suffered, given that ibn Ḥabib died before completing his work on the *En Yaaqov.* In later editions, printers corrected the indexes so that they eventually became more useful. See, for example, *En Yaaqov* (Venice, 1546) and *En Yaaqov* (Venice, 1566).

26. Bella Hass Weinberg notes that even as early as Maimonides, prior to the onset of Hebrew printing, Jews prepared indexes. Maimonides put together an index titled *Mafteaḥ Haderashot* in the twelfth century. See Bella Hass Weinberg, "The Earliest Hebrew Citation Indexes," *Journal of the American Society for Information Science* 48:4 (1997): 318–30. Maimonides' index also points to the fact that there was an age-old interest in creating indexes that would aid in the study of aggadic material.

27. See *EY* (Salonika, 1516), vol. 1, 303 (this page can be found immediately before the first index at the end of volume 1). Ibn Ḥabib also offered the printer, Judah Gedaliah, input with regard to the format of his composition. In his introduction ibn Ḥabib states his intention to create an anthology of commentaries and expresses his desire to align these commentaries with the texts of the Talmud. These were not decisions made solely on the part of the printer. See *EY* (Salonika, 1516), introduction, vol. 1 (= Jerusalem, 1961, introduction, vol. 1).

28. Collections differed from one another because there were no set pages or a sense of uniformity.

29. Prior to the invention of printing with movable type, the text of the Babylonian Talmud was written in codices without commentaries. Commentaries were found in separate books. Although we do have some fragments where Rashi and Tosafot both appear on the Talmudic page (see E. E. Urbach, *Baale hatosafot: Toldotehem, ḥibburehem, shitatam* [Jerusalem: Mossad Bialik, 1980], vol. 2, 29), this format was not common and was not initially utilized in Spain or Portugal. The Soncino press in Italy established a template of commentaries on the Talmud page that included Rashi and Tosafot. Editors and printers followed this template for centuries. See Marvin J. Heller, "Earliest Printings of the Talmud," in *Printing of the Talmud from Bomberg to Schottenstein,* ed. Sharon Liberman Mintz and Gabriel M. Goldstein (New York: Yeshiva University Museum, 2005), 61–62. For a more extensive overview of the history of the printing of the Talmud, see Heller, *Printing of the Talmud.* Also see Shimon Iakerson, *Catalogue of Hebrew Incunabula from the Collection of the Library of the Jewish Theological Seminary of America,* 2 vols. (New York: Jewish Theological Seminary, 2004), 2:319–436; and Iakerson, *Catalogue of Books Printed in the XVth Century Now in the British Library* (Netherlands: Hes & De Graaf, 2004), 82–84. Most especially see Dimitrovsky, ed., *Seride bavli,* to view a collection of fragments of Spanish and Portuguese incunabula. These fragments contain Rashi's commentary but not Tosafot.

30. The Italian printer Joshua Solomon Soncino writes on one of the two colophons found in tractate *b. Berakhot* (Soncino, 1483–84): "I have joined these desirable commentaries [Rashi and Tosafot, *Sefer Mordekhai,* and Maimonides' commentary on the Mishnah] together to be a comely work, for all who know our way, know that no other books are necessary besides these for this tractate." See *b. Berakhot* (Soncino, 1483–84). Also see Heller, "Earliest Printings of the Talmud," 63. In this regard, ibn Ḥabib followed in the footsteps of Soncino with respect to Talmud study by including the "most desirable" commentaries of Rashi and Tosafot (as well as others) in his collection. A comparison between the text of *b. Berakhot* (Soncino, 1483–84) and *EY Berakhot* (Salonika, 1516) shows that ibn Ḥabib had the versions of the texts found within it and relied on it when he prepared the *En Yaaqov.* He relied on other versions of tractate *Berakhot* as well, which were available to him in Salonika.

31. See chapter 2, "The *En Yaaqov:* A Response to the Problems and Challenges of Aggadah," where I discuss the attitudes of Jews toward aggadah.

32. Ta-Shma, "The Study of Aggadah and Its Interpretation in Early Rabbinic Literature," 205–6.

33. The texts of Rashi's commentary found in the first printed edition of the *En Yaaqov* differ from our own versions of Rashi found presently in the *Bavli* (Vilna: Romm, 1880–91). When ibn Ḥabib engaged in the process of anthologizing Rashi's comments, he did not always include Rashi's full comment on a given Talmudic section. He left out portions that related to the halakhic debates found in the *sugyot* (pericopes) of the Talmud when they did not inform the aggadaic passage of interest to him.

34. At times, before ibn Ḥabib begins his own comments, he takes the opportunity to refer to a comment made by Rashi in another tractate in order to guide

the reader's study of the material. For example, in *EY Berakhot* (Salonika, 1516), vol. 1, 6b, ibn Ḥabib wishes to provide some background material on the term *bat qol* (heavenly voice). He states, "[Regarding the term] *bat qol,* Rashi does not say anything in his commentary at all here [in tractate *Berakhot*]. But, in tractate *Sotah,* he explains [it]." Ibn Ḥabib, however, does not quote Rashi's interpretation from *Sotah* (*b. Sotah* 33a). Instead, he notes that Rashi offers a new interpretation of the term *bat qol* and encourages his readers to look at Rashi in tractate *Sotah.*

35. According to Rashi's understanding, the passage in *b. Ber.* 6b should be translated: "The entire world was created only [so that the] community [could gather together to support] this [righteous] person." See *EY Berakhot* (Salonika, 1516), vol. 1, section 21, 15a (= Jerusalem, 1961, vol. 1, section 26, 19a). Also see the following reference works: Moshe Kattan, *Otsar haloazim* (Jerusalem, 1984), 1, where Rashi's use of the old French word *solaz* is translated as "a community that prevents a person who lives within it from becoming bored." And see Israel Gukovitzki, *Targum halaaz al hashas* (London: G. J. George & Co., 1985), 101, who defines the word as "company." See parallels in *b. Shabbat* 30b, *b. Qidd.* 63a, *b. B. Qama* 9b, and *b. B. Metsia* 28a.

36. Eric Lawee, "The Reception of Rashi's *Commentary on the Torah* in Spain: The Case of Adam's Mating with the Animals," *Jewish Quarterly Review* 97:1 (2007): 42–43n41. Also see E. E. Urbach, "How Did Rashi Merit the Title *Parshandata?*" in *Rashi 1040–1090: Hommage à Ephraïm E. Urbach,* ed. Gabrielle Sed-Rajna (Paris: Editions du Cerf, 1993), 390–92, including his comments on how the reference to Rashi as *parshandata* was widespread in the circle that included Isaac Aboab, a disciple of Isaac Canpanton and a contemporary of ibn Ḥabib in Castile.

37. See *EY* (Salonika, 1516), vol. 1, introduction (= Jerusalem, 1961, vol. 1, introduction).

38. Israel M. Ta-Shma, "Halakhah and Reality: The Tosafist Experience," in *Creativity and Tradition: Studies in Medieval Rabbinic Scholarship, Literature, and Thought* (Cambridge, MA: Harvard University Press, 2006), 88.

39. See Israel M. Ta-Shma, *Kenesset meḥqarim: Iyyunim besifrut harabbanit biyeme habenayim* (Jerusalem: Mossad Bialik, 2004), 266–67, where he discusses the fact that the study of Tosafot was not central to Talmud study in the middle of the fifteenth century in Castile. Scholars such as Isaac Aboab more commonly drew from the works of Ran (Nissim ben Reuven Gerondi) and Rosh (Asher ben Yeḥiel) rather than from Tosafot. In addition, the approach of Tosafot was different from the approach adopted by many Jews during this period, that is, the methodology of Isaac Canpanton, who used Aristotelian logic to explicate Talmudic passages (discussed beginning on page 105). Ta-Shma also presents evidence that ibn Ḥabib himself did not have access to Tosafot, for the most part, until he arrived in Salonika. See also *Zera Anashim,* #43, quoted by Ta-Shma, *Kenesset meḥqarim,* 267. In this *teshuvah* (rabbinic response to a legal question), ibn Ḥabib discusses the issue of *sivlonot,* gifts given to a bride prior to marriage, and notes that he could not render an appropriate legal conclusion until he looked at Tosafot, which had become available to him in Salonika. Finally, see Y. Mehlman, "*Peraqim betoldot hadefus besaloniqi,*" *Sefunot* 13 (1976): 215–72, specifically 221–27. There he argues

that Tosafot did not appear on the pages of tractates of the Talmud in the Ottoman empire until 1558. However, an edition of *b. Pesahim* (Constantinople, 1505) in the Rare Book Room of the Jewish Theological Seminary (New York), and fragments of *b. Yoma* and *b. Rosh Hashanah* (Constantinople, 1509) from holdings of the Jewish National and University Library (Jerusalem), have both Rashi and Tosafot. All these tractates were published by David and Samuel ibn Nahmias. See Heller, *Printing of the Talmud,* 14–15; Isaac Yudlov, *Bet hasefarim haleumi vehauniversitah biyerushalayim* (Jerusalem: Jewish National and University Library, 1984), 141.

40. Note that Spanish incunabula of tractates of the Talmud did not contain Tosafot. See Iakerson, *Catalogue of Hebrew Incunabula,* 2:331, 333, 336, 341, 344. See also Iakerson, *Catalogue of Books Printed in the XVth Century,* 82–84. The editors of these catalogues attest that Talmud editions published in Faro, Portugal, also contained only Rashi. For more evidence on the lack of Tosafot in the Spanish academies, see Daniel Chwolson, *Reshit maase hadefus beyisrael* (Warsaw, 1897), 22; Hayim Duberish (Bernard) Friedberg, *Toledot hadefus haivri bimedinat italya, aspanyah-portugalia, togarmah* (Tel Aviv: Bar-Yuda, 1956), 91–92; Herrman M. Z. Meyer, "A Short-Title Catalogue of the Hebrew Incunabulas and Other Books," appended to *Thesaurus Typographiae Hebraicae Saeculi: Hebrew Printing during the Fifteenth Century,* ed. Aron Freimann and Moses Marx (Jerusalem: University Booksellers, 1968). Also see Raphael Rabbinovicz, *Maamar al hadpasat hatalmud* (Jerusalem: Mossad Harav Kook, 1965), 32–35.

41. In Salonika, David Messer Leon became the *marbits torah* (rabbinic leader) of the Calabrian Jewish community, succeeding Jacob ibn Habib. See Tirosh-Rothschild, *Between Worlds,* 84. See Amarillo, "*Hevrat hatalmud torah hagadol besaloniqi,*" 279; David Pipano, "*Shalshelet rabbanei saloniqi,*" *Hagor Haefod,* 3b.

42. David Messer Leon, *Kevod Hakhamim,* ed. S. Bernfeld (Berlin: Meqitse Nirdamim, 1899; repr. Jerusalem: Makor, 1970), 129–30. This text is quoted both in Simha Assaf, *Meqorot letoledot hahinukh beyisrael,* 2 vols. (Tel Aviv: Dvir, 1930), 1:33–35, and in Heller, "Earliest Printings of the Talmud," 65. Note that Dimitrovsky, *Seride bavli,* 17, also suggests that in the Spanish and Portuguese academies, Jews studied *Hiddushe Haramban* instead of Tosafot.

43. Note that both an edition of *b. Pesahim* (Constantinople, 1505), in the Rare Book Room of the Jewish Theological Seminary (New York), and fragments of *b. Yoma* and *b. Rosh Hashanah* (Constantinople, 1509), from holdings of the Jewish National and University Library (Jerusalem), have both Rashi and Tosafot. These were printed in Constantinople and not Salonika.

44. An edition of tractate *Eruvin* whose colophon indicates that it was printed in 1522 contained Rashi and not Tosafot. The place where it was printed has been the subject of dispute. See Raphael Rabbinovicz, *Maamar al hadpasat hatalmud,* 32–34, who suggested, with great hesitation, that it was printed in Salonika, and Haim Dimitrovsky, *Seridei bavli,* 44–45, who believed it was printed in Fez.

45. See Joseph Hacker, "Intellectual Activity," 104–5, who translated this paragraph found in ibn Habib's introduction to *EY* (Salonika, 1516). Also see Rabbinovicz, *Maamar al hadpasat hatalmud,* 34, where he comments that there were many manuscripts of the Talmud circulating in Salonika and Constantinople, and

one did not necessarily know what was in the possession of his neighbor. Thus not only were different versions of the tractates of the Talmud available, but different textual traditions circulated within the same geographical area.

46. See *EY* (Salonika, 1516), vol. 1, introduction.

47. Note that some editions of the Talmud were being printed with Tosafot, and some were not. Fragments available to us at the Jewish National and University Library in Jerusalem indicate that, in 1509, three tractates—*Eruvin, Yoma,* and *Rosh Hashanah*—were printed in Constantinople. The pages from tractate *Eruvin* do not contain Tosafot. Rashi's commentary can be found along the inside margin, and we find only two columns on each page (one of Talmud text and one of Rashi). The format of the pages found in the editions of tractates *Yoma* and *Rosh Hashanah* is different. These tractates contain Tosafot on the outside margins and Rashi on the inside margins. Their format is more similar to Soncino's template; see *b. Berakhot* (Soncino, 1483–84). According to Heller, the Spanish printers David and Samuel ibn Naḥmias printed four tractates in Constantinople—*Eruvin, Pesaḥim, Yoma,* and *Rosh Hashanah*—and all of them contained Rashi and Tosafot. Possibly, he was looking at a different edition of *Eruvin* than the one at the Jewish National and University Library. Heller is correct, however, that it is unusual to find both Rashi and Tosafot on the pages of these tractates given the Spanish roots of these printers. Heller also attributes the inclusion of Tosafot to these printers' familiarity with the Italian Soncino incunabula treatises and to the marketing advantages of printing Tosafot. See Heller, "Earliest Printings of the Talmud," 68.

48. See Ta-Shma, *Hasifrut haparshanit,* 1:153.

49. Ibn Ḥabib also mentions that he intends to follow the example set by the fourteenth-century rabbi Asher ben Yeḥiel (Rosh), who was head of the academy in Toledo and who organized his halakhic collection in accordance with the template set by Alfasi. Rosh's work, *Pisqei Harosh,* offers an overview of the halakhic opinions of earlier scholars and covers most of the Talmudic tractates. See *EY* (Salonika, 1516), vol. 1, introduction (= Jerusalem, 1961, vol. 1, introduction).

50. Although Alfasi used the Talmud as his template, his interests in practical halakhah explain why, for example, he left out material on the Passover sacrifice found in tractate *Pesaḥim* as well as material related to the Temple ceremonies that took place with respect to the observance of Yom Kippur, found in tractate *Yoma.*

51. Menachem Elon argues that Alfasi's *Hilkhot Harif* earned the title *talmud qatan* because of Alfasi's decision to integrate aggadah with halakhah, paralleling the character of the *sugyot* in the Talmud itself. However, Alfasi's inclusion of aggadah is far from comprehensive; he quotes only a limited number of passages and only when they relate to matters of practical behavior. It would seem more likely that *Hilkhot Harif* earned this title because of Alfasi's editorial decision to follow the structure of the Talmud, that is, its structure of tractates and chapters. See Menachem Elon, *Jewish Law: History, Sources, Principles,* 4 vols. (Philadelphia: Jewish Publication Society, 1994), 3:1171. Also see Gerson D. Cohen, *A Critical Edition with a Translation and Notes of the Book of Tradition (Sefer Haqabbalah) by Abraham Ibn Daud* (Philadelphia: Jewish Publication Society, 1967), 84.

52. Menaḥem ibn Zeraḥ, *Tsedah Laderekh* (Feraro, 1554), introduction, 4a. See

Leonard Robert Levy, "R. Yitzhaq Alfasi's Application of Principles of Adjudication," 13n62.

53. Maimonides, *Mishnah im Perush Rabbenu Moshe ben Maimon,* 1:47 (introduction to *Seder Zeraim*); Levy, "R. Yitzhaq Alfasi's Application of Principles of Adjudication," 15–16.

54. *EY Berakhot* (Salonika, 1516), vol. 1, section 13, 12b (= Jerusalem, 1961, vol. 1, section 17, 14a).

55. *EY* (Salonika, 1516), vol. 1, introduction (= Jerusalem, 1961, vol. 1, introduction).

56. See Levy, "R. Yitzhaq Alfasi's Application of Principles of Adjudication," 28.

57. See *EY* (Salonika, 1516), vol. 1, 60b. This passage can be found at the end of ibn Ḥabib's anthology of *Yerushalmi* passages drawn from *Seder Zeraim* (= Jerusalem, 1961, 15a, second pagination following the *Yerushalmi* passages). Note that although this page is numbered 60, it is in fact page 62.

58. Saperstein, *Decoding the Rabbis,* 21, 222n4, notes that he found several quotations from Isaac ben Yedayah's commentary to tractate *Berakhot* in ibn Ḥabib's *En Yaaqov.* This discovery enabled him to conclude that these passages had been mistakenly attributed to Yedayah Hapenini Bedersi. Also see Saperstein, "R. Isaac B. Yeda'ya," 38–42, where he proves through quotations from ibn Ḥabib's commentary in the *En Yaaqov* that Isaac ben Yedayah is the correct author.

59. Stern, *Anthology in Jewish Literature,* 7. Stern uses this term to describe the anthologizing efforts of Bialik and Ravnitzky in their *Sefer haaggadah* and their contribution to modern Jewish culture. He notes, "Not only has the anthology functioned as a medium for retrieving and re-creating tradition . . . but it has also served as a figurative, idealized space for imagining new communities of readers and audiences, for transforming the past into a new entity through conscious fragmentation, literary montage, and collage."

60. Twersky, "Talmudists, Philosophers, Kabbalists," 433. See the late fourteenth-/early fifteenth-century work of Profiat Duran, *Maase Efod* (Vienna: Holtvarteh, 1865; repr. Jerusalem: Makor, 1969–70), introduction. In his introduction Duran distinguishes among three groups of scholars. The first group is composed of masters of the Talmud, the second is composed of philosophers, and the third is composed of Kabbalists.

61. Twersky, "Talmudists, Philosophers, Kabbalists," 432. Also see Moshe Halbertal, *People of the Book,* 106–7.

62. *EY* (Salonika, 1516), vol. 1, introduction (= Jerusalem, 1961, vol. 1, introduction). Also see chapter 4, "From Talmudic Text to Theology: The Search for God, the Search for Home," where I discuss ibn Ḥabib's commentary and his interest in faith in greater detail.

63. See *EY Megillah* (Salonika, 1516), vol. 1, 153b (= Jerusalem, 1961, vol. 2, 7b), where ibn Ḥabib criticizes Joseph Albo for spending too much time investigating what is a "principle," a "root," and a "branch" of faith. I will discuss this at greater length in the next chapter.

64. Tirosh-Rothschild, "Jewish Philosophy on the Eve of Modernity," 509–10.

65. Maimonides, *Guide for the Perplexed,* 1:34.

66. Maimonides, *Guide for the Perplexed,* 1:71.

67. Julius Guttmann, *Philosophies of Judaism,* 225–26.

68. Eliezer Schweid, *The Classic Jewish Philosophers: From Saadia through the Renaissance,* trans. Leonard Levin (Leiden: E. J. Brill, 2008), 425.

69. Joseph Albo, *Sefer Haiqqarim,* ed. Isaak Husik (Philadelphia: Jewish Publication Society, 1946), xv–xvii (Husik's introduction).

70. Albo, *Sefer Haiqqarim* (ed. Husik), xvi.

71. See the beginning of Albo's introduction to *Sefer Haiqqarim* (ed. Husik), 35. Also see Kellner, *Dogma,* 149.

72. See Israel Bettan, "The Sermons of Isaac Arama," *Hebrew Union College Annual* 12–13 (1937–38): 587n6, and 591–93.

73. Bettan, "The Sermons of Isaac Arama," 589.

74. Bettan, "The Sermons of Isaac Arama," 586n2. Bettan indicates that Maimonides' *Guide for the Perplexed* directed Arama extensively in his sermons.

75. See Isaac Arama, *Aqedat Yitshaq* (Venice, 1547; repr. Warsaw, 1904), sermon 96, 101.

76. Arama, *Aqedat Yitshaq,* sermon 80, 129.

77. See Bettan, "The Sermons of Isaac Arama," 587n3, where he notes Arama's use of, and interest in, the *Ethics* of Aristotle (*Aqedat Yitshaq,* sermon 22, 245, and sermon 33, 395). See also Bernard Septimus, "Isaac Arama and the *Ethics,*" in *Jews and Conversos at the Time of the Expulsion,* ed. Yom Tov Assis and Yosef Kaplan (Jerusalem: Zalman Shazar Center for Jewish History, 1999), 23, where he notes that the *Ethics* became for Arama an important instrument of biblical and aggadic interpretation. Arama also referred to Aristotle's *Metaphysics* in his sermons (*Aqedat Yitshaq,* sermon 10, 130) and quoted from Plato (sermon 35, 16, and sermon 73, 20).

78. Bettan, "The Sermons of Isaac Arama," 589–90.

79. See Arama, *Aqedat Yitshaq,* sermon 67. See Kellner, *Dogma,* 159, and Sara Heller-Wilensky, *Rabbi yitshaq arama umishnato* (Jerusalem: Mossad Bialik, 1956), 78–96.

80. See Antius Manlius Severinus Boethius, *De Consolatione Philosophiae traduzione ebraica di Azaria ben R. Joseph ibn Abba Mari* [Translated into Hebrew by Azariah ben R. Joseph ibn Abba Mari], ed. Sergio Joseph Sierra (Jerusalem and Torino: Instituto di Studi Ebraici Scuola Rabbinica S. H. Margulies Disegni, 1967), introduction. Also see Eleazar Gutwirth, "Conversions to Christianity amongst Fifteenth-Century Spanish Jews: An Alternative Explanation," in *Shlomo Simonsohn Jubilee Volume: Studies on the History of the Jews in the Middle Ages and Renaissance Period,* ed. D. Carpi et al. (Tel Aviv: Tel Aviv University Press, 1993), 110.

81. Abraham Bibago, *Derekh Emunah* (Constantinople, 1522; repr. Jerusalem: Sifriyat Meqorot, 1970; Jerusalem: Mossad Bialik, 1978), 45:4. See Saperstein, "The Social and Cultural Context," 306 and 320n76. Saperstein notes that, although it is unclear whether Bibago was head of his own academy in Saragossa, we have some evidence to suggest that philosophy found its way into the curriculum

there as an "adjunct" to Talmud studies. Allan Lazaroff, *The Theology of Abraham Bibago* (Tuscaloosa: University of Alabama Press, 1981).

82. Abraham Bibago, *Derekh Emunah*, 45:2 and 45:4. See Joseph Hacker's discussion of Bibago's attitude toward philosophy, "*Meqomo shel rabbi avraham bibago bamahloqet al limmud hafilosofia umaamadah bisefarad bameah ha-15*," *Proceedings of the Fifth World Congress of Jewish Studies* (1969): 158; Gutwirth, "Conversions to Christianity," 119.

83. See Abraham Gross's critique of Arama, "*Qavim letoledot hayeshivot beqasti-lya bameah ha-15*," *Peamim* 31 (1987): 14n50. Despite this critique, it is important to note that a survey of manuscripts available from fifteenth-century Spain shows a proportionally larger number of philosophic works than Talmud tractates, commentaries, responsa, and code literature (see Jewish National University Library catalogue of manuscripts). It was not until Hebrew printing presses began printing books in 1480 that there was a distinct change. There is no record that any philosophic works were printed between 1480 and 1492. Instead, printers produced bibles and biblical commentaries, tractates of the Talmud, and codes (such as Maimonides' *Mishne Torah* and Jacob ben Asher's *Tur*).

84. Isaac Arama, *Ḥazut Qashah* (Warsaw: Shuldberg, 1884), chapter 12, 24a. Also see Saperstein, "The Social and Cultural Context," 305.

85. Chaim Pearl, *The Medieval Jewish Mind: The Religious Philosophy of Isaac Arama* (London: Vallentine, Mitchell, 1971), 12.

86. Yitzhak Baer, *A History of the Jews in Christian Spain*, 2:255–56.

87. See Adena Tanenbaum, "Arrogance, Bad Form, and Curricular Narrowness: Belletristic Critiques of Rabbinic Culture from Medieval Spain and Provence," in *Rabbinic Culture and Its Critics: Jewish Authority, Dissent, and Heresy in Medieval and Early Modern Times,* ed. Daniel Frank and Matt Goldish (Detroit: Wayne State University Press, 2008), 57–81. Here Tanenbaum captures the tensions between reason and religion that ensued throughout the medieval period in the medium of Hebrew poetry. For example, her discussion of the introductory poem found in Shem Tov Falaquera's *Iggeret Havikkuah* is particularly instructive in its ability to communicate the challenges that a commitment to philosophy posed. Indeed, Falaquera's work draws a negative picture of those who refrain from philosophic study, when he writes, "Believers in the Law and observers of its commandments [who] when they hear a word of the sciences from a scholar, they hasten to spread the report that he is among the infidels without examining whether it is true or not . . . even though this [scientific teaching] may be obligated by our Law and among the things that strengthen our faith, they will out of their stupidity deny it and reproach him who has said it, just because it is mentioned in the philosophical books." See Shem Tov Falaquera, *Iggeret Havikkuah* (see Steven Harvey, ed. and trans., *Falaquera's Epistle of the Debate* [Cambridge, MA: Harvard University Press, 1987], 69–70).

88. See *EY Berakhot* (Jerusalem, 1961), vol. 1, 109a. Note that the 1516 edition of the *En Yaaqov* does not have this passage written by ibn Ḥabib, but it was included in later editions in his name. The editors of *En Yaaqov* (Vilna, 1883), of which the Jerusalem edition (1961) is a an exact reprint, claim that *En Yisrael* (Ven-

ice, 1566) contained this text. While I was unable to locate it in the place where the editors of *En Yaaqov* (Vilna, 1883) claimed it should be, the language of the passage reflects ibn Ḥabib's style of writing, and the perspective conveyed suggests that the comment was authored by him. Therefore I chose to speak about it as if it was original to ibn Ḥabib, in keeping with the observations of the editors of *En Yaaqov* (Vilna, 1883).

89. Neither *Derekh Emunah* nor Bibago's many other works convey that he was disinterested in philosophy. A list of Bibago's extant and lost works has been compiled by Abraham Nuriel, *Galuy vesamuy befilosofiyah heyehudit biyeme habenayim* (Jerusalem: Magnes Press, 2000), 181–92 and 299–300. Many of these works reflect a serious interest in philosophy and counter ibn Ḥabib's perception of Bibago. For example, included in this list is a supercommentary on Averroës' *Middle Commentary* on Aristotle's *Posterior Analytics* and *Metaphysics*. Both were based on Hebrew translations of Averroës's work prepared by Jacob Anatoli and Kalonymous ben Kalonymous. For a more extensive discussion of the influence of philosophy on Bibago, see Mauro Zonta, *Hebrew Scholasticism in the Fifteenth Century: A History and Source Book* (Amsterdam: Springer, 2006), 33–107.

90. In the Ottoman empire Jews began to systemize, summarize, and translate philosophical ideas and works to make them more readily available to the non-scholarly world. See Tirosh-Rothschild, "The Ultimate End of Human Life," 231.

91. See below in this chapter where I discuss ibn Ḥabib's critique of philosophy, as well as my discussion in chapter 4, "From Talmudic Text to Theology: The Search for God, the Search for Home."

92. Twersky, "Talmudists, Philosophers, Kabbalists," 448–49. Also see Jacob Katz, *Halakhah veqabbalah: Meḥqarim betoledot dat yisrael midoreha vezikatah* (Jerusalem: Magnes Press, 1984), 16.

93. Twersky, "Talmudists, Philosophers, Kabbalists," 448.

94. Halbertal, *People of the Book*, 119.

95. Elisheva Carlebach, "The Status of the Talmud in Early Modern Europe," in *The Printing of the Talmud from Bomberg to Schottenstein*, ed. Sharon Liberman Mintz and Gabriel M. Goldstein (New York: Yeshiva University Museum, 2005), 83; Talya Fishman, *Shaking the Pillars of Exile*, 119.

96. Shem Tov ibn Shem Tov wrote *Sefer Haemunot* (Jerusalem, 1968–69) in 1400. See Gutwirth, "Conversions to Christianity," 111.

97. See Halbertal, *People of the Book*, 119, where he discusses the attitudes of some Kabbalists toward Talmud study. Also see Jacob Katz, "*Halakhah vekabbalah kenose limud mitharim*," in *Halakhah veqabbalah*, 82–83.

98. See Halbertal, *People of the Book*, 119–21. Also see Moshe Idel, *Kabbalah: New Perspectives* (New Haven, CT: Yale University Press, 1988).

99. Gutwirth, "Conversions to Christianity," 112.

100. Gutwirth, "Conversions to Christianity," 111–12.

101. Note that Duran, in his work *Maase Efod*, lambastes Talmudists for ignoring biblical studies and for spending too much time focused on Talmud study. See Gutwirth, "Conversions to Christianity," 110, and Duran, in *Maase Efod*, "Introduction." See Kozodoy, "A Study of the Life and Works of Profiat Duran," 336. See

Gampel, "A Letter to a Wayward Teacher," 432.

102. Kozodoy, "A Study of the Life and Works of Profiat Duran," 327–28, 336.

103. Kozodoy, "A Study of the Life and Works of Profiat Duran," 336.

104. Gampel, "A Letter to a Wayward Teacher," 432.

105. Halbertal, *People of the Book*, 126.

106. Ta-Shma, *Kenesset meḥqarim,* 261–62, 264; Abraham Gross, "Qavim," 8–19; Abraham Gross, "Centers of Study and Yeshivot in Spain," in *Moreshet Sepharad: The Sephardi Legacy,* 2 vols., ed. Haim Beinart (Jerusalem: Magnes Press, 1992), 1:407–10; Joseph Hacker, *"Lidemutam haruḥanit,"* 21–59.

107. See Assaf, *Meqorot letoledot haḥinukh beyisrael,* 2:80–84; Yitzhak Baer, *A History of the Jews in Christian Spain,* 259–70; Gross, "Qavim," 12–18.

108. Gross, "Qavim," 10.

109. See Abraham Zacuto, *Yuḥasin Hashalem* (Constantinople, 1566; repr. Frankfurt: M. A. Vohrmann, 1924), 226b; Elijah Capsali, *Seder Eliyahu Zuta* (Jerusalem: Makhon Ben Tsvi, 1975–1983, 179. See these sources quoted in Assaf, *Meqorot letoledot haḥinukh beyisrael,* 2:84–85. Also see Gross, "Qavim," 6–8, who refers to other fifteenth- and sixteenth-century sources that describe Canpanton's prominence.

110. See Gross, "Qavim," 10, 16–17, and "Centers of Study," 408.

111. See Zvi Avneri's bibliography of Isaac Aboab's works: "Isaac Aboab II," in *Encyclopedia Judaica* 2:93. There he notes that Aboab wrote novellae to tractate *Betsah,* published in "*Ḥiddushe Rabbenu Yitsḥaq Aboab,*" in *Shitat Haqadmonim* (Jerusalem: Oraita, 1959), as well as comments on *Baba Metsia* found in Bezalel ben Abraham Ashkenazi, *Shitah Mequbetset.* According to Avneri, Aboab's responsa are appended to *Sheva Enayim* (Leghorn, 1745). Aboab also wrote a commentary on Jacob ben Asher's *Arbaah Turim,* which was quoted and used by Joseph Caro and later authorities, but has been lost.

112. While there is no agreement on the extent to which the study of Kabbalah pervaded the Jewish academies of the Iberian Peninsula, some have argued that it was taught by rabbinic authorities alongside halakhah and philosophy as, for example, in the yeshiva of Canpanton. Isaac de Leon, one of Canpanton's students, became a Kabbalist, as did others. See Hacker, *"Lidemutam haruḥanit,"* 54; Gross, "Qavim," 16–17.

113. This work is sometimes titled *Darkhe Hagemara* (Constantinople, 1515–20; repr. Mantua, 1593).

114. See, for example, Canpanton, *Darkhe Hatalmud* (Jerusalem: Daf Ḥen, 1981), 22, where he refers to *b. Shevuot* 48b to emphasize that one needs to examine each passage of the Talmud carefully to determine its true intent.

115. Also see Haim Z. Dimitrovsky, *"Al derekh hapilpul,"* in *Sefer hayovel likhvod shalom baron,* ed. Saul Lieberman (Jerusalem: American Academy of Jewish Research, 1975), 3:130, and Sergey Dolgopolski's more recent work, *What Is the Talmud? The Art of Disagreement* (New York: Fordham University Press, 2008), 7–13, regarding Canpanton. Abraham Gross disagrees, noting that the great rabbinic personalities of the day, such as Isaac Canpanton, may have been more focused on developing great scholars, especially following the disputation at Tortosa. See

Gross, "*Qavim*," 18. Also see Hacker's description of the academic environment in Castile, "*Lidemutam haruḥanit*," 25–29.

116. Gross, "Qavim," 18–19, and "Centers and Study," 408. Also see Haim Bentov, "*Shitat limmud hatalmud biyeshivot saloniqi veturkya*," *Sefunot* 13 (1979): 30, where he discusses Canpanton.

117. See Daniel Boyarin, "*Meḥqarim befarshanut hatalmud shel megorashe sefarad*," *Sefunot*, n.s. 2 (1983): 165–80. Also see Haim Z. Dimitrovsky, "*Bet midrasho shel rav yaaqov berav bitsfat*," *Sefunot* 7:2 (1964): 43–102, who discusses the method of casuistry employed by the Spanish exiles in their academies following the expulsion from Spain.

118. Daniel Boyarin, "Moslem, Christian, and Jewish Cultural Interaction in Sephardic Talmudic Interpretation," *Review of Rabbinic Judaism* 5:1 (2002): 2. Also see Daniel Boyarin, *Haiyyun hasefaradi: Lefarshanut hatalmud shel megorashe sefarad* (Jerusalem: Makhon Ben Tsvi, 1989). See Dolgopolski, *What Is the Talmud?* 72–116, where he discusses Canpanton's approach in relationship to Boyarin's work.

119. See Isaac Canpanton, *Darkhei Hatalmud;* Daniel Boyarin, *Haiyyun hasefaradi,* 50; Gampel, "A Letter to a Wayward Teacher," 432. Also see Gross, "*Qavim*," 13–14.

120. Avraham Grossman, "Legislation and Responsa Literature," 1:212. Also see Bentov, "*Shitat limmud hatalmud*," 28–32.

121. See Boyarin, *Haiyyun hasefaradi,* 37–42; Bentov, "*Shitat limmud hatalmud*," 28–37, where he discusses Canpanton's approach to the study of Talmud. Although Bentov points to some of Canpanton's predecessors who used logic to explicate the texts of the Talmud, none of the rabbinic scholars whom he mentions composed or utilized the type of carefully explicated methodology that Canpanton proposed. None embraced rules or "*kelale iyyun.*" Avraham Grossman summarizes the contributions of Canpanton in "Legislation and Responsa Literature," 212–13, as does Elisheva Carlebach, "The Status of the Talmud in Early Modern Europe," 80.

122. Gampel, "A Letter to a Wayward Teacher," 432.

123. See Boyarin, *Haiyyun hasefaradi,* 112–15; Hacker, "*Lidemutam haruḥanit*," 50–51; Gross, "Centers of Study," 409.

124. See Daniel Boyarin, *Haiyyun hasefaradi.*

125. See Canpanton's statement at the end of *Darkhe Hatalmud,* 72, where he praises those who buy books, including those that focus on logic and philosophy. Also see Gross, "*Qavim*," 15.

126. Gross, "*Qavim*," 15.

127. Elijah Capsali, *Seder Eliyahu Zuta,* 1:178–79; Gross, "*Qavim*," 15.

128. Avraham ben Shlomo Ardutiel, *Avne Zikkaron* (published by Gershon Scholem in *Kiryat sefer* 7 [1931]: 457–65, specifically 458); Gross, "*Qavim*," 15.

129. Williston Walker et al., *A History of the Christian Church* (New York: Charles Scribner's & Sons, 1985), 324.

130. Boyarin, *Haiyyun hasefaradi;* Carlebach, "The Status of the Talmud in Early Modern Europe," 80.

131. Gross, "Centers of Study," 405.

132. Gross, *"Qavim,"* 14.

133. Judah ibn Abbas, *Yair Netiv,* in Assaf, *Meqorot letoledot haḥinukh beyisrael,* 2:29–30; Gross, "Centers of Study," 405–6; Bentov, *"Shitat limmud hatalmud,"* 73.

134. Joseph Jabetz, *Or Haḥayyim* (Lublin, 1912), 8; Gross, *"Qavim,"* 14n50; Gutwirth, "Conversions to Christianity," 110.

135. See Levi ibn Ḥabib, *EY* (Salonika, 1522), vol. 2, introduction, written by Levi to introduce the second volume of *En Yaaqov,* titled *Bet Yaaqov.* In *EY* (Jerusalem, 1961), Levi's introduction follows immediately after Jacob ibn Ḥabib's introduction in volume 1. Also see Bentov, *"Shitat limmud hatalmud,"* 39n6, who refers to the fact that Rosanes, *Divre yeme yisrael betogarmah,* 1:84, describes ibn Ḥabib as one of the generation's "mediocre rabbis." Bentov is confused by Rosanes's reference, in the wake of Levi ibn Ḥabib's description of his father's commitment to casuistry and to the cultivation of many students. Rosanes's remarks may stem from conclusions he drew from the fact that ibn Ḥabib's only surviving printed work was one of aggadah and not of halakhah. He may have assumed that ibn Ḥabib paled in erudition in comparison to his contemporaries.

136. The Hebrew word used here is *beqiut.* See Hacker, *"Lidemutam haruḥanit,"* 51–52 and 94, where he quotes the eulogy in its entirety.

137. Note that Garson uses the phrase *"ḥokhmot ḥitsoniyot,"* or "external/foreign wisdoms" to refer to the type of study that was less praiseworthy in ibn Ḥabib's eyes. In medieval texts this phrase refers to philosophic texts, such as those written by Aristotle and Averroës. Also see Hacker, *"Lidemutam haruḥanit,"* 51–52, 94.

138. See *EY Berakhot* (Salonika, 1516), vol. 1, section 68, 32b (= Jerusalem, 1961, vol. 1, section 77, 55a–b); and *b. Ber.* 28b.

139. I have translated this passage in accordance with *EY Berakhot* (Salonika, 1516), which has the Hebrew word *arur* (cursed).

140. Rashi claims that *higayon* is the study of the Bible by rote. Accordingly, if children study this way they will be drawn to memorizing biblical verses and will not learn what they need to truly understand the verse in question. Note that this comment made by Rashi does not appear in the *Talmud Bavli* (Vilna: Romm, 1880–91), on which today's editions are based.

141. See *EY Berakhot* (Salonika, 1516), vol. 1, section 68, 32b (= Jerusalem, 1961, vol. 1, section 77, 55a–b); and *b. Ber.* 28b.

142. See Joseph Hacker, *"Rabbi yaaqov ibn ḥabib,"* 126, where he writes that ibn Ḥabib represented "the voices of the Spanish masters of halakhah" who had opposed philosophy as well as Kabbalah. Hacker viewed ibn Ḥabib as the representative of a halakhically inclined Jewish community that refused to see philosophy as offering "an [appropriate] perspective on the world . . . [or] an [effective] means of interpretation."

143. Note that any time Rabbi Eliezer is mentioned without patronymic in the Talmud, he is the tanna Eliezer ben Hyrcanus.

144. See *EY Berakhot* (Salonika, 1516), vol. 1, section 35, 21b (= Jerusalem, 1961, vol. 1, section 40, 28a). Also see *EY Shabbat* (Salonika, 1516), vol. 1, section 2, 61a (= Jerusalem, 1961, vol. 1, 2b).

145. Note that ibn Ḥabib does not quote the entire story from *b. Avodah Zarah*

16b–17a in his commentary. He merely reminds us of it and relies on the reader to recall the details. This presumes a great deal of knowledge about the stories found within the other tractates of the Talmud and raises questions regarding the nature of ibn Ḥabib's targeted readership.

146. See *EY Avodah Zarah* (Salonika, 1522), vol. 2, 348, which has the following version of the text that differs from *Bavli* (Vilna: Romm, 1880–91): "Once I was walking in the upper marketplace of Tsippori and [there] I found a man who was one of the students of Jesus, the Christian (*yeshu hanotsri*)." Also note that tractate *Avodah Zarah* of the *En Yaaqov* was prepared by Levi ibn Ḥabib following his father's death. While it does not absolutely prove that Jacob ibn Ḥabib had a version of *b. Avodah Zarah* 16b–17a that contained a reference to Jesus, it is possible that this was the textual tradition available to him.

147. Hacker, "Intellectual Activity," 116–20.

148. In the Christian community of the fifteenth century, philosophical study flourished in the universities. In the Jewish community, on the other hand, there is evidence that such study was a private affair transmitted from father to son or from master to disciple outside the context of formal institutions. In this environment Jews may have sustained separate academic centers for the study of philosophy and attended them following their studies at Jewish academies. See Saperstein's overview on this issue, "The Social and Cultural Context," 302–6. Also see Hacker, "*Lidemutam haruḥanit*," 55; Hacker, "Intellectual Activity," 116; Tirosh-Rothschild, "Jewish Philosophy on the Eve of Modernity," 503; and Gampel, "A Letter to a Wayward Teacher," 433, who seem more convinced that separate philosophic academies existed.

149. Hacker, "*Lidemutam haruḥanit*," 56; and Hacker, "Intellectual Activity," 116–17.

150. See Hacker, "*Lidemutam haruḥanit*," 94. Also note where Hacker quotes a passage from Garson's writings that reflects his willingness to allow philosophic study. Such study, however, had to take place following one's Torah study in the Jewish academy (Hacker, "*Lidemutam haruḥanit*," 55).

151. *EY Berakhot* (Salonika, 1516), vol. 1, section 109, 44b (= Jerusalem, 1961, vol. 1, 88a).

152. In an attempt to explain why ibn Ḥabib appeared to be less steeped in philosophy than many of his contemporaries, Shlomo Rosanes conjectures that because ibn Ḥabib's teacher, Valensi, died at an early age, he left a void in his student's training (Rosanes, *Divre yeme yisrael betogarmah,* 1:84). Whether Rosanes's conclusion is correct or not is immaterial. What is interesting about his conjecture is the fact that ibn Ḥabib takes him by surprise. Rosanes expects that a scholar reared in the Hispano-Jewish culture of fifteenth-century Spain should be far more knowledgeable in the field of philosophy.

153. See Dolgopolski, *What Is the Talmud?* 79.

154. Bentov, "*Shitat limmud hatalmud*," 41, esp. n15, where Bentov defines the exceptional student as one who investigates halakhah.

155. Gross, "*Qavim*," 16, argues that the essence of study in the academy revolved around Talmud, with a focus on casuistry and the development of a great

breadth of Talmudic knowledge (*beqiut*). However, even within this framework there were those who were experts not only in Mishnah and Talmud but also in aggadah. Gross mentions David, the son of Solomon ibn Yeḥiyah of Portugal, as an example. Unfortunately, I could find no similar examples of "aggadic experts" among the heads of the academies in Castile during the last decades of the fifteenth century, and no evidence suggesting that aggadah played a central role in the curriculum of the academy.

156. Ibn Ḥabib frequently refers to his interest in elucidating aggadah for the populace. See, for example, *EY* (Salonika, 1516), vol. 1, introduction (= Jerusalem, 1961, vol. 1, introduction). But he also makes clear in his commentary that he is speaking to the scholarly elite as well, who are, for example, knowledgeable in the discipline of logic. See *EY Berakhot* (Salonika, 1516), vol. 1, section 68, 32b (= Jerusalem, 1961, vol. 1, section 77, 55a–b); and *b. Ber.* 28b. Additionally, when ibn Habib speaks against the study of philosophy, he is addressing an elite who either are engaged in studying it or who are thinking of pursuing it.

157. See Hacker, *"Rabbi yaaqov ibn ḥabib,"* 126.

158. See Elisheva Carlebach, *The Pursuit of Heresy: Rabbi Moses Hagiz and the Sabbatian Controversy* (New York: Columbia University Press, 1990), 14–17. In Carlebach's assessment of rabbinic historiography, she warns against the writing of rabbinic biographies that couch rabbinic Judaism and its rabbinic leaders as bound to halakhah and as incapable of promoting inner renewal. See Fishman, *Shaking the Pillars of Exile,* 6–7, where she dismisses rigid perceptions of premodern Jewish life and culture put forth by defenders of "Modern Orthodoxy" or "Neo-Orthodoxy" and ideologues of Reform Judaism in the period following the Emancipation. Bonfil adds more recent offenders. See Robert Bonfil, "The Historian's Perceptions of the Jews in the Italian Renaissance: Towards a Reappraisal," *Revue des Études Juives* 134 (1984): 59–82.

Chapter 4

1. Steiner, "Our Homeland," 7.

2. Steiner, "Our Homeland," 12.

3. Steiner, "Our Homeland," 7.

4. John C. Hirsh, *Boundaries of Faith: The Development and Transmission of Medieval Spirituality* (Leiden: E. J. Brill, 1996), 3.

5. See *EY Berakhot* (Salonika 1516), vol. 1, section 4, 9b–10a (= Jerusalem, 1961, vol. 1, section 8, 7b).

6. Note that ibn Ḥabib uses the phrase *"tsarot hagalut"* (the difficulties of exile) to refer to the time following the destruction of the Temple in a general way. This is not a specific reference to the expulsion from Spain. See, for example, *EY Berakhot* (Salonika, 1516), vol. 1, section 1, 7a (bottom) (= Jerusalem, 1961, vol. 1, 3b). Also see *EY Berakhot* (Salonika, 1516), vol. 1, section 4, 10a (= Jerusalem, 1961, vol. 1, section 8, 7b). And see where ibn Ḥabib tries to console his readers about their own travails through a discussion about the rebuilding of the Temple: *EY Berakhot* (Salonika, 1516), vol. 1, section 114, 45b–46b (= Jerusalem, 1961, vol. 1, section 127,

95a–96a). Yosef Hayim Yerushalmi points out that many medieval Jews did not speak about crisis and recovery in terms of recent historical events. Instead, they relied on paradigmatic experiences, such as the destruction of the first and second Temples. See Yerushalmi, "Clio and the Jews: Reflections on Jewish Historiography in the Sixteenth Century," *Proceedings of the American Academy of Jewish Research* 46–47:2 (1978–79): 616.

7. Moshe Idel, "Religion, Thought and Attitudes: The Impact of the Expulsion on the Jews," in *Spain and the Jews,* ed. Elie Kedourie (London: Thames & Hudson, 1992), 123.

8. See Hirsh, *Boundaries of Faith,* 2–3, who speaks more generally about the significance of creating timeless messages. Also see Neusner, *Judaism in Society,* 15, who writes the following about the failure of the *Yerushalmi* to respond to its historical context: "A document so reticent about events in its own day clearly wishes to claim that it be read as if composed in a vacuum" unconcerned about time and place.

9. Hacker, *"Rabbi yaaqov ibn ḥabib,"* 123–26.

10. *EY Berakhot* (Salonika, 1516), vol. 1, section 55 (aggadic passage only; the commentary does not match this number), 27b–28a (= Jerusalem, 1961, vol. 1, section 68, 45b); see my discussion of this text below. Note that although the first page is numbered 28, it is actually page 27. The second page numbered 28 is, in fact, page 28. Additionally, page 29 is mistakenly numbered page 26. I am referring here to what should be 27b–28a, despite the fact that both printed page numbers read 28. I will refer to this discrepancy each time it occurs in references to the *En Yaaqov* throughout this chapter.

11. Hacker, *"Rabbi yaaqov ibn ḥabib,"* 126, where he points to ibn Ḥabib's critique of Maimonidean philosophy.

12. Kellner, *Must a Jew Believe Anything?* 21.

13. See, for example, ibn Ḥabib's comment found on *EY Berakhot* (Salonika, 1516), vol. 1, 7b (= Jerusalem, 1961, vol. 1, 3b); *EY Berakhot* (Salonika, 1516), vol. 1, 9a (= Jerusalem, 1961, vol. 1, 6b), where ibn Ḥabib uses the words *"metsuyyar belibbo"* ("inscribed in his heart"); *EY Berakhot* (Salonika, 1516), vol. 1, 17b (= Jerusalem, 1961, vol. 1, 21a); *EY Berakhot* (Salonika, 1516), vol. 1, 21b (= Jerusalem, 1961, vol. 1, 28a); *EY Berakhot* (Salonika, 1516), vol. 1, 28a (this is the second page numbered 28) (= Jerusalem, 1961, vol. 1, 45b); *EY Berakhot* (Salonika, 1516), vol. 1, 45a (bottom) (= Jerusalem, 1961, vol. 1, 89a), where ibn Ḥabib states that one's fear of God should be "fixed in one's heart"; *EY Berakhot* (Salonika, 1516), vol. 1, 54a–55b (*Yerushalmi* section) (= Jerusalem, 1961, vol. 1, 5a [second pagination]); *EY Kilayim* (Salonika, 1516), vol. 1, 57b–58b (*Yerushalmi* section) (= Jerusalem, 1961, vol. 1, 11b, 12b, 13a [second pagination]). Many of these comments insist that a particular dogmatic principle, such as a belief that God created the world or will resurrect the dead, should be inscribed in one's heart.

14. Ibn Ḥabib states that one should "establish a belief in one's heart" and notes that eternal life requires both the performance of external deeds as well as *"ḥovot levavot"* "[inner] duties of the heart." See, for example, *EY Berakhot* (Salonika, 1516), vol. 1, section 36, 21b (= Jerusalem, 1961, vol. 1, section 40, 28a); *EY Berakhot*

(Salonika, 1516), vol. 1, section 5, 54b–55a (*Yerushalmi* section) (= Jerusalem, 1961, vol. 1, 5a [end]); *EY Kilayim* (Salonika, 1516), vol. 1, 57b–58b (*Yerushalmi* section) (= Jerusalem, 1961, 11b, 12b, 13a).

15. See *EY Berakhot* (Salonika, 1516), vol. 1, section 35, 21b (as I discuss later in this chapter) (= Jerusalem, 1961, vol. 1, section 40, 28a). Also see *EY Shabbat* (Salonika, 1516), vol. 1, section 2, 61a (= Jerusalem, 1961, vol. 1, section 2, 2b).

16. See ibn Ḥabib's comment on *b. Ber.* 12a, where he elaborates on the prayers recited following the *Shema*. There he writes that one's belief in the "principles of faith must not depend upon [one's] study [of the ideas about faith] (*iyyun*) alone, rather faith should gird one's loins [that is, give one strength]." See *EY Berakhot* (Salonika, 1516), vol. 1, section 52, 25b (end of comment) (= Jerusalem, 1961, vol. 1, section 56, 38b [end of comment]). Also see page 131 and note 78 of this chapter, where I discuss ibn Ḥabib's definition of the word *iyyun*.

17. That said, on occasion ibn Ḥabib made allowances in his commentary for the use of philosophy. He seemed open to the idea that, for some, philosophy was an acceptable means of approaching Torah study. See *EY Berakhot* (Salonika, 1516), vol. 1, section 68, 32b (= Jerusalem, 1961, vol. 1, section 77, 55a–b), which is a comment on *b. Ber.* 28b. Also see my discussion of this text in chapter 3, "Rethinking the Image of the Talmud," pages 110–11.

18. One finds ibn Ḥabib making other statements where he uses philosophical terms, such as the word *sekhel* in the following phrase, "*veen hasekhel sovel shenaḥshov*" ([and our] intellect cannot endure thinking that . . .), *EY Berakhot* (Salonika, 1516), vol. 1, section 26, 18b (= Jerusalem, 1961, vol. 1, section 30, 22b)—or where ibn Ḥabib states that one should develop an "*emunah shelemah ḥaquqah besikhlo*," that is, a "complete faith ingrained in one's intellect." See *EY Berakhot* (Salonika, 1516), vol. 1, section 4, 9b (= Jerusalem, 1961, vol. 1, section 8, 7a).

19. Ibn Ḥabib warns in his commentary that philosophy can contradict the principles of faith that are written in the Torah; see *EY Berakhot* (Salonika, 1516), vol. 1, section 4, 10a (= Jerusalem, 1961, vol. 1, section 8, 7b). Interestingly, despite ibn Ḥabib's interest in discussing the principles of faith, he chooses to distance himself from the approach of Joseph Albo who, he argues, went too far in investigating the principles of faith in *Sefer Haiqqarim*. See *EY Megillah* (Salonika, 1516), vol. 1, 153b (= Jerusalem, 1961, vol. 2, 7b). Ibn Ḥabib prefers to embrace Maimonides' position outlined in *Mishnah im Perush Rabbenu Moshe ben Maimon*, introduction to *Pereq Ḥeleq*, 4:210–17.

20. See Hacker, "*Lidemutam haruḥanit*," 54–56, on the challenges posed to the study of Talmud by those interested in philosophy. More specifically, see Hacker, "*Lidemutam haruḥanit*," 94, where he quotes a text written to eulogize ibn Ḥabib, which makes reference to ibn Ḥabib's disinterest in "foreign wisdoms" and to his belief that such wisdom could never satiate the soul. Also see Tirosh-Rothschild, "Jewish Philosophy on the Eve of Modernity," 500–501, where she connects the desire of Jewish intellectuals in Spain to question their conduct and cultural orientation in the wake of the traumatic events of 1391. This self-examination, she argues, provoked a debate on the role of the "foreign wisdoms" or philosophy.

21. Hirsh, *Boundaries of Faith,* 177.

22. See *EY Berakhot* (Salonika, 1516), vol. 1, section 52, 25a–b (= Jerusalem, 1961, vol. 1, section 56, 37b–38b).

23. See *EY Berakhot* (Salonika, 1516), vol. 1, section 52, 25a–b (= Jerusalem, 1961, vol. 1, section 56, 37b–38b).

24. Tirosh-Rothschild, "Jewish Philosophy on the Eve of Modernity," 501.

25. *EY Berakhot* (Salonika, 1516), vol. 1, section 79, 35a–b (= Jerusalem, 1961, vol. 1, 63b). Note that in *EY Berakhot* (Salonika, 1516), vol. 1, there are two pages numbered 36. I am referring here to the first of two pages, that is, to the page that should be numbered 35.

26. *EY Berakhot* (Salonika, 1516), vol. 1, section 52, 25a–b (= Jerusalem, 1961, vol. 1, section 56, 38b).

27. *EY Berakhot* (Salonika, 1516), vol. 1, section 1, 7b (= Jerusalem, 1961, vol. 1, section, 3, 3b); *EY Shabbat* (Salonika, 1516), vol. 1, section 4, 61b (= Jerusalem, 1961, vol. 1, section 3, 5a). Also note that in *EY Shabbat* (Salonika, 1516), vol. 1, the page numbered 61 is in fact page 63, due to some extra pages that are not numbered.

28. *EY Berakhot* (Salonika, 1516), vol. 1, section 110, 45a (= Jerusalem, 1961, vol. 1, section 123, 89a).

29. *EY Shabbat* (Salonika, 1516), vol. 1, section 2, 61a–b (= Jerusalem, 1961, vol. 1, section 2, 2b). Note that in *EY Shabbat* (Salonika, 1516), vol. 1, the page numbered 61 is in fact page 63. There are a few pages that have no numbers. I am referring to it here as page 61. Also see *EY Megillah* (Salonika, 1516), vol. 1, 152a (= Jerusalem, 1961, vol. 2, 2a).

30. *EY Berakhot* (Salonika, 1516), vol. 1, section 127, 48b (= Jerusalem, 1961, vol. 1, section 139, 103a).

31. *EY Berakhot* (Salonika, 1516), vol. 1, section 5, 54b–55a (*Yerushalmi* section) (= Jerusalem, 1961, vol. 1, section 5, 5a).

32. *EY Berakhot* (Salonika, 1516), vol. 1, section 35, 21a–b (= Jerusalem, 1961, vol. 1, section 39, 28a).

33. *EY Shabbat* (Salonika, 1516), vol. 1, section 4, 61b (= Jerusalem, 1961, vol. 1, section 3, 5a). Note that this page is numbered 61 but is in fact page 63, due to some extra pages that are not numbered.

34. *EY* (Salonika, 1516), vol. 1, introduction (= Jerusalem, 1961, vol. 1, introduction). See, for example, *EY Berakhot* (Salonika, 1516), vol. 1, section 4, 9b (= Jerusalem, 1961, vol. 1, section 8, 7a).

35. See *EY Megillah* (Salonika, 1516), vol. 1, 153b (= Jerusalem, 1961, vol. 2, 7b), where ibn Ḥabib discusses the study of the principles of faith. See also Maimonides, *Mishnah im Perush Rabbenu Moshe ben Maimon,* introduction to *Pereq Ḥeleq,* 4:210–17.

36. See Tirosh-Samuelson, "The Ultimate End of Human Life," 223. And yet, as Tirosh-Samuelson readily points out, most of the technical philosophic works, including those that served as commentaries on Aristotle and Averroës, were never published and remained in manuscript. In fact, when one looks at the lists of Jewish books published during the first decade of the sixteenth century in the Ottoman

empire, one finds no published philosophical works; see Vinograd, *Otsar hasefer haivri*, 2:602–4, 666. The only possible exception is the philosopher Solomon Almoli's work on dreams, *Pitron Ḥalomot* (see Vinograd, *Otsar hasefer haivri*, 666). Given that publishers produced what they thought would sell, this evidence suggests that books on philosophy were not viewed as profitable. However, this does not discount the amount of philosophic material that remained in manuscript. See Hacker, "Intellectual Activity," 112–13.

37. Hacker, "Intellectual Activity," 110–11; Tirosh-Rothschild, "Jewish Philosophy on the Eve of Modernity," 530.

38. Tirosh-Samuelson, "The Ultimate End of Human Life," 233–35.

39. Tirosh-Rothschild, "Jewish Philosophy on the Eve of Modernity," 532; Tirosh-Samuelson, "The Ultimate End of Human Life," 235.

40. Tirosh-Rothschild, "Jewish Philosophy on the Eve of Modernity," 530. In such an environment, one could find individuals like the Spanish refugee Solomon Almoli devoting their energies to systematizing and summarizing centuries of Jewish philosophy for a more popular audience. Almoli believed that a widespread study of philosophy would perfect the community and even bring about the messianic age. However, as Tirosh-Samuelson points out, Almoli printed only the introduction to his digest or philosophic encyclopedia, *Measef Lekhol Hamaḥanot*, fearing that philosophy could be harmful in the hands of those unable to study it properly. For this reason, he preserved the core of this work in manuscript. See also Tirosh-Samuelson, "The Ultimate End of Human Life," 230–32, and Almoli, *Sefer Measef Lekhol Hamaḥanot* (Constantinople, 1530). Sections from the introduction were published by Hanokh Yalon, *"Peraqim min hameasef lekhol hamaḥanot larav shlomo almoli," Areshet* 2 (1960): 96–108.

41. Tirosh-Samuelson, "The Ultimate End of Human Life," 235.

42. See Twersky, "Talmudists, Philosophers, Kabbalists," 440, where he argues that Jews wondered what would lead them to "higher levels of religious understanding." Would it be natural science and metaphysics or halakhah?

43. Tirosh-Samuelson, "The Ultimate End of Human Life," 232.

44. Hirsh, *Boundaries of Faith*, 1.

45. Hacker, *"Rabbi yaaqov ibn ḥabib,"* 126, uses this passage to demonstrate what he correctly observed as ibn Ḥabib's anti-Maimonidean stance.

46. *EY Berakhot* (Salonika, 1516), vol. 1, section 4, 9b (= Jerusalem, 1961, vol. 1, section 8, 7a).

47. *EY Berakhot* (Salonika, 1516), vol. 1, section 4, 9b (= Jerusalem, 1961, vol. 1, section 8, 7a). In this comment, ibn Ḥabib also states that faith should be "ingrained in one's intellect." However, he had no intention of connecting philosophy to this goal. Ibn Ḥabib was merely using terminology with which he was familiar to advocate for a nonrational type of faith.

48. Note that ibn Ḥabib uses the term *sekhel* in his commentary numerous times. However, he employs it more generally to refer to a person who possesses the ability to process an idea clearly (*baal sakhla*); see *EY Berakhot* (Salonika, 1516), vol. 1, section 52, 25a–b (for ibn Ḥabib's commentary see the bottom of 25a) (= Jerusalem, 1961, vol. 1, section 56, 37b), which has *baal sekhel.* It does not connote

philosophical intellection. Also see *EY Berakhot* (Salonika, 1516), vol. 1, section 23, 15b (bottom) (= Jerusalem, 1961, vol. 1, 19b).

49. *EY Berakhot* (Salonika, 1516), vol. 1, section 4, 9b (= Jerusalem, 1961, vol. 1, section 8, 7a).

50. *EY Berakhot* (Salonika, 1516), vol. 1, section 52, 25a–b (= Jerusalem, 1961, vol. 1, section 56, 38b).

51. See *m. Abot* 1:3, and also see *b. Avodah Zarah* 19a, which quotes *m. Abot* 4:2. See Maimonides, *Mishnah im Perush Rabbenu Moshe ben Maimon*, introduction to *Pereq Ḥeleq*, 4:199.

52. See Maimonides, *Mishnah im Perush Rabbenu Moshe ben Maimon*, introduction to *Pereq Ḥeleq*, 4:199. Also Albo, *Sefer Haiqqarim*, 3:32, where he points out that one who fulfills the commandments out of a love for reward and/or a fear of punishment is considered as though he performed them "not for their own sake." The goal is to observe the commandments without any ulterior motive. Also see Joseph Heinemann, *The Reasons for the Commandments in Jewish Thought from the Bible to the Renaissance,* trans. Leonard Levin (Boston: Academic Studies Press, 2008), 144.

53. Maimonides, *Guide for the Perplexed*, 3:51, 639.

54. See David Hartman, *Maimonides: Torah and Philosophic Quest* (Philadelphia: Jewish Publication Society, 1976), 212–13.

55. See Maimonides' definition of wisdom, *Guide for the Perplexed*, 3:54, 632–38.

56. See *b. Ber.* 10a; *EY Berakhot* (Salonika, 1516), vol. 1, section 46, 22b–23a (= Jerusalem, 1961, vol. 1, section 50, 32a–b).

57. See *b. Ber.* 10a; *EY Berakhot* (Salonika, 1516), vol. 1, section 46, 22b–23a (= Jerusalem, 1961, vol. 1, section 50, 32a–b).

58. The phrase that ibn Ḥabib uses is "*ḥokhmat teva*." Also see Israel Efros, *Philosophical Terms in the Moreh Nebukhim* (New York: AMS Press, 1966), 50, for his definition of *ḥakhame teva*.

59. See *b. Ber.* 10a; *EY Berakhot* (Salonika, 1516), vol. 1, section 46, 22b–23a (= Jerusalem, 1961, vol. 1, section 50, 32a–b).

60. Maimonides also used Solomon as an example of someone who, despite his wisdom, could not understand the reasons for all of the commandments. See Maimonides, *Sefer Hamitsvot Lerabbenu Moshe ben Maimon* (Jerusalem: Mossad Harav Kook, 1971), 347 negative commandment #365.

61. Moses Maimonides, *Guide for the Perplexed*, 3:54, 632–38.

62. See *b. Ber.* 10a; *EY Berakhot* (Salonika, 1516), vol. 1, section 46, 22b–23a (= Jerusalem, 1961, vol. 1, section 50, 32a–b).

63. Naḥmanides, *Perushe Hatorah Lerabbenu Moshe ben Naḥman*, ed. Ḥayyim Dov Shavel (Jerusalem: Mossad Harav Kook, 1959), 346–47 (*ad* Ex. 13:12). Naḥmanides writes: "Accordingly, it follows that the great signs and wonders constitute faithful witness to the truth of the belief in the existence of the creator and the truth of the whole Torah."

64. See *b. Ber.* 10a; *EY Berakhot* (Salonika, 1516), vol. 1, section 46, 22b–23a (= Jerusalem, 1961, vol. 1, section 50, 32a–b).

65. Naḥmanides, *Perushe Hatorah*, 346–47 (*ad* Exodus 13:12).

66. Eliezer Schweid, *Classic Jewish Philosophers,* 306.

67. See Maimonides, *Guide for the Perplexed,* 3:52, 629–30, where he points out that the person who has achieved intellectual perfection achieves "such humility, such awe and fear of God, such reverence and such shame before Him." With the help and guidance of the performance of mitsvot, individuals develop both "love" and "fear" of God. As such, mitsvot are for "the benefit of those who know the true reality."

68. See *b. Ber.* 10a; *EY Berakhot* (Salonika, 1516), vol. 1, section 46, 22b–23a (= Jerusalem, 1961, vol. 1, section 50, 32b).

69. *EY Berakhot* (Salonika, 1516), vol. 1, section 55 (aggadic passage only), 27b–28a (= Jerusalem, 1961, vol. 1, section 68, 45b). Oddly, ibn Ḥabib does not use the term "Torah study" to define what he means by *ḥokhmah.* However, earlier, in his commentary on *b. Ber.* 17a, he specifically refers to the occupation of the wise person, the *ḥakham,* as Torah study. Note also that page 27 is mistakenly marked as page 28. I am referring to it here as page 27 despite this error.

70. Ibn Ḥabib uses the same term "*maasim tovim*" (literally, good deeds), as the aggadic passage in his commentary. He uses this term, however, as a way to refer to both ethical and ritual commandments.

71. See Maimonides, *Guide for the Perplexed,* 3:51, 622–23, regarding *Shema,* and 3:52, 629–30. Also see Schweid, *Classic Jewish Philosophers,* 306.

72. Note that ibn Ḥabib refers to Rabbi Yannai as a *ḥakham* in his commentary and does not mention him by name. I added the sage's name as it appears in the *Bavli.* See *b. Shabb.* 31b.

73. Note *EY Berakhot* (Salonika, 1516), vol. 1, section 55 (aggadic passage only), 28a (the second page numbered 28). Also note that *EY Berakhot* (Jerusalem, 1961), vol. 1, section 68, 45b, has a different version of this text from *b. Shabb.* (Vilna ed.). Ibn Ḥabib uses the term *beta,* the Aramaic word for house, based presumably on a different manuscript of *b. Shabb.* Many later versions of the *En Yaaqov* followed suit. *Tractate b. Shabb.* uses the term *darta,* the Aramaic word for "courtyard" (see *b. Shabb.* 31b).

74. *EY Berakhot* (Salonika, 1516), vol. 1, section 55, 28a (the second page numbered 28) (= Jerusalem, 1961, vol. 1, section 68, 45b).

75. See *EY Berakhot* (Salonika, 1516), vol. 1, section 85, 36b–37b (the second page numbered 36) (= Jerusalem, 1961, vol. 1, section 94, 67a–b).

76. Ibn Ḥabib relies on *m. Abot* 3:10 to make his point: "Rabbi ben Dosa said, 'He whose fear of sin comes before his wisdom, his wisdom endures; but he whose wisdom comes before his fear of sin, his wisdom does not endure.'" See *EY* (Salonika, 1516), vol. 1, introduction (= Jerusalem, 1961, vol. 1, introduction).

77. Compare this to the following passage found in the writings of ibn Ḥabib's contemporary, Isaac Caro: "I shall have peace because I follow the dictates of my heart and my good thoughts [based on Deut. 29:18]—such a person desires two Torahs . . . the Torah of God in his heart, and the teaching of the gentiles in his hand. He supposes that he will be forgiven because he believes in the principles of faith." See Isaac Caro, *Toledot Yitsḥaq* (Mantua, 1558), to parashat *Vayelekh,* 78a,

and Haim Hillel Ben-Sasson, *"Dor gole sefarad al atsmo,"* 46.

78. Note that there is an error in the phrase that reads *"iqqarim toraniyyim am-itiyyim."* It should read *"iqqarim toraniyyim* emuniyyim." The phrase appears in its corrected form in *EY Berakhot* (Salonika, 1516), vol. 1, section 4, 9b (= Jerusalem, 1961, vol. 1, section 8, 7a). I have therefore translated it in accordance with the correct reading. Also see ibn Ḥabib's introduction to the *En Yaaqov,* where he defines *iyyun.* In interpreting *m. Abot* 1:2, where Simon Hatsaddiq argues that the world is built on three things (Torah, worship, and good deeds), ibn Ḥabib defines Torah as the "study (*iyyun*) of ideas about faith." Also see, for example, *EY Berakhot* (Salonika, 1516), vol. 1, section 52, 25a–b (esp. 25b) (= Jerusalem, 1961, vol. 1, section 56, 37b–38a), where ibn Ḥabib discusses the principles of faith in his interpretation of *b. Ber.* 12a.

79. *EY Berakhot* (Salonika, 1516), vol. 1, section 85, 37a (= Jerusalem, 1961, vol. 1, section 94, 67b).

80. See *EY Berakhot* (Salonika, 1516), vol. 1, section 85, 36b–37b (the second page numbered 36) (= Jerusalem, 1961, vol. 1, section 94, 67b).

81. Earlier in this comment, ibn Ḥabib expresses the importance of maintaining both a *"sekhel iyyuni"* and a *"sekhel maasi."* This means that individuals must not only engage in the type of study that yields an understanding of the principles of faith, as I will discuss below, but also comprehend the importance of the performance of mitsvot at the same time. Both must exist in tandem in the worship of God. See *EY Berakhot* (Salonika, 1516), vol. 1, section 85, 36b–37b (= Jerusalem, 1961, vol. 1, section 94, 66b).

82. See Maimonides, *Guide for the Perplexed,* 3:51, 619, where the word *iyyun* in the Hebrew translation is used to refer to philosophic speculation. He wrote, "Those who have plunged into speculation (*iyyun*) concerning the fundamental principles of religion have entered the antechambers [of the palace]."

83. See *EY Berakhot* (Salonika, 1516), vol. 1, section 85, 37b (= Jerusalem, 1961, vol. 1, section 94, 67b).

84. See *EY Berakhot* (Salonika, 1516), vol. 1, section 52, 25a–b (esp. 25b) (= Jerusalem, 1961, vol. 1, section 56, 37b).

85. Hirsh, *Boundaries of Faith,* 5.

86. See *EY Berakhot* (Salonika, 1516), vol. 1, section 52, 25a–b (= Jerusalem, 1961, vol. 1, section 56, 37b). Also see *EY Berakhot* (Salonika, 1516), vol. 1, section 4, 10a (= Jerusalem, 1961, vol. 1, section 8, 7b).

87. *EY Berakhot* (Salonika, 1516), vol. 1, section 52, 25a–b (= Jerusalem, 1961, vol. 1, section 56, 37b). Also see *EY Berakhot* (Salonika, 1516), vol. 1, section 4, 10a (= Jerusalem, 1961, vol. 1, section 8, 7b).

88. See Gen. 6:9.

89. *EY Berakhot* (Salonika, 1516), vol. 1, section 2, 7b–8a (= Jerusalem, 1961, vol. 1, section 6, 4a).

90. *EY Berakhot* (Salonika, 1516), vol. 1, section 2, 7b–8a (= Jerusalem, 1961, vol. 1, section 6, 4a).

91. *EY Berakhot* (Salonika, 1516), vol. 1, section 2, 7b–8a (= Jerusalem, 1961, vol. 1, section 6, 4a).

92. *EY Berakhot* (Salonika, 1516), vol. 1, section 36, 21b (= Jerusalem, 1961, vol. 1, section 41, 28b–29b).

93. Maimonides, *Guide for the Perplexed,* 3:54, 635–38.

94. *EY Berakhot* (Salonika, 1516), vol. 1, section 21, 15a (= Jerusalem, 1961, vol. 1, section 25, 19a).

95. Maimonides also held that the community should aid its elite in achieving perfection. See Shweid, *Classic Jewish Philosophers,* 178.

96. See Kellner, *Dogma,* 11, 109, 143.

97. Maimonides, *Guide for the Perplexed,* 1:56, 120; Marvin Fox, *Interpreting Maimonides: Studies in Methodology, Metaphysics, and Moral Philosophy* (Chicago: University of Chicago Press, 1994), 306–7.

98. Maimonides, *Guide for the Perplexed,* 1:36, 84; Fox, *Interpreting Maimonides,* 307.

99. Fox, *Interpreting Maimonides,* 307.

100. Note that I have quoted the version of the aggadic story found in *EY Berakhot* (Salonika, 1516), section 89, 38a. Ibn Ḥabib had different manuscripts of the aggadic texts from those found in the *Bavli* (Vilna: Romm, 1880–91).

101. The *Bavli* text of this aggadah reads: "Are you a prophet?"

102. The *Bavli* has, "I am neither a prophet nor the son of a prophet."

103. The *Bavli* (Vilna, 1880–91) has, "Had [I] ben Zakkai stuck my head between my knees all day long . . ." (*b. Ber.* 34b).

104. *EY Berakhot* (Salonika, 1516), vol. 1, section 89, 38a–b (= Jerusalem, 1961, vol. 1, section 98, 69b–71a).

105. Here ibn Ḥabib uses the term *ḥokhmah* to refer to the great Toraitic knowledge of these great rabbis.

106. *EY Berakhot* (Salonika, 1516), vol. 1, section 89, 38a–b (= Jerusalem, 1961, vol. 1, section 98, 69b–71a.

107. See Fox, *Interpreting Maimonides,* 300–305.

108. Albo, *Sefer Haiqqarim,* 4:164.

109. See the beginning of the comment on *EY Berakhot* (Salonika, 1516), vol. 1, section 55 (aggadic passage only), 27b–28a (note that page 27 is mistakenly numbered 28). Here ibn Ḥabib specifically defines the person who works in the city as the one who chooses to study Torah as a profession and the one who works in the field as an *am haaretz,* an ignorant person, lacking Torah knowledge.

110. *EY Berakhot* (Salonika, 1516), vol. 1, section 55, 27b–28a (= Jerusalem, 1961, vol. 1, section 68, 45b).

111. Daniel Abrams, "From Divine Shape to Angelic Being: The Career of Akatriel in Jewish Literature," *Journal of Religion* 76:1 (1996): 60–61.

112. *EY Berakhot* (Salonika, 1516), vol. 1, section 23, 15a–16b (note that the aggadic passage begins on 15a, but Akatriel is mentioned on 15b) (= Jerusalem, 1961, vol. 1, section 27, 19a–20b).

113. Ibn Ḥabib was not alone in choosing to focus on *b. Ber.* 7a, where Akatriel asks Rabbi Yishmael to bless him, as a way to discuss the meaning of the liturgical term "blessing." See, for example, Joshua ibn Shu'eib, *Sefer Derashot al Hatorah* (Cracow, 1573; repr. facsimile Jerusalem, 1969), 52a–b, as referred to by Carmi

Horowitz, *The Jewish Sermon*, 131. Horowitz notes that ibn Shu'ieb drew from a number of Kabbalistic texts, starting with *Sefer Habahir,* as well as those written by Rabbi Ezra, Rabbi Azriel, Rashba, Joseph Gikatilla, Baḥya ben Asher, and Recanati, for each showed how the Bible and the Talmud alluded to God's need for human blessings.

114. See Albo, *Sefer Haiqqarim,* 2:28, 158. Also see *EY Berakhot* (Salonika, 1516), vol. 1, section 23, 16a (= Jerusalem, 1961, vol. 1, 19b), where ibn Ḥabib refers to this passage found in *Sefer Haiqqarim.* I have quoted here a larger portion from Albo's *Sefer Haiqqarim* than was quoted by ibn Ḥabib in order to guide the reader. Ibn Ḥabib was, however, drawing from this context. Also note that ibn Ḥabib's perception of God as emanating goodness on those who were deserving had its roots not only in the philosophy of Joseph Albo but also in the philosophy of Ḥasdai Crescas. As a staunch critic of Maimonides and Aristotelian philosophy, Crescas sought to unravel the notion that God's desire to impart goodness was related to intellection. For Crescas it became imperative to reconstruct a God-idea that was not premised on thought, that is, on the view that thinking was a central aspect of God. Goodness was the common denominator that united all of God's attributes. In His essence, Crescas had argued, God was supreme goodness. He allowed this goodness to overflow in order to create in an ongoing fashion. Ibn Ḥabib drew from this context. See Ḥasdai Crescas, *Or Adonai* (Johannesberg, 1861; based on the first printed edition, Ferrara, 1555), book 1, 3:3–5, 17a–19d; book 2, 6:1, 40d–41a. Also see Julius Guttmann, *Philosophies of Judaism,* 265–66.

115. Ibn Ḥabib does not quote Rashba's comment in full within his own, but he includes Rashba's comment in the anthology that he compiled and included in the *En Yaaqov.* See *EY Berakhot* (Salonika, 1516). Also note that ibn Ḥabib included a brief reference to Baḥya's commentary on Deut. 8:10, but the overall tenor of his remark shows that he agreed with Baḥya's general position on the meaning of the *berakhah.* See Baḥya ben Asher, *Rabbenu Baḥya: Biur al Hatorah,* ed. Charles Ber Chavel (Jerusalem: Mossad Harav Kook, 1974), 3:300 (*ad* Deut. 8:10).

116. Joshua ibn Shu'eib, *Sefer Derashot al Hatorah,* 52a–b, as referred to by Horowitz, *The Jewish Sermon,* 131.

117. See Horowitz, *The Jewish Sermon,* 131.

118. See Joseph Gikatilla, *Sefer Shaare Orah* (Warsaw, 1883), 5a.

119. Comparing ibn Ḥabib's comment to the following statement made by Moses de Leon, in his thirteenth-century Kabbalistic exposition of the reasons for the commandments titled *Sefer Harimmon,* highlights the absence of a full commitment to Kabbalistic theosophy on the part of ibn Ḥabib: "When a person prays and offers thanks to his Creator, he draws down an influx of blessing from above to below . . . And, thus when we bless [God], for example, we augment the flow by our drawing down the influx of blessings from the source [*binah*] of the Place where they camp [that is, the *shekhinah*] . . . And, the matter is correct to the enlightened person [the Kabbalist] for God emanates the blessing of that gradation [*shekhinah*] to pour forth to the lower beings. And, therefore, it says, 'And bless the Lord your God' (Deut. 8:10), that is, draw down by prayer in order to increase the flow in that place [that is, from *shekhinah*]." See Moses de Leon, *Sefer Ha-rimmon: Critical*

Edition, ed. Elliot R. Wolfson (Ann Arbor, MI: University Microfilms, 1986), 371. The translation is excerpted from Byron L. Sherwin, *Kabbalah: An Introduction to Jewish Mysticism* (Lanham, MD: Rowman & Littlefield, 2006), 124.

120. Note that I have skipped several lines of ibn Ḥabib's comment here.

121. *EY Berakhot* (Salonika, 1516), vol. 1, section 23, 15a–16a (note that the aggadic passage begins on 15a, but Akatriel is mentioned on 15b) (= Jerusalem, 1961, vol. 1, section 27, 19a–20b).

122. See the portion of the passage found directly above the portion I translated. *EY Berakhot* (Salonika, 1516), vol. 1, section 23, 15a–16a (= Jerusalem, 1961, vol. 1, section 27, 19a–20b).

123. *EY Berakhot* (Salonika, 1516), vol. 1, section 4, 9b (= Jerusalem, 1961, vol. 1, section 8, 7a).

124. See Fox, *Interpreting Maimonides*, 321, where he makes a similar point describing how to confront analogous contradictions in Maimonidean thought regarding prayer.

125. This tension emerges on several occasions in ibn Ḥabib's commentary. He moves back and forth between a description of a God who answers one's prayer requests and the importance of cultivating a type of faith that is not dependent on what God provides.

126. Maimonides, *Mishnah im Perush Rabbenu Moshe ben Maimon*, introduction to *Pereq Ḥeleq*, 4:199.

127. See Heinemann, *The Reasons for the Commandments*, 144.

128. *EY Berakhot* (Salonika, 1516), vol. 1, section 4, 9b (= Jerusalem, 1961, vol. 1, section 8, 7a).

129. Medieval thinkers invoked the same idea. For example, in his discussion regarding the thirteen dogmatic principles of faith, Maimonides stated, "The obedient person and the rebellious person would reach [a point] with Him . . . where [God] would reward the one and punish the other." See the end of Maimonides' introduction to his commentary on the tenth chapter of *m. Sanhedrin* (*Pereq Ḥeleq*), *Mishnah im Perush Rabbenu Moshe ben Maimon*, 4:195–217. Also see Kellner, *Must a Jew Believe Anything?* 149–74, where he discusses Maimonides' view on reward and punishment.

130. Maimonides, among others, also struggled. On the one hand, he insisted that the belief in an exact system of reward and punishment was a principle of faith that could not be disregarded. On the other hand, Maimonides specifically stated that individuals were not to observe the commandments expecting that they would be rewarded for their commitment to Torah law. The ultimate goal of studying wisdom, for example, was to be nothing more than knowing that the Torah was truth. See Isadore Twersky, *A Maimonides Reader* (New York: Behrman House, 1972), 405, for a translation of this passage from Maimonides' commentary on *m. Sanhedrin*. Also see Kellner, *Must a Jew Believe Anything?* 151–52. Joseph Albo went so far as to say that, without a belief in reward and punishment, the Torah would have no purpose. "If there is no corporeal reward and punishment in this world and spiritual reward in the next, what need is there of divine law?" He also pointed out that the dogmatic principle of reward and punishment made no sense without

an understanding of God's ubiquitous knowledge, the extent of man's freedom, and God's providence. He thus devoted the fourth volume of *Sefer Haiqqarim* to explaining how the system of reward and punishment could operate in the face of the facts that God had foresight, that God was protective, and that man had free will. See Albo, *Sefer Haiqqarim,* 1:10, 97; 4:1, 2.

131. I have chosen to leave out a portion of this aggadic pericope, which offers different answers to Moses's question from the one offered below, attributed to Rabbi Meir. The passage puts forth three additional responses: (1) that the behaviors of fathers determine the fates of their children; (2) that children are rewarded depending on whether they follow in their fathers' footsteps; and (3) that there are degrees of righteousness. In fact, ibn Habib spends a significant portion of his comment struggling with these possibilities; before presenting his overall view, he suggests that we adopt the understanding of the biblical prophet Habbakuk. Habbakuk argued that justice would occur eventually and that one needed to trust God that all would work out fairly in the end (Hab. 2:1–4). Interestingly, ibn Habib does not reject this position. However, he does move on to offer another answer to Moses's question, as I discuss below.

132. *b. Ber.* 7a; also see *EY Berakhot* (Salonika, 1516), vol. 1, section 26, 18a–b (= Jerusalem, 1961, vol. 1, section 30, 22a–23a). Note that the opinion of Rabbi Meir was not the only answer to the question why it appears that God does not exact reward and punishment fairly. Three other answers were offered in the aggadic passage. However, the opinion of Rabbi Meir was well represented in rabbinic literature. The notions that one cannot understand the workings of God in the universe and that the concept of exact retribution is beyond human comprehension can be found elsewhere. See, for example, *m. Abot* 4:15, where Rabbi Yannai argued that it was not within the power of human beings to understand why the righteous suffer and the wicked prosper.

133. Sirat, *A History of Jewish Philosophy,* 348.

134. See *EY Berakhot* (Salonika, 1516), vol. 1, section 26, 18a–b (= Jerusalem, 1961, vol. 1, section 30, 22a–23a). Ibn Habib's point, that the adoption of Rabbi Meir's approach would overturn a fundamental principle of faith, can be found only in ibn Habib's commentary in the 1516 edition and not in the 1961 edition.

135. Note that I have corrected the word *omanut,* which appears both in *EY Berakhot* (Salonika, 1516) and in *EY Berakhot* (Jerusalem, 1961). There is a printing error, and the word should be *emunot.* Compare this to where ibn Habib uses the term *omanut* correctly to refer to one's craft. See his comment on *EY Berakhot* (Salonika, 1516), section 55 (aggadic passage only), 27b (bottom) (note that page 27 is mistakenly numbered 28).

136. *EY Berakhot* (Salonika, 1516), vol. 1, section 26, 18a–b (= Jerusalem, 1961, vol. 1, section 30, 22a–23a).

137. EY *Berakhot* (Salonika, 1516), vol. 1, section 26, 18a–b (= Jerusalem, 1961, vol. 1, section 30, 22a–23a).

138. *EY Berakhot* (Salonika, 1516), vol. 1, section 26, 18a–b (= Jerusalem, 1961, vol. 1, section 30, 23a).

139. EY *Berakhot* (Salonika, 1516), vol. 1, section 26, 18a–b (= Jerusalem, 1961,

vol. 1, 23a). For another example, see *EY Berakhot* (Salonika, 1516), vol. 1, section 85, 36b–37b (the second page numbered 36) (= Jerusalem, 1961, vol. 1, section 94, 67a–b). In this source, ibn Ḥabib reiterates that *iyyun* and the performance of deeds are central components in the formation of one's spirituality. However, according to this passage, individuals are encouraged to embrace them to the extent that it is possible given the circumstances of the day. See my discussion earlier in this chapter regarding the definition of *iyyun*.

140. Refer back to chapter 1, pages 38–39 where I deal with this source through the lens of the conversos. There, I refer to the midrashic passage that ibn Ḥabib quotes from *Shemot Rabbah,* where one finds God granting free rewards from a treasure. This was the treasure where the excess merit of others had been stored and that was used in situations where individuals appeared less deserving.

141. Eric Lawee, *Isaac Abarbanel's Stance toward Tradition,* 128. Regarding the lack of unified vision with respect to the matter of messianism, see E. E. Urbach, *The Sages: Their Concepts and Beliefs,* trans. Israel Abrahams (Cambridge, MA: Harvard University Press, 1987), 649. Also see Moshe Idel, introduction to *Hatenuot hameshihiyot beyisrael,* by Aaron Zev Aescoly (Jerusalem: Mossad Bialik, 1987), 10.

142. Lawee, *Isaac Abarbanel's Stance toward Tradition,* 132.

143. Note that the Palestinian amora Rabbi Hillel, noted above, and the tanna Hillel are not the same individual.

144. There has been much debate among modern Jewish historians about the extent to which interest in messianism intensified as a response to the crisis of the Spanish expulsion. Evidence of this debate emerges in Idel, introduction to *Hatenuot hameshihiyot beyisrael,* where he argues against Gershom Scholem, in particular. See also Tirosh-Samuelson, "The Ultimate End of Human Life," 353–54n10. See Gershom Scholem, "Opening Address," in *Types of Redemption: Contributions to the Theme of the Study-Conference Held at Jerusalem, 14th–19th of July, 1968,* ed. R. J. Z. Werblowsky and C. Joyce Bleeker (Leiden: E. J. Brill, 1970), 1–12. See also Elior, "Messianic Expectations," 35–36n2.

145. See Lawee, *Isaac Abarbanel's Stance toward Tradition,* 137–38, who summarizes the various approaches to Rabbi Hillel's statement concerning the messiah, including those of Maimonides, Shem Tov ibn Shaprut, and Albo, in light of Abarbanel's understanding of this passage.

146. Rabbi Hillel's dictum had posed challenges for many medieval thinkers, including Crescas (*Or Adonai,* Treatise II, introduction); Albo (*Sefer Haiqqarim* 1:1, 44–47); and Isaac Arama (*Aqedat Yitshak,* sermon 67). The fifteenth-century thinker Abraham Bibago, with whom ibn Ḥabib was familiar, had posed the question in his treatise *Derekh Emunah:* How could Maimonides count the coming of the messiah as a principle of faith when Rabbi Hillel of the Talmud had denied his coming in *b. San.* 99a? In raising this question, Bibago intended to strengthen the dogmatic principle established by Maimonides that one needed to believe that the messiah would come. See *Derekh Emunah* 3:4, 95a. See Kellner, *Dogma,* 151, 172, and 216.

147. See Rashi *ad b. San.* 99a, s.v. *En lahem mashiaḥ leyisrael.* Note, however, that ibn Ḥabib quotes a different version of Rashi in his introduction from the one

present in contemporary printings of the Talmud. This indicates that he had a different printed edition or manuscript tradition in front of him. Also note that ibn Ḥabib includes the text from *b. Sanhedrin* in his introduction to the *En Yaaqov* not to make a point about messianism necessarily, but to emphasize the importance of Rashi's commentary in explicating aggadic texts. Ibn Ḥabib was arguing for the value of including Rashi's commentary in the *En Yaaqov*. In doing so, however, he offers a lengthy explanation of the statement made by Rabbi Hillel that is relevant to my discussion here regarding messianism.

148. Ibn Ḥabib had a similar perspective to that of Abarbanel. See Lawee, *Isaac Abarbanel's Stance toward Tradition,* 138, for Abarbanel's perspective. For Abarbanel, who spoke at greater length about messianism than ibn Ḥabib in his treatise devoted to this subject, *Yeshuot Meshiḥo,* the verse in Ezekiel (37:25) claiming that David would act as the "prince over [Israel] forever" became a reference to a limited monarch who would lead the Jews in a war against the gentiles, but who was not the Davidic savior *par excellence.* See Lawee, *Isaac Abarbanel's Stance toward Tradition,* 138.

149. Note that the word *shoresh* used here is a catchphrase employed by ibn Ḥabib to signify that he is referring to a principle of faith. It was used by medieval Jewish philosophers who were interested in dogmatics. While many medieval thinkers were careful to distinguish the word *shoresh* from other terms, like *iqqar* and *anaf,* in generating systematic presentations of Jewish dogma, ibn Ḥabib was not as precise.

150. *EY* (Salonika, 1516), vol. 1, introduction (= Jerusalem, 1961, vol. 1, introduction).

151. Rashi, for example, held this opinion, as ibn Ḥabib notes. In addition, in writings such as Maimonides' *Epistle to Yemen,* one finds more blatant discussions regarding how to identify a messiah. Maimonides hoped to arm the Yemenite Jewish community with the facility to recognize theological misrepresentations made by fraudulent individuals. See Halkin and Hartman, *Crisis and Leadership: Epistles of Maimonides,* 190–91; Martin Kafka, *Jewish Messianism and the History of Philosophy* (Cambridge: Cambridge University Press, 2004), 91.

152. Rachel Elior, "Messianic Expectations," 35–49. Also see Shalom Rosenberg's discussion of the link that some Jews drew between suffering and the coming of the messianic age, "Exile and Redemption in Jewish Thought in the Sixteenth Century: Contending Conceptions," in *Jewish Thought in the Sixteenth Century,* ed. Bernard Dov Cooperman (Cambridge, MA: Harvard University Press, 1983), 405.

153. Elior, "Messianic Expectations," 36–38.

154. Abraham Halevi, *Mashre Qitrin* (Constantinople, 1510), repr. in *Qiryat sefer* 2 (1925): 101–4, 269–73, and *Qiryat sefer* 7 (1930): 149–65; 440–56.

155. Elior, "Messianic Expectations," 37–38.

156. See Tirosh-Samuelson, "The Ultimate End of Human Life," 2–3, and esp. 353–55n9 and n11, regarding the effects of the expulsion on messianism. See also Idel, introduction to *Hatenuot hameshiḥiyot beyisrael,* 10, 21–22, where he highlights the fact that there were Kabbalistic works written prior to the expulsion, such as *Sefer Hameshiv,* which discussed the nature of the messiah, the date of his arrival,

and the means by which one might hasten his arrival. Idel cites *Sefer Hameshiv* as evidence that there was no direct relationship between the crisis of the expulsion and the rise of messianism, or even a different form of Kabbalah tied to messianic longings, during the early sixteenth century. He attempts to diminish the link, embraced by several scholars, between crisis and changes in intellectual and spiritual attitudes following crisis. See also Moshe Idel, "Spanish Kabbalah after the Expulsion," in *Moreshet Sepharad: The Sephardi Legacy,* 2 vols., ed. Haim Beinart (Jerusalem: Magnes Press, 1992), 2:166–78 (English version). Also see Gershom Scholem, *Major Trends in Jewish Mysticism* (New York: Schocken Books, 1974), 244–51.

157. See, for example, Maimonides' twelfth principle of faith in *Mishnah im Perush Rabbenu Moshe ben Maimon,* introduction to *Pereq Ḥeleq,* 4:216; Crescas, *Or Adonai* 3:2; Albo, *Sefer Haiqqarim* 1:23, 186. See Kellner, *Dogma,* and his treatment of several dogmatists on this issue.

158. Note that ibn Ḥabib comments on the continuation of the aggadic passage as well. I have left out this portion in order to focus on ibn Ḥabib's references to messianism. See *EY Berakhot* (Salonika, 1516), vol. 1, section 1, 6b–7a (= Jerusalem, 1961, vol. 1, section 3, 2a–b).

159. The prophet Elijah appears frequently in rabbinic literature, revealing secrets to pious individuals and solving halakhic issues (*b. B. Metsia* 59b; *m. Ed.* 8:7). In several midrashic works, however, Elijah is given the role of recording the deeds of the righteous, presumably in preparation for the coming of the messiah, e.g. *Vayiqra Rab.* 34:8 (Vilna, 1878), *Ruth Rab.* 5:6 (Jerusalem, 1971). He was also associated with the ability to bring about the resurrection of the dead, e.g., *Shir Hashirim Rab.* 2:13, 4 (Vilna, 1878). This may be connected to the fact that in 1Kings 17:17–24, he revived the son of the widow of Tsorfat. See Moses Aberbach, "Elijah," in *Encyclopedia Judaica* 6: 632–38. See also Kris Lindbeck, "Story and Theology: Elijah's Appearance in the Babylonian Talmud" (Ph.D. diss., Jewish Theological Seminary, 1999).

160. Ibn Ḥabib quotes passages from Daniel 9:2–3, where the prophet attempts to determine the length of Israel's exile saying, "I, Daniel, consulted books concerning the number of years that, according to the word of the Lord, had come to Jeremiah the prophet and were to be the term of Jerusalem's desolation—seventy years. I turned my face to the Lord God, devoting myself to prayer and supplication." By drawing this parallel, ibn Ḥabib intends to show that Rabbi Yose acted similarly. He, too, turned to God to seek information regarding the coming of the messiah and prayed that God would foretell the future.

161. Note the addition here from *EY Berakhot* (Salonika, 1516).

162. Note that "among the nations" can be found only in *EY Berakhot* (Salonika, 1516); *EY Berakhot* (Jerusalem, 1961) has "among the idolators."

163. In *b. Shabb.* 30b, Rabban Gamaliel states: "When the messiah comes, the soil of the land of Israel is destined to bring forth bread rolls and fine woolen clothing, so that Israel will have food and clothing without hardship. 'May there be an abundance of corn in the land, may it rustle on top of the mountains, may its fruit be like Lebanon' (Ps. 72:16)."

164. *EY Berakhot* (Salonika, 1516), vol. 1, section 1, 6b–7a (= Jerusalem, 1961, vol. 1 section 3, 2a–b).

165. See Maimonides, *Mishnah im Perush Rabbenu Moshe ben Maimon,* introduction to *Pereq Ḥeleq,* 4:207. See Maimonides, *Mishne Torah, Hilkhot Melakhim* 12:2. Also see Aviezer Ravitzky, *History and Faith: Studies in Jewish Philosophy* (Amsterdam: J. C. Gieben, 1996), 73–112, for a complete overview of Maimonides' conception of the messianic age.

166. *EY Berakhot* (Salonika, 1516), vol. 1, section 59 (the first aggadic section labeled 59 in small letters), 28a–b, end of comment (= Jerusalem, 1961, vol. 1, section 68, 46a). Note that there are two pages in *EY* (Salonika, 1516), vol. 1, that are numbered 28. My reference here is to the second of those two pages, which is actually page 28.

167. Ibn Ḥabib specifically referred in his comment to the shortened version of the *Amidah* (the main section of daily prayer) known as *havinenu,* which summarizes the *Amidah*'s main themes. Individuals could pray using this prayer if they were in danger. See the Talmud's larger discussion on *b. Ber.* 30a.

168. Lawee, *Isaac Abarbanel's Stance toward Tradition,* 138.

169. See *y. Ber.* 1:6, 3d; *EY Berakhot* (Salonika, 1516), section 5, 54b–55b (*Yerushalmi* section) (= Jerusalem, 1961, section 5, 4b–5a) (second pagination).

170. See *y. Ber.* 1:6, 3d; *EY Berakhot* (Salonika, 1516), vol. 1, section 5, 54b–55b (= Jerusalem, 1961, vol. 1, section 5, 4b–5a) (second pagination, *Yerushalmi Berakhot*).

171. See *y. Ber.* 1:6, 3d; *EY Berakhot* (Salonika, 1516), vol. 1, section 5, 54b–55b (*Yerushalmi* section) (= Jerusalem, 1961, vol. 1, section 5, 4b–5a) (second pagination). Also see *EY Berakhot* (Salonika, 1516), vol. 1, section 59 (the first aggadic section, marked 59 in small letters), 27b–28a (specifically 28a) (= Jerusalem, 1961, vol. 1, section 68, 46a–47b). Note that there are two pages in *EY* (Salonika, 1516), vol. 1, that are numbered as page 28. My reference here to 27b can be found on the first page numbered 28, which is in fact page 27. This is a comment on *b. Ber* 17a, where Rav distinguishes this world from the World to Come. Ibn Ḥabib states at the end of this comment that earning life in the World to Come is dependent on one's commitment to the performance of good deeds and on one's commitment to Torah.

172. Also see *EY Berakhot* (Salonika, 1516), vol. 1, section 73, 33b–34a (ibn Ḥabib's commentary can be found on 34a) (= Jerusalem, 1961, vol. 1, section 82, 59a), where ibn Ḥabib points out in his commentary that when the righteous heap on themselves opportunities to study Torah and to perform God's commandments in this world, they receive the reward of being connected to God for all eternity.

173. See *y. Ber.* 1:6, 3d; *EY Berakhot* (Salonika, 1516), vol. 1, section 5, 54b–55b (*Yerushalmi* section) (= Jerusalem, 1961, vol. 1, section 5, 4b–5a) (second pagination).

174. See *y. Ber.* 1:6, 3d; *EY Berakhot* (Salonika, 1516), vol. 1, section 5, 54b–55b (*Yerushalmi* section) (= Jerusalem, 1961, vol. 1, section 5, 4b–5a) (second pagination). Also note that Isaiah continues in 52:10 to describe the redemption of Jerusalem as a time when God will "bare His holy arm in the sight of all the nations [so that] at the very ends of the earth [the people will] see the victory of God."

175. See *EY Berakhot* (Salonika, 1516), vol. 1, section 5, 54b–55b (*Yerushalmi* section) (= Jerusalem, 1961, vol. 1, section 5, 4b–5a) (second pagination). Also see *EY Kilayim* (Salonika, 1516), vol. 1, section 25, 58b (*Yerushalmi* section) (= Jerusalem, 1961, vol. 1, section 26, 12b–13a).

176. *EY Kilayim* (Salonika, 1516), vol. 1, section 25, 58b (*Yerushalmi* section) (= Jerusalem, 1961, section 26, 12b–13a).

177. A. P. Coudert, "Kabbalistic Messianism versus Kabbalistic Enlightenment," in *Millenarianism and Messianism in Early Modern Culture: Jewish Messianism in the Early Modern World,* 2 vols., ed. Matt Goldish and Richard H. Popkin (Dordrecht: Kluwer, 2001), 1:112–13.

178. See Septimus, *Hispano-Jewish Culture in Transition,* 39–60.

179. *EY Berakhot* (Salonika, 1516), vol. 1, section 59 (the first aggadic section labeled 59 in small letters), 28a–b (= Jerusalem, 1961, vol. 1, section 68, 46a). Note that there are two pages in *EY* (Salonika, 1516), vol. 1, that are numbered 28. My reference here is to the second of those two pages, which is actually page 28.

180. See Maimonides, *Mishnah im Perush Rabbenu Moshe ben Maimon,* introduction to *Pereq Ḥeleq,* 4:205.

181. See Maimonides, *Mishnah im Perush Rabbenu Moshe ben Maimon,* introduction to *Pereq Ḥeleq,* 4:216.

182. Septimus, *Hispano-Jewish Culture in Transition,* 40–42.

183. Hava Tirosh-Samuelson, *Happiness in Premodern Judaism* (Cincinnati: Hebrew Union College Press, 2003), 239.

184. See ibn Ḥabib's comment on *b. Ber.* 17a, *EY Berakhot* (Salonika, 1516), vol. 1, section 59 (see the first aggadic section marked 59 in small letters), 28a–b (= Jerusalem, 1961, vol. 1, section 68, 46a–47a). Note that there are two pages in *EY* (Salonika, 1516), vol. 1, that are numbered 28. My reference here is to the second of those two pages, which is actually page 28.

185. Also see *EY Berakhot* (Salonika, 1516), vol. 1, section 36, 21b (= Jerusalem, 1961, vol. 1, section 40, 28a).

186. See Elliot R. Wolfson, *Language, Eros, Being: Kabbalistic Hermeneutics and Poetic Imagination* (New York: Fordham University Press, 2005), 252–53, where he discusses Naḥmanides' view of the World to Come, situating it within a Kabbalistic framework. Halevi did not embrace the full force of Naḥmanides' more Kabbalistic view on the subject of the World to Come, and this may be the reason ibn Ḥabib chose to quote from Halevi's interpretation of *b. Ber.* 17a rather than to refer to Naḥmanides.

187. Also see Bernard Septimus's discussion of the Spanish rabbi Meir Halevi Abulafia (Ramah, 1165–1244), who opposed Maimonides on similar grounds. Abulafia attacked Maimonides' naturalistic interpretation of rabbinic eschatology, stating that "he who attaches greater importance to the soul than to the body in [the final] judgment is, it would seem, of the opinion that reward and punishment in *olam haba* are not in accordance with men's deeds and the requirements of justice, but rather in accordance with nature; for, in this view the soul, which is by nature immortal, remains in existence, while the body, which is by nature mortal, ceases to exist . . . and the soul of the righteous and the wicked, according to this

view, are judged not according to their deeds, but according to their intellects. For, the soul that knows its Creator through philosophical proof is immortal by reason of its knowledge which is everlasting. But, the soul that does not know its Creator by way of philosophical proof shall be cut off—though it be possessed of Torah and good deeds. It follows that there is no lasting benefit to Torah and good deeds, since the matter is determined by nature." For this reason, Abulafia rejected Maimonides' position. See Septimus, *Hispano-Jewish Culture in Transition,* 59. Also see 146n146.

188. *EY Berakhot* (Salonika, 1516), vol. 1, section 59 (the first aggadic section labeled 59 in small letters), 28a–b (= Jerusalem, 1961, vol. 1, section 68, 46a). Note that there are two pages in *EY* (Salonika, 1516), vol. 1, that are numbered 28. My reference here is to the second of those two pages, which is actually page 28.

189. Maimonides, *Guide for the Perplexed,* 1:59; Gershom Scholem, *Major Trends in Jewish Mysticism,* as cited in Septimus, *Hispano-Jewish Culture in Transition,* 76 and 153n5.

190. Ibn Ḥabib refers to his belief that the Torah "speaks in the language of human beings" several times in his commentary. For example, see *EY Berakhot* (Salonika, 1516), vol. 1, section 1, 7a (bottom) (= Jerusalem, 1961, vol. 1, section 3, 3a–4a) (discussed above); *EY Berakhot* (Salonika, 1516), vol. 1, section 46, 23b (= Jerusalem, 1961, vol. 1, section 50, 33b); *EY Berakhot* (Salonika, 1516), vol. 1, section 89, 38a (= Jerusalem, 1961, vol. 1, section 98, 70b); *EY Berakhot* (Salonika, 1516), vol. 1, section 114, 45b (= Jerusalem, 1961, vol. 1, section 127, 94a). See also Hai Gaon's comment in Benjamin M. Lewin, ed., *Otsar Hageonim: Teshuvot Geone Bavel Uferusham al pi Seder Hatalmud,* 13 vols. (Haifa: 1928–62) 1:1, 131; Baḥya ibn Pakuda, *Ḥovot Halevavot,* ed. Moses Hyamson (Jerusalem: Feldheim, 1962), 106–7; Maimonides, *Guide for the Perplexed,* 1:59. Also see Isaak Husik, *The History of Medieval Jewish Philosophy* (New York: Meridian, 1958), 261. There he notes that anthropomorphic references were necessary for convincing the masses that God was "perfect . . . existent, living, wise, powerful, and active."

191. *EY Berakhot* (Salonika, 1516), vol. 1, section 27, 19a (= Jerusalem, 1961, vol. 1, section 31 [end of comment], 23b). Note that the larger passage in *EY Berakhot* contains the only reference to aggadic material not found in the *Bavli* and *Yerushalmi* Talmudim. A passage is quoted from *Shemot Rab.* 3:1 (Vilna, 1878).

192. Ibn Ḥabib lauds Rashba for citing the position of Hai Gaon with respect to this aggadic passage (*b. Ber* 7a). However, he also notes that in Rashba's commentary on the aggadot, Rashba offers a different interpretation of the passage, one that ibn Ḥabib did not embrace. Nevertheless, ibn Ḥabib decides to include Rashba's comment, following his discussion of the preferable interpretation of Hai Gaon.

193. Despite ibn Ḥabib's discontent with the figurative interpretive approach to difficult aggadot that referred to God in anthropomorphic ways, he included Rashba's analysis of *b. Ber.* 7a. In contrast to the position offered by Hai Gaon, Rashba's comment highlighted the idea that tefillin were an instrument of sight, because they were worn between one's eyes. The straps that extended from the tefillin and encircled one's head symbolized that God was the cause of everything and that everything returned to His will. Just as the base of the tefillin was connected to the

knot by the straps, so too the knot in the back was connected to the base, the first cause of the straps. In the same way, when Moses saw the knot of God's tefillin, he did not actually see God wearing them. Instead, he saw or came to understand the ways of God, who controlled the universe. Relying on a Maimonidean/Aristotelian description of the universe (*Guide for the Perplexed,* 2:4), Rashba argued that God willed the creation of ten intelligences. These intelligences acted on the corresponding spheres and kept them in motion. The tenth intelligence, the Active Intellect, did not act on a sphere. Its sphere of operation was the world of matter, the sublunar world. The intelligence that caused each sphere to move had as its cause the intelligence that was higher than it, with the ultimate cause being God. The process was therefore cyclical, beginning from God and ultimately returning to Him, like the tefillin straps that encircled the head and returned to the base. Thus when Moses saw the knot of God's tefillin, he perceived the ways of God. Everything was connected to and controlled by God.

194. See Exodus 25:9, which Hai Gaon quotes in his interpretation.

195. *EY Berakhot* (Salonika, 1516), vol. 1, section 27, 19a (= Jerusalem, 1961, vol. 1, section 31, 23b).

196. See Daniel J. Lasker, "Chasdei Crescas," in *Routledge History of World Philosophies: History of Jewish Philosophy,* 2 vols., ed. Daniel H. Frank and Oliver Leaman (London: Routledge, 1996), 2:405, where he discusses Crescas's reliance on Maimonides regarding the issue of proving God's existence. Indeed, while Crescas's own philosophy remains largely within the framework established by Maimonides, he differs on many details, which represent a critique of Maimonidean philosophy in his work, *Or Adonai.*

197. *EY Berakhot* (Salonika, 1516), vol. 1, section 1, 7a (bottom) (= Jerusalem, 1961, vol. 1, section 3, 3a–4a).

198. See Maimonides, *Mishnah im Perush Rabbenu Moshe ben Maimon,* introduction to *Pereq Ḥeleq* 4:211.

199. See, for example, *EY Berakhot* (Salonika, 1516), section 24, 16b–17a (= Jerusalem, 1961, vol. 1, section 28, 20a–22a; ibn Ḥabib's commentary begins on 20b), where ibn Ḥabib discusses God's emotional expression of anger. Also note, in contrast, that Maimonides had argued in the *Guide* that "God does not receive impressions and affections . . . nor does He have dispositions . . . Nor is He, may He be exalted, endowed with a soul, so that He may have habits pertaining to Him—such as clemency, modesty, and similar things." According to Maimonides, God cannot express emotion (*Guide for the Perplexed,* 1:52).

200. *EY Berakhot* (Salonika, 1516), vol. 1, section 23, 15a–16b (= Jerusalem, 1961, vol. 1, section 27, 19a–20b).

201. Guttmann, *Philosophies of Judaism,* 265–67.

202. The aggadic passage repeats the same dialogue with two different amoraim, Rabbi Yirmiyah and Rabbi Zera, immediately following the exchange between Rabbah and Abbaye. Ibn Ḥabib includes both passages in his anthology. See *EY Berakhot* (Salonika, 1516), vol. 1, section 72, 33a–b (= Jerusalem, 1961, vol. 1, section 81, 57b–58b).

203. Note that ibn Ḥabib had a slightly different version of *b. Ber* 30b from the

version found in the Vilna edition. See *EY Berakhot* (Salonika, 1516), vol. 1, section 72, 33a–b (= Jerusalem, 1961, vol. 1, section 81, 57b–58b).

204. *EY Berakhot* (Salonika, 1516), vol. 1, section 94, 39a–b (= Jerusalem, 1961, vol. 1, section 103, 72b–73a).

205. *EY Berakhot* (Salonika, 1516), vol. 1, section 67, 32a–b (= Jerusalem, 1961, vol. 1, section 76, 53b–54b [ibn Ḥabib's comment is on 54a]).

206. Note that in ibn Ḥabib's introduction, he specifically refers to his desire to bring the aggadic texts to the entire populace (*hamon*) in keeping with the model set by Alfasi, who aimed to present the populace with a clear presentation of the halakhic material drawn from the Talmud.

Chapter 5

1. Shulamit Soloveitchik Meiselman, *The Soloveitchik Heritage: A Daughter's Memoir* (Hoboken, NJ: Ktav, 1995), 127–28.

2. Don Seeman and Rebecca Kobrin, "'Like One of the Whole Men': Learning, Gender and Autobiography in R. Barukh Epstein's *Mekor Barukh*," *Nashim: A Journal of Jewish Women's Studies and Gender Issues* 2 (1999): 72.

3. Yitzhak Buxbaum, *Light and Fire of the Baal Shem Tov* (New York: Continuum, 2005), 214.

4. Some studied the *En Yaaqov* once they had advanced beyond learning the Bible as well as the *Shulḥan Arukh* and prior to their study of the Talmud with Tosafot. See Assaf, *Meqorot letoledot haḥinukh beyisrael,* 2:155. For some children, the study of the *En Yaaqov* was a part of their daily curriculum (Assaf, 2:157, 163). Others studied the *En Yaaqov* if they could not master the Talmudic page with Tosafot (Assaf, 1:92).

5. Thomas R. Adams and Nicholas Barker, "A New Model for the Study of the Book," in *A Potencie of Life: Books in Society,* ed. Nicolas Barker (London: British Library, 1993), 8–10.

6. Adams and Barker, "A New Model for the Study of the Book," 29.

7. Josiah Pinto (1565–1648) wrote a commentary on the *En Yaaqov, Meor Enayim* (part 1: Amsterdam, 1643; part 2: Mantua, 1743). He was, for most of his life, a rabbi in Damascus before resettling in Safed.

8. The first English translation of the *En Yaaqov* was published in New York in 1916. See S. H. Glick, trans., *En Jacob: Aggada of the Babylonian Talmud* (New York: Traditional Press, 1916).

9. Adams and Barker, "A New Model for the Study of Book," 27–28, 37. Also see Robert Bonfil, "Reading in the Jewish Communities of Western Europe in the Middle Ages," in *A History of Reading in the West,* ed. Guglielmo Cavallo and Roger Chartier (Amherst: University of Massachusetts Press, 1999), 149–78. In this article Bonfil discusses the reading habits of Jews during the Middle Ages. However, there is little written material available regarding the seventeenth and eighteenth centuries, when the *En Yaaqov* was published more frequently. Also see Zeev Gries, *The Book in the Jewish World: 1700–1900* (Oxford: Littman Library of Jewish Civilization, 2007), 20.

10. Roger Chartier and Maurice Elton, "Crossing the Borders in Early Modern Europe: Sociology of Texts and Literature," *Book History* 8 (2005): 39–40. Also see D. F. McKenzie, *Bibliography and the Sociology of Texts* (Cambridge: Cambridge University Press, 1999), 13.

11. See ibn Ḥabib's comments found at the end of his work on *Seder Zeraim, EY* (Salonika, 1516), vol. 1, 60b (= Jerusalem, 1961, vol. 1, 15a). Note that this page is numbered 60, but is in fact page 62.

12. See Levi ibn Ḥabib, *Sheelot Uteshuvot*, #126, where he states that there are many things in the aggadot that are not fitting to speak about and should not be written down. Presenting *b. B. Metsia* 54a as an example, he notes that such aggadot have little purpose and few delight in them. Also see Jacob Elbaum, *Lehavin divre ḥakhamim*, 21n13. See Levi ibn Ḥabib, *En Yaaqov/Bet Yaaqov* (Salonika, 1522–23), vol. 2, introduction (= Jerusalem, 1961, vol. 1, introduction of Levi ibn Ḥabib), where he notes that he cannot produce a collection that will match his father's. Lauding his father, he bemoans his own deficiencies regarding the endeavor of completing the *En Yaaqov.*

13. See Levi ibn Ḥabib, *En Yaaqov/Bet Yaaqov* (Salonika, 1522–23), vol. 2 of the *En Yaaqov.*

14. See below where I discuss the fact that during the sixteenth century in Italy the title of the *En Yaaqov/Bet Yaaqov* was changed to *En Yisrael/Bet Yisrael.*

15. See Marjorie Lehman, "A Talmudic Anthology of Aggada: Examining the *En Yaaqov*" (Ph.D. diss., Columbia University, 1993), 385–404 ("Appendix of Printed Editions").

16. Adams and Barker, "A New Model for the Study of the Book," 8.

17. In Venice, the first volume of the *En Yaaqov* retained its original name, and the second volume was titled *Bet Yaaqov,* as in its first printed edition.

18. See Vinograd, *Otsar hasefer haivri,* "Venice," 2:287. See Heller, *The Printing of the Talmud,* 183.

19. This list included books that had a relationship to the Talmud, as well as *Sheelot Uteshuvot* of Rabbi Asher ben Yeḥiel and *Sefer Mitsvot Gadol* of Moses ben Jacob of Coucy. See Heller, *The Printing of the Talmud,* 222–23.

20. See Heller, *The Printing of the Talmud,* 222–23. Also see Benjamin Ravid, "The Prohibition against Jewish Printing and Publishing in Venice and the Difficulties of Leone Modena," in *Studies in Medieval Jewish History and Literature,* ed. Isadore Twersky (Cambridge, MA: Harvard University Press, 1979), 135–53.

21. See Heller, *The Printing of the Talmud,* 224.

22. Giorgio di Cavalli was a Venetian printer of Hebrew books from 1566 to 1567. See S. Van Straalen and Brad Sabin Hill, *Catalogue of Hebrew Printers: 1500–1900* (London: British Library, 1995), lxiv. Also see Friedberg, *Toledot hadefus haivri bimedinat italya,* 73–74; David Werner Amram, *The Makers of Hebrew Books in Italy* (Philadelphia: Julius H. Greenstone, 1909), 346–49. Amram argues that at the time Cavalli began printing, Jews focused mostly on the study of compendia of the law and traditional religious texts (like the *En Yaaqov*). Therefore, these types of books were most desirable and sellable. The printer's mark used by Cavalli, of an elephant carrying a castle, was a sign that "slowly, but surely" (*tarde*

sed tuto) men would be led out of darkness and into enlightenment, that is, away from their traditional legal works and toward the study of different types of works, like philosophical ones (Amram, 349). Interestingly, the title page of the *En Yisrael* (Venice, 1566) did not have this mark. Instead, it was printed with two winding pillars (see appendix, figure 2).

23. See *En Yaaqov* (Salonika, 1516), vol. 1, introduction (= Jerusalem, 1961, vol. 1, introduction), where ibn Ḥabib describes his indexes. There are two indexes included at the end of the first volume. The same types of indexes appear at the end of the second volume of the *En Yaaqov*, the *Bet Yaakov* (Salonika, 1522–23). The first index is divided in accordance with a set of themes referred to as "twelve pillars," describing the main ideas on which Judaism stands. The second is organized in accordance with the *parshiyot* (sections) of the Torah read each week in the synagogue. In addition, this index also provides aggadic references regarding the biblical books of the Prophets and the Writings. Also note that volume 2 has two biblical indexes: the first is the index reprinted from volume 1; the second is an index of references to volume 2. Unfortunately, the indexes that Jacob ibn Ḥabib organized are not useful. References in his indexes do not point to the correct sections in the *En Yaaqov*. Those produced by Levi ibn Ḥabib, found at the end of volume 2, are correct and do guide the user to the aggadot of the second volume of the *En Yaaqov*. Indexes found in two editions of the *En Yaaqov* (Venice, 1546 and 1566) are also usable, as indexers corrected the problems they found in ibn Ḥabib's *En Yaaqov* (1516).

24. One can see more evidence of this title change by comparing the title page and Jacob ibn Ḥabib's introduction in *En Yaaqov* (Salonika, 1516) to the 1566 edition (Venice, 1566). Each instance where ibn Ḥabib referred to the *En Yaaqov* by name in the 1516 edition now reads *En Yisrael* in the 1566 edition. One can also see evidence of attempts to rub out the word "*Yaaqov*" from the title page in 1546 editions that were printed under the title *En Yaaqov* in Venice. See, for example, the edition of *En Yaaqov* (Venice, 1546) in the rare book collection at the Jewish Theological Seminary. Also note that the title change from *En Yaaqov* to *En Yisrael* is derived from Gen. 32:29, where God says to Jacob, "Your name shall no longer be Jacob, but Israel, for you have striven with beings divine and human and have prevailed."

25. The editions printed by Isaac ben Aharon of Prostitz in Cracow in 1587–88 were titled *En Yisrael/Bet Yisrael*. See Vinograd, *Otsar hasefer haivri*, "Cracow," 2:116. (See, for example, appendix, figure 4).

26. Brad Sabin Hill, *Hebraica: Manuscripts and Early Printed Books from the Library of the Valmadonna Trust* (Oxford: Oxford University Press, 1989), entry 40.

27. See *En Yisrael/Bet Yisrael* (Venice, 1566) and other books published by Cavalli during the time when his printing press produced Hebrew books (approximately, 1566–67). They exhibit the brown marks of censors throughout their pages. Also see Heller, *The Printing of the Talmud*, 243.

28. The Talmud was given the title *Gemara*, and any mention of the word "Talmud" was changed to "Gemara" as well. See Heller, *The Printing of the Talmud*, 243–44.

29. Heller, *The Printing of the Talmud*, 244.

30. Heller, *The Printing of the Talmud*, 243–44.

31. This edition was called *En Yisrael,* and there were swirly pillars on the title page. This was an exact copy of the title page found in Cavalli's *En Yisrael* (Venice, 1566). See appendix, figure 2.

32. *En Yisrael/Bet Yisrael* (Salonika: Matityah Bat Sheva and Yehudah Bigah, 1595–1601).

33. *En Yisrael/Bet Yisrael* (Cracow, 1587). See appendix, figure 4. The collection was so popular that its printer, Isaac ben Aharon of Prostitz, noted on the title page of this edition that the collection had already been reprinted two to three times. The same type of comment appears on the title page of *En Yisrael/Bet Yisrael* (Salonika: Matityah Bat Sheva and Yehudah Bigah, 1595–1601).

34. *En Yisrael/Bet Yisrael* (Prostitz, 1603).

35. See *En Yisrael/Bet Yisrael* (Verona, 1649), which was a reprint of *En Yisrael/Bet Yisrael* (Venice, 1566), except in a far smaller size (4 by 6 inches). Indeed, the availability of versions of the *En Yaaqov* in small sizes also attests to the number of people who wished to study it. Its size enabled individuals to carry it from place to place and allowed for sellers to market the book at a cheaper price.

36. See n23, where I discuss ibn Ḥabib's indexes, as well as my discussion in chapter 3.

37. Note that one of the earliest citation indexes was compiled by Maimonides, *Mafteaḥ Haderashot,* in the twelfth century. Although there is some scholarly disagreement as to whether Maimonides was the author of this index, its existence indicates that there was age-old interest in creating indexes that would aid in the study of Jewish works of aggadah or of midrash aggadah. See Bella Hass Weinberg, "Predecessors of Scientific Indexing Structures in the Domain of Religion," in *The History and Heritage of Scientific and Technological Information Systems: Proceedings of the 2002 Conference,* ed. W. Boyd Rayward and Mary Ellen Bowden (Medford, NJ: Information Today, 2004), 130. Also see Weinberg, "The Earliest Hebrew Citation Indexes," *Journal of the American Society for Information Science* 48:4 (1997): 318–30.

38. *En Yisrael* (Cracow, 1587) had the same section and page numbers as *En Yisrael* (Venice, 1566). (See appendix: compare figure 3 to figure 5.)

39. Modena's index, which was published separately in 1625, was also included in *En Yisrael/Bet Yisrael* (Venice, 1625). Despite the fact that Modena makes reference in his alphabetical index to aggadot that appear in tractates found in volume 1 and volume 2 of the *En Yisrael/Bet Yisrael,* the index was oddly placed at the end of volume 1. Also note that Modena refers to aggadot in volume 1 by section number, but refers to the aggadot in volume 2 by page number. See Modena's introduction to *Bet Leḥem Yehudah* (Venice, 1625), where he warns his reader of this discrepancy. In fact, early editions of the *En Yaaqov* had only section numbers in volume 1. Ibn Ḥabib's edition had virtually no section numbers beginning with tractate *Megillah.* Note that in the copy of the *En Yisrael/Bet Yisrael* (Venice, 1625) in the Rare Book Room at the Jewish Theological Seminary, volumes 1 and 2 are bound together.

40. Note that this edition published in Cracow bore the title *En Yisrael* and not *En Yaaqov* (see appendix, figure 4).

41. See *En Yisrael* (Cracow, 1587).

42. See Modena's introduction found at the beginning of *Bet Leḥem Yehudah* (Venice, 1625) and his introduction to *Bet Yehudah* (Venice, 1635).

43. Mark R. Cohen, *The Autobiography of a Seventeenth-Century Venetian Rabbi: Leon Modena's Life of Judah* (Princeton, NJ: Princeton University Press, 1989), 141. In this autobiography, Modena also describes the difficulties his printers experienced in keeping the print shop open and operating. His grandson was primarily responsible for typesetting the *Bet Yehudah,* despite risking imprisonment by the local authorities for his printing work. Modena was determined, even in the face of these obstacles, that the *Bet Yehudah* would be finished and available for sale. For an extensive discussion of Modena's critique of rabbinic Judaism, see Fishman, *Shaking the Pillars of Exile.*

44. Judah Modena, *Bet Yehudah* (Venice, 1635).

45. See Rosanes, *Divre yeme yisrael betogarmah* 3:231–32. Also see Meir Beneyahu, *"Rabbi moshe castilats meḥakhame mitsrayim, rabbo shel qehillat qodesh ashkenazim bitsefat," Tarbiz* 29 (1959–60): 74.

46. See Edels's (Maharsha's) introduction to his commentary on the *En Yaaqov,* where he specifically states that he is commenting on the *En Yaaqov* and not simply writing a running commentary on the aggadot of the Talmud, in *Qotnot Or [En Yisrael]* (Amsterdam: Joseph Athias and David de Castro Tartas, 1683 [vol. 1]); *Qohelet Shlomo [En Yaaqov im Qotnot Or]* (Amsterdam: Herts Levi Rofe, 1740); *En Yaaqov* (Jerusalem, 1961), vol. 1. Maharsha's commentary on the *En Yaaqov* became one of the most cited commentaries. At times, his commentary was included instead of ibn Ḥabib's *Hakotev.* See, for example, *En Yaaqov* (Vilna: Samuel Joseph Fuen and Abraham Hirsch [Tsvi] Rosenkranz, 1869), where Maharsha's commentary was included and ibn Ḥabib's was left out. See appendix, figures 13 and 14.

47. Shmuel Ashkenazi, "Edels, Samuel Eliezer Ben Judah Ha-Levi," in *Encyclopedia Judaica,* 6 vols., ed. Cecil Roth and Geoffrey Wigoder (New York: Macmillan, 1971–72), 6:363.

48. See *Qotnot Or [En Yisrael]* (Amsterdam: David de Castro Tartas, 1684) and *Qohelet Shlomo [En Yaaqov im Qotnor Or]* (Amsterdam: Herts Levi Rofe, 1740). The latter volume has Pinto's introduction. It was not included in *Qotnot Or [En Yisrael]* (Amsterdam: David de Castro Tartas, 1684) alongside ibn Ḥabib's and Maharsha's introductions. Also see Natan Shapira's (d. 1662), *He'arot al Sefer En Yaaqov [He'arot Kabaliyot],* a seventeenth-century Kabbalistic commentary on the aggadot of the *En Yaaqov.* This commentary exists in manuscript in the rare book room at Columbia University. Many thanks to the cataloger at Columbia, Yoram Bitton, for pointing out this manuscript to me.

49. The period between 1683 and 1740 in Amsterdam was one in which different types of editions of the *En Yaaqov* were published by different printers. An Amsterdam edition of the *En Yaaqov* published by Joseph Athias is titled *Qotnot Or* (Amsterdam, 1683 [vol. 1]; Amsterdam, 1685 [vol. 2]). Despite the use of this title, *Qotnot Or,* the title page indicates that its compilers intended to create a new

edition of the *En Yaaqov,* adding to its contents to improve on it. David de Castro Tartas assisted Athias with the printing. This edition included the commentaries of Pinto (Harif) and Edels (Maharsha) alongside ibn Ḥabib's commentary. See L. Fuks and R. G. Fuks-Mansfeld, *Hebrew Typography in the Northern Netherlands 1585–1815,* 2 vols. (Leiden: E. J. Brill, 1987), 2:338 (entry 432). Two other editions were published in 1684. One edition was published in two volumes. The first volume was published by Athias (see appendix, figure 6) and the second volume by Tartas. The second volume also has a title page that reads *Qotnot Or/En Yisrael.* Levi ibn Ḥabib's introduction was included in this volume. Another edition was published by Tartas and was also titled *Qotnot Or* (see appendix, figure 7). It too contained the commentaries of Pinto and Edels alongside ibn Ḥabib's commentary, *Hakotev.* Levi ibn Ḥabib's second volume was included with the first volume under the same title. Athias's and Tartas's 1684 editions were very similar, but the title pages point to the fact that different printers took an interest in publishing them. According to Moritz Steinschneider, *Catalogus Librorum Hebraeorum in Bibliotheca Bodleiana* (Berlin: Friedlaender, 1852–60), 2:1200–02, there was a fourth edition of the *En Yaaqov* that was published by Athias in the same year (Amsterdam, 1684–85). It included the alphabetical index of the Venetian rabbi Eliezer Reiti and a note that Christian editors aided in its preparation for printing. In 1698, an entirely different type of edition was printed that contained only an abridged commentary, similar to Rashi's Talmud commentary (see appendix, figures 8 and 9). Ibn Ḥabib's commentary was left out. It was published by Caspar Steen, who was able to secure a contract for its reprinting in 1700. He was supposed to print 5,300 copies largely for sale in Poland, but the money never came through and therefore he never reprinted it (Fuks and R. G. Fuks-Mansfeld, *Hebrew Typography,* 2: 412–14). Several editions of the *En Yaaqov* were published by Solomon Proops (Amsterdam, 1714, 1725, 1726). *En Yaaqov* (Amsterdam, 1740), which has the title *Qohelet Shlomo,* was printed by Herts Levi Rofe. Also see A. E. Cowley, *A Concise Catalogue of the Hebrew Printed Books in the Bodleian Library* (Oxford: Clarendon Press, 1929), 294–95.

50. Interestingly, neither the 1684 editions nor the 1740 edition of the *En Yaaqov* published in Amsterdam contained Modena's commentary, *Haboneh.* See also Isaac Ben-Yaakov, *Otsar hasefarim* (Vilna: Romm, 1880), 438. The flower symbols, which reflect additions to ibn Habib's collection of aggadot from Modena's *Beit Yehudah,* are in evidence for the first time in *Qohelet Shlomo [En Yaaqov im Qotnot Or]* (Amsterdam, 1740). A large flower symbol in the appendix, figure 11, in the righthand column, next to *"amar r. yossi,"* for example, is clear in the original, though difficult to see in this reproduction. Smaller stars were inserted to highlight quotes from the Bible and are already in evidence in Amsterdam editions printed in 1684.

51. Editions of *Qohelet Shlomo [En Yaaqov im Qotnot Or]* (Amsterdam, 1740) were printed in two-volume sets as well as in one large volume on blue paper.

52. To cite one example, *Qohelet Shlomo [En Yaaqov im Qotnot Or]* (Amsterdam, 1740) displayed in bold Hebrew letters at the top of its title page the title *Qohelet Shlomo.* This title referred to Shlomo Yequtiel Zalman, a judge in the religious

court (*bet din*) of the city of Glokhov, in the Ukraine, who had arranged this "new and improved" edition of the *En Yaaqov.* He relied on the work of Isaac Meir, the son of Yonah Teomim-Fraenkel, who was from the small town of Chmielnik, in southeastern Poland, and was known as *Qotnot Or.* In *Qohelet Shlomo [En Yaaqov im Qotnot Or]* (Amsterdam, 1740), *Qotnot Or* is also mentioned on the title page, signifying that this new edition was built not only on the work of ibn Ḥabib but also on the work of others. Indeed, Jacob ibn Ḥabib's name was recognized on the title page, and he was praised for his endeavor. However, the less prominent, undersized font used to describe his efforts also diminished his role as the sole author of the *En Yaaqov* (see appendix, figure 10).

In *Otsar hasefarim,* Ben-Yaakov also notes that the first edition to rely on *Qotnot Or* was *En Yisrael* (Amsterdam, 1683). See Ben-Yaakov, *Otsar hasefarim,* 250, 438.

53. See "*Haqdamat hamadpisim*" in the *En Yaaqov* (Jerusalem, 1961), 2–3. Also note that editions of the *En Yaaqov* published in nineteenth-century Slawita (Slawita, 1818, 1819, and 1860) not only bore a striking resemblance to each other but also to Amsterdam-printed editions, such as *Qohelet Shlomo [En Yaaqov im Qotnot Or]* (Amsterdam, 1740). Despite the fact that the Slawita editions inverted *Qotnot Or* and *Qohelet Shlomo* on their title pages, as compared to the Amsterdam editions that listed *Qohelet Shlomo* first and *Qotnot Or* beneath it, the editions were similar. While page numbers varied slightly from Slawita edition to Slawita edition, the texts of the aggadot and the commentaries contained therein are virtually the same.

54. Natan Goren, ed., *Yehadut lita,* 3 vols. (Tel-Aviv: Am Hasefer, 1959), 3:348.

55. Two Warsaw editions of the *En Yaaqov,* for example, did not contain ibn Ḥabib's commentary. In addition, each reflected a desire to maintain a sense of flexibility in that each was quite distinct from the other. The *En Yaaqov* (Warsaw: Joel Lebensohn, 1857) contained aggadic passages with a commentary that summarized many commentaries. Humorously, the title page describes this commentary as a "*perush maspiq,*" a "sufficient commentary," signifying that this was all the reader needed for his or her study of the *En Yaaqov.* On the other hand, a Warsaw edition published in 1895 contained an expanded Yiddish translation, that is, a "*perush ivre taytsh,*" which incorporated explanations by Rashi without explicitly attributing them to him, and which contained extra words and phrases aimed at paraphrasing the aggadic material so that it would be more understandable to the reader (see appendix, figure 12). This was clearly an appeal to a popular but literate audience that knew little Hebrew. In addition, English translations of the *En Yaaqov* were printed, the first of which was published in New York in 1916; see S. H. Glick, trans., *En Jacob: Aggada of the Babylonian Talmud* (New York: Traditional Press, 1916). Once again, ibn Ḥabib's contributions to the *En Yaaqov* were virtually ignored, despite mention made of him on the title page. His commentary was omitted, his introduction was excised, and even the anthology of aggadot present in the collection was not his own. Oddly, the only essay that appeared at the beginning of the collection was that written by Abraham, the son of Maimonides. Another English translation was published in 1999; see Avraham Yaakov Finkel, trans., *En Yaaqov: The Ethical and Inspirational Teachings of the Talmud* (Northvale, NJ: Jason Aronson, 1999). Although Finkel provided his own commentary in Eng-

lish, testifying to the continued interest in the aggadot of the *En Yaaqov,* he did not include any other commentaries.

56. See *En Yaaqov* (Vilna, 1876), printed by Romm. Specifically note "*Haqdamat hamadpisim,*" found at the beginning of the edition, where the printers discuss the difficulties they encountered in printing the *En Yaaqov.*

57. The Romm family had also published earlier editions of the *En Yaaqov* in Vilna in 1837, 1838, 1840, 1857, and 1863. See Vinograd, *Otsar hasefer haivri,* "Vilna," 2:395, 421, 476, 958, 1175. Note that entries 421 and 476 are listed as the work of the printer Menaḥem Mann, who was also a member of the Romm family, and who worked with Simḥa Zymel. See Van Straalen and Hill, *Catalogue of Hebrew Printers,* lxvi. See also Hayim Duberish (Bernard) Friedberg, *Toledot hadefus haivri befolania* (Tel Aviv, 1950), 125. Another edition published in Vilna in 1874 by a different printer (Jabetz) contained a commentary written by Jacob ben Joseph Reischer, *Iyyun Yaaqov* (Wilhermsdorf, 1729), which had circulated independently for a time before becoming part of editions of the *En Yaaqov* years later. It was added to *En Yaaqov* (Vilna, 1874) for the first time, as the title page of that edition notes.

58. See Yehudah Slutsky, "Romm," in *Encyclopedia Judaica,* 16 vols., ed. Cecil Roth and Geoffrey Wigoder (New York: Macmillan, 1971–72), 15:255.

59. Essays on aggadah included one written by Abraham, the son of Maimonides, years before the birth of ibn Ḥabib; one by Yeshayah Halevi Hurvitz; one by Moshe Ḥayyim Luzatto of Padua, Italy (1701–46); as well as one by Zvi Hirsch Chajes of Brody, Galicia (1805–55). Note that Chajes's essay also appeared in *En Yaaqov* (Vilna, 1876), where it accompanied his commentary. For some reason, his commentary did not appear in *En Yaaqov* (Vilna, 1883).

60. *En Yaaqov* (Vilna: Romm, 1883) was republished many times. Reprints of it were produced in Vilna (1923) and in Jerusalem (1961; 2000), to name a few (see appendix, figures 15, 16, and 17). However, this edition did not prevent the printing of variant editions over the past century that differed from it, including a more recent edition, *En Yaaqov Mevoar* (Jerusalem, 1994). Ibn Ḥabib's commentary does not appear in this edition. Rather, Rashi's commentary is included, along with that of Ḥayim Joseph Waldman, a later commentary that had not appeared in Romm's edition. Also see *En Yaaqov,* 7 vols. (Jerusalem: Mesoret Hashas, 2008), which has vocalized texts and citations in ibn Ḥabib's commentary indicating his sources (although it is incomplete and not always correct); this edition has different section numbers from those of *En Yaaqov* (Vilna, 1883). Greater differences can be seen in other editions, such as *En Yaaqov* (Warsaw, 1895). See appendix, figure 12.

61. I do not discount here that the folios of the *Bavli* came to include a wider number of commentaries over time than just Rashi and Tosafot. See Eliezer Segal, "Anthological Dimensions of the Babylonian Talmud," in *The Anthology in Jewish Literature,* ed. David Stern (Oxford: Oxford University Press, 2004), 81–107.

62. Also note that the *En Yaaqov* served as a resource for those wishing to design more popular collections of aggadah. The *Mayse Buch,* for example, was a seventeenth-century collection of aggadic material translated into Yiddish and drawn,

in part, from the *En Yaaqov.* For an overview of this collection, see Moses Gaster, trans., *Ma'aseh Book: The Book of Jewish Tales and Legends* (Philadelphia: Jewish Publication Society, 1934). In the early twentieth century, H. N. Bialik joined Y. H. Ravnitzky in producing a collection of aggadot translated into Hebrew, *Sefer Haaggadah,* which was a type of updated *En Yaaqov.* Bialik used *Sefer Haaggadah* to draw from his past while looking to participate in the revival of Jewish culture in the present. See Alan Mintz, *"Sefer Ha'aggadah:* Triumph or Tragedy?" in *History and Literature: New Readings of Jewish Texts in Honor of Arnold J. Band,* ed. William Cutter and David C. Jacobson (Providence, RI: Brown University Press, 2002), 17–26, and Mark W. Kiel, *"Sefer Ha'aggadah:* Creating a Classic Anthology," in *The Anthology in Jewish Literature,* ed. David Stern (Oxford: Oxford University Press, 2004), 226–43.

63. See Adam Shear's *The Kuzari and the Shaping of Jewish Identity, 1167–1900* (Cambridge: Cambridge University Press, 2008), 14, where he poses these questions regarding the reception history of Judah Halevi's *Kuzari.* Jacob Elbaum has begun to probe sixteenth- and seventeenth-century commentaries written on the *En Yaaqov,* and Avraham Eisen of Ben Gurion University of the Negev has completed a master's thesis on *Derash Moshe,* a sixteenth-century Ashkenazic commentary on the *En Yaaqov.*

64. Adams and Barker, "A New Model for the Study of the Book," 38.

Bibliography

Primary Sources

Rabbinic

Finkelstein, Louis, ed. *Sifre Devarim.* Berlin, 1939. Repr. New York: Jewish Theological Seminary, 1969.

Lauterbach, Jacob Z., ed. *Mekhilta Derabbi Yishmael.* New York: Jewish Theological Seminary, 1976.

Lieberman, Saul, ed. *Devarim Rabbah.* Jerusalem, 1940.

Margulies Mordecai, ed. *Midrash Vayiqra Rabbah.* New York: Jewish Theological Seminary, 1956–58. Repr. 1993.

Midrash Rabbah. Vilna, 1878.

Schechter, Solomon, ed. *Abot Derabbi Natan.* Vienna, 1887.

Talmud Bavli. Vilna: Romm, 1880–91. Repr. Jerusalem, 1995.

Talmud Bavli Massekhet Berakhot. Soncino, 1483–84.

Talmud Yerushalmi. Krotoshin, 1866 (based on Venice: Bomberg, 1523–24). Repr. Jerusalem, 1969.

Talmud Yerushalmi. Jerusalem, 1922. Repr. Jerusalem, 1968.

Theodor, Jehuda, and Hanokh Albeck, eds. *Midrash Bereshit Rabbah: Critical Edition with Notes and Commentary.* 3 vols. Berlin, 1929. Repr. Jerusalem: Wahrmann Books, 1965.

Medieval

Abarbanel, Isaac. *Mashmia Yeshuah.* Offenbach, 1767. Repr. Tel Aviv, 1960.

———. *Perush al Neviim Aharonim.* Jerusalem: Torah Vedaat, 1956.

———. *Yeshuot Meshiḥo.* Königsberg, 1861.

Abarbanel, Judah. *Sefer Havikkuaḥ.* Lyck, 1871. Repr. in *Mivḥar hashirah haivrit bietalyah,* edited by Jefim Hayim Schirman. Berlin, 1934.

Aboab, Isaac. *Menorat Hamaor.* Jerusalem: Mossad Harav Kook, 1961.

Aboab, Samuel. *Devar Yisrael.* Venice, 1702.

Abulafia, Meir Halevi. *Kitab al-rasa'il.* Edited by J. Brill. Paris, 1871.

Abulafia, Todros ben Joseph Halevi. *Otzar Hakavod.* Warsaw, 1879.

Albo, Joseph. *Sefer Haiqqarim.* Edited by Isaak Husik. Philadelphia: Jewish Publication Society, 1946.

Alfasi, Isaac. *Hilkhot Rav Alfas [Hilkhot Harif].* Edited by Nissan Zaks. Jerusalem:

Mossad Harav Kook, 1969, 2 vols. (Based on the first print edition, Constantinople, 1509.)

———. *Hilkhot Rav Alfas [Hilkhot Harif]*. In *Talmud Bavli*. Vilna: Romm, 1880–91. Repr. Jerusalem, 1995.

Alfonsi, Petrus. *Dialogu, PL*. Edited by J. P. Migne. Paris, 1854.

Almoli, Solomon. *Pitron Ḥalomot*. Salonika, 1515.

———. *Sefer Measef Lekhol Hamaḥanot*. Constantinople, 1530.

Arama, Isaac. *Aqedat Yitsḥaq*. Venice, 1547. Repr. Warsaw, 1904.

———. *Ḥazut Qashah*. Warsaw: Shuldberg, 1884.

Ardutiel, Avraham ben Shlomo. *Avne Zikkaron*. Published by Gershon Scholem in *Qiryat sefer* 7 (1930): 457–65.

Ashkenazi, Samuel Jaffee. *Yefe Anaf*. Frankfurt, 1696.

———. *Yefe Mare*. Constantinople, 1587.

———. *Yefe Qol*. Smyrna, 1739.

———. *Yefe Toar*. Venice, 1597–1606. Repr. Constantinople, 1648.

ben Asher, Baḥya. *Kitve Rabbenu Baḥya*. Edited by Charles Ber Chavel. Jerusalem: Mossad Harav Kook, 1969.

———. *Rabbenu Baḥya: Biur al Hatorah*. Edited by Charles Ber Chavel. Jerusalem: Mossad Harav Kook, 1974.

ben Asher, Jacob. *Tur*. Jerusalem, 1957–1960.

ben Yeḥiel, Asher. *Piskei Harosh [Hilkhot Harosh]*. In *Talmud Bavli*. Vilna: Romm, 1880–91. Repr. Jerusalem, 1995.

Berav, Jacob. *Sheelot Uteshuvot*. Jerusalem, 1958.

Bibago, Abraham. *Derekh Emunah*. Constantinople, 1522. Repr. Jerusalem: Sifriyat Meqorot, 1970; Jerusalem: Mossad Bialik, 1978.

Boethius, Antius Manlius Severinus. *De Consolatione Philosophiae traduzione ebraica di Azaria ben R. Joseph ibn Abba Mari*. [Translated into Hebrew by Azariah ben R. Joseph Ibn Abba Mari]. Edited by Sergio Joseph Sierra. Jerusalem and Torino: Instituto di Studi Ebraici Scuola Rabbinica S. H. Margulies Disegni, 1967.

Canpanton, Isaac. *Darkhe Hagemara*. Constantinople, 1515–20. Repr. Mantua, 1593.

———. *Darkhe Hatalmud*. Jerusalem: Daf Ḥen, 1981.

Capsali, Elijah. *Seder Eliyahu Zuta*. Jerusalem: Makhon Ben Tsvi, 1975–83.

Caro, Isaac. *Toledot Yitsḥaq*. Mantua, 1558. Repr. Amsterdam, 1708; Jerusalem: H. Vagshal, 1993–94.

Caro, Joseph. *Avqat Rokhel*. Salonika, 1791.

———. *Bet Yosef*. Jerusalem, 1993–94.

———. *Shulḥan Arukh*. Jerusalem, 1992.

Crescas, Ḥasdai. *Or Adonai*. Johannesberg, 1861. (Based on the first printed edition, Ferrara, 1555.)

———. *Or Adonai*. (See Natan Ophir, *"Harav ḥasdai crescas kefarshan filosofi lemaamare ḥazal."* Ph.D. dissertation, Hebrew University, 1993 [appendix].)

Davidson, Israel. *Sefer Milḥamot Hashem*. New York: Jewish Theological Seminary, 1934.

de Leon, Moses. *Sefer Ha-rimmon: Critical Edition.* Edited by Elliot R. Wolfson. Ann Arbor, MI: University Microfilms, 1986.

de Medina, Samuel. *Sheelot Uteshuvot.* Salonika, 1598. Repr. Lemberg, 1862.

Duran, Profiat. *Maase Efod.* Vienna: Holtvarteh, 1865. Repr. Jerusalem: Makor, 1969–70.

Falquera, Shem Tov. *Iggeret Havikkuah.* (See Steven Harvey, ed. and trans., *Falaquera's Epistle of the Debate* [Cambridge, MA: Harvard University Press, 1987].)

Frenkel, David, ed. *Zera Anashim.* Husiyatin, 1902.

Gikatilla, Joseph. *Sefer Shaare Orah.* Warsaw, 1883.

Halevi, Abraham. *Mashre Qitrin.* Constantinople, 1510. Repr. in *Qiryat sefer* 2 (1925): 101–4, 269–73, and *Qiryat sefer* 7 (1930): 149–65; 440–56.

Hapenini, Yedayah. *Ketav Hahitnatslut.* Printed in Solomon ibn Adret, *Sheelot Uteshuvot* (Hanover, 1610), 65d–67a (416–18).

ibn Adret, Solomon ben Abraham. *Hiddushe Harashba al Aggadot Hashas.* Jerusalem: Shalom Meshulam Weinberger, 1966.

———. *Sheelot Uteshuvot.* Hanover, 1610.

———. *Sheelot Uteshuvot.* Ashdod and Jerusalem: Mir, 2004.

ibn al-Nakawa, Israel. *Menorat Hamaor.* 2 vols. Edited by Hyman Gerson Enelow. New York: Bloch, 1929.

ibn Habib, Levi. *Sheelot Uteshuvot.* Venice, 1565.

ibn Lev, Joseph. *Sheelot Uteshuvot.* Bene Beraq, 1988.

ibn Pakuda, Bahya. *Hovot Halevavot.* Edited by Moses Hyamson. Jerusalem: Feldheim, 1962.

ibn Shahin, Nissim. *Hibbur Yefe Mehayeshuah.* Edited by H. Z. Hirschberg. Jerusalem: Mossad Harav Kook, 1954.

ibn Shem Tov, Shem Tov. *Sefer Haemunot.* Jerusalem, 1968–69.

ibn Shu'eib, Joel. *Nora Tehillot.* Salonika, 1568.

ibn Shu'eib, Joshua. *Sefer Derashot al Hatorah.* Cracow, 1573. Repr. Jerusalem, 1969.

ibn Zerah, Menahem. *Tsedah Laderekh.* Feraro, 1554.

Jabetz, Joseph. *Magen Avot.* Leipzig, 1855.

———. *Or Hahayyim.* Lublin, 1912.

Leon, David Messer. *Kevod Hakhamim.* Edited by S. Bernfeld. Berlin: Meqitse Nirdamim, 1899. Repr. Jerusalem: Makor, 1970.

Lewin, Benjamin M., ed. *Otsar Hageonim: Teshuvot Geone Bavel Uferusham al pi Seder Hatalmud.* 13 vols. Haifa, 1928–62.

Maimonides, Abraham. *Milhamot Hashem.* Jerusalem, 1953.

Maimonides, Moses. *Guide for the Perplexed.* Translated by Shlomo Pines. Chicago: University of Chicago Press, 1963.

———. *Iggerot Harambam.* 2 vols. Edited by Y. Shailat. Jerusalem: Hotsaat Maaliyot, 1987–88.

———. *Mishnah im Perush Rabbenu Moshe ben Maimon.* 6 vols. Translated by Joseph Kafih. Jerusalem: Mossad Harav Kook, 1963.

———. *Mishne Torah.* Jerusalem: Hotsaat Shivte Frankel, 2007.

———. *Sefer Hamitsvot Lerabbenu Moshe ben Maimon.* Jerusalem: Mossad Harav Kook, 1971.

Mizraḥi, Elijah. *Sheelot Uteshuvot.* Constantinople, 1560. Repr. Jerusalem: Darom, 1937.

Naḥmanides, Moses. *Perushe Hatorah Lerabbenu Moshe ben Naḥman.* Edited by Ḥayyim Dov Shavel. Jerusalem: Mossad Harav Kook, 1959.

Pipano, David. *Sefer Shalshelet Rabbane Saloniq Verabbane Sofia,* published with *Ḥagor Efod.* Sofia, 1925.

Recanati, Menachem. *Taamei Hamitsvot.* Constantinople, 1544.

Saadya Gaon. *Emunot Vedeot.* Translated by Samuel Rosenblatt. New Haven, CT: Yale University Press, 1948.

Saba, Abraham. *Eshkol Hakofer.* Venice, 1567. Repr. Warsaw, 1879; Bartfeld, 1907.

———. *Tseror Hamor.* Venice, 1522. Repr. Warsaw, 1879; Bene Beraq: Hekhal Hasefer, 1989–90.

Shalom, Abraham. *Neve Shalom.* Venice, 1525.

Shaprut, Shem Tov ben Isaac. *Pardes Rimonim.* Zhitomir, 1866.

Weinberger, Shalom Meshulam, ed. *Ḥiddushe Harashba al Aggadot Hashas.* Jerusalem, 1966.

Zacuto, Abraham. *Yuḥasin Hashalem.* Constantinople, 1566. Repr. Frankfurt: M. A. Vohrmann, 1924.

Editions of the *En Yaaqov*

En Yaaqov. Salonika: Judah Gedaliah, 1516.

En Yaaqov/Bet Yaaqov. Salonika: Judah Gedaliah, 1522–23.

En Yaaqov/Bet Yaaqov. Venice: Marco Antonio Giustiniani, 1546.

En Yisrael/Bet Yisrael. Venice: Giorgio di Cavalli, 1566.

En Yisrael/Bet Yisrael. Cracow: Isaac ben Aharon of Prostitz, 1587.

En Yisrael/Bet Yisrael. Salonika: Matityah Bat Sheva and Yehudah Bigah, 1595–1601.

En Yisrael/Bet Yisrael. Cracow: Isaac ben Aharon of Prostitz, 1603.

En Yisrael/Bet Yisrael. Venice: Pietro Aluife and Lorenzo Bragadini, 1625.

En Yisrael/Bet Yisrael. Verona: No printer on title page, 1649.

Qotnot Or [En Yisrael]. Amsterdam: Joseph Athias and David de Castro Tartas, 1683 (vol. 1), and 1685 (vol. 2).

Qotnot Or [En Yisrael]. Amsterdam: David de Castro Tartas, 1684.

Qotnor Or [En Yisrael]. Amsterdam: Joseph Athias, 1684 (vol. 1); David de Castro Tartas, 1684 (vol. 2).

En Yisrael. Amsterdam: Joseph Athias, 1684.

En Yisrael. Amsterdam: Caspar Steen, 1698.

En Yaaqov. Amsterdam: Solomon Proops, 1714.

En Yaaqov. Amsterdam: Solomon Proops, 1725.

En Yaaqov. Amsterdam: Solomon Proops, 1726.

Qohelet Shlomo [En Yaaqov im Qotnot Or]. Amsterdam: Herts Levi Rofe, 1740.

En Yaaqov. Slawita: Moshe Shapira, 1818.

En Yaaqov. Slawita: Moshe Shapira, 1819.

En Yaaqov. Vilna: Romm, 1837.
En Yaaqov. Vilna: Romm, 1838.
En Yaaqov. Vilna: Romm, 1840.
En Yaaqov. Vilna: Romm, 1857.
En Yaaqov. Warsaw: Joel Lebensohn, 1857.
En Yaaqov. Slawita: No printer on title page, 1860.
En Yaaqov. Vilna: Romm, 1863.
En Yaaqov. Vilna: Samuel Joseph Fuen and Abraham Hirsch (Tsvi) Rosenkranz, 1869.
En Yaaqov. Vilna: Jabetz, 1874.
En Yaaqov. Vilna: Romm, 1876.
En Yaaqov. Vilna: Romm, 1883. Repr. Vilna, 1923; Jerusalem, 1961; Jerusalem, 2000.
En Yaaqov. Warsaw, 1895.
En Yaaqov Mevoar. Jerusalem, 1994.
En Yaaqov. 7 vols. Jerusalem: Mesoret Hashas, 2008.

English Editions of the *En Yaaqov*

Finkel, Avraham Yaakov, trans. *En Yaaqov: The Ethical and Inspirational Teachings of the Talmud.* Northvale, NJ: Jason Aronson, 1999.
Glick, S. H., trans. *En Jacob: Aggada of the Babylonian Talmud.* New York: Traditional Press, 1916.

En Yaaqov–Associated Works and Commentaries

ben Moshe, Yedidyah. *Liqqute Aggadah Misefer En Yaaqov.* 1602–3 (manuscript).
Haggadot Hatalmud. Constantinople, 1511.
Modena, Judah Aryeh (Leone). *Bet Leḥem Yehudah.* Venice, 1625.
———. *Bet Yehudah.* Venice, 1635.
Pinto, Josiah. *Meor Enayim.* Part 1: Amsterdam, 1643. Part 2: Mantua, 1743.
Reischer, Jacob ben Joseph, *Iyyun Yaaqov.* Wilhermsdorf, 1729.
Reiti, Eliezer. *Luaḥ Maamare En Yisrael.* Venice, 1612.
Shapira, Natan. *He'arot al Sefer En Yaaqov [He'arot Kabaliyot]* (seventeenth-century Italian manuscript).

Secondary Sources

Aberbach, Moses. "Elijah." In *Encyclopedia Judaica,* vol. 6. Edited by Cecil Roth and Geoffrey Wigoder, 632–38. 16 vols. New York: Macmillan, 1971–72.
Abrams, Daniel. "From Divine Shape to Angelic Being: The Career of Akatriel in Jewish Literature." *Journal of Religion* 76:1 (1996): 43–63.
Ackerman, Ari. "Jewish Philosophy and the Jewish-Christian Philosophical Dialogue in Fifteenth-Century Spain." In *The Cambridge Companion to Medieval Jewish Philosophy,* edited by Daniel H. Frank and Oliver Leaman, 371–90. Cambridge: Cambridge University Press, 2003.

Adams, Thomas R., and Nicholas Barker. "A New Model for the Study of the Book." In *A Potencie of Life: Books in Society,* edited by Nicolas Barker, 5–43. London: British Library, 1993.

Amarillo, Avraham Shaul. *"Ḥevrat hatalmud torah hagadol besaloniqi"* [The great Talmud Torah society in Salonika]. *Sefunot* 13 (1971–8): 275–308.

Amram, David Werner. *The Makers of Hebrew Books in Italy.* Philadelphia: Julius H. Greenstone, 1909.

Ashkenazi, Shmuel. "Edels, Samuel Eliezer Ben Judah Ha-Levi." In *Encyclopedia Judaica,* vol. 6. Edited by Cecil Roth and Geoffrey Wigoder, 363. 16 vols. New York: Macmillan, 1971–72.

Assaf, Simḥa. *"Anuse sefarad ufortugal besifrut hateshuvot"* [The forced converts of Spain and Portugal in responsa literature]. *Zion* 5 (1932–33): 19–60.

———. *Meqorot letoledot haḥinukh beyisrael* [Sources for the history of Jewish education]. 2 vols. Tel Aviv: Dvir, 1930.

———. *"Mikhtavim meet gedole saloniqi"* [Letters from the great rabbis of Salonika]. In *Meqorot umeḥqarim betoledot yisrael,* 209–17. Jerusalem, 1946.

Avneri, Zvi. "Isaac Aboab II." in *Encyclopedia Judaica,* vol. 2. Edited by Cecil Roth and Geoffrey Wigoder, 93. 16 vols. New York: Macmillan, 1971–72.

Bacher, Wilhelm. *Erkhe midrash* [Midrashic terminology]. Tel Aviv, 1922/1923.

Baer, Marc. "Islamic Conversion Narratives on Women: Social Change and Gendered Religious Hierarchy in Early Modern Istanbul." *Gender and History* 16:2 (2004): 425–58.

Baer, Yitzhak. *A History of the Jews in Christian Spain.* 2 vols. Philadelphia: Jewish Publication Society, 1992.

Becker, Hans-Jürgen. "Die Yerushalmi-Midrashim der Ordnung Zeraim in Ya'akov ibn Ḥabib's *En Ya'aqov.*" *Frankfurter Judaistische Beiträge* 18 (1990): 77.

Beinart, Haim. "The Conversos and Their Fate." In *Spain and the Jews: The Sephardi Experience 1492 and After,* edited by Elie Kedourie, 92–122. London: Thames & Hudson, 1992.

———. *The Expulsion of the Jews from Spain.* Translated by Jeffrey Green. Oxford: Oxford University Press, 2002.

———. "The Great Conversion and the Converso Problem." In *Moreshet Sepharad: The Sephardi Legacy,* vol. 1, edited by Haim Beinart, 355–92. 2 vols. Jerusalem: Magnes Press, 1992.

———. "The Judaizing Movement in the Order of San Jeronimo in Castile." *Scripta Hierosolymitana* 7 (1961): 167–92.

Benayahu, Meir. *"Rabbi moshe castilats meḥakhame mitsrayim, rabbo shel qehillat qodesh ashkenazim bitsefat"* [Rabbi Moshe Castillas of Egypt, rabbi of the Ashkenazi community in Safed]. *Tarbiz* 29 (1959–60): 71–74.

———. *"Rav yosef taitazak misaloniqi: Rosh golat sefarad"* [Rabbi Joseph Taitazak of Salonika: Leader of the Spanish exile]. In *Meaz vead ata,* edited by Zvi Ankori, 21–34. Tel Aviv: Tel Aviv University Press, 1984.

Ben-Sasson, Haim Hillel. *"Dor gole sefarad al atsmo"* [The generation of the Spanish exiles (reflects) on itself]. *Zion* 26 (1961): 23–64.

Ben-Shalom, Ram. "The Ban Placed by the Community of Barcelona on the Study of Philosophy and Allegorical Preaching: A New Study." *Revue des Études Juives* 3:4 (2000): 387–404.

———. "Communication and Propaganda between Provence and Spain: The Controversy over Extreme Allegorization (1303–1306)." In *Communication in the Jewish Diaspora,* edited by Sophia Menache, 171–224. Leiden: E. J. Brill, 1996.

———. "The Typology of the Converso in Isaac Abravanel's Biblical Exegesis." *Jewish History* 23:3 (2009): 281–92.

Bentov, Haim. *"Shitat limmud hatalmud biyeshivot saloniqi veturkya"* [The method of Talmud study in the yeshivot of Salonika and Turkey]. *Sefunot* 13 (1979): 7–102.

Ben-Yaakov, Isaac. *Otsar hasefarim* [Catalog of books]. Vilna: Romm, 1880.

Bettan, Israel. "The Sermons of Isaac Arama." *Hebrew Union College Annual* 12–13 (1937–38): 564–83.

———. *Studies in Jewish Preaching, Middle Ages.* Cincinnati: Hebrew Union College Press, 1939.

Blair, Ann. "Reading Strategies for Coping with Information Overload, ca. 1550–1700." *Journal of the History of Ideas* 64:1 (2003): 11–28.

Blumberg, Harry. "The Problem of Immortality in Avicenna, Maimonides, and St. Thomas Aquinas." In *Essays in Medieval Jewish and Islamic Philosophy,* edited by Arthur Hyman, 95–115. New York: Ktav, 1977.

Bodian, Miriam. *Dying in the Law of Moses: Crypto-Jewish Martyrdom in the Iberian World.* Bloomington: Indiana University Press, 2007.

———. *Hebrews of the Portuguese Nation: Conversos and Community in Early Modern Amsterdam.* Bloomington: Indiana University Press, 1999.

———. " 'Men of the Nation': The Shaping of Converso Identity in Early Modern Europe." *Past and Present* 143 (1994): 48–76.

Bonfil, Roberto. "Dubious Crimes in Sixteenth-Century Italy: Rethinking the Relations between Jews, Christians, and *Conversos* in Pre-modern Europe." In *The Jews of Spain and the Expulsion of 1492,* edited by Moshe Lazar and Stephen Haliczer, 299–310. Lancaster, CA: Labyrinthos, 1997.

———. "The Historian's Perceptions of the Jews in the Italian Renaissance: Towards a Reappraisal." *Revue des Études Juives* 134 (1984): 59–82.

———. "Reading in the Jewish Communities of Western Europe in the Middle Ages." In *A History of Reading in the West,* edited by Guglielmo Cavallo and Roger Chartier, 149–79. Amherst: University of Massachusetts Press, 1999.

Borenstein-Makovetzki, Leah. "Tendencies of Separation and Unification in Greek-Jewish Communities during the Sixteenth and Seventeenth Centuries." *Annual of Bar-Ilan Studies in Judaica and Humanities* 20–21 (1983): 246–70.

Boyarin, Daniel. *Haiyyun hasefaradi: Lefarshanut hatalmud shel megorashe sefarad* [The Spanish method: The Talmudic exegesis of the Spanish exiles]. Jerusalem: Makhon Ben Tsvi, 1989.

———. *"Meḥqarim befarshanut hatalmud shel megorashe sefarad"* [Studies in the Talmudic exegesis of the Spanish exiles]. *Sefunot,* n.s. 2 (1983): 165–80.

———. "Moslem, Christian, and Jewish Cultural Interaction in Sephardic Talmudic Interpretation." *Review of Rabbinic Judaism* 5:1 (2002): 1–33.

Bregman, Marc. "Midrash Rabbah and the Medieval Collector Mentality." *Proof-texts* 17 (1997): 63–76. Repr. in *The Anthology in Jewish Literature*, edited by David Stern, 196–208. Oxford: Oxford University Press, 2004.

Breuer, Edward. "Maimonides and the Authority of Aggadah." In *Be'erot Yitzhak: Studies in Memory of Isadore Twersky*, edited by Jay Harris, 25–45. Cambridge, MA: Harvard University Press, 2005.

Broadie, Alexander. "The Nature of Medieval Jewish Philosophy." In *Routledge History of World Philosophies: History of Jewish Philosophy*, vol. 2, edited by Daniel H. Frank and Oliver Leaman, 83–92. 2 vols. London: Routledge, 1996.

Brown, Peter. *Religion and Society in the Age of Saint Augustine*. New York: Harper & Row, 1972.

Buxbaum, Yitzhak. *Light and Fire of the Baal Shem Tov*. New York: Continuum, 2005.

Carlebach, Elisheva. *The Pursuit of Heresy: Rabbi Moses Hagiz and the Sabbatian Controversy*. New York: Columbia University Press, 1990.

———. "The Status of the Talmud in Early Modern Europe." In *The Printing of the Talmud from Bomberg to Schottenstein*, edited by Sharon Liberman Mintz and Gabriel M. Goldstein, 79–89. New York: Yeshiva University Museum, 2005.

Carrete Parrondo, Carlos. "Jews, Castilian Conversos, and the Inquisition: 1482–1492." In *The Jews of Spain and the Expulsion of 1492*, edited by Moshe Lazar and Stephen Haliczer, 147–51. Lancaster, CA: Labyrinthos, 1997.

Chartier, Roger, and Maurice Elton. "Crossing the Borders in Early Modern Europe: Sociology of Texts and Literature." *Book History* 8 (2005): 37–50.

Chavel, Charles Ber. *Rabbenu moshe ben nahman* [Rabbi Moses ben Nahman]. Jerusalem: Mossad Harav Kook, 1973.

Chazan, Robert. *Barcelona and Beyond: The Disputation of 1263 and Its Aftermath*. Berkeley: University of California Press, 1992.

———. *Daggers of Faith: Thirteenth-Century Missionizing and the Jewish Response*. Berkeley: University of California Press, 1989.

Chwolson, Daniel. *Reshit maase hadefus beyisrael* [The beginnings of Jewish printing]. Warsaw, 1897.

Cohen, Gerson D. *A Critical Edition with a Translation and Notes of the Book of Tradition (Sefer Haqabbalah) by Abraham Ibn Daud*. Philadelphia: Jewish Publication Society, 1967.

———. "[On] Ben Zion Netanyahu, *The Marranos of Spain* (1966)." *Jewish Social Studies* 29 (1967): 178–84.

Cohen, Jeremy. *The Friars and the Jews: The Evolution of Medieval Anti-Judaism*. Ithaca, NY: Cornell University Press, 1982.

Cohen, Mark R. *The Autobiography of a Seventeenth-Century Venetian Rabbi: Leon Modena's Life of Judah*. Princeton, NJ: Princeton University Press, 1989.

Cohen, Martin A. "Reflections on the Text and Context of the Disputation of Barcelona." *Hebrew Union College Annual* 35 (1964): 157–92.

———. *Samuel Usque's Consolation for the Tribulations of Israel*. Philadelphia: Jewish Publication Society, 1965.

Cohen, Norman. "Leviticus Rabbah, Parashah 3: An Example of a Classic Rabbinic Homily." *Jewish Quarterly Review* 72:1 (1981): 18–31.

Cohen, Rivka. *"Lisheelat qelitatam shel anusim lisheavar biyehadut haotomanit beferuts hahagirah haportugezit leaḥar 1536"* [The absorption of conversos in Ottoman Judaism after the beginning of the Portuguese immigration in 1536]. In *Milisbon lesaloniqi vequshta,* edited by Zvi Ankori, 11–26. Jerusalem: Geref Ḥen, 1988.

———. *Yehude yavan ledorotam* [History of Greek Jewry]. Tel Aviv: Tel Aviv University Press, 1984.

Coudert, A. P. "Kabbalistic Messianism versus Kabbalistic Enlightenment." In *Millenarianism and Messianism in Early Modern Culture: Jewish Messianism in the Early Modern World,* vol. 1, edited by Matt Goldish and Richard H. Popkin, 107–24. 2 vols. Dordrecht: Kluwer, 2001.

Cowley, A. E. *A Concise Catalogue of the Hebrew Printed Books in the Bodleian Library.* Oxford: Clarendon Press, 1929.

Dan, Joseph. "Midrash Aseret Hadibberot." In *Encyclopedia Judaica,* vol. 11. Edited by Cecil Roth and Geoffrey Wigoder, 1514–15. 16 vols. New York: Macmillan, 1971–72.

Danon, Abraham. "La Communauté Juive de Salonique au XVIe siècle." *Revue des Études Juives* 40 (1900): 206–30.

Danzig, Neil. *Mavo lesefer halakhot pesuqot* [An introduction to *Sefer Halakhot Pesuqot*]. New York: Jewish Theological Seminary, 1999.

Davidson, Hannah. "Communal Pride and Feminine Virtue: 'Suspecting *Sivlonot'* in the Jewish Communities of the Ottoman Empire in the Early Sixteenth Century." In *Sephardi Family Life in the Early Modern Diaspora,* edited by Julia R. Lieberman, 23–69. Waltham, MA: Brandeis University Press, 2011.

Davidson, Herbert A. *The Philosophy of Abraham Shalom: A Fifteenth-Century Exposition and Defense of Maimonides.* Berkeley: University of California Press, 1964.

Dimitrovsky, Haim Z. *"Al derekh hapilpul"* [On the pilpul method]. In *Sefer hayovel likhvod shalom baron,* vol. 3, edited by Saul Lieberman, 111–81. 3 vols. Jerusalem: American Academy of Jewish Research, 1975.

———. *"Bet midrasho shel rav yaaqov berav bitsfat"* [The bet midrash of Jacob Berav in Tsefat]. *Sefunot* 7:2 (1964): 43–102.

———, ed. *Seride bavli* [Fragments of the *Bavli*]. New York: Jewish Theological Seminary, 1979.

Dolgopolski, Sergey. *What Is the Talmud? The Art of Disagreement.* New York: Fordham University Press, 2008.

Efros, Israel. *Philosophical Terms in the Moreh Nebukhim.* New York: AMS Press, 1966.

Elbaum, Jacob. *Lehavin divre ḥakhamim: Mivḥar divre mavo laaggadah ulemidrash mishel ḥakhame yeme habenayim* [Toward an understanding of the words of our sages: Selected introductions to aggadah and midrash from medieval Jewish scholars]. Jerusalem: Bialik Institute, 2000.

———. *Petiḥut vehistagrut: Hayetsirah hasifrutit befolin uveartsot ashkenaz beshilhe *hameah ha-16* [Openness and insularity: Late sixteenth-century Jewish literature in Poland and Ashkenaz]. Jerusalem: Magnes Press, 1990.

———. "*Yalqut Shim'oni* and the Medieval Midrashic Anthology." *Prooftexts* 17 (1997): 133–47. Repr. in *The Anthology in Jewish Literature,* edited by David Stern, 159–75. Oxford: Oxford University Press, 2004.

Elior, Rachel. "Messianic Expectations and Spiritualization of Religious Life in the Sixteenth Century." *Revue des Études Juives* 145 (1986): 35–49.

Elon, Menachem. *Jewish Law: History, Sources, Principles.* 4 vols. Philadelphia: Jewish Publication Society, 1994.

Emmanuel, Yitzḥak. *Matsevot saloniqi betseruf toledot ḥayyehem shel gedole haqehillah* [Grave markers of Salonika and lives of prominent members of the community]. 2 vols. Jerusalem: Ben Tzvi Institute, 1963.

Epstein, Isadore. "Haggadah." In *The Interpreter's Dictionary of the Bible,* vol. 2. Edited by G. A. Buttrick, 509. 4 vols. Nashville, TN: Abingdon, 1962.

Epstein, Mark A. "The Leadership of the Ottoman Jews in the Fifteenth and Sixteenth Centuries." In *Christians and Jews in the Ottoman Empire: The Functioning of a Plural Society,* edited by Benjamin Braude and Bernard Lewis, 1:101–16. 2 vols. New York: Holmes & Meier, 1982.

Faur, Jose. "Four Classes of Conversos: A Typological Study." *Revue des Études Juives* 149:1–3 (1990): 113–24.

———. *In the Shadow of History.* Albany: State University of New York Press, 1992.

Feinstein, Moshe. *Iggerot Moshe.* (*Yoreh Deah.*) New York, 1959–73.

Feldman, Leon A. "*Perush haaggadot lerashba lemasekhet baba batra*" [Rashba's aggadic commentary to tractate *Baba Batra*]. *Bar Ilan University Studies in Judaica* 7–8 (1969–70): 138–53.

———. "*Perush haaggadot lerashba lemasekhet ḥullin*" [Rashba's aggadic commentary to tractate *Ḥullin*]. *Sinai* 64:5–6 (1969): 243–47.

———. "*Perush haagadot lerashba lemasekhet nedarim*" [Rashba's aggadic commentary to tractate *Nedarim*]. In *Hagut ivrit beamerika,* vol. 1, edited by Menaḥem Zohari, Aryeh Tartakover, and Haim Ormian, 421–25. 2 vols. Tel Aviv: Yavne, 1972.

———. "R. Solomon ibn Adret: Commentary on the Legends in the Talmud, Tractate Megillah." In *Rabbi Joseph H. Lookstein Memorial Volume,* edited by Leo Landman, 119–24. New York: Ktav, 1980.

Finkelstein, Louis. "*Midrash halakhah veaggadot*" [Halakhic midrash and aggadah]. In *Yitzhak F. Baer Jubilee Volume on the Occasion of His Seventieth Birthday,* edited by Salo W. Baron, 28–47. Jerusalem: Historical Society of Israel, 1960.

Fishbane, Michael A. *Biblical Myth and Rabbinic Mythmaking.* Oxford: Oxford University Press, 2003.

Fishman, Talya. *Shaking the Pillars of Exile: "Voice of a Fool," an Early Modern Jewish Critique of Rabbinic Culture.* Stanford, CA: Stanford University Press, 1997.

Fox, Marvin. *Interpreting Maimonides: Studies in Methodology, Metaphysics, and Moral Philosophy.* Chicago: University of Chicago Press, 1994.

———. "Naḥmanides on the Status of Aggadot: Perspectives on the Disputation at Barcelona, 1263." *Journal of Jewish Studies* 40 (1989): 95–109.

Fraenkel, Jonah. *Darkhe haaggadah vehamidrash* [Principles of aggadah and midrash]. Masada: Yad Letalmud, 1991.

———. "*Sheelot hermeneutiyot beḥeqer sippur haaggadah*" [Hermeneutical questions in the investigation of the aggadic tale]. *Tarbiz* 47 (1978): 139–72.

Fram, Edward. "Perception and Reception of Repentant Apostates in Medieval Ashkenaz and Premodern Poland." *Association for Jewish Studies Review* 21:2 (1996): 299–339.

Friedberg, Hayyim Duberish (Bernard). *Toledot hadefus haivri befolania* [History of Jewish printing in Poland]. Tel Aviv, 1950.

———. *Toledot hadefus haivri bimedinat italya, aspanyah-portugalia, togarmah* [History of Jewish printing in Italy, Spain-Portugal, and Turkey]. Tel Aviv: Bar-Yuda, 1956.

Friedman, Shamma. "*Sippur rav kahana verabbi yoḥanan* (b. B. Qam. *117a–b*) *veanaf nusaḥ genizah hamburg*" [The story of Rav Kahana and Rabbi Yoḥanan (*b. B. Qam.* 117a–b) and the manuscript tradition of Ms. Hamburg]. *Bar-Ilan* 30–31 (2006): 409–90.

Fuks, L., and R. G. Fuks-Mansfeld. *Hebrew Typography in the Northern Netherlands 1585–1815*. 2 vols. Leiden: E. J. Brill, 1987.

Gampel, Benjamin. "A Letter to a Wayward Teacher: The Transformation of Sephardic Culture in Christian Iberia." In *Cultures of the Jews: A History,* edited by David Biale, 389–447. New York: Schocken Books, 2002.

Gaster, Moses, trans. *Ma'aseh Book: The Book of Jewish Tales and Legends*. Philadelphia: Jewish Publication Society, 1934.

Gecas, Viktor. "Value Identities, Self-Motives, and Social Movements." In *Self, Identity, and Social Movements,* edited by Sheldon Stryker, Timothy J. Owens, and Robert W. White, 93–109. Minneapolis: University of Minnesota Press, 2000.

Gerber, Jane. *The Jews of Spain: A History of the Sephardic Experience*. New York: Free Press, 1992.

Ginio, Eyal. "The Administration of Criminal Justice in Ottoman Selanik." *Turcia* 30 (1998): 185–209.

Goldin, Judah. "The Freedom and Restraint of Haggadah." In *Studies in Midrash and Related Literature,* edited by Barry L. Eichler and Jeffrey Tigay, 57–76. Philadelphia: Jewish Publication Society, 1988.

Goldish, Matt. "Rabbinic Culture and Dissent." In *Rabbinic Culture and Its Critics: Jewish Authority, Dissent, and Heresy in Medieval and Early Modern Times,* edited by Daniel Frank and Matt Goldish, 1–53. Detroit: Wayne State University Press, 2008.

Goodblatt, Morris S. *Jewish Life in Turkey in the Sixteenth Century as Reflected in the Legal Writings of Samuel de Medina*. New York: Jewish Theological Seminary, 1952.

Goren, Natan, ed. *Yehadut lita* [Lithuanian Jewry]. 3 vols. Tel Aviv: Am Hasefer, 1959.

Graizbord, David. "Religion and Ethnicity among 'Men of the Nation': Toward a Realistic Interpretation." *Jewish Social Studies* 15:1 (2008): 32–65.

———. *Souls in Dispute: Converso Identities in Iberia and the Jewish Diaspora, 1580–1700.* Philadelphia: University of Pennsylvania Press, 2004.

Gries, Zeev. *The Book in the Jewish World: 1700–1900.* Oxford: Littman Library of Jewish Civilization, 2007.

Gross, Abraham. "Centers of Study and Yeshivot in Spain." In *Moreshet Sepharad: The Sephardi Legacy,* vol. 1, edited by Haim Beinart, 407–10. 2 vols. Jerusalem: Magnes Press, 1992.

———. *Iberian Jewry, from Twilight to Dawn: The World of Rabbi Abraham Saba.* Leiden: E. J. Brill, 1995.

———. "*Qavim letoledot hayeshivot beqastilya bameah ha-15*" [A sketch of the history of the yeshivot in fifteenth-century Castile]. *Peamim* 31 (1987): 3–21.

Grossman, Avraham. "Legislation and Responsa Literature." In *Moreshet Sepharad: The Sephardi Legacy,* vol. 1, edited by Haim Beinart, 188–219. 2 vols. Jerusalem: Magnes Press, 1992.

Gukovitzki, Israel. *Targum halaaz al hashas* [Translation of (Rashi's) vernacular (in his commentary) on the Talmud]. London: G. J. George, 1985.

Guttmann, Julius. *Philosophies of Judaism: A History of Jewish Philosophy from Biblical Times to Franz Rosenzweig.* New York: Schocken Books, 1964.

Gutwirth, Eleazar. "Conversions to Christianity amongst Fifteenth-Century Spanish Jews: An Alternative Explanation." In *Shlomo Simonsohn Jubilee Volume: Studies on the History of the Jews in the Middle Ages and Renaissance Period,* edited by D. Carpi et al., 97–121 (English section). Tel Aviv: Tel Aviv University Press, 1993.

Hacker, Joseph. "Elijah Mizrahi." In *Encyclopedia Judaica,* vol. 8. Edited by Cecil Roth and Geoffrey Wigoder, 1176–78. 16 vols. New York: Macmillan, 1971–72.

———. "*Gaon vedikkaon: Ketavim behavayatam haruhanit vehahevratit shel yotse sefarad ufortugal baimperyah haotomanit*" [Genius and depression: Writings on the spiritual and social lives of Spanish and Portuguese exiles in the Ottoman empire]. In *Tarbut vehevrah betoldot yisrael biyeme habenayim,* edited by Reuven Bonfil, Menahem Ben-Sasson, and Joseph Hacker, 541–86. Jerusalem: Zalman Shazar Center for Jewish History, 1989.

———. "*Hahevrah hayehudit besaloniqi veagapeha bemeot ha-15 veha-16*" [Jewish society in Salonika and its environs in the fifteenth and the sixteenth century]. Ph.D. dissertation, Hebrew University, 1978.

———. "*Hamidrash hasefardi: Sifriyah tsiburit yehudit*" [Public libraries of Hispanic Jewry in the late medieval and early-modern periods]. In *Rishonim veaharonim: Mehkarim betoldot yisrael mugashim leavraham grossman,* edited by Joseph R. Hacker, Yosef Kaplan, and B. Z. Kedar, 263–83. Jerusalem: Zalman Shazar Center, 2010.

———. "*'Im shakhahnu shem elohenu venifros kappenu leel zar': Gilgulah shel parshanut al reqa hametsiut bisfarad biyme habenayim*" ["If we have forgotten the name of our God or stretched out our hand to a strange god": The evolution of interpretation in the context of life in medieval Spain]. *Zion* 57 (1992): 247–74.

———. "The Intellectual Activity of the Jews of the Ottoman Empire during the Sixteenth and Seventeenth Centuries." In *Jewish Thought in the Seventeenth Century,* edited by Isadore Twersky and Bernard Septimus, 95–135. Cambridge, MA: Harvard University Press, 1987.

———. "*Lidemutam haruḥanit shel yehude sefarad besof hameah ha-15*" [On the spiritual character of Spanish Jewry in the late fifteenth century]. *Sefunot* n.s. 2 (1983): 21–95.

———. "*Meqomo shel rabbi avraham bibago bamaḥloqet al limmud hafilosofia umaamadah bisefarad bameah ha-15*" [Rabbi Abraham Bibago's role in the debate over the study of philosophy and its standing in fifteenth-century Spain]. *Proceedings of the Fifth World Congress of Jewish Studies* (1969): 161–69.

———. "*Rabbi yaaqov ibn ḥabib: Lidmutah shel hahanhagah hayehudit besaloniqi bereshit hameah ha-16*" [Rabbi Jacob ibn Ḥabib: Toward the image of Jewish leadership in early sixteenth-century Salonika]. *Proceedings of the Sixth World Congress of Jewish Studies* 2 (1975): 117–26.

———. "The Sephardim in the Ottoman Empire in the Sixteenth Century." In *Moreshet Sepharad: The Sephardi Legacy,* vol. 2, edited by Haim Beinart, 109–33. 2 vols. Jerusalem: Magnes Press, 1992.

Halbertal, Moshe. *People of the Book: Canon, Meaning, and Authority.* Cambridge, MA: Harvard University Press, 1997.

Halkin, Abraham. "Yedayah Bedershi's Apology." In *Jewish Medieval and Renaissance Studies,* edited by Alexander Altmann, 165–84. Cambridge, MA: Harvard University Press, 1967.

Halkin, Abraham, and David Hartman. *Crisis and Leadership: Epistles of Maimonides.* Philadelphia: Jewish Publication Society, 1985.

Handelman, Susan. "The 'Torah' of Criticism and the Criticism of Torah: Recuperating the Pedagogical Moment." In *Interpreting Judaism in a Postmodern Age,* edited by Steven Kepnes, 221–37. New York: New York University Press, 1996.

Harris, Jay M. *Nachman Krochmal: Guiding the Perplexed of the Modern Age.* New York: New York University Press, 1991.

Hartman, David. *Maimonides: Torah and Philosophic Quest.* Philadelphia: Jewish Publication Society, 1976.

Harvey, Warren Zev. "Ḥasdai Crescas's Critique of the Theory of the Acquired Intellect." Ph.D. dissertation, Columbia University, 1973.

Heinemann, Joseph. "*Hapetiḥtot bemidrashe haaggadah: Meqoran vetafqidan*" [*Petiḥot* (Proems) in midrash aggadah: Source and function]. *Proceedings of the Fourth World Congress of Jewish Studies* (1969): 2:43–47.

———. "The Proem in the Aggadic Midrashim: A Form-Critical Study." *Scripta Hierosolymitana* 22 (1971): 100–122.

———. *The Reasons for the Commandments in Jewish Thought from the Bible to the Renaissance.* Translated by Leonard Levin. Boston: Academic Studies Press, 2008.

Heller, Marvin. "Earliest Printings of the Talmud." In *Printing of the Talmud from*

Bomberg to Schottenstein, edited by Sharon Liberman Mintz and Gabriel M. Goldstein, 61–78. New York: Yeshiva University Museum, 2005.

———. *The Printing of the Talmud.* Brooklyn: Im Hasefer, 1992.

———. *The Sixteenth Century Hebrew Book.* Leiden: E. J. Brill, 2004.

Heller-Wilensky, Sara. *Rabbi yitsḥaq arama umishnato* [Rabbi Isaac Arama and his teaching]. Jerusalem: Mossad Bialik, 1956.

Herculano, Alexandre. *History of the Origin and Establishment of the Inquisition in Portugal.* New York: Ktav, 1972.

Herr, Moshe David. "Aggadah." In *Encyclopedia Judaica,* vol. 2. Edited by Cecil Roth and Geoffrey Wigoder, 354–64. 16 vols. New York: Macmillan, 1971–72.

———. "Midrash." In *Encyclopedia Judaica,* vol. 11. Edited by Cecil Roth and Geoffrey Wigoder, 1507–14. 16 vols. New York: Macmillan, 1971–72.

Hill, Brad Sabin. *Hebraica: Manuscripts and Early Printed Books from the Library of the Valmadonna Trust.* Oxford: Oxford University Press, 1989.

Hirsh, John C. *Boundaries of Faith: The Development and Transmission of Medieval Spirituality.* Leiden: E. J. Brill, 1996.

Horowitz, Carmi. *"Al perush haaggadot shel harashba: Ben kabbalah lefilosofia"* [On the Rashba's aggadic commentary: Between Kabbalah and philosophy]. *Daat* 18 (1987): 15–27.

———. *The Jewish Sermon in Fourteenth-Century Spain: The Derashot of Rabbi Joshua ibn Shu'eib.* Cambridge, MA: Harvard University Press, 1989.

Husik, Isaak. *The History of Medieval Jewish Philosophy.* New York: Meridian, 1958.

Hyman, Arthur. "Maimonides on Religious Language." In *Studies in Jewish Philosophy,* edited by Norbert Samuelson, 351–67. New York: University Press of America, 1987.

Iakerson, Shimon. *Catalogue of Books Printed in the XVth Century Now in the British Library.* Netherlands: Hes & De Graaf, 2004.

———. *Catalogue of Hebrew Incunabula from the Collection of the Library of the Jewish Theological Seminary of America.* 2 vols. New York: Jewish Theological Seminary, 2004.

Idel, Moshe. "From Italy to Ashkenaz and Back: On the Circulation of Jewish Mystical Traditions." *Kabbalah: Journal for the Study of Jewish Mystical Texts* 14 (2006): 47–94.

———. Introduction to *Hatenuot hameshiḥiyot beyisrael* [Jewish messianic movements], by Aaron Zev Aescoly. Jerusalem: Mossad Bialik, 1987.

———. *Kabbalah: New Perspectives.* New Haven, CT: Yale University Press, 1988.

———. "Maimonides and Kabbalah." In *Studies in Maimonides,* edited by Isadore Twersky, 31–81. Cambridge, MA: Harvard University Press, 1990.

———. "Religion, Thought and Attitudes: The Impact of the Expulsion on the Jews." In *Spain and the Jews: The Sephardi Experience 1492 and After,* edited by Elie Kedourie, 123–39. London: Thames & Hudson, 1992.

———. "Spanish Kabbalah after the Expulsion." In *Moreshet Sepharad: The Sephardi Legacy,* vol. 2, edited by Haim Beinart, 166–79. 2 vols. Jerusalem: Magnes Press, 1992.

Kafka, Martin. *Jewish Messianism and the History of Philosophy.* Cambridge: Cambridge University Press, 2004.

Kattan, Moshe. *Otsar haloazim* [Dictionary of (Rashi's) vernacular]. Jerusalem, 1984.

Katz, Jacob. *"Af al pi shehata yisrael hu"* [Though he has sinned, he remains a Jew]. *Tarbiz* 27 (1958): 203–17.

————. *Halakhah veqabbalah: Mehqarim betoledot dat yisrael midoreha vezikatah* [Halakhah and Kabbalah: Studies in the history of the Jewish religion, its various faces, and social relevance]. Jerusalem: Magnes Press, 1984.

————. *"Mahloket hasemikhah ben rabbi yaaqov berav veharalbah (levi ibn habib)"* [The ordination debate between Jacob Berav and Levi ibn Habib]. *Zion* 17 (1959): 28–45.

Kayserling, Meyer. *Geschichte der Juden in Spanien und Portugal.* Berlin, 1861. Repr., Hildesheim: Gerstenberg, 1978.

Kellner, Menachem. *Dogma in Medieval Jewish Thought: From Maimonides to Abravanel.* Oxford: Littman Library of Jewish Civilization, 1986.

————. *Maimonides' Confrontation with Mysticism.* Oxford: Littman Library of Jewish Civilization, 2006.

————. "Maimonides' Critique of the Rabbinic Culture of His Day." In *Rabbinic Culture and Its Critics: Jewish Authority, Dissent, and Heresy in Medieval and Early Modern Times,* edited by Daniel Frank and Matt Goldish, 83–116. Detroit: Wayne State University Press, 2008.

————. *Must a Jew Believe Anything?* Oxford: Littman Library of Jewish Civilization, 1999.

Kiel, Mark W. *"Sefer Ha'aggadah:* Creating a Classic Anthology." In *The Anthology in Jewish Literature,* edited by David Stern, 226–43. Oxford: Oxford University Press, 2004.

Kobler, F. *Letters of the Jews through the Ages.* Philadelphia: Jewish Publication Society, 1978.

Kohut, Alexander, ed. *Notes on a Hitherto Unknown Exegetical, Theological and Philosophical Commentary to the Pentateuch Composed by Aboo Manzur Al-Dhamari.* New York: A. Ginsberg, 1892.

Kozodoy, Maud. "A Study of the Life and Works of Profiat Duran." Ph.D. dissertation, Jewish Theological Seminary, 2006.

Lasker, Daniel J. "Chasdei Crescas." In *Routledge History of World Philosophies: History of Jewish Philosophy,* vol. 2, edited by Daniel H. Frank and Oliver Leaman, 399–414. 2 vols. London: Routledge, 1996.

————. *Jewish Philosophical Polemics against Christianity in the Middle Ages.* New York: Ktav, 1977.

Lawee, Eric. *Isaac Abarbanel's Stance toward Tradition: Defense, Dissent, and Dialogue.* Albany: State University of New York Press, 2001.

————. "The Reception of Rashi's *Commentary on the Torah* in Spain: The Case of Adam's Mating with the Animals." *Jewish Quarterly Review* 97:1 (2007): 33–66.

Lazaroff, Allan. *The Theology of Abraham Bibago.* Tuscaloosa: University of Alabama Press, 1981.

Lehman, Marjorie. "The Ein Ya'akov: A Collection of Aggadah in Transition." *Prooftexts* 19 (1999): 21–40.

———. "A Talmudic Anthology of Aggada: Examining the *Ein Yaaqov*." Ph.D. dissertation, Columbia University, 1994.

Levy, Leonard Robert. "R. Yitzhaq Alfasi's Application of Principles of Adjudication in 'Halakhot Rabbati.'" Ph.D. dissertation, Jewish Theological Seminary, 2002.

Lieberman, Saul. *Sheqiin: Midrashe teman.* Jerusalem: Wahrmann, 1970.

Lindbeck, Kris. "Story and Theology: Elijah's Appearance in the Babylonian Talmud." Ph.D. dissertation, Jewish Theological Seminary, 1999.

Lorberbaum, Yair. *"Temurot beyahaso shel harambam lemidreshot hazal"* [Changes in Maimonides' approach to rabbinic midrash]. *Tarbiz* 78:1 (2009): 81–122.

Marcus, Jacob Rader. *The Jew in the Medieval World.* New York: Athenuem, 1938.

Mazower, Mark. *Salonika: City of Ghosts.* New York: Alfred A. Knopf, 2004.

McKenzie, D. F. *Bibliography and the Sociology of Texts.* Cambridge: Cambridge University Press, 1999.

Mehlman, Yisrael. *Genuzot sefarim: Maamarim bibliografiyyimm* [Bibliographical essays]. Jerusalem: Jewish National and University Library Press, 1976.

———. *"Peraqim betoldot hadefus besaloniqi"* [Chapters in the history of the Salonika printing press]. *Sefunot* 13 (1976): 215–72.

Meir, Ofra. "Hademuyot hapoalot besippure hatalmud vehamidrash" [The active characters in the stories of the Talmud and midrash]. Ph.D. dissertation, Hebrew University, 1976.

———. *Hasippur hadarshani bivereshit rabbah* [The midrashic story in Genesis Rabbah]. Tel Aviv: Hakibbuts Hameuhad, 1987.

Meiselman, Shulamit Soloveitchik. *The Soloveitchik Heritage: A Daughter's Memoir.* Hoboken, NJ: Ktav, 1995.

Meyer, Herrman M. Z. "A Short-Title Catalogue of the Hebrew Incunabulas and Other Books." Appended to *Thesaurus Typographiae Hebraicae Saeculi: Hebrew Printing during the Fifteenth Century,* edited by Aron Freimann and Moses Marx. Jerusalem: University Booksellers, 1968.

Mintz, Alan. *"Sefer Ha'aggadah:* Triumph or Tragedy?" In *History and Literature: New Readings of Jewish Texts in Honor of Arnold J. Band,* edited by William Cutter and David C. Jacobson, 17–26. Providence, RI: Brown University Press, 2002.

Molcho, Mikhael. *"Bate eqed sefarim"* [Libraries of books]. *Mahberet* 2 (1954): 23–24.

Netanyahu, Benzion. *The Marranos of Spain: From the Late Fifteenth to the Early Sixteenth Century.* New York: American Academy of Jewish Research, 1966.

Neusner, Jacob. *Judaism in Society: The Evidence of the Yerushalmi.* Chicago: University of Chicago Press, 1983.

Nirenberg, David. "Enmity and Assimilation: Jews, Christians, and Converts in Medieval Spain." *Common Knowledge* 9:1 (2003): 137–55.

———. "Mass Conversion and Genealogical Mentalities: Jews and Christians in Fifteenth-Century Spain." *Past and Present* 174 (2002): 3–41.

Novak, David. *The Election of Israel: The Idea of a Chosen People.* Cambridge: Cambridge University Press, 1995.

Noy, Dov. *"Tippusim ben-leumiyyim viyehudiyyim bemidrash aseret hadibberot"* [International and Jewish motifs in midrash aseret hadibberot]. *Proceedings of the Fourth World Congress of Jewish Studies* (1968): 2:353–55.

Nuriel, Abraham. *Galuy vesamuy befilosofiyah hayehudit biyeme habenayim* [Concealed and revealed in medieval Jewish philosophy]. Jerusalem: Magnes Press, 2000.

Ophir, Natan. *"Harav ḥasdai crescas kefarshan filosofi lemaamare ḥazal"* [Rabbi Hasdai Crescas as a philosophical commentator on rabbinic statements]. Ph.D. dissertation, Hebrew University, 1993.

———. *"Qeriah ḥadashah beor hashem lerabbi ḥasdai crescas uveayat haanusim"* [A new reading in the *Or Hashem* of Rabbi Hasdai Crescas, and the converso problem]. *Proceedings of the Eleventh World Congress of Jewish Studies,* 3:2, 41–47. Jerusalem: World Union of Jewish Studies, 1994.

Orfali, Moisés. "Jeronimo de Santa Fe y la Polémica Cristiana Contra el Talmud" [Jeronimo de Sante Fe and the Christian Polemic against the Talmud]. *Annuario Di Studi Ebraici* 10 (1984): 157–78.

Pearl, Chaim. *The Medieval Jewish Mind: The Religious Philosophy of Isaac Arama.* London: Vallentine, Mitchell, 1971.

Popkin, Richard. "Marranos, New Christians and the Beginnings of Modern Anti-Trinitarianism." In *Jews and Conversos at the Time of the Expulsion,* edited by Yom Tov Assis and Yosef Kaplan, 143–60. Jerusalem: Zalman Shazar Center for Jewish History, 1999.

Pullan, Brian. " 'A Ship with Two Rudders': Righetto Marrano and the Inquisition in Venice." *Historical Journal* 20:1 (1977): 25–58.

Rabbinovicz, Raphael. *Maamar al hadpasat hatalmud* [An essay on the printing of the Talmud]. Jerusalem: Mossad Harav Kook, 1965.

Ravid, Benjamin. "The Prohibition against Jewish Printing and Publishing in Venice and the Difficulties of Leone Modena." In *Studies in Medieval Jewish History and Literature,* edited by Isadore Twersky, 135–53. Cambridge, MA: Harvard University Press, 1979.

Ravitzky, Aviezer. *History and Faith: Studies in Jewish Philosophy.* Amsterdam: J. C. Gieben, 1996.

Regev, Shaul. "The Attitude Towards the Conversos in Fifteenth and Sixteenth Century Jewish Thought." *Revue des Études Juives* 156:1–2 (1997): 117–34.

Rodrigue, Aron. "The Sephardim in the Ottoman Empire." In *Spain and the Jews: The Sephardi Experience 1492 and After,* edited by Elie Kedourie, 162–88. London: Thames & Hudson, 1992.

Rosanes, Shlomo. *Divre yeme yisrael betogarmah* [History of the Jews of Turkey]. 4 vols. Tel Aviv: Dvir, 1930.

Rosenberg, Shalom. "The Concept of *Emunah* in Post-Maimonidean Philosophy." In *Studies in Medieval Jewish History and Literature II,* edited by Isadore Twersky, 273–307. Cambridge, MA: Harvard University Press, 1984.

———. "Exile and Redemption in Jewish Thought in the Sixteenth Century:

Contending Conceptions." In *Jewish Thought in the Sixteenth Century*, edited by Bernard Dov Cooperman, 399–430. Cambridge, MA: Harvard University Press, 1983.

Roth, Cecil. *A History of the Marranos*. New York: Hermon Press, 1974.

Rozen, Minna. *A History of the Jewish Community in Istanbul: The Formative Years, 1453–1566*. Leiden: E. J. Brill, 2002.

———. "Individual and Community in the Jewish Society of the Ottoman Empire: Salonika in the Sixteenth Century." In *The Jews of the Ottoman Empire*, edited by Avigdor Levy, 215–73. Princeton, NJ: Darwin Press, 1994.

Rubenstein, Jeffrey M. *Talmudic Stories: Narrative Art, Composition, and Culture*. Baltimore, MD: Johns Hopkins University Press, 1999.

Saperstein, Marc. "The Conflict over the Rashba's Herem on Philosophical Study: A Political Perspective." *Jewish History* 1:2 (1986): 27–38.

———. *Decoding the Rabbis: A Thirteenth-Century Commentary on the Aggadah*. Cambridge, MA: Harvard University Press, 1980.

———. "R. Isaac b. Yeda'ya: A Forgotten Commentator on the Aggada." *Revue des Études Juives* 138:1–2 (1979): 17–45.

———. "Selected Passages from Yedayah Bedersi's Commentary on the Midrashim." In *Studies in Medieval Jewish History II,* edited by Isadore Twersky, 423–40. Cambridge, MA: Harvard University Press, 1984.

———. "The Social and Cultural Context: Thirteenth–Fifteenth Centuries." In *Routledge History of World Philosophies: History of Jewish Philosophy,* vol. 2, edited by Daniel H. Frank and Oliver Leaman, 294–330. 2 vols. London: Routledge, 1996.

———. *"Your Voice Like a Ram's Horn": Themes and Texts in Traditional Jewish Preaching*. Cincinnati: Hebrew Union College Press, 1996.

Scheindlin, Raymond P. "Judah Abarbanel to His Son." *Judaism* 41 (1992): 190–99.

Schirman, Jefim Hayim. *Mivḥar hashirah haivrit bietalyah* [A selection of Italian Jewish poetry]. Berlin, 1934.

Scholem, Gershom. *Major Trends in Jewish Mysticism*. New York: Schocken Books, 1974.

———. "Opening Address." In *Types of Redemption: Contributions to the Theme of the Study-Conference Held at Jerusalem, 14th–19th of July, 1968,* edited by R. J. Z. Werblowsky and C. Joyce Bleeker, 1–12. Leiden: E. J. Brill, 1970.

Schweid, Eliezer. *The Classic Jewish Philosophers: From Saadia through the Renaissance*. Translated by Leonard Levin. Leiden: E. J. Brill, 2008.

Seeman, Don, and Rebecca Kobrin. " 'Like One of the Whole Men': Learning, Gender and Autobiography in R. Barukh Epstein's *Mekor Barukh*." *Nashim: A Journal of Jewish Women's Studies and Gender Issues* 2 (1999): 52–94.

Seeskin, Kenneth. "Judaism and the Linguistic Interpretation of Jewish Faith." In *Studies in Jewish Philosophy: Collected Essays of the Academy for Jewish Philosophy, 1980–1985,* edited by Norbert Samuelson, 215–34. Lanham, MD: University Press of America, 1987.

Segal, Eliezer. "Anthological Dimensions of the Babylonian Talmud." In *The An-*

thology in Jewish Literature, edited by David Stern, 81–107. Oxford: Oxford University Press, 2004.

Septimus, Bernard. *Hispano-Jewish Culture in Transition: The Career and Controversies of Ramah.* Cambridge, MA: Harvard University Press, 1982.

———. "Isaac Arama and the *Ethics.*" In *Jews and Conversos at the Time of the Expulsion,* edited by Yom Tov Assis and Yosef Kaplan, 1–24 (English section). Jerusalem: Zalman Shazar Center for Jewish History, 1999.

———. "'Open Rebuke and Concealed Love': Naḥmanides and the Andalusian Tradition." In *Rabbi Moses Naḥmanides (Ramban): Explorations in His Religious and Literary Virtuosity,* edited by Isadore Twersky, 11–34. Cambridge, MA: Harvard University Press, 1983.

———. "Piety and Power in Thirteenth-Century Catalonia." In *Studies in Medieval Jewish History and Literature,* edited by Isadore Twersky, 197–230. Cambridge, MA: Harvard University Press, 1979.

Shapira, Anat. *Midrash aseret hadibberot* [Midrash on the Ten Commandments]. Jerusalem: Mossad Bialik, 2005.

Shear, Adam. *The Kuzari and the Shaping of Jewish Identity, 1167–1900.* Cambridge: Cambridge University Press, 2008.

Sherwin, Byron L. *Kabbalah: An Introduction to Jewish Mysticism.* Lanham, MD: Rowman & Littlefield, 2006.

Shmuelevitz, Aryeh. "The Responsa as a Source for the History of the Ottoman Empire." In *Ottoman History and Society,* edited by Aryeh Shmuelevitz, 19–28. Istanbul: Isis Press, 1999.

Shulman, Lee S. *The Wisdom of Practice: Essays on Teaching, Learning, and Learning to Teach.* San Francisco: Jossey-Bass, 2004.

Sirat, Colette. *A History of Jewish Philosophy in the Middle Ages.* Cambridge: Cambridge University Press, 1985.

Slutsky, Yehudah. "Romm." In *Encyclopedia Judaica,* vol. 15. Edited by Cecil Roth and Geoffrey Wigoder, 255. 16 vols. New York: Macmillan, 1971–72.

Steiner, George. "Our Homeland, the Text." *Salmagundi* 66 (1985): 4–25.

———. *Real Presences.* Chicago: University of Chicago Press, 1989.

Steinsalz, Adin. *The Talmud: A Reference Guide.* New York: Random House, 1989.

Steinschneider, Moritz. *Catalogus Librorum Hebraeorum in Bibliotheca Bodleiana* [A catalog of Hebrew books in the Bodleian Library]. Berlin: Friedlaender, 1852–60.

Stern, David. *The Anthology in Jewish Literature.* Oxford: Oxford University Press, 2004.

———. "Midrash and the Language of Exegesis: A Study of *Vayikra Rabbah* Chapter 1." In *Midrash and Literature,* edited by Geoffrey H. Hartman and Sanford Budick, 105–24. New Haven, CT: Yale University Press, 1986.

Strayer, Joseph R., ed. *Dictionary of the Middle Ages.* 13 vols. New York: American Council for Learned Societies, 1982–89.

Subtelny, Maria E. "The Tale of the Four Sages Who Entered Pardes: A Talmudic Enigma from a Persian Perspective." *Jewish Studies Quarterly* 11 (2004): 3–58.

Talmage, Frank. "Apples of Gold: The Inner Meaning of Sacred Texts in Medieval Judaism." In *Jewish Spirituality: From the Bible through the Middle Ages,* edited by Arthur Green, 313–55. New York: Crossroad, 1987. Repr. in *Apples of Gold in Settings of Silver: Studies in Medieval Jewish Exegesis and Polemics,* edited by Barry Dov Walfish, 108–50. Toronto: Pontifical Institute of Mediaeval Studies, 1999.

———. *David Kimhi: The Man and His Commentaries.* Cambridge, MA: Harvard University Press, 1975.

Tanenbaum, Adena. "Arrogance, Bad Form, and Curricular Narrowness: Belletristic Critiques of Rabbinic Culture from Medieval Spain and Provence." In *Rabbinic Culture and Its Critics: Jewish Authority, Dissent, and Heresy in Medieval and Early Modern Times,* edited by Daniel Frank and Matt Goldish, 57–81. Detroit: Wayne State University Press, 2008.

Ta-Shma, Israel M. "Halakhah and Reality: The Tosafist Experience." In *Creativity and Tradition: Studies in Medieval Rabbinic Scholarship, Literature, and Thought,* 87–101. Cambridge, MA: Harvard University Press, 2006.

———. *Hasifrut haparshanit latalmud beeropah uvitsfon Africa* [Talmudic commentary in Europe and North Africa]. 2 vols. Jerusalem: Magnes Press, 1999–2000.

———. *Kenesset meḥqarim: Iyyunim besifrut harabbanit biyeme habenayim* [Collected essays: Studies in medieval rabbinic literature]. Jerusalem: Mossad Bialik, 2004.

———. "The Study of Aggadah and Its Interpretation in Early Rabbinic Literature." In *Creativity and Tradition: Studies in Medieval Rabbinic Scholarship, Literature, and Thought,* 201–11. Cambridge, MA: Harvard University Press, 2006.

Tavares, Maria José Pimenta Ferro. "Expulsion or Integration? The Portuguese Jewish Problem." In *Crisis and Creativity in the Sephardic World: 1391–1648,* edited by Benjamin Gampel, 95–103. New York: Columbia University Press, 1997.

Tirosh-Rothschild, Hava. *Between Worlds: The Life and Thought of Rabbi David ben Judah Messer Leon.* Albany: State University of New York Press, 1991.

———. "Jewish Philosophy on the Eve of Modernity." In *Routledge History of World Philosophies: History of Jewish Philosophy,* vol. 2, edited by Daniel H. Frank and Oliver Leaman, 499–573. 2 vols. London: Routledge, 1996.

Tirosh-Samuelson, Hava. *Happiness in Premodern Judaism.* Cincinnati: Hebrew Union College Press, 2003.

———. "The Ultimate End of Human Life in Postexpulsion Philosophic Literature." In *Crisis and Creativity in the Sephardic World: 1391–1648,* edited by Benjamin R. Gampel, 223–54. New York: Columbia University Press, 1997.

Tishby, Isaiah. *"Dape genizah miḥibbur meshiḥi-misti al gerushe sefarad ufortugal"* [Pages from a messianic-mystical composition on the Spanish and Portuguese exiles from the genizah]. *Zion* 48 (1983): 55–102, 347–85, and *Zion* 49 (1984): 20–60.

Twersky, Isadore. "Aspects of the Social and Cultural History of Provencal Jewry." In *Jewish Society through the Ages,* edited by H. H. Ben-Sasson and S. Ettinger,

190–202. London: Vallentine, 1971.

———. "Joseph ibn Kaspi: Portrait of a Medieval Jewish Intellectual." In *Studies in Medieval Jewish History and Literature,* edited by Isadore Twersky, 231–57. Cambridge, MA: Harvard University Press, 1979.

———. *A Maimonides Reader.* New York: Behrman House, 1972.

———. *Rabad of Posquieres.* Philadelphia: Jewish Publication Society, 1980.

———. "*R. yedayah hapenini uferusho laaggadah*" [Rabbi Yedayah Hapenini and his aggadic commentary]. In *Studies in Jewish Religion and Intellectual History Presented to A. Altman,* edited by Siegfried Stein and Raphael Loewe, 63–82. Tuscaloosa: University of Alabama Press, 1979.

———. "Talmudists, Philosophers, Kabbalists: The Quest for Spirituality in the Sixteenth Century." In *Jewish Thought in the Sixteenth Century,* edited by Bernard Dov Cooperman, 431–59. Cambridge, MA: Harvard University Press, 1983.

Urbach, E. E. *Baale hatosafot: Toldotehem, ḥibburehem, shitatam* [The Tosafists: Their history, writings, and methods]. 2 vols. Jerusalem: Mossad Bialik, 1980.

———. "How Did Rashi Merit the Title *Parshandata?*" In *Rashi 1040–1090: Hommage à Ephraïm E. Urbach,* edited by Gabrielle Sed-Rajna, 387–98. Paris: Editions du Cerf, 1993.

———. *The Sages: Their Concepts and Beliefs.* Translated by Israel Abrahams. Cambridge, MA: Harvard University Press, 1987.

Van Straalen, S., and Brad Sabin Hill. *Catalogue of Hebrew Printers: 1500–1900.* London: British Library, 1995.

Vinograd, Yeshayahu. *Otsar hasefer haivri* [A catalog of Jewish books]. 2 vols. Jerusalem: Institute for Computerized Hebrew Bibliography, 1993–95.

Visotzky, Burton L. *Golden Bells and Pomegranates: Studies in Midrash Leviticus Rabbah.* Tübingen: Mohr Siebeck, 2003.

———. "The Literature of the Rabbis." In *From Mesopotamia to Modernity,* edited by Burton L. Visotzky and David E. Fishman, 83–92. Boulder, CO: Westview Press, 1999.

Wald, Stephen. "Bavli pesaḥim pereq elu overin: Mahadurah madait uviur meqif" [Bavli tractate *Pesaḥim,* chapter *Elu Overin:* Critical edition and exhaustive commentary]. Ph.D. dissertation, Hebrew University, 1994.

Walker, Williston, Richard A. Norris, David W. Lotz, and Robert T. Handy. *A History of the Christian Church.* New York: Charles Scribner's Sons, 1985.

Weinberg, Bella Hass. "The Earliest Hebrew Citation Indexes." *Journal of the American Society for Information Science* 48:4 (1997): 318–30.

———. "Predecessors of Scientific Indexing Structures in the Domain of Religion." In *The History and Heritage of Scientific and Technological Information Systems: Proceedings of the 2002 Conference,* edited by W. Boyd Rayward and Mary Ellen Bowden, 126–34. Medford, NJ: Information Today, 2004.

Wolfson, Elliot R. "'By Way of Truth': Aspects of Naḥmanides' Kabbalistic Hermeneutic." *Association for Jewish Studies Review* 14 (1989): 103–78.

———. *Language, Eros, Being: Kabbalistic Hermeneutics and Poetic Imagination.* New York: Fordham University Press, 2005.

Yahalom, Yosef. "A Hebrew Renaissance in the Sephardi Diaspora." *Peamim* 26 (1986): 9–28.

Yalon, Hanokh. *"Peraqim min hameasef lekhol hamaḥanot larav shlomo almoli"* [Chapters from Solomon Almoli's *Hameasef Lekhol Hamaḥanot*]. *Areshet* 2 (1960): 96–108.

Yerushalmi, Yosef Hayim. "Clio and the Jews: Reflections on Jewish Historiography in the Sixteenth Century." *Proceedings of the American Academy of Jewish Research* 46–47:2 (1978–79): 607–38.

———. "Exile and Expulsion in Jewish History." In *Crisis and Creativity in the Spanish World: 1391–1648,* edited by Benjamin R. Gampel, 3–22. New York: Columbia University Press, 1997.

———. *From Spanish Court to Italian Ghetto: Isaac Cardoso, A Study in Seventeenth-Century Marranism and Jewish Apologetics.* Seattle: University of Washington Press, 1981.

———. "A Jewish Classic in Portuguese Language." Introduction to *Consolação às Tribulações de Israel,* by Samuel Usque. 2 vols. Lisbon: Fundação Calouste Gulbenkian, 1989.

———. *The Lisbon Massacre of 1506 and the Royal Image of Shevet Yehudah.* HUCA Supplements 1. Cincinnati: Hebrew Union College Press, 1976.

———. *Zakhor: Jewish History and Jewish Memory.* Seattle: University of Washington Press, 1982.

Yovel, Yirmiyahu. *The Other Within: The Marranos—Split Identity and Emerging Modernity.* Princeton, NJ: Princeton University Press, 2009.

Yudlov, Isaac. *Bet hasefarim haleumi vehauniversitah biyerushalayim* [The national library and (Hebrew) university of Jerusalem]. Jerusalem: Jewish National and University Library, 1984.

Zagorin, Perez. *Ways of Lying: Dissimulation, Persecution, and Conformity in Early Modern Europe.* Cambridge, MA: Harvard University Press, 1990.

Zimmels, Hirsch Jakob. *Die Marranen in der rabbinischen Literatur: Forschungen und Quellen zur Geschichte und Kulturgeschichte der Anussim* [The marranos in rabbinic literature: Research and sources for the history and cultural history of the marranos]. Berlin: R. Mass, 1932.

Zonta, Mauro. *Hebrew Scholasticism in the Fifteenth Century: A History and Source Book.* Amsterdam: Springer, 2006.

Zunz, Leopold. *Haderashot beyisrael* [The sermons of the Jews]. Jerusalem: Mossad Bialik, 1974.

Index